CHINESE JUSTICE

This volume analyzes whether China's thirty years of legal reform have taken root in Chinese society by examining how ordinary citizens are using the legal system in contemporary China. It is an interdisciplinary look at law in action and at legal institutions from the bottom up – that is, beginning with those at the ground level who are using and working in the legal system. It explores the emergent Chinese conception of justice – one that seeks to balance Chinese tradition, socialist legacies, and the needs of the global market. Given the political dimension of dispute resolution in creating, settling, and changing social norms, this volume contributes to a greater understanding of political and social change in China today and of the process of legal reform generally.

Margaret Y. K. Woo is Professor of Law at Northeastern University School of Law and co-director of the law school's program on Human Rights in the Global Economy. She has written and spoken widely on U.S. procedural justice and the issue of Chinese legal reform. She was formerly a Fellow at the Bunting Institute of Radcliffe College and is a research associate with the Program on East Asian Legal Studies at Harvard Law School. Her publications include *Litigating in America* (2006) and *East Asian Law – Universal Norms and Local Cultures* (2003).

Mary E. Gallagher is Associate Professor of Political Science at the University of Michigan, where she is also the director of the Center for Chinese Studies. She is also a faculty associate at the Center for Comparative Political Studies at the Institute for Social Research. Gallagher is the author of *Contagious Capitalism: Globalization and the Politics of Labor in China* (2005) and the forthcoming *The Rule of Law in China: If They Build It, Who Will Come?*, which was funded by the Fulbright Association and the National Science Foundation.

Chinese Justice

CIVIL DISPUTE RESOLUTION IN CONTEMPORARY CHINA

Edited by

Margaret Y. K. Woo

Northeastern University School of Law

Mary E. Gallagher

University of Michigan, Department of Political Science

CAMBRIDGE
UNIVERSITY PRESS

CAMBRIDGE UNIVERSITY PRESS
Cambridge, New York, Melbourne, Madrid, Cape Town,
Singapore, São Paulo, Delhi, Mexico City

Cambridge University Press
32 Avenue of the Americas, New York, NY 10013-2473, USA

www.cambridge.org
Information on this title: www.cambridge.org/9781107006249

First published 2011
Reprinted 2012

A catalog record for this publication is available from the British Library.

Library of Congress Cataloging in Publication data
Contemporary Chinese Justice : civil dispute resolution in China / [edited by] Margaret Y. K. Woo, Mary E. Gallagher.
p. cm
Includes bibliographical references and index.
ISBN 978-1-107-00624-9 (hardback)
1. Justice, Administration of – China. 2. Dispute resolution (Law) – China. 3. Civil procedure – China. 4. Law reform – China. I. Woo, Margaret Y. K.
II. Gallagher, Mary Elizabeth, 1969–
KNQ1572.C656 2011
347.51'094 – dc22 2010045090

ISBN 978-1-107-00624-9 Hardback

Contents

Tables and Figures — *page* vii

Contributors — xi

Acknowledgments — xiii

Abbreviations — xv

Glossary — xvii

Introduction — 1
Margaret Y. K. Woo and Mary E. Gallagher

PART I: LEGAL DEVELOPMENT AND INSTITUTIONAL TENSIONS

1 From Mediatory to Adjudicatory Justice: The Limits of Civil Justice Reform in China — 25
Fu Hualing and Richard Cullen

2 Judicial Disciplinary Systems for Incorrectly Decided Cases: The Imperial Chinese Heritage Lives On — 58
Carl Minzner

3 Legalizing the Local State: Administrative "Legality" at China's Grassroots — 91
Douglas B. Grob

4 Economic Development and the Development of the Legal Profession in China — 114
Randall Peerenboom

PART II: *PU FA* AND THE DISSEMINATION OF LAW IN THE CHINESE CONTEXT

5 The Impact of Nationalist and Maoist Legacies on Popular Trust in Legal Institutions 139
Pierre F. Landry

6 Public Attitudes toward Official Justice in Beijing and Rural China 169
Ethan Michelson and Benjamin L. Read

7 Users and Non-Users: Legal Experience and Its Effect on Legal Consciousness 204
Mary E. Gallagher and Yuhua Wang

8 With or without the Law: The Changing Meaning of Ordinary Legal Work in China, 1979–2003 234
Sida Liu

PART III: LAW FROM THE BOTTOM UP

9 A Populist Threat to China's Courts? 269
Benjamin L. Liebman

10 Dispute Resolution and China's Grassroots Legal Services 314
Fu Yulin

11 The Constitution in the Courtroom: Constitutional Development and Civil Litigation in China 340
Thomas E. Kellogg

Conclusion: Chinese Justice from the Bottom Up 380
Margaret Y. K. Woo

Index 403

Tables and Figures

TABLES

1.1 When, Where, and How Shenzhen Judges Conducted Mediation *page* 35
5.1 Multilevel Variance of Trust in Legal Institutions 153
5.2 Summary of the Evolution of Legal Institutions in 87 ILRC Counties 156
5.3 Ordered Probit Model of Trust in Legal Institutions 166
6.1 Experience-Based Assessments of Official Justice, Chicago (1984), Beijing (2001), and Rural China (2002) 179
6.2 Overlap between Experience-Based Assessments of Official Justice Outcomes and Procedures, Chicago (1984), Beijing (2001), and Rural China (2002) 180
6.3 Prevalence of Direct Experience with Official Justice, Chicago (1984), Beijing (2001), and Rural China (2002) 190
A6.1 Perceptions of the Courts 198
A6.2 Perceptions of the Police 201
7.1 Judgment of a Vignette: Work-Unit Actions Legal or Not 215
7.2 Reasons Provided for Saying Illegal 216
7.3 If You Were Mr. Chen, What Would You Do? 217
7.4 Use Mediation? 218
7.5 Use Administrative Methods? 218
7.6 Use Arbitration? 219
7.7 Use Litigation? 219
7.8 Which Method Would You Use First? 219
7.9 Which Method Is Most Effective? 220
7.10 Political Identity and Mobilization 225

8.1 Distribution of Case Types (Percentage), DALS Legal-Advice Column, 1979–2003 244
8.2 Statutes Cited More than Ten Times in the DALS Column, 1979–2003 247

FIGURES

1.1 Percentage of Civil Cases Concluded by Mediation (1956–2006) 43
5.1 Distribution of KMT Membership by Province, 1937 143
5.2 Scatterplots of Trust in Legal Institutions, Aggregated by County (1–4 scale) 152
5.3 Comparison of Random Effects at the Province and County Levels 155
5.4 Respondents' Exposure to Their County of Residence 160
5.5 Mentions of Legal Institutions in the *People's Daily* (1946–2006) 162
6.1 General Perceptions of Official Justice, Chicago (1984), Beijing (2001), and Rural China (2002) 176
6.2 General Perceptions of the Performance of Courts and Police by Economic Development, Beijing (2001) and Rural China (2002) 177
6.3 Experience-Based Assessments by Competing Sources of Help, Beijing (2001) and Rural China (2002) 182
6.4 Incidence of Negative Experience-Based Assessments of Court Performance by Locality, Beijing (2001) and Rural China (2002) 183
6.5 General Perceptions of Courts, by Personal Experience, Chicago (1984), Beijing (2001), and Rural China (2002) 185
6.6 General Perceptions of Police by Personal Experience, Chicago (1984), Beijing (2001), and Rural China (2002) 186
6.7 General Perceptions of Official Justice, by Personal Experience, Disaggregated by Evaluations of Personal Experience, Chicago (1984) 186
6.8 General Perceptions of Courts by Personal Experience, Disaggregated by Experience-Based Assessments, Beijing (2001) and Rural China (2002) 187
6.9 General Perceptions of Police by Personal Experience, Disaggregated by Experience-Based Assessments, Beijing (2001) and Rural China (2002) 188

6.10 Incidence of Escalating Grievances to Lawyers and Courts, by Locality, Beijing (2001) and Rural China (2002) 191
7.1 Dispute "Pyramid" 208
8.1 Changes in the Average Number of Cases per Issue, 1979–2003 242
8.2 Average Number of Statutes Cited per Year, 1979–2003 246

Contributors

Editors

Margaret Y. K. Woo Professor of Law, School of Law, Northeastern University

Mary E. Gallagher Associate Professor, Department of Political Science, University of Michigan

Contributors

Richard Cullen Visiting Professor, Department of Law, University of Hong Kong

Fu Hualing Associate Professor and Head, Department of Law, University of Hong Kong

Fu Yulin Associate Professor of Civil Procedure and Legal Practice, School of Law, Peking University

Douglas B. Grob Assistant Professor, Department of Government and Politics, University of Maryland

Thomas E. Kellogg Program Officer and Advisor to the President, Open Society Institute

Pierre F. Landry Associate Professor, Department of Political Science, Yale University

Benjamin L. Liebman Professor of Law and Director, Center for Chinese Legal Studies, Columbia Law School

Sida Liu Assistant Professor of Law and Sociology, Department of Sociology, University of Wisconsin

Ethan Michelson Associate Professor, Department of Sociology and Department of East Asian Languages and Cultures and Associate Professor of Sociology and Law, Maurer School of Law, Indiana University Bloomington

Carl Minzner Associate Professor of Law, Washington University in St. Louis School of Law

Randall Peerenboom Associate Fellow, Oxford University Centre for Socio-Legal Studies; Director, Oxford Foundation for Law, Justice and Society China Rule of Law Programme; and Professor of Law, La Trobe University, Melbourne

Benjamin L. Read Assistant Professor, Politics Department, University of California, Santa Cruz

Yuhua Wang Assistant Professor, Department of Political Science, University of Pennsylvania

Acknowledgments

This book is the result of a workshop generously funded by the Chiang Ching Kuo Foundation for International Scholarly Exchange and the Center for Chinese Studies at the University of Michigan. We also benefited tremendously from the wise counsel and encouragement of Merle Goldman. Professor Goldman has been an unfailing intellectual force behind the efforts of many young and women scholars, and we are truly grateful to have such a path breaker at the Fairbank Center at Harvard. Similarly, we would like to thank Professor William Alford and the Program for East Asian Legal Studies of Harvard Law School for their financial support. Under the directorship of Professor Alford, the Program on East Asian Legal Studies has been an active intellectual base for Asian scholars here and abroad. Additionally, we would like to thank Professor Elizabeth Perry and the Lam Fund, whose enthusiasm and generosity made the workshop possible. Of course, the workshop discussion greatly benefited from all those who participated as well as from the thoughtful comments by discussants Cai Yanmin, Donald Clarke, Jerome Cohen, Sally Merry, Frank Upham, and Robert Weller. Nancy Hearst provided excellent editorial expertise, as usual. Finally, we would like to acknowledge the institutional support of the Fairbank Center for Chinese Research, Harvard University, who graciously hosted the workshop.

Abbreviations

ALL	Administrative Litigation Law
ARL	Administrative Reconsideration Law
ARR	Administrative Reconsideration Regulation
BPC	basic people's court
CASS	Chinese Academy of Social Sciences
CCP	Chinese Communist Party
DALS	*Democracy and the Legal System* (*Minzhu yu fazhi*)
FZB	legal affairs office (*fazhi bangongshi*)
HLM	hierarchical linear modeling
HPC	higher people's court
ICS	individual case supervision
ILCR	Institutionalization of Legal Reforms
IPC	intermediate people's court
KMT	Guomindang (Kuomintang)
LAO	legislative affairs office
LPC	local people's congress
MoJ	Ministry of Justice
NPC	National People's Congress
PLC	Political-Legal Committee
PRC	People's Republic of China
PSB	Public Security Bureau
PSU	primary sampling unit
SFT	local justice department (*sifa ting*)
SOE	state-owned enterprise
SPC	Supreme People's Court
SPP	Supreme People's Procuratorate

Glossary

bangong bumen
办公部门
operational department of government

baogao qingkuang
报告情况
reporting

bei'an (review)
备案
file the case record (for review)

bijiao xinren
比较信任
somewhat trust

butai xinren
不太信任
somewhat distrust

chouxiang xingzheng xingwei
抽象行政行为
abstract administrative acts

dang de zuzhibu
党的组织部
Party Organization Department

dang zhengban
党政办
party political office

dang zhibu
党支部
party branch

diaocha yanjiu, tiaojie wei zhu, jiu di jiejue
调查研究, 调解为主, 就地解决
investigate and research, taking mediation as the principal method, and solving disputes where they arise

diaopan jiehe, anjie liaoshi
调判结合, 案结了事
combine adjudication and mediation; resolve the dispute and conclude the litigation

difang zhengfu
地方政府
local government

diji chengshi
地级城市
prefectural level city

fazhi bangongshi or *fazhiban*
法制办公室 or 法制办
legal affairs office

fazhichu
法制处
legal affairs section

fazhiyuan
法制员
legal affairs officer

feichang xinren
非常信任
trust a great deal

feinongye hukou
非农业户口
urban registration

fugaimiande
覆盖面的
overlay

fu xianzhang
副县长
deputy county head

fuyi keyi jiejue xinfang de bu fangbian
复议可以解决信访的不方便
reconsideration can solve many of the inconveniences of *xinfang* (petition)

gaodeng fayuan
高等法院
high court

gaodeng fayuan fenyuan
高等法院分院
divisional courts of high court

gongan sifa
公安司法
public security and justice

gongshang
工商
Industry and Commerce (Bureau)

guizhang
规章
administrative rules

guoshui and *dishui*
国税 and 地税
national and real estate tax

hai you kongbaidian
还有空白点
bare patches

he li
合理
be reasonable (a rule)

jiandu
监督
supervise, inspect, review

jiaoda de shi
较大的市
large cities

jiguan
籍贯
native place

jingji hetong zhongcai weiyuanhui
经济合同仲裁委员会
economic contract arbitration committees

jishu jiandu
技术监督
Technical Supervision (Bureau)

nengdiao zediao, dangpan zepan, diaopan jiehe, anjie liaoshi
能調則調, 當判則判, 調判結合, 案結了事
mediate cases that can be mediated, adjudicate cases that should be adjudicated, combine mediation with adjudication to resolve the dispute and conclude the litigation

paichu
派出
sent out (an individual)

pu fa
普法
(legal) awareness

renda fagui chu
人大法规处
legislative affairs office of the people's congress

shefa
涉法
law related

shizhang or xianzhang
市长 or 县长
head (of a city or a county)

shuofa
说法
an explanation

sifa bu
司法部
Ministry of Justice

sifa jiguan
司法机关
legal organs

sifasuo
司法所
local justice office

sifa ting
司法厅
local justice departments

sifa weimin
司法为民
legality serving the people

wanquan buxinren
完全不信任
completely distrust

xian
县
county

xianshi gongzheng
显失公正
manifest lack of fairness

xianzhi
县志
County gazetteer

xinfang
信访
petition

xingzheng fuyi
行政复议
administrative reconsideration

xingzheng fuyi fa
行政复议法
Administrative Reconsideration Law

xingzheng fuyi weiyuanhui
行政复议委员会
Administrative Reconsideration Committee

xingzheng shenpan ting
行政审判庭
administrative trial court

yantaohui
研讨会
seminar/discussion group

yifa banshi
依法办事
do things according to law

yifa xingzheng
依法行政
administrate according to law

yikao qunzhong, diaocha yanjiu, iaojie weizhu, jiudi jiejue
依靠群众, 调查研究, 调解为主, 就地解决
rely on the masses, investigate and research, take mediation as the principal method, solve disputes where they arise

yizhi
一致
consistency

you fazhi yishi de guanyuan
有法制意识的官员
those officials with a sense of acting according to the law

zhengfa wei
政法委
Political and Legal Affairs Committee (of the CCP)

zhengfazu
政法组
political and legal committee

zhengfu bangong huiyi
政府办公会议
government working conference

zhengfu changwei hui [fu]huizhang
政府常委会(副)会长
chairman (or vice chairman) of the standing committee of the government

zhengfu xinxi gongkai
政府信息公开
open government information

zhineng bumen
职能部门
administrative department

zhuren
主任
head (of the local FZB)

Introduction

Margaret Y. K. Woo and Mary E. Gallagher

> *[I]t is in its legal institutions that the characteristics of a civilized society are most clearly reflected, not only, and not so much, in its substantive law as in the practice and procedure of its courts. Legal procedure is a . . . ritual of extreme social significance.*[1]

If how a society decides its disputes is "a ritual of extreme social significance," then China's thirty years of legal reform can inform our understanding of how the Chinese state relates to its society and how Chinese citizens relate to one another. Since 1978, China has embarked on legal reforms to promote law as a main mode of dispute resolution. But critics argue that China is establishing legal institutions more to promote economic development and coalesce state power and less to empower ordinary citizens.[2] It is said that ordinary citizens shy away from formal legal mechanisms to resolve disputes because of an historical distrust of the law that is reinforced by recent experiences with Chinese courts. At the same time, the state's distrust of civil society institutions renders bottom-up initiatives unpromising.

This volume takes an on-the ground look at how civil disputes of ordinary citizens are being resolved in China today. In identifying what is going on at the ground level, this volume "disaggregates the Chinese state and society" to focus on the hows and whys – that is, the *process* of "law in action." This approach includes analyses of the process of ideas transmission and the dissemination of law in the Chinese context, discussions of legal institutional dynamics as they affect Chinese legal development,

[1] C. J. Hamson, "In Court in Two Countries: Civil Procedure in England and France," *The Times*, November 15, 1949, p. 5.

[2] *See* e.g., Donald C. Clarke, "The Chinese Legal System Since 1995," *The China Quarterly*, no. 191 (2007): 555–566.

and descriptions of the contours of legal mobilization by different social actors. As a whole, the chapters focus on "law in action" rather than on "law on the books," as well as on legal institutions from the "bottom up" – that is, those at the implementation level who are using and working in the legal system.

The authors take advantage of the growing body of "law and society" literature as well as the body of work on comparative judicial politics. In *Engaging the Law in China*, Neil Diamant, Stanley Lubman, and Kevin O'Brien challenge scholars to recognize the relevance of interdisciplinary research on legal developments in China.[3] In recent years, the growth of scholarship on law and society has meant an increasing number of Sinologists exploring the terrains of Chinese law. At the same time, those in the legal academy have steadily incorporated social science research and methodology into their pedagogy and scholarship. Legal scholars and social scientists are no longer constrained by the belief that law and adjudication are sui generis subjects that can be understood only through specialized legal training.

Yet there is still far too little collaboration among law scholars and social scientists in the area of Chinese law. This volume evolved from a workshop we held at the Fairbank Center for Chinese Studies at Harvard University in the fall of 2007. It was a conversation between those traditionally recognized as legal scholars and social scientists on the growth of law and legality in China and the challenge of rule of law reforms. The workshop brought together leading legal scholars from China, Taiwan, and the United States who have gained unusual access to mainland Chinese courts and other legal institutions. Rather than talking across disciplines, this volume encourages conversations among disciplines to add to our current understanding of these Chinese legal reforms.

This inquiry is particularly timely as China marks its thirty-year anniversary of legal reforms. By sharing existing findings about Chinese legal reforms across disciplines (law and the social sciences) and across regions (the United States, Taiwan, and China), we hope to explore contemporary Chinese notions of justice that seek to balance Chinese traditions, socialist legacies, foreign adaptations, social realities, and the needs of the global market. By providing a state-of-the-field report based on empirical data, we present a retrospective assessment of the thirty

[3] Neil J. Diamant, Stanley B. Lubman, and Kevin J. O'Brien, eds., *Engaging the Law in China: State, Society, and Possibilities for Justice* (Stanford: Stanford University Press, 2005).

years of legal reforms and identify connections that may not have been obvious in the past.

The focus of this volume is on civil dispute resolution – in particular, how once defined as legal, disputes are resolved in China. Civil disputes, along with commercial disputes, are those with which ordinary citizens are most involved. The authors examine what social scientists call "third party (triad) dispute resolution" – that is, when parties delegate a dispute to a third party for resolution. As Alec Stone Sweet has pointed out, triad dispute resolution – two contracting parties and a dispute "decider" – constitutes a primal social institution, a microcosm of governance.[4] By organizing disputes about a community's normative structure, triad dispute resolution performs an important governance function by adapting general rules to the specific experiences and exigencies of those who live under them. In turn, those who initiate the triad learn something about the rules governing their exchange and the normative structure that sustains it. This dynamic of change is observable at both the micro level – the behavior of individual actors – and at the macro level – the institutional environment or social structure in which the dispute is situated. In other words, the individual dispute in China and the manner of its resolution can be reflective of individual identities and motivations as well as a statement of macro-level interactions of power and contestation.

More importantly, under certain circumstances, triad dispute resolutions can be a powerful engine for social change, as the dispute resolution can either reinforce existing structures or adapt or reinterpret existing rules. In the latter scenario, if the agent of dispute resolution has authoritative value and the resolution is taken as the legitimate restructuring of social norms for future cases, triadic decision resolution will be a powerful mechanism of social cohesion and political change.[5] Disputants, in turn, will adapt their own behavior to increasingly differentiated sets of rules, thus (re)making themselves and their community. Systemic change, then, implies the transformation of collective and individual entity and can be observed at the micro level, that is, at the level of individual disputants in seeking resolution.

There are multiple civil dispute resolution methods in China, ranging from formal court adjudication to arbitration (as in labor disputes), mediation, petitions (or "letters and visits"), and even protests in the streets.

[4] Martin Shapiro and Alec Stone Sweet, *On Law, Politics and Judicialization* (New York: Oxford University Press, 2002), pp. 15, 57–60.
[5] Ibid.

Although recognizing that a vast majority of disputes are resolved before their recognition as formal "lawsuits," this volume nevertheless takes as a starting point the view that, increasingly, the "rules of the game" are in fact legal rules. We ask how legal doctrine is shaping the strategies of those who pursue their interests within or without the courts and look at how law has or has not infiltrated and shaped triad dispute resolution in China. We recognize that law is only one set of normative structures in dispute resolution, but we are interested in how law intersects, integrates, and competes with the variety of triadic dispute resolution methods from adjudication to nonadjudicatory methods of resolution, such as petitions, mediation, and arbitration. In each method, parties fight by raising alternative views of the facts and relevant legal norms, with the outcome determining entitlements, governing the power to own and control property, and conferring the right to marry, divorce, work, and live in various places. Even in the recent protest movements in China, we see how concepts of legal rights and entitlements can inform and shape contentious behavior as the legal language leaves the courtroom and appears on the streets and in the media.

We apply what Martin Shapiro calls "political jurisprudence," or "sociological jurisprudence" – that is, recognizing that those working in law are political actors – and apply the same modes of analysis that are applied to other political actors and institutions.[6] We ask the same questions that are asked of other political actors. How do these legal institutions make policy decisions, and how do they relate to other institutional actors? We know that legal institutions, once created, often take on an independent dynamic of their own, including both political self-preservation and institutional competition for expansion. In the Chinese context, we explore legal institutions for public redress – how they have developed and evolved. What are the dynamics among legal institutional players, and how do their organization and work style affect efficacy? But our lens is from the perspective of how Chinese citizens are accessing "justice" mechanisms and how the changes and dynamics in legal institutions impact the daily lives of ordinary Chinese citizens.[7]

In the last decade, scholars have questioned the link of law, markets, and development as key to improved governance. Observers of China's legal reform have long noted that Chinese leaders embrace the economic

[6] Ibid.

[7] The identity of a citizen has been defined as "a personal status consisting of a body of universal rights and duties held equally by all legal members of a nation-state." T. H. Marshall, *Class, Citizenship, and Social Development* (New York: Anchor, 1964).

growth-enhancing effects of "rule by law," but not the "rule of law" reforms that can challenge Communist Party power and authority. As Sally Merry pointed out in her opening remarks at our workshop, law is connected to relations of power. It allocates power through the construction of identities that have consequences, such as citizens/aliens, criminals, urban dwellers/rural migrants, licensed/nonlicensed. In its ability to distribute power, law can be a double-edged sword (used for or against the people). When combined with state and economic power, law can concentrate on oppression as it is used by the state to govern the people (rule by law) rather than used by the people to check the state (rule of law).

"Rule of law" means that law distributes power to ordinary citizens as against the state in subjecting state authority to legal rules and norms as any other citizen. In practice, a system of rule of law must feature independent and impartial decision makers, transparent and open rules that apply uniformly to all (including governmental powers), and a process that ensures the protection of fundamental rights and interests. This means that attention must be paid not only to bolstering institutions such as the legislature, the judiciary, and the legal profession, but also to promoting a legal consciousness and acceptance of the law on the part of ordinary citizens and nongovernmental organizations to whom these laws apply. In other words, "rule of law" requires the use of legal triad dispute resolution by ordinary citizens in ways that directly or indirectly challenge state authority.

We know from law and society scholars that at a minimum, the power of law lies in its discourse and in serving to provide a narrative frame. In other words, law's power lies not only in its ability to settle disputes or to establish social norms, but also in its power to give a name to moral and ethical claims. The law label "legitimizes" an otherwise contentious claim, imbuing it with greater social significance and lessening its political dimension. In other words, law provides a framework within which a victim can connect an injury with a normative violation, blame a violator, and claim relief.[8] Legal process provides a platform on which substantive issues can be contested and debated. A "rule of law" state develops when the law gives context, legitimacy, a name, and a framework to disputes, even when the disputes involve powerful state actors.

[8] William L. F. Felstiner, Richard L. Abel, and Austin Sarat, "The Emergence and Transformation of Disputes: Naming, Blaming, Claiming...," *Law & Society Review* 15, no. 3–4 (1980–1981): 631–654; Lynn Mather and Barbara Yngvesson, "Language, Audience, and the Transformation of Disputes," *Law & Society Review* 15, no. 3–4 (1980–1981): 775–821.

In this volume, we seek to identify when the law works as a narrative frame rather than as an oppressive command – as a platform for debate rather than as a hurdle to overcome. In the ongoing conversation about the nature of the Chinese legal system, we have given much attention to the intentions and desires of leaders with a utilitarian approach to "rule of law" – those who take law to be a new tool for social control and effective governance. But to more fully understand the societal effects of legal development, we also need to investigate the unintended consequences on the actors below, be they the judges who enforce the law, the lawyers who use the law, or the ordinary citizens who rely on the law. This requires analysis of the historical and cultural attitudes toward legal phenomena in China. Rules are not self-enforcing, but rather require internalization of the norms by those to whom they are directed as well as the sanctioning of mechanisms for noncompliance. Thus, an integral aspect of understanding the effectiveness of legal systems requires an investigation into the similarities between rules and norms and the knowledge (misinformation) that laypeople and legal professionals possess about rules, as well as the incentives and disincentives facing them in the use of these rules. This involves a better understanding of the popular attitudes ordinary Chinese citizens have toward legal institutions and legal norms, the origins of such attitudes, and their variation across time, geography, and individual attributes.

We separate the chapters in this volume into three themes. Yet, reflective of how integrally intertwined these questions are and how important it is to bridge disciplines, one or more of these themes flow in and out of every chapter. First, we focus on the dynamics and tensions between the institutions in legal triad dispute resolution. We examine the adjudicatory and mediation systems, with a focus on the judiciary in some detail and its incentives and interactions with other institutions. We also examine the intermediaries of the law, such as lawyers and other quasilegal professionals – what they do, how they developed, and how they compete, interact, and otherwise undermine or sustain the legal system.

Second, we focus on *pu fa* (the dissemination of law) – that is, how legal culture and legal consciousness are developed in contemporary China among Chinese citizens. What are the popular attitudes toward contemporary legal processes and institutions? How do historical traditions and individual attributes affect popular attitudes toward legal institutions? How is the legal consciousness of ordinary citizens changing and coalescing as the use of law to settle disputes increases?

Third, how has law been used to provide a narrative frame for ordinary citizens? If law is invoked by private citizens, does it have the power to challenge the state? Is there an evolving concept of the "private attorney general," that is, enforcement of legal norms through private litigation, to bolster application of the administrative state? Are courts being used as a "democratic" vehicle for ordinary citizens to shape and adjust, if not directly challenge, state-imposed norms?

LEGAL DEVELOPMENT AND INSTITUTIONAL TENSIONS

Legal institutions serve as the mediators of the law and as the site for the "performances of law." Yet, as social scientists have long pointed out, after legal institutions are put in place, the forces of institutional dynamics follow, adding texture to the picture. In several chapters, our authors explore legal institutions according to not only how they are designed, but also how they have meaningfully evolved through use in ways that were unintended. They also look at the institutional dynamics and competition that have added to or detracted from the development of law. In recent years, the Chinese state has implemented and encouraged the development of a wide array of competing legal institutions, ranging from the judiciary, the justice offices, and the legal affairs office to legal journals and periodicals – as well as a wide array of legal actors including judges, private lawyers, legal-service workers, and legal-affairs workers. Authors in this volume assess whether these institutions enforce rights or simply diffuse the bubbling dissatisfaction of public discord, or both. How do these legal institutions adjust state-society relations? In some ways, these institutions may be working at cross-purposes, even as they are reaffirming one another's legitimacy.

In Chapter 1, Fu Hualing and Richard Cullen trace the course of legal reforms from mediatory to adjudicatory justice and back to what they term "neo-mediation." Through this development, Fu and Cullen reveal the growing strength of the Supreme People's Court (SPC) as an institution in determining how civil disputes are to be handled when brought before the courts. Because civil matters historically did not rise to central government attention, the SPC has had unusual liberty in interpreting civil legislation and controlling the form and method of civil litigation in the courts. It is here, according to Fu and Cullen, that a limited form of "civil society" might operate within the parameters of China's current one-party state.

With this limited autonomy, through a series of five-year plans, it was the SPC that moved the civil courts away from "coercive" mediation to adjudication, from Communist Party–centric justice to judge-centric justice. By 1997, the quantity of mediated cases had decreased both in terms of real numbers and percentages. Under adjudication, the burden is placed on the parties to find and present evidence, and the judges, now relieved from time-consuming fact investigation and mediation, can simply decide the facts according to the law.

Yet, as Fu and Cullen point out, more formality has not led to greater satisfaction. Higher expectations and more formal but complex procedures have meant that litigants are less inclined to accept the legitimacy of court decisions. As a result, by the early 2000s, public discontent had led to a dramatic increase in petitions to the central authorities. Concerned with growing unrest, the Chinese Communist Party (CCP) turned its attention to the courts to demand that they fulfill the essential political duty of preventing disputes from occurring or ending them where they occurred – in other words, demanding that the courts refocus attention from the legal aspect to the political and social contexts of disputes and "mediate" toward a "harmonious society." Judges are pushed back from a "public and general role of norm-finding and norm-application to settling private disputes."

But a more interesting observation is the SPC's measured and slow response to this new dictate. As Fu and Cullen note, because judicial reform has taken place only within the judiciary, one would assume that the judiciary is particularly vulnerable to changing party policies. Yet today's more professionalized Chinese judiciary may be more defiant toward political incursions than expected. Hence, to date, while giving lip service to mediation, the SPC has limited this enhanced mediation to specified categories of cases and has reemphasized the importance of court processes and the voluntariness of parties. How this resistance plays out may well foretell important directions of future Chinese judicial reforms and will lend insight into how an institution, once established, may create dynamics of its own.

Whereas Fu and Cullen focus on the interplay between mediation and adjudication and the evolving role of the SPC, Carl Minzner examines the delicate process of discipline and rewards within the judiciary. Of course, "rule of law" requires an independent and competent judiciary on the ground level. Yet Chinese judges are often criticized for their lack of judicial independence and, on the flip side, lack of judicial accountability. In Chapter 2, Carl Minzner examines the constraints on lower court judges in China today. Going beyond the accepted assumptions of the Chinese judiciary as under the political control of the Chinese state, Minzner examines how the internal institutional structure of incentives and promotions can work to inhibit the everyday workings of individual judges. Minzner reveals how the layered hierarchy of judicial discipline is a disincentive to judicial independence and how historical legacies compete with foreign ideas of legality.

Chapter 2 focuses on the Chinese court responsibility system, which promotes and disciplines judges based on a range of factors, including reversals by higher courts for legal errors. Meticulously researched, Minzner's surveys of various provincial regulations uncover an elaborate point system that is used to hold judges both individually and collectively responsible. This has led to lower courts evading responsibility in deciding cases and instead seeking informal advisory opinions from higher courts prior to decision making to avoid reversals. Importantly, Minzner traces this system to the imperial court system, in which Chinese judges are more a part of the bureaucracy than independent professional actors separate from the state. The chapter then supports the argument that Chinese legal reforms are path dependent and not divorced from its historical past. Although it notes the importance of changing legal culture, the chapter also emphasizes the importance of changing structural and institutional incentives in the development of an independent judiciary.

Chapter 3, meanwhile, returns to the theme of bureaucratic competition. Moving away from a focus on courts, Douglas Grob presents a study of the dynamics between China's administrative institutions that preside at the "large city" (*jiaoda de shi*) level and above and China's "legalized local states" below: the legal affairs offices at the county and city level.

Grob's analysis on the legal affairs offices (*fazhiban* or FZBs) of local governments is a much-needed study of a nonjudicial institution that is playing a growing but yet unnoticed role in reconciling local policy with central law dictates. FZBs do not have any legislative capabilities of their own, but they draw their power and influence from their roles in coordinating rule making among competing government departments and hearing grievances against local administrative offices under the Administrative Reconsideration process. As Grob finds, the importance of FZBs grows in settled ways, because in interpreting higher-up laws, the FZB is a gatekeeper in the administrative rule-making process and a gateway to redress for ordinary citizens. Furthermore, tracing each institution's strategic use of legal procedures to enhance its standing and local reputation, Grob concludes that the resultant competition between FZBs and the Justice department offices, such as the *sifa ting* (SFT), can, under some circumstances, actually be beneficial to the rule of law project as each strives to best the other in establishing legality.

Given that lawyers often are the first intermediaries between rules and norms, a number of chapters in this volume focus on the legal profession, its development and growth over time, and the changing relationship between lawyers and their clients. Rule of law requires empowered legal professionals who are accessible to ordinary citizens. Historically, lawyers were viewed with distrust as "litigation tricksters," with Chinese citizens resolving their disputes without any professional assistance. But even as the numbers of lawyers, as well as the use of lawyers, have grown in recent years, the question of whether and how the legal profession can empower ordinary citizens remains.

Chapter 4 provides a useful and timely overview of the legal profession in China as it has developed during the past thirty years. Rejecting the premise that lawyers must be idealized as noble statesmen or vilified as "self-interested actors" or "deeply embedded politically or dependent on social networks," Randall Peerenboom disaggregates the Chinese legal profession, from the professional and newly privatized lawyer in elite law firms to the nonelite, legal-service workers in rural areas to the "barefoot lawyer" activists who have no formal legal training whatsoever. He is optimistic as he traces the development of the legal profession according to economic growth patterns, noting that the development of the legal profession in China by and large has been similar to its development in many other countries. Hence, Peerenboom predicts that a competitive legal market will lead to greater professionalism at every level, that a more robust economy will support more lawyers, and that as the market for legal services matures, individual consumers will become more sophisticated, leading to greater checks on lawyer misconduct. Ultimately, the general modernization story of economic growth, according to Peerenboom, will continue to fuel legal reforms for a long time.

PU FA AND THE DISSEMINATION OF LAW IN THE CHINESE CONTEXT

Institutions (even competing ones) are meaningless without a legal consciousness on the part of ordinary citizens and those whom these institutions address. What are the experiences of ordinary citizens with the legal system? In what ways is law synchronized with local dynamics, culture, and history? Is the legal system, including the procedures underlying it, deemed legitimate by society?

Social scientists examine how knowledge is disseminated and thus how it is distributed. Raising legal consciousness and encouraging people to trust the legal system and respect the law is no easy task.[9] In the context of China, the accepted assumption is that there is an historical distrust of the courts as punitive and as a place of last resort. As such, rather than focusing on building a body of legal professionals, some law reformers have focused on developing a legal culture and consciousness on the part of ordinary citizens and supporting the establishment of law-based civil society groups. The following four chapters explore popular attitudes of Chinese citizens toward the legal system and reveal some surprising results on how legal consciousness is shaped as much by historical legacy as by individual status and institutional changes.

In Chapter 5, Pierre Landry's important work examines popular attitudes of Chinese citizens toward legal institutions as they changed over time. Landry compares survey data collected by Peking University in 2003–04 on the attitudes and behavior of more than seven thousand respondents located in one hundred county units with data in the comparable historical provincial gazetteers. Landry proposes not only that the institutional features of the Nationalist and Maoist eras are still relevant to how these institutions are perceived today, but also that their past performance has a detectable impact on the trust that ordinary citizens are willing to put in them.

Given the role that the people's courts played in the repression of various groups during the 1950s and their presumed paralysis during the Cultural Revolution, one would expect the contemporary Chinese citizen to place less trust in the courts and greater trust in more recent and presumably better-performing non-court institutions. Yet Landry concludes the contrary.

Instead, Landry's survey data reveal that trust is institution specific: that is, non-court organizations that are frequently involved in dispute resolution (such as village committees) receive the lowest rankings, whereas formal legal institutions such as the courts and the procuracy are held

[9] China's latest economic development is enviable in terms of its tremendous growth, but it has also created a rural/urban divide, with the rural areas having limited access to justice. Furthermore, civil society groups are still carefully regulated in China. National regulations issued in 1998 require that to register and obtain legal status civil society organizations must have a government-approved sponsor organization. The government limits sponsor organizations to designated government and party bureaus.

in relatively high regard. Surprisingly, most respondents trust institutions that are closely associated with the state to a far greater extent than they trust nonbureaucratic actors. Similarly, private lawyers are less trusted than courts or public security organs.

Landry concludes that the "trust" is tied to historical legacy. By matching "trust" results with the timing of the original establishment of legal institutions such as the courts, procuracy, and legal-affairs offices, Landry traces the impact of an institution's longevity on popular attitudes. The data reveal that the longer an institution is present in a county, the likelier it is that its past performance still shapes its trustworthiness in the eyes of county residents. The fact that these institutions often bear the same name as during the Nationalist and early Mao periods suggests that the degree of popular trust or distrust in these institutions accumulated before the post-Mao reforms continues to affect how citizens evaluate them today. Thus, in counties that introduced courts early in the Mao regime, when courts performed useful social functions, the level of trust in the people's courts is higher than in localities where courts were introduced later.

According to Landry, then, perceptions of trustworthiness will differ by geography and generation depending on the longevity of the courts, not the longevity of the Communist Party, with trust in legal institutions higher in counties that committed to the revolution late. Significantly, if historical memory of those institutions that predate the reform era still has a powerful impact on contemporary levels of trust in legal institutions, then the strength of Chinese attitudes to endure even in the face of radical reforms cannot be underestimated. The experience of law in China, according to Landry, is not one of discovery but rather one of resurrection and regeneration of legality.

Landry's results contrast somewhat with those of Ethan Michelson and Benjamin Read. In Chapter 6, Michelson and Read present results from their two 2001–02 surveys (adapting the famous 1984 Chicago survey on legal attitudes) of 1,124 households in seven urban districts of Beijing and 2,902 rural households in five provinces (Shaanxi, Henan, Jiangsu, Hunan, and Shandong) and one centrally administered city (Chongqing). Perhaps unsurprisingly, their survey results indicate that in both rural and urban areas, disputes taken to courts are rare (only 0.9% in the Beijing survey and 2.7% of the rural survey reported direct experience with the courts). Even Beijing residents tend to "lump" their disputes or resolve them bilaterally, with the next-most-common response being seeking the help of the police, followed by administrative solutions (at the workplace or government agencies) as well as neighborhood mediation. The likelihood of going to court varied according to the nature of the problem, with personal injuries and criminal matters, property rights, and divorces likelier than other kinds of disputes to go to court. According to Michelson and Read, legal utilization rates are strongly and positively related to the level of economic development, whereby economic development facilitates access to legal system.

More interestingly, those with experience with courts assess the legal system far more negatively than those without, and rural residents are far more negative toward the courts than are Beijing residents. Generally, the closer to courts and the legal system people brought their disputes, the more negatively they assessed their experiences. Furthermore, popular assessments of distributive justice (satisfaction with the outcome) and procedural justice (fairness of the process) were the same, indicating that traditional Chinese cultural values that privilege substantive justice over procedural justice still dominate. Rural Chinese prefer bilateral negotiation and informal relations for dispute resolution, followed by resolution by community leaders and higher-level government agencies, and last by courts, lawyers, and police.

Although Michelson and Read's findings, at first glance, may appear contradictory to Landry's, their results are not irreconcilable. Indeed, as Michelson and Read pointed out, actual experience leading to "informed disenchantment" may lie at the root of negative perceptions of rural residents – whether of the village committees (Landry) or of the courts (Michelson and Read). As pointed out by the latter, this negative perception contrasts starkly with generally positive impressions or, as they termed it, "uninformed enchantment" of the legal system. If so, then legal popularization will need to raise public awareness of both the fallibility and the possibilities of the legal system and lower expectations. Otherwise, whereas popular confidence in the legal system in the most developed parts of China seems to be the norm, "informed disenchantment" may undermine the legal system in the countryside.

In Chapter 7, Mary Gallagher and Yuhua Wang also explore the dimensions of legal consciousness and the dynamics of legal mobilization across the population. They argue that the effects of legal experiences are mediated by an individual's political identity as defined by citizenship status, the nature (and time) of political socialization, and whether the state's role in the dispute is fused as employer and political/legal authority. Based on a four-city household survey on employment and labor law issues, as well as on in-depth return interviews, Gallagher and Wang find that legal experience leads to higher levels of disillusionment and more negative perceptions of the legal system's effectiveness and fairness (external efficacy). However, disillusionment is mitigated by increased feelings of personal efficacy and a sense that one has become educated about the law (internal efficacy). These feelings are most evident among legal-aid plaintiffs whose legal experiences are improved by constant contact with legal-aid staff and their supportive social network.

Most interestingly, different political generations have varied responses to the legal process. Older, urban disputants employed in the state sector are more prone to feelings of disillusionment, powerlessness, and inefficacy. Younger, rural disputants employed in the non-state sectors are likelier to have positive evaluations of their legal experience and to embrace the legal system as a potential space for rights protection. The construction of "rule of law" in China has attenuated the previously strong bonds between the party-state and urban workers in the public sectors but has also created new constituents from groups that previously were ignored or actively discriminated against in the old socialist order. "Rule of law" may be creating new identities that can be supportive of future political changes.

Finally, to complete this section on *pu fa*, in Chapter 8 Sida Liu traces the changing meaning of ordinary legal work in China by analyzing 2,077 cases raised by readers in a legal advice column in the *Democracy and the Legal System* journal from 1979–2003. The evolution of this column "not only witnessed the formal rationalization of Chinese law and its gradual detachment from society . . . , but also the interactions between legal professionals and ordinary citizens and the changing meaning of law constructed through these public correspondences."

Liu analyzes the cases through the lens of the Weberian School (macro-level analysis of the formal rationalization of a modern legal system) and the Amherst School (micro-level interactions in which the meaning of law is constructed through social interactions in everyday life). According to Liu, lawyers' prescriptions for the readers' problems became increasingly rational, shifting the meaning of ordinary legal work from an organic part of social life to a logical, authoritative, yet sometimes incoherent system. Like other authors in this volume, Liu concludes that the progression of advice given in these columns demonstrates the gap between readers' expectations and lawyers' interpretations of the law, often leaving the substantive problem unresolved.

The advice column was first dominated by questions dealing with criminal, family, and inheritance cases. In the 1980s, cases related to contract labor and administrative law emerged and became important categories, whereas the 1990s saw an increase in debt and loan and consumer rights cases (as well as cases on criminal procedure in 1994–98 related to the 1996 revision of the criminal procedure law). The advice initially focused more generally on moral and social norms, but with each successive year, it became increasingly more formalistic and "legal."

In examining three kinds of cases – family and inheritance, debt and contract, and labor disputes – Liu traces the advice column's trajectory from espousing moral norms and social customs and conciliation to legal formality. Ultimately, Liu expresses concerns that the legal system has become overly technocratic, losing sight of the "spirit of the law" in promoting justice. Read in conjunction with the other chapters in this volume, Chapter 8 shows that greater formality does not necessarily mean greater acceptance of law in China. Legitimacy of the legal system would require a delicate balance in which law is publicized but not idealized, imposed from above but diffused from below. There is a need for more areas of dispute resolution in which ordinary citizens can participate and have a say in defining the meaning of the law that is used to resolve the dispute.

LAW FROM THE BOTTOM UP

The next three chapters raise the question of whether the experiences of everyday Chinese life are linked by law to larger social and political forces. They focus on how the current law frame is being utilized by civil society to identify, categorize, and resolve everyday disputes. How are issues framed in the legal context to render its dissemination and ultimate adoption? How are the ideas of "rights" and "law" mediated at the local level? Specifically, has law merely preserved existing power structures, or has it expanded rights and provided the seeds of democratic governance?

In Chapter 9, Benjamin Liebman examines the surprisingly effective popular pressure on the people's courts. He examines the work of the lower civil courts and how the system of letters and petitions serves as a competing site for dispute resolution and as pressure points for changing judicial outcomes. Petitioning, even as it threatens unrest, is consistent with China's embrace of institutional competition and the reliance on multiple party-state entities to serve as checks on malfeasance. According to Liebman, populist justice in China means that a single individual, standing with a sign stating "grievance" outside a local court, has the ability to sway a court's decision. But rather than adjudicating right from wrong and developing a normative prescription for the future, courts are used to "assuage petitioners" to the detriment of "rule of law" principles.

Indeed, according to Liebman, populist pressures on the courts may be greater in nondemocratic systems such as China, where there are few other outlets for expressing popular views. China's letters and visits system, or *xinfang*, refers to the offices that exist at most levels of the party-state to handle both written and in-person complaints. The actual number of petitions remains quite high, and their effects on courts, according to Liebman's interviews of judges, are substantial. Most complaints are from litigants who lack legal expertise or those who may have valid grievances but lack legal recourse; often these are "problems in society" and not issues that the courts can resolve on their own. Court responses can range from changing decisions to reopening decisions to compensating complainants. Some courts have even established "assistance funds" specifically for such purposes.

Like Minzner, Liebman confirm that courts and judges are evaluated and rewarded based on their success in reducing the number of petitions, and they are punished for failing to do so. Certainly, the emphasis on addressing the petitioners' complaints reflects the party-state emphasis on stability. And significantly, courts are concerned not only with collective grievances, but also with individual petitioners, and are swayed even when the chances of unrest are remote. In many instances, a petitioner's ability to persuade or pressure courts is tied to his or her ability to attract the attention of senior party officials or the media. Judges acknowledge ignoring laws on the books or reaching strained interpretations to assuage the petitioners. Interestingly, although petitioning places pressures on courts, it may also sometimes relieve the courts by providing them with strategic arguments to resist pressures from powerful state interests.

Whereas petitioning the courts may reflect the perseverance of problems that undermine court authority, petitioning also speaks to the range of roles that the courts are expected to perform. Courts do not appear to be distinguishing themselves from other state institutions in the minds of those who use them. The increase of letters and petitions to the courts reflects an increasing turn to the courts for social problems. The use of the courts as a locus of protest reflects the fact that courts are increasingly an important space for the resolution of social disputes, but it is also a sign that courts remain political institutions closely tied to the local party-state. More pessimistically, Chapter 9 demonstrates that the Chinese legal system is one in which formal legal rules are increasingly diverging from popular views of justice and in which regime legitimacy continues to be based more on the ability to maintain social stability than on the fairness of the legal system.

In Chapter 10, Fu Yulin continues the focus on the legalized local states by examining legal services at the grassroots level. In providing basic legal services, the legal-services offices and the local justice offices promote legal consciousness in the rural areas and serve as a critical intermediary where the state meets society. Fu examines the role of these offices in disseminating law and shows how the rural residents view the law and its ambassadors. In her study of the legal-services offices; its successor, the local justice offices; and mediation in four counties, she concludes that these offices ascend and decline depending on central policy dictates rather than reflecting populist needs and demands. Problematically, then, when central policy emphasized adjudication, legal-services offices were promoted, and most recently, when central policy retracted adjudication, mediation committees were reinstated.

Fu points out that the reality of economic and political constraints has led, problematically, to the phenomenon of "one group of personnel with three names," with one director simultaneously and alternately performing the functions of the director of the local justice office, the legal-services office, and the mediation committee, depending on the sway and turn of official policy. Such adaptation can but has not led to confusion among the grassroots population. Rather, in their minds, there is no difference between lawyers and non-lawyers, legal-services offices and justice offices, adjudication and mediation. What is important to the grassroots population is not so much expertise or the official name, but that they are familiar with those in the office and that those personnel are from the same home village. In such a way, use and trust in the legal system rely as much on the "personalities" of the individuals and their ability to instill trust in the office as on historical memories and actual experiences with the legal institutions, as argued by Landry and Michelson and Read in Chapters 5 and 6, respectively.

Finally, in Chapter 11 on "judicialization of the constitution" (*xianfa sifahua*), Thomas Kellogg explores both the extent of Chinese citizens' ability to use constitutional litigation to hold the Chinese state accountable and the extent to which litigation (as a whole) adds to the growing group identity of individuals as Chinese citizens. Kellogg examines attempts by actors outside, and to a lesser extent inside, the government to make the constitution a legally operative document, both as a basis for constitutional rights protection and as a check on legislation.

Recognizing that Article 67 of the Chinese Constitution vests the National People's Congress Standing Committee with the power to "interpret" and "supervise the enforcement" of the Constitution, reformers pushing for judicialization are careful in treading around the constitution, rendering sufficiently narrow arguments so as to be at the "very edge of political feasibility." They do not question party authority or the overall structure of the one-party state. Instead, they argue for the court's sharing, rather than displacing, the Standing Committee's authority to interpret the Constitution, and they focus their argument on the SPC rather than lower-level courts.

In a series of seemingly garden-variety civil cases, Kellogg points out the implicit attempts by litigants, activist lawyers, and courts to refer to constitutional norms as a basis for resolving disputes. According to Kellogg, courts act when two private parties, in the absence of specific legal norms that would justify such an outcome, implicitly import constitutional norms such as the right to free expression, right to reputation, right to education, and most recently, in a series of cases challenging hepatitis B discrimination, right to equal protection.

Since 2002, more than forty hepatitis B discrimination cases have been brought to challenge provincial health test standards under the right to equal protection as guaranteed by the Chinese Constitution. Although the courts by and large have been conservative in not ruling on the constitutional claims, these courts did note the arguments. More important than the case outcomes is the fact that by framing hepatitis B carriers as a constitutional antidiscrimination issue, advocates were able to capture the attention of the media, mobilize the public, and force central government attention to the issue. The "legal" frame gave reformers legitimacy and political cover as they argued that the Constitution is a source of law on which courts can draw in adjudicating cases and that courts, as adjudicators, should hear these claims. Needless to say, judicialization of the constitution has enormous democratic benefits. By giving voice to constitutional interpretations in the context of ordinary individuals raising legal claims (rather than on the initiative of the NPC), the process potentially gives enormous power to the judiciary as well as to those ordinary citizens seeking constitutional protection.

Margaret Y. K. Woo's concluding contribution returns to the examination of China's thirty years of legal reform and what it has meant for China's ordinary citizens. Noting that "rule of law" can be co-opted into serving primarily state goals, she nevertheless argues that the legal system, when structured appropriately, can also be an important source of citizen empowerment and participation. Balancing the conflicting goals of justice and efficiency, while maintaining sociopolitical stability and rapid economic growth, the Chinese government continuously experiments with new legal mechanisms, reform of existing mechanisms, and a return to older mechanisms. Yet how these top-down reforms have fared in China depends largely on how law has been received by ordinary Chinese citizens.

In part, Woo argues that use of the legal system, while serving the goal of dispute resolution, also can be an important component of democracy. Even as it funnels social discontent back to the state, civil litigation, if structured liberally, can provide the opportunity for participation by ordinary citizens in both norm setting and norm application. In a society where policy and norms primarily come from the central government, litigation may be one vehicle in which citizens can voice their views and assist in norm setting and norm application by adapting general norms to their specific situations. Litigation, in particular group litigation, can lead to identities of citizenship and empowerment, identities that make a difference in terms of broader political outcomes. This has rendered civil litigation both attractive as well as a source of concern to the Chinese government, resulting in policy ebbs and flows that fluctuate between emphasizing and deemphasizing litigation and the courts.

However, Woo warns that although the use of Chinese courts by ordinary citizens is on the rise, such use is promising only if there are "democratic professionals" to serve as mediators to translate, assist, and otherwise educate the citizens on the technicalities and decisions of the legal system. "Democratic professionals" do not allow their expertise to drown out the local knowledge of the disputants, but rather share their authority to delineate tasks and collaborate in the construction of norms that constrain and direct professional action.[10] Absent such mediators of justice, it is not surprising that heightened legal consciousness and increased use of the courts have only led to greater disillusionment.

[10] Susan M. Olson and Albert W. Dzur, "Revising Informal Justice: Restorative Justice and Democratic Professionalism," *Law & Society Review* 38, no. 1 (March 2004): 150.

In sum, Woo notes that wealth and economic development alone will not guarantee the growth of rule of law. Rather, legal reformers must bear in mind the constant tug and pull between historical determinism and actual experiences on legal culture and the disjuncture such pulls can create; the potential fragmentation of diffuse sources of law despite central dictates; and finally, the growing technical alienation and the danger of high levels of unmet expectations facing Chinese citizens today. Thus, rising legal consciousness has led to wide disenchantment, top-down discipline has led judges to adhere technically to black letter law, and undue pressures on the courts have led to greater corruption rather than greater accountability.

Woo points out that while legal institutions do matter, they exist in a broad inter-dependent matrix, the dynamics of which cannot be ignored, particularly as they play out in the local context where law is adjusted to local conditions. Additionally, even as historical legacy is important for the reception of legal reforms, legal culture is further defined by an individual's actual experience in the legal system. Finally, while formal legal process can create greater predictability, if ossified, formal process can impede the development of courts as a participatory forum.

For Chinese litigants, legal consciousness is growing along with higher expectations for the law and legal process. However, as has been pointed out by other contributors to the volume, "discontent" and "disenchantment" are also increasingly voiced by those with actual experience in the litigating process. When Chinese legal professionals serve more as technocrats or bureaucrats than as "democratic professionals," even objectively fair procedures can be alienating and disempowering. As such, ordinary citizens revert back to paralegal professionals and informal dispute mechanisms, and those moving through the legal process are left with a negative sense of the system. What is developing, then, is a "multi-tracked" legal system in which litigants seek out mediation, litigation, administrative reviews and petitions successively not only to resolve their disputes, but in hopes of a greater voice.

China's thirty years of legal reform have reached a critical juncture. Throughout the years, the legal system has supported China's economic transition to a booming market economy, but for reformers, the question is whether the next thirty years will see law furthering political reforms as well. Considering China's size, geographic variation, and investment in legal change, whether legal reforms are achieving political change will depend both on historical and local contexts. Indeed, one lesson from this volume is the persistence of legal continuity and legal change; that is, legal reformers must recognize how underlying existing law, legal institutions, and legal traditions affect the pattern of reception and change. This means that legal reform does not progress in a direct trajectory but rather meanders along a course that is characterized by as many peaks as valleys as it seeks pockets of space for infiltration. It also means that equal attention must be paid to promoting change in legal culture and legal consciousness and to restructuring umbrella legal institutions.

Given the tremendous inertia of institutional change and the unpredictable tensions that can develop between institutions, change may not necessarily occur from top-down reforms, as in the restructuring of institutions, but rather from bottom-up "bubblings" of local experimentations in how the law is implemented, utilized, and received by ordinary citizens. Sometimes reforms find unexpected space for growth and develop in unexpected ways, as in the interesting interaction of populist pressures on courts. It is how individual citizens creatively use the courts, or how local legislative affairs offices implement the rules, or how individual judges resist political and structural constraints, that are most illuminating and promising for the development of rule of law in China.

PART I

Legal Development and Institutional Tensions

I

From Mediatory to Adjudicatory Justice: The Limits of Civil Justice Reform in China

Fu Hualing and Richard Cullen

INTRODUCTION

One of the most conspicuous changes in judicial policy toward the end of Xiao Yang's two terms (1999–2008) as president of the Supreme People's Court (SPC) was the retreat from a concerted period of civil justice reform, the origins of which can be traced back to 1979 and which was at its most intense during the decade prior to 2006. The hallmark of this recent change in approach has been a shift of priority from adjudicatory to mediatory justice.

By 2006, the SPC had openly conceded the failure of judicial reform programs aimed at enhancing judicial professionalism. The SPC had also issued a series of judicial interpretations to steer the judiciary toward settlement of disputes through court-based mediation. Because of this policy change, local courts are revising their incentive mechanisms to encourage judges to privilege mediation in resolving disputes and to reward them for doing so. Judges and legal scholars are rediscovering the virtues of court-based mediation, including its efficiency, cost-effectiveness, and humanity.[1]

This chapter, in seven parts, studies this transition by examining the rise, demise, and partial resurgence of court mediation in Chinese justice. Section I details the development of the civil justice system of the People's Republic of China (PRC) and explains how its political marginalization helped create the space for its subsequent reform. Section II analyzes what might be termed phase one of the reform process, including the factors driving the striking shift from mediatory

[1] Huang Songyou, ed., *Susong tiaojie yaowu* (Important Matters in Court Mediation) (Beijing: Renmin fayuan chubanshe, 2006).

toward adjudicatory justice. Section III considers the additional momentum of phase two of the reform process, which commenced with the appointment in 1998 of Xiao Yang as president of the SPC. Section IV reviews and clarifies the factors leading to the stalling and partial reversal of civil justice reform. Section V examines how court mediation is used in implementing the political agenda in the construction of a socialist, harmonious society. Section VI is the conclusion.

I. CIVIL DISPUTES AND THE AUTONOMY OF CIVIL JUSTICE

The rise of civil justice came about as a result of three significant changes in China's political and legal matrix since the late 1970s. The first was the open-door policy of the Chinese Communist Party (CCP) and the shift of core state policy from revolution to modernization. The CCP was determined to develop the legal system to serve economic modernization. The second was the diminished use in both quality and quantity of political trials. Counterrevolutionary cases, which dominated the work of the courts, dropped to such a small percentage that they no longer influenced the development of the judiciary.

Indeed, by the end of the 1970s, it was clear that the vast majority of crimes were no longer committed by class enemies – the criminal population was principally composed of juvenile and young offenders. As such, the old mechanisms and procedures associated with "dictatorship" and "class struggle" were no longer applicable, and the entire criminal process needed to be redesigned and softened to address what essentially were contradictions among the people.[2]

The third change was the quantitative and qualitative change in civil disputes. Not only was the number of civil cases rising and expected to continue to do so, but the courts were also experiencing new types of disputes associated with economic liberalization and reform. Civil justice prior to the 1980s was responsible mainly for handling matrimonial matters, disputes between neighbors, small interpersonal debts, and tortuous liability among acquaintances. There were indications by this time, however, that the economic modernization was likely to generate new commercial disputes among strangers and place new demands on the courts.

It was at this pivotal moment that the SPC started to recognize and promote the importance of civil justice. Within the court, the predominance

[2] Fu Huliang, "Juvenile Delinquency in Post-Mao China," *International Journal of Comparative and Applied Criminal Justice* 16, no. 1 (1992): 263–272.

of civil cases and the conspicuous role of civil justice also caused a paradigmatic change. Less "political work" meant that courts became less politicized. This created breathing space for thinking about and formulating judicial policies autonomously. Institutionally, courts were unconstrained by other powerful players (the police in particular) in the areas of civil justice, as they were in criminal justice. Courts in the civil justice system, facing two private parties, act largely on their own. It is true that external authorities have designed numerous mechanisms and procedures, including the CCP leadership, the people's congresses, and procuracy, to hold all courts accountable. However, this external control was indirect and remote and did not touch on the rules of civil procedure and their implementation.

Judicial autonomy was reflected clearly in the power of the civil courts in lawmaking and law implementation. Civil courts are largely free to formulate and implement court rules for handling civil and commercial disputes. One neglected aspect of the operation of the Chinese court system has been the near monopoly of the lawmaking power of the SPC in matters relating to civil justice.

With the CCP withdrawing into the background on civil and commercial matters, the judiciary, because of its institutional capacity to apply the law and resolve disputes, was in an advantageous position vis-à-vis other institutions. The courts may be weak in an authoritarian state, but the legislature often is even weaker. The SPC was the principal sponsor of any civil procedure legislation, and the legislative drafts prepared by the SPC were accepted and passed as law with few amendments by lawmakers. Rules of civil procedures were regarded as highly technical, and the CCP, and the legislature for that matter, were content to leave the drafting and consultation to the SPC itself.

More significantly, the SPC is unconstrained in interpreting national legislation. In 1981, the Standing Committee of the National People's Congress (NPC) authorized the SPC to interpret national laws on its own when dealing with civil disputes. Armed with this delegation of interpretive authority, the SPC has developed the habit of essentially rewriting national legislation to suit judicial practice. SPC interpretations are more specific and can be applied directly to cases at hand. Gradually, it has become the case that what is binding in Chinese courts is not national law but SPC interpretations.[3]

[3] Liu Nanping, *Judicial Interpretation in China: Opinions of the Supreme People's Court* (Hong Kong: Sweet & Maxwell Asia, 1997).

The SPC has the power to not only make and interpret the rules of civil procedure but also to apply the rules and to reform civil justice in the national judicial system. Indeed, the SPC, as the highest judicial authority, is free to push through major civil justice reform with few external constraints. Much has been written about the local control of the PRC judiciary in both the Chinese and English literature. The dependence of the local judiciary on local CCP and government branches is stressed because of the latter's control over judicial appointments and court budgets. However, the SPC and higher people's courts (HPCs) dominate the agenda on professional matters, especially regarding the running of civil justice, including the structure of civil courts, trial procedures, and rules on evidence.[4] The role of mediation and its relations to adjudication are matters for the SPC to decide.

The Paradigm of Civil Justice

The principles guiding civil justice in China evolved from the 1950s to the 1980s, but the general principle of preferring mediation to adjudication remained unchanged. From the establishment of the PRC in 1949 to the late 1980s, the political ideology of the CCP demanded that courts settle disputes using "democratic methods" – that is, by persuading and educating disputants rather than adjudicating their disputes according to established legal principles.[5] The government generally regarded mediation as a necessary and key component of judicial dispute resolution, mandating courts to mediate before adjudicating a case. By 1958, the requirement to mediate became concrete and clear. Judges were required to follow a twelve-character directive: investigation and research, taking mediation as the principal method, and solving disputes when they arise (*diaocha yanjiu, tiaojie weizhu, jiudi jiejue*). Later the directive evolved

[4] Hou Meng, *Zhongguo zuigao renmin fayuan yanjiu: Yi sifa de yingxiangli qieru* (Research of the Supreme People's Court of the PRC: Using Judicial Influence as an Entry Point) (Beijing: Falü chubanshe, 2007).

[5] Stanley B. Lubman, *Bird in a Cage: Legal Reform in China After Mao* (Stanford: Stanford University Press, 1999); Michael Palmer, "The Revival of Mediation in the People's Republic of China (2): Judicial Mediation." In *Yearbook on Socialist Legal Systems 1989*, ed. W. E. Butler (Dobbs Ferry, N.Y.: Transnational Publishers, Inc., 1990), pp. 145–171; Donald C. Clarke and James V. Feinerman, "Antagonistic Contradictions: Criminal Law and Human Rights in China," *The China Quarterly*, no. 141 (1995): 135–154; Fu Hualiang, "Putting China's Judiciary into Perspective: Is it Independent, Competent and Fair?" In *Beyond Common Knowledge: Empirical Approaches to the Rule of Law*, ed. Erik G. Jensen and Tom C. Heller (Stanford: Stanford University Press, 2003), chap. 6.

into sixteen characters: relying on the masses, investigation and research, taking mediation as the principal method, and solving disputes when they arise (*yikao qunzhong, diaocha yanjiu, tiaojie weizhu, jiudi jiejue*).[6]

When the SPC initiated civil justice reform in the late 1970s, the early civil justice rejuvenation was limited to a few fundamental, yet formal, issues. The SPC first demanded a public trial of civil cases, forcing judges to act formally, openly, and responsibly. In particular, open trials demanded formal rules and procedures for judges to follow and set the stage for further procedural innovation and reform. Second, the SPC recognized the substantive and procedural rights of parties in civil justice. This allowed the parties to play a more active and meaningful role in the process, again setting the stage for the development of a more adversarial procedure in the next decade.

Although the judiciary was searching for new forms of civil justice, it had to handle the increasing disputes at hand and rely on what it knew best. Thus, it continued to depend on mediation. Mediation remained the key principle of Chinese civil justice throughout the 1980s, and civil litigation was characterized as a four-steps-to-court procedure, with mediation as one of the essential steps: interview, investigation, mediation, and adjudication.

It was expected that judges, upon receiving a complaint, would interview both parties to understand the claims and defenses. Then the judges would investigate the dispute and gather evidence to substantiate claims and verify defenses. After they became certain about the facts and the law, they (the same judges) were to assemble the disputing parties for mediation. Only after repeated mediation attempts had failed would the matter proceed to adjudication. Proactive judging thus was the key to civil justice. Judges dominated the process because of the extensive pretrial investigation process. The parties, on the other hand, were passive participants and had to place great reliance on the competency and integrity of judges.

Mediation constituted the paradigm for civil justice in China before the end of the 1980s. Trial judges were trained primarily in the Maoist "two contradictions theory" and lacked an alternative approach to civil justice.

[6] Xu Hui, "Dalü minshi susong zhidu de guoqu, xianzai yu weilai" (The Past, Present and Future of the Mainland's Civil Justice System). In *Liang'an sidi falü fazhan, xiace: Minshi susong yu xinshi susong* (Cross-Strait, Four-Region Law Development in Taiwan, China, Hong Kong, and Macau, Volume Two: Civil Procedure and Criminal Procedure), ed. Dennis T. C. Tang and Peng-Hsiang Wang (Taipei: Zhongyang yanjiuyuan falü xueyuan yanjiusuo choubeibuchu, 2007), pp. 201–229.

Courts considered mediation the core of civil justice, and adjudication was rendered as a default position. With few judges being formally educated in law, it was natural for them to rely on mediation and for the court to impose a high rate of successful mediations.

II. JUDICIAL REFORMS

The shift in judicial policy toward settlement has taken place at three levels. At the personnel level, formally trained judges have been replacing the old generation of revolutionary cadres; at the ideological level, the judiciary has been promoting judicial professionalism and formalism in civil justice; and at the policy level, the judiciary has been emphasizing the importance of adjudication in developing rules and the rule of law. The shift in judicial policy began gradually and steadily to limit the use of mediation.

A New Generation

Chinese law schools reopened and recruited law students on a large scale in 1978. In that year, six law schools admitted a total of 729 students; the number increased to 1,947 in 1979, 2,557 in 1980, 3,483 in 1981, and 3,678 in 1982.[7] The legal education that the students, especially those admitted in 1978 and 1979, received was more political than legal and more ideal than pragmatic. China had very little law at that time but had high expectations as to what the law could provide. Students studied more legal history and legal philosophy (both Chinese and Western) than technical legal rules. There was much less cynicism regarding what the law could and should provide. Immediately after the end of the Cultural Revolution, there was a consensus within the CCP and society in general that the chaos and violence that had taken place in China should never occur again and that the best route to prevent a recurrence was through the institutions of law and the rule of law.

The fact that a large proportion of the students, like the political leaders, had personally suffered during the Cultural Revolution only reinforced their faith in the law. The new generation was not merely to apply or practice law; they were to change the law and use it to change society.

[7] Huo Xiandan, *Bujie zhi yuan: Ershi nian faxue jiaoyu zhi jianzheng* (The Indissoluble Bound: The Witness of the Twenty Years of Legal Education) (Beijing: Falü chubanshe, 2003).

The new generation of students regarded themselves as the watershed in Chinese legal development, representing the division between lawlessness and the rule of law. There was a strong sense of mission on the part of the fresh graduates to subvert the existing (and discredited) system and to start a new way of doing things.

When the first batch of law students graduated in 1982, their practicing opportunities were equally unprecedented. At the time, there was a serious shortage of legal expertise in key positions at every level of the judiciary. The logical decision for most of the graduates was to join the courts, procuracy, and justice at the central and provincial levels.[8] The legal profession was in its infancy and attracted only a minority of the graduates. There was such a thirst for expertise in these formative years that the new graduates were immediately useful and instrumental in reforming the judiciary. The combination of talent and opportunity provided the catalyst for legal reform in China.

The large number of law school graduates entering the judiciary formed an important faction within the courts. They formed a new identity and developed new interests that were different from and challenged those of their revolutionary comrades. The overall percentage of formally trained law school graduates is still small in the judiciary in China. But the percentage was even smaller in the 1980s. In 1983, for example, among the 130,000 court personnel in China, only about 8,000 had received a tertiary education, accounting for 7 percent of the total number of court personnel in China in that year. Fewer than 3 percent of the total number of court cadres and the police were university law school graduates,[9] most of whom had been legally trained in the 1960s.[10] According to an SPC report, only five hundred university students were allocated to the courts in the entire country in the three years from 1980 to 1983.[11]

[8] For an interesting study of the career path of 389 law students who graduated in 1985 from an unnamed law school, see Chen Huigu, "Xunzhao shehui bianqian de yinji: Yi biye 20 nian de falü daxuesheng qunti wei fenxi danwei" (Searching for the Footprints of Social Change: An Analysis of a Group of Law Students Twenty Years after Their Graduation), *Bijiaofa yanjiu* (Studies of Comparative Law), no. 3 (2006): 138–146.

[9] Su Zelin, "Sifa kaoshi dazao zhiye menkan" (Judicial Exam Creates Professional Requirements), *Renmin wang*, n.d., http://www2.qglt.com.cn/wsrmlt/jbzl/s/suzelin/su1.html (accessed September 12, 2007).

[10] Zhang Jianjun, "Woguo sifaguan linxuan zhidu de jiangou" (Construction of the System for the Selection of Judicial Officers of our Country), *Guojia jianchaguan xuexiao xuebao* (Journal of the National Procurators College), no. 5 (2005): 50.

[11] See Huo Xiandan, *Bujie zhi yuan*.

Yet those percentages may be misleading. During the 1980s, more than 80 percent of the law school graduates joined various legal organs (*sifa jiguan*) at the central or provincial levels or in the coastal cities.[12] Many of them joined the SPC, the Supreme People's Procuratorate (SPP), and the Ministry of Justice (MoJ) in Beijing or their provincial counterparts. These are high-level decision-making bodies. This was especially true for the graduates in the first half of the 1980s.

Another cohort of graduates joined legal institutions in the large coastal cities, such as Shanghai, Guangzhou, and Shenzhen.[13] This was particularly true in the second half of the 1980s. By the late 1980s, judges in the SPC, HPCs, and courts in the coastal, economically advanced cities were highly professionalized (if formal legal training of judges is used as the yardstick). A third group of graduates joined legal academia after graduate studies in China or overseas. They immediately started to introduce (often idealized) foreign legal practices and to promote legal reform in civil procedure to modernize and institutionalize China's civil justice. Through their teaching and publications, they also influenced generations of future judges who would carry on the reforms.

Together, these groups of lawyers formed a liberal-minded iron triangle that maintained a common conception of legal reform and also often knew one another. Jointly, they initiated and carried out a liberal judicial reform of China's civil justice system. Academic lawyers, using the freedom associated with their position, launched critical reviews of existing practices and put forward and supported reform proposals. Judges in the SPC formulated and made decisions based on the work of the academic experts and on the experience of the legal reforms in the coastal cities.

Each party in the community contributed to civil justice reform in its own way. Judges in the SPC, with the support of HPC judges, played a leading role in the reform process. Courts in the coastal cities provided sites for pilot projects and, more importantly, an actual model for the operation of reformed civil justice in the late 1980s and early 1990s. Legal academics drummed up support for the reform programs. There

[12] Zhao Xiaoqiu, "Huifu, shi yiqie de kaishi: Faxue jiaoyu 30 nian de bianqian" (Restoration is the Beginning of Everything: Changes in Legal Education in the Past Thirty Years), *Falü yu shenghuo* (Law and Life), no. 14 (2007): 22.

[13] Pan Jianfeng, "Zhongguo sifa zhidu gaige de ruogan wenti" (On Several Questions concerning the Reform of China's Judicial System), *Yantai daxue xuebao (zhexue shehui kexue ban)* (Journal of Yantai University) (Philosophy and Social Science) 14, no. 2 (2001): 145–153.

was a gradual, but fundamental, shift in the understanding of the proper role and function of the judiciary in society.

Attack on Mediation

For the new Chinese judges, a court was not a "court" if it principally performed the function of keeping peace and order rather than determining right or wrong and distinguishing the guilty from the innocent.[14] If the incentive structure in the court process was such that the courts and judges aimed primarily at ending disputes and the judges were rewarded and sanctioned accordingly, the resulting process was hardly "judicial." A settlement court, the defining characteristic of Chinese civil courts in Maoist China, did not satisfy these key hallmarks of a modern, common rule defining the judiciary. Chinese judicial reformers wanted their courts to play a more general, public, and normative role in applying and proclaiming rules. After this conceptual foundation against mediation was formulated, judges and legal academics joined forces to challenge the cost-effectiveness, efficiency, and fairness of mediation.

First, mediation as practiced was not voluntary. Parties settled mainly because of the pressures applied by the trial judges. To increase the amount of mediation, the courts imposed a quota for the judges and rewarded those who were able to achieve a higher rate of mediation among their cases. The judges, in turn, transferred the political pressure to the parties, inducing or forcing them to settle.[15] Because of the political demand for settlements, court mediation turned out to be "far more adjudicatory, aggressive, and interventionist."[16]

Because of the lack of genuine consent, the agreement that the court imposed was often unfair. Likelier than not, it was the weaker party, the plaintiffs in particular, who compromised their interests to reach a settlement. In a study in Shenzhen in which 210 judges in the Shenzhen courts were asked 34 questions relating to court mediation,[17] about

14 Theodore L. Becker, *Comparative Judicial Politics: The Political Functionings of Courts* (Chicago: Rand McNally, 1970), p. 100.

15 Lubman, *Bird in a Cage*, p. 275.

16 Philip C. C. Huang, "Court Mediation in China, Past and Present," *Modern China* 32, no. 3 (2006): 287.

17 Wang Yong, Wen Changzhi, and Wang Dejun, "Zhuanbian tiaojie guannian, shenhua tiaojie gaige, chongfen fahui tiaojie zuoyong" (Changing the Understanding about Mediation, Deepening Mediation Reform, and Fully Promoting the Functions of Mediation). In *Tiaojie zhidu gaige yu tansuo* (Reforming and Exploring the Mediation System), ed. Deng Jilian (Shenzhen: Haitian chubanshe, 2003), p. 20.

two-thirds admitted that mediation has been directly or indirectly imposed on the parties. This was done by pressuring and inducing the parties to settle or by stalling the parties through repeated mediation. In addition, the judges initiated a mediation process in 66.3 percent of the cases, and 66.5 percent of the judges reported that the judges, rather than the parties, played the main role in mediation, including facilitating mediation sessions and reaching a mediation agreement.[18]

Mediation also bred corruption. In settling a case, the courts enjoyed wide discretion. Judges decided on the facts and the evidence. They also chose which process to apply – mediation, adjudication, or anything in between. Worst of all, there were few rules of procedure regarding mediation – at least the judges themselves felt they were not guided by any rules. In the Shenzhen survey, 62 percent of the judges reported that there was little or no guidance on mediation, and 38 percent said there were only indirect rules and constraints.[19]

There was little accountability in mediation. First, the process was secretive, informal, and invisible, and there were no regular accountability mechanisms. Many judges preferred this decreased accountability. Second, it was much easier to achieve the end product of the process than through an adjudicative process. It was easier to write a mediation agreement than a judgment for the simple reason that it was supposed to be an agreement between the parties. In mediation, the parties' participation and consent replaced the reasoning of the judges, and it generally sufficed that the judges provide an accurate record of the consent.

Third, and most importantly, after an agreement is reached, the entire matter generally is ended, as far as court procedure is concerned. There is no appeal and thus no supervision from an appellate court and the associated risk of a change of decision, reversal, or retrial. The principal risk to which a judge is exposed in a regular judicial process thus is avoided. Despite all of the criticisms of mediation by the judges, on balance, some judges preferred mediation because of the ultimate perceived advantages, especially in difficult cases.

Mediation could take place at different stages during the trial process. The following statistics (see Table 1.1) demonstrate the informal and irregular nature of mediation.

18 Ibid., p. 23.

19 Ibid. The indirect constraints include the time limit within which a judge is required to complete a case.

TABLE 1.1. *When, where, and how Shenzhen Judges conducted mediation*

How many times mediation was conducted in one case	Once (44%)	Twice (42.5%)	Three times (13.5%)
When	Pretrial (23.7%)	During trial (29%)	After trial (22.4%)
Where	In court (66.2%)	In office (31.6%)	Out of court (2.2%)
How	With both parties (67.8%)	Ex parte (32.2%)	

Source: Wang Yong, Wen Changzhi, and Wang Dejun, "Zhuanbian tiaojie guannian, shenhua tiaojie gaige, chongfen fahui tiaojie zuoyong" (Changing the Understanding about Mediation, Deepening Mediation Reform, and Fully Promoting the Functions of Mediation). In *Tiaojie zhidu gaige yu tansuo* (Reforming and Exploring the Mediation System), ed. Deng Jilian (Shenzhen: Haitian chubanshe, 2003), p. 22.

There was no formal record kept of the process. Because the same judges who mediated disputes also adjudicated them if the mediation failed, those judges were in a strong position to influence the choices of the parties. Given the nature of mediation, there were ample opportunities for ex parte contacts between the parties and their lawyers.

Mediation was more labor intensive and time-consuming. It was common that mediated settlements would take longer than adjudication. Because this process was more time-consuming, city courts, facing a surge in civil cases, moved to abandon mediation in favor of speedier adjudication.[20] It is important to note that the amount of time, as calculated by days, was shorter for mediation than for adjudication.[21] But a careful reading of the studies suggests that although it took fewer days to achieve a mediated result, it actually took more hours. Judges tended to work in a labor-intensive manner to iron out an agreement as quickly as possible before one of the parties changed his or her mind. As one author comments, although adjudication puts additional mental pressure on the judges because of the accountability mechanism, mediation puts pressure

[20] Ibid., p. 23.

[21] The rest of the 284 cases were classified as others, including withdrawal, transfer of jurisdiction, et cetera, which took an average of 66 days. Tang Yingmao, "Yige guanyu panjue, tiaojie he zhixing guanxi de shizheng yanjiu" (An Empirical Study of the Relations between Judgment, Mediation, and Enforcement), *Zhongwai faxue* (Peking University Law Journal) 18, no. 6 (2006): 752–760.

on the judges physically because of the additional time and energy needed to achieve a result.[22]

Mediation was not necessarily more effective than adjudication in resolving disputes. Although judges could press the parties to enter into a mediation agreement by prolonging the trial or by other means, the agreement was not legally binding until the court served the signed agreement on the involved parties.[23] Naturally, some parties used mediation as a stalling tactic: agreeing to settle but engaging in lengthy negotiation and then refusing to honor the agreement.

Mediation was expected to improve enforcement because of the consensual decision making, so that after the parties left the court, the matter would end – by immediate execution of the agreed-upon settlement. However, empirical evidence shows that enforcing a mediation agreement is just as difficult as enforcing a court judgment.[24]

Most importantly for the SPC judges, mediation deterred the development of judicial professionalism and the rule of law. In court mediation, the judges were not only lawyers and educators, but also social workers tackling the deeper causes of a dispute.[25] Mediation in China relies on life experiences and people skills and places little emphasis on legal knowledge and legal skills or on what may be legally right or wrong.[26] The model judge/mediators traditionally have been dedicated CCP members with little education, not to mention little legal education. There were few incentives for judges to develop legal skills.[27] Younger judges in particular prefer adjudication to mediation. It is their basic skills that determine this preference. Increasingly, Chinese courts are filled with law graduates with few incentives and little ability to solve cases through mediation.[28]

[22] Ibid.

[23] Civil Procedure Law, Art. 191.

[24] Fan Meiqing, Mei Xianming, and He Xiaohui, "Tiaojie: Yao fang 'anjie shi weiliao'" (Mediation: Must Prevent Cases Completed But Disputes Continue), *Renmin fayuan bao* (People's Courts Post), April 26, 2007, http://rmfyb.chinacourt.org/public/detail.php?id=108145 (accessed September 28, 2007); Tang Yingmao, "Yige guanyu panjue."

[25] Huang, "Court Mediation in China," 298–299.

[26] This in part explains the lack of training and training materials for mediators. Because mediation is treated mainly as an art, not a science, the passing of mediation skills from one person to another becomes difficult.

[27] During interviews with judges, one factor that affects whether mediation is preferred is a judge's educational background. Young judges with a formal education tend to prefer adjudication to mediation. In the Shenzhen survey, when asked, "Why not resort more to mediation?" 44.9 percent of the judges responded that they did not know how. Wang Yong et al., "Zhuanbian tiaojie guannian," p. 22.

[28] Huang Songyou, ed., *Susong tiaojie yaowu*, p. 25.

At a deeper level, mediation privatizes disputes and issues of social concern and blocks the development of general legal norms and the rule of law. This concern as it relates to China is best explained by Owen Fiss and David Luban, who succinctly point out how and why such widespread mediated settlement erodes the public realm and reduces the opportunities to produce, clarify, and reaffirm norms that are fundamental to society. For Luban, a court is a public forum engaging a much wider audience than the parties to a case. The public has a vested interest in the adjudicative process because a court distinguishes between right and wrong, defines the rules, and confirms social values, thus building a sociolegal framework to govern citizen behavior. Mediation, according to Luban, compromises principles and privatizes public issues, creating a "private peace" and avoiding public participation and accountability.[29]

For the (new) professional judges in China, justice demands, privileges, and also depends on the existence and use of legal principles and rules to resolve disputes. The Shenzhen survey presented in Table 1.1 is illustrative of the tensions between mediation and justice. Slightly more than 40 percent of the judges said that mediation could not bring justice and fairness,[30] and nearly 40 percent said that the rights of the parties were not clearly stated in mediation and thus could not be effectively protected.[31] This unfairness was reflected in the fact that in 85.8 percent of the mediated cases, it was the plaintiff (the right-claiming party) who made concessions to accept a mediated result, and in only 14.2 percent of the cases did the defendant (the duty-owing party) make concessions.[32]

The Reform of Court Mediation

The shift of focus in judicial policy from mediation to adjudication was gradual but highly visible. Once they occupied key positions in the judiciary, the fresh law-school-graduate judges, encouraged and assisted by their liberal-minded teachers, put their beliefs and ideals into practice, initiating a series of civil justice reforms.

[29] David Luban, "Bargaining and Compromise: Recent Work on Negotiation and Informal Justice," *Philosophy and Public Affairs* 14 (1985): 397–416; David Luban, "Settlements and the Erosion of the Public Realm," *Georgetown Law Journal* 83, no. 7 (1995): 2,619–2,662.

[30] Wang Yong et al., "Zhuanbian tiaojie guannian," p. 23.

[31] A minority of 20 percent of the judges preferred mediation because it was informal and could not be supervised by an appelate court. It was regarded as a low risk method of dispute resolution. Ibid., p. 22.

[32] Ibid., p. 26.

The SPC began to rethink the role of mediation in civil justice in 1979 when China started to draft the first Civil Procedure Law. One product of the resulting debate was the replacement of "taking mediation as the principal method" with "emphasizing mediation" in the Civil Procedure Law (Trial) in 1982. Although the new directive may have alleviated forced "mediation," civil justice remained tied to mediation, only supplemented by adjudication.

The SPC officially initiated civil trial reform in 1988. A key component of this reform was to limit the role of mediation and prevent the abuse of mediation that was common within the judicial process. Stressing the importance of mediation in solving disputes, the SPC nevertheless denied the legitimacy of using the rate of mediation to evaluate the performance of the courts and judges and strongly criticized the common practice of unlawful and coercive mediation.

By the second half of the 1980s, the judiciary no longer privileged mediation. Rather than emphasizing mediation, the court started to use voluntariness and lawfulness as the core tests to measure the legitimacy and efficiency of mediation. The talk of the day was that a court should not impose an agreement without the genuine consent of the parties involved and that mediation should comply with the law both substantively and procedurally.

The 1991 Civil Procedure Law was an important milestone in the transition from mediatory to adjudicatory justice. As a matter of legal principle, the new law emphasized that mediation must be voluntary and lawful. Upon the failure of mediation, judges should proceed immediately to adjudication.[33] The SPC further clarified that if one or both parties to a dispute declined mediation, the judges should give a prompt judgment. Even in the case of a petition for divorce in which mediation was the precondition for adjudication, judges were not to repeat mediation without rendering a decision if one or both parties declined mediation.[34] Although judges could try to persuade the parties to settle through mediation, ultimately they were required to respect, and give effect to, party autonomy in civil justice.

Lawfulness was an even more important requirement. Mediation was lawful only if it was based on a clear finding of the facts and a clear distinction between right and wrong.[35] A more significant constraint on

[33] Civil Procedure Law, Art. 9.

[34] SPC Opinion on Several Questions on the Implementation of the Civil Procedure Law, Art. 92.

[35] SPC Opinion on Several Questions on the Implementation of the Civil Procedure Law, Art. 85.

mediation was the newly imposed time limit in which a court had to dispose of a case. According to the law, a court had to complete a case within six months for regular proceedings or three months for summary proceedings (after the court accepted the case).[36] This legal mandate deprived judges of the opportunity to solve cases through prolonged and repeated mediation.

New judges understood the role of the courts, the commitment to the law, and the value of settlement through mediation differently from their predecessors. Yet their understanding of the law and the courts was also shaped by the surrounding circumstances and the cases they handled. Court cases have been growing steadily, and more importantly, the pressure of this growth has been disproportionately felt by the urban courts, especially those in the large, coastal cities. Pressures to complete the cases within a specified time limit force the judges to adopt a more formal(istic) model of judging, relying on formal rules and evidence as produced, and to dispose of cases as quickly as they arrive. Judges in such courts have little time, resources, or patience to think carefully about the immediate (or longer-term) social consequences of their judgments.

III. XIAO YANG'S JUDICIAL REFORMS

It is within the above context that Xiao Yang initiated his Five-Year Plan for Court Reform,[37] commencing in 1999. When Xiao Yang took the helm at the SPC, the time was ripe to accelerate and systematize the piecemeal judicial reform that previously had been achieved. Xiao Yang was confident of his ability to implement systematic judicial reforms.

The core of the judicial reform under Xiao Yang was the promotion of judicial justice and efficiency. Each term has a specific meaning, and each highlights the new function and role of the courts in China. Judicial reformers clearly distinguished substantive justice from procedural justice, arguing that justice in China was principally defined in substantive terms and was results oriented. Little attention had been paid to procedural fairness and justice. Thus, there had to be a shift in Chinese civil

[36] Civil Procedure Law, Arts. 135 and 146. Another significant development was the ban on mediation in judicial review cases because of the power disparities between the two parties and because of the public nature of the cases. For a discussion of the significance and challenges, see Michael Palmer, "Controlling the State? Mediation in Administrative Litigation in the People's Republic of China," *Transnational Law and Contemporary Problems* 16, no. 1 (2006–2007): 165–186.

[37] Zuigao renmin fayuan yanjiushi, ed., *Renmin fayuan wunian gaige gangyao* (Outline of the People's Courts' Five-Year Plan) (Beijing: Renmin fayuan chubanshe, 2000).

justice toward a much greater emphasis on procedure. Judges and legal scholars reiterated the importance of the appearance of justice.

What are the components of procedural justice? The quality of the judges became a foundational issue. If judges without a formal education are ideal for mediation and for providing substantive justice, a law school education and legal training are essential for providing procedural justice. Procedural justice relies on judges who are well versed in the law and who can act judicially. Many such judges joined the SPC and the provincial courts, taking positions that allowed them to make and shape important judicial policies. Young judges institutionalized their professional ideologies by designing specific rules and putting their beliefs about justice into practice. Throughout the late 1980s and early 1990s, the SPC issued a series of rules on civil procedure. As lawyers and judges started to use the rules, civil justice became more procedurally complicated. Gradually, the conceptual distinction between issues of law and issues of fact became clear and relevant, and judges considered their responsibilities in the law/fact equation and became aware of the methodological issues in finding the distinctions. Judicial reformers dreamed of a modern and formalistic legal system characterized by its ability to elevate legal principles above messy factual situations.

Justice means party autonomy in civil cases, with a corresponding shift in the burden of proof from the judges to the litigants. The core of this phase of civil justice reform was to shift from judge-centric justice to party-centric justice. In this system, the inquisitorial judges were withdrawn to the background, whereas the parties (and their representatives) were allowed, and indeed required, to play a more active and assertive role, contributing meaningfully to a more adversarial process. The courts shifted most of the responsibilities to the parties, relieving the judges of most of the fact finding. Judges, as legal specialists, were to take care of the legal delicacies, leaving the factual issues to the parties themselves. As it happens, the judges likely were also making a virtue out of necessity by moving to a party-centric approach and allowing more party freedom. The sudden increase in disputes made it impossible for the judges to continue their inquisitorial styles, time-consuming factual investigations, and repetitive mediation.[38]

[38] Huang observes that although the horizontal jurisdiction of the courts may have expanded, "the (vertical) interventionist reach of the courts into the private lives of people has diminished." Philip C. C. Huang, *Civil Justice in China: Representation and Practice in the Qing* (Stanford: Stanford University Press, 1996), p. 167.

Once the parties were required to produce evidence, the SPC created new evidence rules for civil justice. Important rules governed the time limit for the parties to produce evidence; the admissibility of evidence after the time limit elapsed; the exchange of evidence between parties before the trial; and exclusionary rules limiting the production of new evidence at the appellate level. These new rules not only shifted the burden to produce evidence to the parties raising an issue, but they also compelled the parties to act expediently, responsively, and professionally.

Given the new requirement for pretrial preparation by the parties, the role of the judges changed accordingly. Sitting in on his or her court hearing submissions and evaluating evidence became not only possible but necessary. A natural follow-up change abolished all of the pretrial judicial investigations for a case, changing the procedure from *four-steps to court* to *one-step to court* in the early 1990s. As part of the measures against judicial corruption, judges were now prohibited from making any ex parte contacts with the parties or their lawyers (a key component of how the mediation was practiced) to ensure both the reality and appearance of justice.

The final component in the reform process was the requirement for prompt in-court delivery of decisions upon hearing the cases. The SPC required judges to decide their cases and announce their decisions immediately following the trial in the majority of the cases they adjudicated. In-court deliveries of judgments were a key component in Xiao Yang's first Five-Year Reform Plan.[39] Although a prompt in-court delivery of the judgments may strengthen the decision-making power of individual judges during a trial, it also reduces the opportunities for court mediation.

Judicial efficiency was narrowly defined, and the judicial bureaucracy defined judicial effectiveness largely according to either political imperatives or bureaucratic interests. One key measure of effectiveness is the three-month time limit for civil litigation, which is rigidly followed. Under the Civil Procedure Law, after receiving and accepting a civil case, a court should render a decision within three or six months depending on whether regular or summary proceedings are to apply. Although the time limit is frequently violated in both county and city courts,[40] it is an issue that

[39] The Five-Year Plan and other SPC documents required a "gradual increase" in in-court delivery of decisions throughout the courts. See Zuigao renmin fayuan yanjiushi, ed., *Renmin fayuan wunian gaige gangyao*.

[40] The common explanation for the delay in city courts is the increase in caseloads, so judges are unable to complete the trial within the specified time limit. The explanation for the delay in rural courts is usually the geographic distance between the courts and the

judges need to face constantly. Senior judges in charge of case management closely monitor the time limit and constantly remind others judges accordingly.

Another measure used to enhance judicial efficiency, which is more political than legal, is the case completion rate. Case completion requires that the courts finish by the end of the year most, if not all, of the court cases received and accepted during that year. Most courts achieve a near 100 percent completion rate, meaning they complete all the cases they accepted within the year. This time limit produces further strains on court mediation, which, as noted above, is often both time and labor intensive.

Under the combined "assault" of judicial professionalism, procedural justice reform, and the introduction of adversarial proceedings, mediated cases declined steadily from the mid-1980s to the mid-2000s (see Figure 1.1). The procedural reforms and the new efforts to enhance procedural justice and efficiency have rendered mediation much less likely in civil disputes.

The decline in mediated cases occurred in courts across China. Beginning in 1982 and continuing steadily, the decline was sharper in the city courts than in the county courts. Before 1996, the annual number of mediated cases increased, although their percentage declined. But after 1997, both the number and percentage of mediated cases dropped.[41] In the Guangdong courts, for example, the mediation rate declined from 67.7 percent in 1989 to 23.6 percent in 2001.[42] In 2001, the mediation rate was as low as 12 percent in courts in Shenzhen,[43] and in one

litigants, in particular the transportation and communication problems. In Guangzhou Intermediate People's Court, 61 percent of the civil cases (a total of 11,086 cases) in 2003 were completed within the time limit. See Sun Hailong and Deng Juanrun, "Lun chao shenxian zhi keguan chengyin jiqi yingdui" (Objective Cause of Exceeding the Time Limit and the Countermeasures), *Beida falü xinxi wang*, http://article.chinalawinfo.com/article/user/article_display.asp?ArticleID=30393 (accessed October 7, 2008) (on file with the authors). For the problems facing the county courts, see Ji Bumin and Ji Jinlin, "Wosheng fating chao shenxian minshi anjian de chengyin yu duice" (Causes for Exceeding the Time Limit in Civil Cases in our Province and the Countermeasures), *Tianya falü wang*, August 13, 2004 (on file with the authors).

41 Huang Songyou, ed., *Susong tiaojie yaowu*, p. 25.

42 Ji Yuan, "Minshi susong zhong de tiaojie yanjiu" (Research on Mediation in the Judicial Process). In *Tiaojie zhidu gaige yu tansuo* (Reforming and Exploring the Mediation System), ed. Deng Jilian, pp. 43–51.

43 Wang Yong et al., "Zhuanbian tiaojie guannian." The mediation rate for civil cases in the appelate court fell to 2 percent.

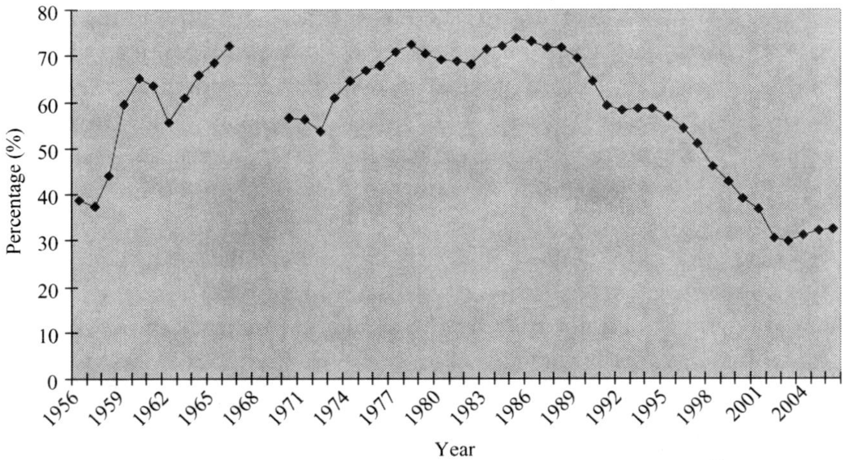

FIGURE 1.1. Percentage of Civil Cases Concluded by Mediation (1956–2006)
Source: For figures between 1956 and 1998, see Zuigao renmin fayuan yanjiushi, ed., *Quanguo renmin fayuan sifa tongji lishi ziliao huibian, 1949–1998* (Judicial Statistical Compendium of the Courts) (Beijing: Renmin fayuan chubanshe, 2000); for figures between 1999 and 2006, see *Zhongguo falü nianjian* (China Law Yearbook). Statistics were not available in the late 1960s. *Note:* For some years, the figures reported in the *Zhongguo falü nianjian* (China Law Yearbook) are slightly different from those reported in the *Zuigao renmin fayuan gongzuo baogao* (SPC Work Reports).

Shenzhen district court, it was as low as 8 percent.[44] This steady decline and low rate of mediation were common in urban courts, especially those in the major coastal cities. However, mediation remained relatively high in the county courts and in the courts in small cities, even though a decline was also visible.

IV. DISPUTES, STABILITY, AND THE POLITICIZATION OF THE COURTS

Civil justice reform has been self-contained in the sense that its impact has been felt mainly within the courts and among the judges. It has not affected any other key, powerful state institutions. Indeed, some have watched the judicial reform with admiration, but more with amazement

[44] Zhu Zhu, "Tiaojie zhidu chonggou zhi yanjiu" (Studying the Restructuring of Mediation). In *Tiaojie zhidu gaige yu tansuo*, ed. Deng Jilian, p. 91. Among 6,577 civil cases decided in Futian District Court, only 578 were resolved through mediation.

and amusement. As long as the CCP remained largely uninterested in civil cases, the courts achieved autonomy by default and the reform continued. Yet the CCP's lack of interest in civil justice reform is a result of the perceived triviality of case matters. After civil cases move from the periphery to the center, one can expect the CCP to take serious notice.

Judicial Effectiveness

The CCP began to pay attention to civil cases in the early 2000s. It became increasingly alarmed not only by the significant increase in the number of civil justice cases in dispute, but also by the public manifestations of discontent and the persistent and confrontational approach adopted by the disputants. The number of citizen petitions has been huge in China,[45] but what attracted the attention of the central leaders was the sudden surge in the number of petitions to the central authorities in Beijing in the early 2000s. In 2003, the number of petitioners that the State Administration of Petitions received surpassed the figure for 2002 by 29.9 percent, and there was a 94.9 percent increase in the first three quarters of 2004. Yu Jianrong argues that the failure to satisfy the demand of petitioners was diminishing the credibility of the central authorities, and as a result, the petitioners were becoming radicalized and seeking remedies outside the political system.[46]

What relevance does this have for the courts and court mediation? The courts are directly blamed for this upsurge in petitions because a large proportion of the petitions to the central authorities involved cases that were "law related" (she*fa*). Among the 632 petitioners whom Yu Jianrong interviewed, 401 (63.4 percent) had first resorted to the courts for legal solutions to their problems before petitioning in Beijing. In 172 cases (42.9 percent) the courts had declined to accept their cases; in 220 cases (54.9 percent) the courts had adjudicated the cases but ruled against the petitioners; and in nine cases (2.2 percent) the courts were unable to enforce judgments in favor of the petitioners. The petitioners brought their cases to the central authorities because of the alleged failure of the

[45] The number has been rising steadily since 1993. Wang Yongqian and Huang Haiyan, "Guojia xinfangju juzhang: 80% shangfang you daoli" (Bureau Chief of the State Petition Bureau: 80% of the Petitions have Grounds), *Banyue tan* (Bi-monthly Talks), November 20, 2003 (on file with the authors).

[46] Yu Jianrong, "Xinfang de zhiduxing queshi jiqi zhengzhi houguo" (The Defects of the Petition System and its Political Consequences), *Zhongguo xuanju yu zhili* (China Elections and Governance), http://www.chinaelections.org/NewsInfo.asp?NewsID=84598 (accessed October 7, 2008) (on file with the authors).

courts.[47] Yu's research is supported by official estimates. The Petitions Bureau of the NPC Standing Committee estimated that about 40 percent of the petitions that were perceived to be unfair were against decisions made in the legal system, including the courts. The bureau further asserted that 80 percent of the petitions were well grounded.[48]

Litigants, dissatisfied with a court decision, continue to petition political institutions and higher-level institutions. Ultimately, all of the anger and frustration centers on Beijing. For the CCP, the courts not only have failed to end many disputes, but they actually have aggravated the problems because of bureaucratic case handling, exorbitant court fees, and real or perceived corruption. There is also the problem of enhanced expectations. The reform of court procedures, judicial formality, and the rhetoric of fairness may have amplified the expectations of consumers who become disappointed and frustrated when their expectations do not comport with the results.

More important than the courts' reputation as ineffective or the wasted judicial resources resulting from the repeated petitions, as the judiciary is ready to concede, is the failure of the courts to make positive contributions to maintaining social stability by containing disputes (and by establishing and maintaining public sphere, law-based social contract norms). The CCP's primary strategy of social control is to impose responsibilities on institutions or a level of government to prevent disputes from occurring or to end them when and where they occur. Although this demand may be simply unrealistic, given the steadily increasing number of civil court cases, the courts, in the eyes of the CCP, have failed to fulfill an essential political duty because of their professionalization.

Many critics blame the court reform, and particularly the increasingly reliance on adjudication, as the principal method of dispute resolution. The ideal model of mediation works differently from the ideal model of adjudication. In mediation, the judges play an active role in persuading the parties to compromise and settle. This process, as described earlier, is often painstaking, long, and demanding. Ultimately, according to the CCP's experiences and expectations, the judges should be able to persuade the parties to accept a compromise (or should be able to impose one)

[47] Ibid. There are no consistent figures on the percentage of law-related petitions, however. It is generally stated that law-related petitions represent more than 40 percent of the total petitions. See Li Changfeng, "Zhuanxing shiqi nongmin shefa xinfang wenti tanxi" (Exploration of Petitions by Peasants in the Transition Period), *Sheke zongheng* (Social Sciences Review), 20, no. 2 (2005): 48–50.

[48] Wang Yongqian and Huang Haiyan, "Guojia xinfangju juzhang."

and, happily or reluctantly, the parties should agree to put an end to the dispute. Because most cases were settled, relatively few were appealed to a higher court and even fewer eventually migrated from the judicial system into the political sphere.

But adjudication, in the way it has been implemented in China, represented a drastic change. Judges are required to act as a neutral third party in applying the law in an impartial, fair manner. An unbiased judge listens to the evidence produced by the parties and rules according to what he or she deems to be the proper law. There is no ex parte contact and no persuasion. The courts have not built (or have been unable to build) a "basis" for strongly reasoned, norm-reinforcing decisions covering the vast array of different types of civil disputes that arise. The parties, mostly pro se, are expected to understand the judgments, accept the results, and get on with their lives.

Critics of the civil justice reform have pointed out that the results did not conform with the expectations of the judges or the reformers. Formalized procedures and courtroom formalities failed to enhance the legitimacy or the validity of court decisions. The parties refused to end their disputes when the judges wanted them to. The law, as found and applied by the judges, did not have sufficient persuasive power over a sizable number of the parties who felt largely both unbound by and dissatisfied with the court decisions. In other words, the new judicial process confronted an early and growing legitimacy crisis.

Facing an increase in the number of cases in which the parties refused to accept the finality of the court decisions, critics of the judicial reform, including many in the CCP and government, blamed the reform-minded judges who allegedly displayed an excess of loyalty to the law and insufficient loyalty to the party and to the communal task of maintaining social stability. The judges, it was said, blindly followed the law without considering the social context of the cases and the political consequences.

In modern Western judicial systems, it is clear that the responsibility – and the impact – of the work of the courts extends well beyond the court doors. However, the strict legal position is that the courts need only to solve the disputes at hand. Of course, powerful, organic norm setting unfolds over time. Yet this role is not articulated as a direct and immediate public responsibility of the courts. For the CCP, however, this role is crucial in the sense that the courts must be a major contributor toward maintaining broad social order. This is a task that the courts cannot ignore.

Judicial Responsiveness

The experiences during the recent attempts at judicial reform of the civil justice system demonstrate that judiciary reform is not feasible when it takes place only within the judiciary. It also requires key external support mechanisms. It is true that the courts, because of the new formalism and procedural complexity, have become increasingly bureaucratic, distancing themselves from the public. Judicial trappings make the judiciary less responsive to social needs. A direct concern relates to the developing evidential rule in civil procedure and the burdens that are placed on the parties.

The new evidence rules necessitate a passive judiciary. For the reformers, this passivity is a symbol of judicial rationality and professionalism. But for the critics, it indicates judicial bureaucracy, insensitivity, unresponsiveness, and even arrogance. It has been rightly pointed out that the judiciary has a vested interest in shifting the burden of proof to the parties. The judges prefer the newly developed "adversarial system" simply because they no longer need to perform the due diligence work associated with the pretrial investigation and/or the tedious mediation.

The shift in the burden of proof needs to be studied in the context of the developing judicial professionalism and rule-oriented judgments in China. Legal thinking is specialized, and in applying the laws in adjudication, the lawyers and the judges need to organize the chaotic factual situations and to place them into neatly categorized legal boxes, separating them from the political and social contexts. The judges are becoming more responsive to the law and to their own bureaucratic interests and less responsive to the social needs of the parties. China is developing specialist legal knowledge and procedures; lawyers and judges are developing a monopoly over this knowledge and are tending to use their knowledge to legitimize their power and to generate respect and consent (and wealth). However, this specialist legal knowledge has yet to establish its authority and legitimacy over political demands and social morality. The process has begun, but progress has been unsteady.

Legal reasoning in litigation is also narrow compared with political and moral persuasion. In mediation, judges examine a dispute in a much wider context and situate the disputants in broader social relations. Judges consider the case in its totality, taking into account legal and extralegal considerations. Mediation, on the one hand, tackles a dispute and also may tackle the cause of the dispute. Litigation, on the other hand, is expected to be largely rule-based dispute resolution that distinguishes legal considerations from political and social considerations. It is a less useful tool to solve conflicts deeply embedded in certain particular social settings and social relations.

The main criticisms against judicial reform are aimed not at professionalism or bureaucratization but at the reform's social impact (or lack thereof). Judges become elitists, and the courts lose their skill (and former responsibility) in maintaining a touch on the pulse of society. They are no longer focused on responding to societal needs. The bureaucratization, and the resulting elitist way of judging, has driven many cases away from the courts. Even worse, these disputes have been separated from access to legal remedies, which might play a real role in alleviating the mounting social problems. Too many cases that have entered the judicial process are not solved in a meaningful manner. Judges may write longer and better legally qualified decisions, but they are doing less to understand the disputes and to help the disputants resolve their problems. Judgments may contain more legal reasonings in an effort to provide legal justifications, but they have little persuasive authority over the involved parties. Hence, the legitimacy problem persists.

The shift to adversarial civil justice represents an especially serious challenge in a country with an underdeveloped legal profession and a poor legal aid system, in which most litigants are unrepresented in litigation. Civil justice in any mature legal system would collapse without the support of a strong, professionalized legal profession. Lawyers are effective in a strong system to reach settlements for their clients and also serve as a buffer zone between the courts and the parties, absorbing most of the tensions that are bound to occur in a contentious legal process.

V. MEDIATION IN A HARMONIOUS SOCIETY

However, judicial reform took place within the judiciary and largely was limited to the civil justice system dealing with ordinary civil and commercial disputes. It has had no impact on the political system, and the reform has not resulted in any significant increase in judicial authority and independence relative to other state institutions. Because of the lack of real political power within the judiciary during these reforms, the process of judicial reform and autonomy within the area of civil justice were not entrenched. They remained vulnerable to political influences. When social conflicts began to intensify in 2003, with the sudden increase in petitions and social unrest and when disgruntled peasants, workers, and others started to bypass the judiciary in civil disputes and resort directly to the central authorities in Beijing, the courts became the scapegoats and were blamed for the real and perceived judicial ineffectiveness. As a result, judicial reform was first halted and then partially reversed.

The recent resurgence of court mediation is a direct attack, largely from outside the court system, on the decade-long reforms to promote judicial professionalism and formalism. The defining characteristic of the recent promotion of mediation is the instrumentalist focus on judicial effectiveness in containing and resolving disputes. Formal (adversarial) adjudication allegedly has failed to provide an effective resolution to the growing social conflicts. It has failed to build legitimacy for the reformed system. Mediation is now preferred because of the claimed failure of adjudicatory justice and the perceived effectiveness of mediatory justice. Judges, as a result of this political assault, have been relegated to settling private disputes, rather than serving a more public and general role of norm finding and norm application. The political pressures and rhetoric seem to suggest there is now a single "ground norm" to resolve disputes, with which all other norms must conform. The reality as it is playing out is less basic and drastic, as explained in the following.

The SPC started to reemphasize court mediation in 2002. In that year, with the MoJ, it passed the Opinions of the Supreme People's Court and the Ministry of Justice on Further Strengthening the Work of People's Mediation in the New Era.[49] Although the Opinions aimed mainly to enhance judicial support for extrajudicial mediation by formally linking people's mediation and civil litigation, court mediation was put firmly on the agenda.[50]

Following this ideological change, the SPC began to redesign civil procedure to encourage the use of court mediation. The first clear sign of an active use of mediation based on an instruction of the SPC occurred in 2003.[51] In February 2003, the SPC, in a judicial interpretation on adjudicating cases involving false representation with respect to the

[49] Fan Yu, "Tiaojie de chonggou (shang): Yi fayuan tiaojie de gaige wei zhongdian" (Reconstructing Mediation: Focusing on the Reform of Court Mediation [Part 1]), *Fazhi yu shehui fazhan* (Law and Social Development) no. 2 (2004): 113–125.

[50] "Zuigao renmin fayuan gongzuo baogao 2003" (SPC Work Report 2003), National People's Congress of the People's Republic of China, http://www.npc.gov.cn (accessed March 6, 2008); Yao Zhijian, "'Tiaojie re' yu fayuan tiaojie zhidu de xiandai zhuanxing" (The Modern Transformation of the 'Tidal Wave of Mediation' and the Court Mediation System), *Falü shiyong* (Application of the Law), no. 9 (2005): 69–72.

[51] Fan Yu, "Tiaojie de chonggou."

securities market,[52] expressly provided that people's courts should put more emphasis on mediation and encouraged litigants to settle their disputes when handling civil compensation cases related to false representation of securities information. In 2004, the SPC promulgated the Provisions on Several Questions Concerning the People's Courts' Civil Mediation Work,[53] providing much-needed flexibility in the mediation processes and certain incentives for both judges and the parties to opt for mediation.[54]

Serving the people (*sifa weimin*), instead of effectiveness and justice, gradually became the overarching principle for the judiciary.[55] It has become a common criticism that judicial reform under Xiao Yang served mainly the interests of the courts and judges. The people-based doctrine necessitates a responsive judiciary that actively serves the interests of the people. Court mediation is considered the most appropriate means to achieve this goal.

Court mediation received another political boost after President Hu Jintao called for the construction of a harmonious society in 2005. Court mediation is not only a key component of this service-based doctrine; it also is closely linked to the creation of a harmonious society.[56] In

[52] Provisions of the Supreme People's Court on Several Questions Concerning the Adjudication of Civil Compensation Cases Arising from False Representation Relating to the Securities Market, Art. 4.

[53] For the full text of these provisions and other relevant background information, see Yang Runshi, *Zuigao renmin fayuan minshi tiaojie gongzuo sifa jieshi de lijie yu shiyong* (Meaning and Application of the Judicial Interpretation of the Supreme People's Court on Civil Mediation Work) (Beijing: Renmin fayuan chubanshe, 2004).

[54] For example, mediation is possible at any time before a judgment is rendered (Art. 1); the time limit stops running after mediation starts (Art. 6); confidentiality is allowed for mediation (Art. 7); and mediation may touch upon issues not accepted for litigation (Art. 9). The provisions are also stronger in enforcing a mediation agreement (Arts. 10 and 13). For a study of the implementation of the provisions, see Han Bo, "Susong tiaojie de shizheng fenxi yu fali sibian: Dui zuigao renmin fayuan 'Guanyu renmin fayuan minshi tiaojie gongzuo ruogan wenti de guiding' de shishi diaocha" (Empirical Analysis of Court Mediation and the Jurisprudential Thinking: An Empirical Study of the Implementation of the Provisions of the Supreme People's Court on Several Questions concerning the People's Courts' Civil Mediation Work), *Falü shiyong* (Application of the Law), no. 4 (2007): 75–79.

[55] In the Directive on Opinions of the Supreme People's Court on the Implementation of 23 Concrete Measures of the "Judiciary Serves the People." Liu Rong, "Shuli sifa weimin sixiang, jianxing gongzheng yu xiaolü zhuti: Ji quanguo gaoji fayuan yuanzhang zuotanhui" (Establishing the Thinking of the Judiciary Serves the People, Implementing the Theme of Justice and Efficiency: Note of the National Conference for Presidents of the Higher Courts), *Renmin sifa* (People's Judicature), no. 9 (2003): 14–15.

[56] Zhang Weiping, "Susong tiaojie: Shixia shitai de fenxi yu sikao" (Court Mediation: Analysis and Reflection of the Current Situation), *Faxue* (Law Science), no. 5 (2007): 18–27.

March 2005, Xiao Yang gave a clear direction to the people's courts to "mediate cases that could be mediated, adjudicate cases that should be adjudicated, combining mediation with adjudication, concluding the case and ending the dispute concurrently" (*neng diaozediao, dang panze pan diaopan jiehe, anjie liaoshi*).[57] Subsequently, the SPC, on numerous occasions, pledged following the sixteen-character guideline closely and containing and resolving disputes that are accepted by the courts , thus reducing the number of cases that may be brought to the attention of other branches of the government.[58]

The SPC's U-turn on mediation is a reluctant response to political demands to maintain social stability. The courts are to use mediation instrumentally to achieve a particular result. In spelling out the goal of court mediation, Xiao Yang stated that "there should not be petitions or continuous litigation, or failure to bring the disputes to an end, for cases concluded through mediation."[59] The ultimate goal is to end adjudication; mediation or anything in-between is merely a means to achieve this goal. In the process, law is merely one consideration. Thus, judges are required to go beyond legal issues in deciding cases and are required to keep in mind the likely social impacts of a court decision.

The CCP has not sent out clear guidelines on the broad topic of legal reform. The recently revived principle of socialist legality emphasizes the

[57] According to the explanatory note to the 2007 SPC Work Report: *neng tiaozediao, dang panze pan* means a case should be promptly mediated by the court if the parties to the case voluntarily make a concession and all the legal requirements of court mediation have been complied with; a case should be promptly adjudicated by the court if the parties are reluctant to make any concessions, or if the conducting of court mediation in the case would harm the interests of the state, a collective, or a third party. *Diaopan jiehe, anjie liaoshi* refers to the emphasis that both adjudication and court mediation are effective means in handling civil cases, and the common goal of both methods is to resolve disputes, minimize social conflicts, and maximize social harmony. "Zuigao renmin fayuan gongzuo baogao – 2007 nian 3 yue 13 ri zai dishijie quanguo renmin daibiao dahui diwuci huiyishang" (SPC Work Report – Presented at the Fifth Session of the Tenth National People's Congress on March 13, 2007), *Zhonghua renmin gongheguo quanguo renmin daibiao dahui changwu weiyuanhui gongbao* (Gazette of the Standing Committee of the National People's Congress of the People's Republic of China), no. 2 (2007): 232–233.

[58] "Zuigao renmin fayuan guanyu jiaqiang shenpan gongzuo jiandu qingkuang de baogao" (Report of the SPC on the Situation of Strengthening the Supervision over Adjudication), *Zhonghua renmin gongheguo quanguo renmin daibiao dahui changwu weiyuanhui gongbao* (Gazette of the Standing Committee of the National People's Congress of the People's Republic of China), no. 7 (2005): 723–730.

[59] Xiao Yang, "Chongfen fahui sifa tiaojie zai goujian shehui zhuyi hexie shehui zhong de jiji zuoyong" (Fully Demonstrate the Pragmatic Function of Court Mediation in the Construction of a Socialist Harmonious Society), *Renmin sifa* (People's Judicature), no. 10 (2006): 4–6.

rule of law and equality, on the one hand, and CCP leadership and the social impact, on the other. The SPC is equally inconsistent. It emphasizes the importance of mediation in creating social harmony and the imperative to consider the social and political consequences of a judgment, but at the same time, it insists repeatedly on the legality of civil procedure.

In sending mixed messages, the SPC is indicating a clear defiance from a now more professionalized judiciary toward political incursions. At the same time it is promoting mediation, the SPC is also calling for the exercise of caution in expanding mediation. This is done in two ways: First, the SPC stresses the importance of the legality of court processes and the voluntariness of the involved parties. The SPC is firm in prohibiting prolonged or coercive mediation that was characteristic of the mediation in the 1980s. Second, the SPC has selected specific cases for enhanced mediation efforts instead of reinforcing mediation in all court cases. In a 2003 judicial interpretation, the SPC set out six categories of cases in which the courts should apply mediation before adjudication. They included small disputes occurring within families, between neighbors, and among acquaintances.[60]

In 2006, the SPC selected further categories of cases subject to enhanced mediation: 1) cases involving public interests that require the collaboration of the government and other relevant departments; 2) class actions involving a great number of people; 3) complicated cases in which the relationship among the parties is tense and neither party has a stronger case according to the evidence; 4) cases involving matters that are not governed by any legislation, or there is no specific legislation governing the respective matters, thus making the application of the law in adjudicating the cases difficult; 5) very sensitive cases and cases of great social concern; and 6) reviews of petitions and retrials.[61] Clearly, most of the court cases do not fall within these categories.

So far, the government has not taken drastic action to push the court onto a more "hard line" mediation track. The changes made to facilitate court mediation have been minor and do not alter the existing court

[60] Provisions of the Supreme People's Court on Several Questions Concerning the Application of Summary Procedure in Adjudicating Civil Cases (entering into force on December 1, 2003), Art. 14. See also Fan Yu, "Tiaojie de chonggou."

[61] Zuigao renmin fayuan guanyu kaizhan guifan sifa xingwei zhuanxiang zhenggai qingkuang de baogao" (Report of the SPC on the Situation of Launching Rectification and Reform to Regulate Judicial Behavior), *Zhonghua renmin gongheguo quanguo renmin daibiao dahui changwu weiyuanhui gongbao* (Gazette of the Standing Committee of the National People's Congress of the People's Republic of China), no. 8 (2006): 772–778.

procedures.[62] Rhetoric aside, most of the actual actions in terms of forcing the judges to mediate by changing the incentive structure are limited to lower-level courts, especially in the rural areas.[63] The overall rate of mediation has grown slowly, and the urban courts, both trial and appelate, are responding cautiously. The overall court mediation rate in China was 31 percent,[64] 32.1 percent,[65] and 30.41 percent[66] in 2004, 2005, and 2006, respectively, whereas the rate in many grassroots courts reached more than 70 percent, especially in courts with a lesser caseload. The main coping strategy is to count cases that have been withdrawn by plaintiffs as cases mediated. In doing so, judges appear to have embraced the rhetoric of mediation and, at the same time, diluted its impact. In general, it is common that civil justice as it is designed weighs heavily against mediation, and the courts are effective in limiting the use of court mediation. As many judges and commentators have asserted, mediation and litigation are "irreconcilable" in the Chinese judicial context."[67]

Despite the comparative political weakness of the judiciary, that judiciary – now unprecedentedly more professionalized – still runs the courts on a day-to-day basis and still is the operational "overseer" of "neo-mediation." This allows some real scope to shape the implementation of neo-mediation and to retain adherence to certain principles underlying the civil justice reform program.

62 Ibid.

63 Yao Zhijian, "Fazhi xiandaihua jincheng zhong de fayuan tiaojie – Dui woguo fayuan tiaojie chongxing xianxiang de fali fenxi" (Court Mediation in the Process of Legal System Modernization: Analyzing the Legal Reasoning behind the Phenomenon of a Re-emphasis on Court Mediation in our Country), *Nanjing shehui kexue* (Social Sciences in Nanjing), no. 7 (2005): 88–94.

64 Zuigao renmin fayuan gongzuo baogao – 2005 nian 3 yue 9 ri zai dishijie quanguo renmin daibiao dahui disanci huiyishang" (SPC Work Report – Presented at the Third Session of the Tenth National People's Congress on March 9, 2005), *Zhonghua renmin gongheguo quanguo renmin daibiao dahui changwu weiyuanhui gongbao* (Gazette of the Standing Committee of the National People's Congress of the People's Republic of China), no. 4 (2005): 7–13.

65 "Zuigao renmin fayuan gongzuo baogao – 2006 nian 3 yue 14 ri zai dishijie quanguo renmin daibiao dahui disici huiyishang" (SPC Work Report – Presented at the Fourth Session of the Tenth National People's Congress on March 14, 2006), *Zhonghua renmin gongheguo quanguo renmin daibiao dahui changwu weiyuanhui gongbao* (Gazette of the Standing Committee of the National People's Congress of the People's Republic of China), no. 4 (2006): 274–284.

66 "Zuigao renmin fayuan gongzuo baogao 2007."

67 Xiao Yang, "Rang 'dongfang jingyan' chongfang guangcai: Zai yatai shouxi dafaguan huiyi shang de yanjiang" (Let the "Eastern Experience" Shine Again: Speech Presented at the Conference of Chief Justices of the Asia-Pacific in 2004), *Panjie yanjiu* (Studies of Precedents), no. 5 (2004): 1–5.

VI. CONCLUSION

A key purpose of this chapter has been to summarize the history of the operation of court mediation in the PRC. Historically, the civil justice system has been regarded by the CCP as being of comparatively minor political importance. Even during the Mao era, civil justice was seen as a zone where ordinary citizen-to-citizen civil disputes were mediated. An important consequence was that the civil justice system was left to operate within its own "paddock," as it were, with minimal interference from party and government cadres and officials. It was here that a limited form of "civil society" could operate within the oppressively, micromanaged Maoist state.

Lawyers and lawyer-scholars discovered the civil justice "paddock" – and began to see, over time, its rather remarkable possibilities. This was a very large zone in the legal realm where CCP influence was limited. The initial process of reform saw a serious challenge launched against the fundamental mediatory role of the Mao-era civil justice system. During that period, the crucial task of the system was to resolve citizen-to-citizen disputes and to maintain stability. The open-door era witnessed a rise in the number of civil law disputes, but these were much more commercial in nature.

Thus began what might be regarded as the first phase of PRC civil justice reform. The old system, it was said, was time consuming, especially vulnerable to corruption, and worst of all, unable to develop and establish clear legal norms to guide the building of a Chinese rule of law system. The latter arose from the reality that mediation generated context-based individual settlements in which getting the parties to agree always trumped any quest to identify the "right or wrong" legal positions of each party. Various key leaders and opinion shapers in the SPC became convinced of the serious drawbacks of the dominance of mediation within the civil justice system.

The initial reform groundwork began as early as 1979. Thereafter, the SPC drafted new Civil Procedure Laws in 1982, 1988, and 1991. A hallmark of these reforms was a major move in the direction of adjudicatory justice. Civil justice courts were to become more professional and more formal, and, over time, consistent, detailed legal procedures were to become the crucial operating norm for the courts. The former inquisitorial role of judges under the mediatory system had to be abolished. The parties were to take over responsibility for gathering and presenting evidence. The judges would evaluate the evidence (not excluded by the new rules) and apply the law and pronounce an explained verdict. Consistent rules of procedure and the consistent application of the law would, it was argued, help build a body of legal norms that would, in turn, enter the social landscape to guide a gradual but major enhancement of a (modern) citizenry and a community of self-regulation. New foundations for social stability would be crafted. These foundations would be constantly maintained and enhanced by the ongoing operation of the reformed civil justice system. The vision was to create a sound, modern private law system that would help boost the credibility of the public law system. This, the advocates explained, was how the the most effective rule of law systems worked in the developed West.

With the elevation of Xiao Yang to head the SPC in 1998, what might be termed the second phase of civil justice reform commenced. This second phase continued the already established reform priorities and reenergized the reform process. Courts in urban centers, especially in the coastal cities, embraced the reform agenda with renewed force.

However, by this stage, the reformers had made the entire reform process a hostage to fortune. The rhetoric of reform raised expectations of real benefits among almost all the stakeholders. Litigants were meant to enjoy fairer dispute outcomes; society was to profit from the growing creation of positive, behavior-regulating legal norms; and the CCP was to benefit from enhanced stability – and, ultimately, legitimacy.

By this time, highly bureaucratic accountability mechanisms had been established. The civil justice systems were required to adjudicate all disputes within three to six months, and all cases were to be completed by the end of each calendar year. In addition, the number of first-instance decisions that were reversed on appeal was monitored. These "quality control" measures drew on the deep tradition and habits of the centralized, premarket economy state. They did little to build enhanced performance into the system and contributed to distorting the autonomy and judicial soundness of the operating structure.

Losing litigants in the reformed system were displeased and looked for an arena to air their views. The CCP felt a perceived growth in complaints to Beijing. Critics of the reforms concluded that the justice reform had coincided with growing and increasingly vociferous social grumbling that frequently was spilling over into mass street protests. It thus followed that the civil justice reform, rather than being part of the solution, was part of the problem. Disputants in the civil justice system continued to dispute.

CCP detractors hankered after a lost "golden age" when mediatory justice provided contextual settlements that helped to maintain stability among the masses.

"Back to the future" seemed to be the answer. By 2006, the SPC openly conceded the failure of part of the judicial reform program. It issued a series of judicial interpretations to steer the judiciary back toward the settlement of disputes through court-based mediation. This policy change encouraged some local courts to revise their incentive mechanisms. Judges were rewarded for privileging mediation in resolving disputes. Judges and legal scholars began to rediscover the virtues of court-based mediation.

In fact, the responsibility for the faltering and uneven outcome of this long-term, massive attempt at civil justice reform in the PRC was widespread. It seemed clear that the reformers were overreaching in their claims that civil justice reforms could open the door to some sort of fast-track implementation of the rule of law. In addition, the CCP and various levels of government failed to support the reform consistently and substantially. Strangely, they saw the civil justice reform as some kind of black-hand driver of growing social discontent. This was rather like blaming inadequate new levees for flood damage while ignoring evidence of record river water levels.

What are some of the important lessons of the post-Mao civil justice reform project in China? And how can this understanding be applied to ensure greater long-term traction for any next phase of the reforms? We fully recognize that providing a complete response to these questions requires much more research. However, some preliminary points can be suggested.

One basic insight of the reformers remains as sound as ever: Over time, China must build a better, more modern and fair civil justice system if it is ever to create any sort of enduring rule of law system. In the West, the crucial way in which an operative civil justice system is fundamental to the maintenance of the public law system is often taken for granted. Yet any basic examination of such developed systems reveals this underlying basis. Next, there is no handy short cut to a Chinese-envisaged rule of law system. In particular, the basic building blocks – for instance, a much enhanced legal-aid regime and continuing greater dispersal of legal expertise – are needed for the long-term process of phase three of the civil justice reform.

Finally, the next phase of the reform will have to draw on even greater political will. Thus far, the CCP has "fostered" civil justice reform by allowing it rather than by actively promoting it. It is very difficult to imagine real progress being made – progress that could build on the partial gains to date – unless the CCP commits itself to supporting further civil justice reform, consistently and substantially. This is a "big task." Yet it is in this reform zone that serious long-term efforts are likely to contribute significantly to the building of the "harmonious society," that is the present anchor of CCP policy.

2

Judicial Disciplinary Systems for Incorrectly Decided Cases: The Imperial Chinese Heritage Lives On

Carl Minzner

INTRODUCTION

Local Chinese courts commonly use responsibility systems (*mubiao guanli zeren zhi, zeren zhuijiu zhi*) to evaluate and discipline judges. Judges receive sanctions under these systems for a wide range of behavior, such as illegal or unethical dealings with parties and lawyers, inappropriate courtroom behavior, and neglect of duty.

Many local court Chinese responsibility systems also discipline judges for simple legal error. Judges may face sanctions linked to the number of cases that are reversed on appeal simply because the interpretation of law made by a higher court differs from that of the original trial judge. Sanctions include monetary fines and negative notations in a judge's career file. Such practices violate Chinese Supreme People's Court (SPC) judicial directives specifically barring the use of responsibility systems to sanction judges for simple legal error. Local Chinese courts, however, have continued to promulgate such systems.

Court responsibility systems that discipline judges for simple legal error also create a perverse set of incentives for Chinese judges. To avoid appellate reversal, lower Chinese courts and judges rely on an ill-defined

Associate Professor, Washington University in St. Louis, School of Law. This chapter is an edited version of an article that was first published in vol. 39, no. 1 (winter 2009) of the *New Mexico Law Review*. I thank Margaret Woo, Mary Gallagher, and Merle Goldman for organizing the October 2007 workshop on Chinese civil dispute resolution at the Fairbank Center for Chinese Studies, and the students of the University of Michigan Law School Asia Law Society for organizing the March 2008 symposium on pressures for legal reform in China, where this piece was presented. I thank the participants in both events, particularly Don Clarke, Randy Pereenboom, and Nico Howsen, for their comments on this piece, and the staff of the *New Mexico Law Review* and Cambridge University Press for their work in publishing it. Special thanks go to my family, particularly my mother, for their support.

system of advisory requests (*qingshi*) to solicit the views of higher courts and judges on how to decide pending cases. As Chinese judges themselves note, excessive resort to *qingshi* practices has many negative effects. It undermines appellate review, because the court or judge that reviews the case on appeal may have responded to the initial *qingshi* request regarding how to decide the case in the first place. It creates a relatively passive Chinese judiciary reliant on top-down direction. Finally, it contributes to an overload of higher-level judicial authorities forced to handle a myriad of requests for guidance from lower-level courts. Unsurprisingly, the SPC has made *qingshi* reform a key component of both their 2004–08 and 2009–13 plans for court reform.

Why, then, do local Chinese courts continue to use internal disciplinary systems that violate Chinese law and negatively affect daily operations of the judiciary? Historically, the use of disciplinary sanctions to punish judges for cases of simple legal error reversed on appeal is deeply rooted in imperial Chinese legal practices dating back to the Qin dynasty. Politically, the disciplinary sanctions employed by modern Chinese court responsibility systems and their imperial analogues reflect a comprehensive governance strategy employed by generations of centralized, authoritarian Chinese rulers to address pervasive principal-agent problems in a sprawling bureaucracy.[1] However, these policies are generating conflict with rule of law norms established in the post-1978 reform period and incarnated SPC judicial directives issued in 1998.

Existing literature on the post-1978 Chinese legal system has devoted significant attention to formal legal norms promulgated by central institutions such as the SPC and the National People's Congress (NPC) but ignores the underlying incentive structures that can drive judicial behavior. Local court responsibility systems and the incentives they create for individual Chinese judges are "*terra incognita* in terms of published systematic studies."[2]

This chapter presents an overview of Chinese court responsibility systems and their disciplinary treatment of incorrectly decided cases (*cuo'an*) and analyzes the important practical problems created in the Chinese legal

[1] For a more extensive discussion, see Carl Minzner, "Riots and Cover-Ups: Counterproductive Control of Local Agents in China," *University of Pennsylvania Journal of International Law* 30 (2009). A separate article by this author, currently in progress, links these practices to the Legalist branch of classical Chinese philosophy.

[2] Donald Clarke, "Empirical Research in Chinese Law." In *Beyond Common Knowledge: Empirical Approaches to the Rule of Law*, ed. Erik G. Jensen and Thomas C. Heller (Stanford: Stanford University Press, 2003), p. 178.

system as a result of official use of responsibility systems to discipline judges for legal error. It also identifies the extent to which key elements of modern People's Republic of China (PRC) court responsibility systems are grounded in prior imperial precedent.

I. LEGAL FRAMEWORK OF JUDICIAL DISCIPLINARY SYSTEMS

The Chinese Constitution and the 1979 Organic Law of the Courts establish the broad contours of the Chinese judicial system, but they lack any detailed provisions regarding the operation of judicial discipline. Both the Constitution and Organic Law provide that "courts shall exercise trial authority independently in accordance with the law, and shall not be subject to the interference from administrative organs, social organizations, and individuals."[3] This language, however, does not address the extent to which individual judges should independently exercise trial authority or sanctions that should apply for misdeeds. By contrast, the Organic Law does contemplate some limitations on judges' independent exercise of their trial authority, as it establishes court adjudication committees, headed by court presidents, as the highest authority within each court.[4]

The 1995 Law on Judges sets the general outlines for the evaluation and discipline of judges. It provides that judges may not be "suspended, demoted, removed from office, or disciplined" for reasons other than those specified by law or pursuant to procedures other than designated by law.[5] It requires each court to establish regular procedures for the evaluation of individual judges.[6] Judges who demonstrate exemplary work performance are to be rewarded.[7] Those who engage in proscribed conduct, such as corruption, concealing evidence, obtaining forced confessions, engaging in speech that "harms the national honor," or participating in demonstrations that oppose the government, are to be disciplined.[8] "Dereliction of duty that results in an incorrectly decided case" is also grounds for sanction.[9] The law states that "the results of judicial

[3] PRC Constitution, Art. 126; Zhonghua renmin gongheguo renmin fayuan zuzhi fa (Organic Law of the PRC Courts), issued July 1, 1979, amended September 2, 1983, Art. 4 (hereafter Organic Law).

[4] Organic Law, Art. 11.

[5] Zhonghua renmin gongheguo faguan fa (PRC Law on Judges), issued February 28, 1995, amended June 30, 2001, Art. 8(3).

[6] Ibid., Art. 21. Articles 46–48 require each court to form a committee, headed by the court president, to oversee the evaluation process.

[7] Ibid., Art. 30.

[8] Ibid., Art. 32.

[9] Ibid., Art. 32(10).

evaluations are to be used as the basis for the reward, sanctioning, training, removal from office, and expulsion of judges as well as their adjustment in rank and salary." Precise implementation of the above directions is left to each court.[10]

In 1998, the SPC issued two directives that expanded on the broad provisions of the 1995 law.[11] They specified a range of cases for which court personnel must bear responsibility, including altering or fabricating court transcripts,[12] concealing evidence from the court panel hearing the case,[13] interfering with the work of lower courts in hearing cases,[14] and failing to assist court personnel from other jurisdictions in the handling of cases.[15] The 1998 directives enumerated a list of disciplinary sanctions that court personnel may receive, ranging from warnings to reduction in rank to expulsion from the court.[16]

The 1998 SPC directives also provided that court personnel who "intentionally ignore law or facts and issue an incorrect verdict" must bear responsibility.[17] This is grounds for at least a severe notation (*ji daguo*) in one's personnel file. In cases in which "serious consequences" have resulted, anything from a reduction in rank to expulsion is warranted. If "negligence [on the part of court personnel] leads to the issuance of an incorrect verdict that causes serious consequences," the responsible court official may receive anything from a warning to a severe notation in one's personnel file.[18] Court adjudication authorities are responsible for determining whether a specific case is "incorrect" (and thus the subject of disciplinary sanctions).[19]

[10] Ibid., Arts. 21, 46–48.
[11] Renmin fayuan shenpan renyuan weifa shenpan zeren zhuijiu banfa (shixing) (Experimental Responsibility Measures for the Illegal [Behavior] of Court Personnel), issued August 26, 1998 (hereafter Experimental Responsibility Measures), and the Renmin fayuan shenpan jilü chufen banfa [shixing] (Experimental Disciplinary Measures for Court Trials), issued September 7, 1998 (hereafter Experimental Disciplinary Measures).
[12] Experimental Responsibility Measures, Art. 11.
[13] Ibid., Art. 12.
[14] Ibid., Art. 7.
[15] Experimental Disciplinary Measures, Art. 55.
[16] Ibid., Art. 13.
[17] Experimental Responsibility Measures, Art. 14.
[18] Experimental Disciplinary Measures, Art. 40. See also Renmin fayuan gongzuo renyuan chufen tiaoli [Disciplinary Regulations for People's Court Personnel], Art. 83, issued January 27, 2010, incorporating the same language.
[19] Specifically, the Experimental Responsibility Measures state that "trial organizations" (*shenpan zuzhi*) are to make the determination. Experimental Responsibility Measures, Art. 27.

Both directives specifically exempted judges from disciplinary sanctions for cases that result from simple legal error. Article 22 of the Experimental Responsibility Measures provides that court personnel do not bear responsibility in erroneous cases due to "different views or understanding" of the law, facts, or evidence, or those in which "new evidence" or "amendment of law" or "alteration of policy" has led to the alteration or reversal of the case. Under article 4 of the 1998 Experimental Disciplinary Measures, disciplinary sanctions are not to be applied to erroneous cases that result from unclear law or regulations or from errors in understanding of the law or facts.

When responsibility for error is found, it rests individually with the court officials who cause the errors. Individual members of a three-judge collegiate judicial panel (or court adjudication committee) who cause the panel (or committee) to incorrectly decide a case by intentionally distorting the facts or interpretation of the law must bear individual responsibility for the collective incorrect tribunal decision.[20] Court presidents and tribunal heads bear only collateral liability for errors by subordinate judges and collegiate judicial panels when their own "intentional violation of the law or serious lack of responsibility" leads them to fail to correct the errors of their subordinates.[21]

The two 1998 SPC directives thus theoretically created the framework for a judicial disciplinary system run by the courts themselves. Furthermore, they barred the application of disciplinary sanctions for simple legal error and restricted liability for errors to the individual judicial personnel who actually cause them.

In 2010, the SPC issued new Disciplinary Regulations for People's Court Personnel that replace (and nullify) the 1998 Experimental Disciplinary Measures, but maintained the 1998 Experimental Responsibility Measures.[22]

Just like their 1998 experimental counterparts, the 2010 Disciplinary Regulations specify a range of sanctions for negligence on the part of court personnel that leads to the issuance of an incorrect verdict.[23] But in an intriguing departure from the 1998 version, they do *not* include the protective language exempting judges from sanctions for simple legal error, such as in situations in which unclear laws or regulations result in appellate reversal of a lower court decision.

[20] Ibid., Arts. 24, 25.

[21] Ibid., Art. 26.

[22] Renmin fayuan gongzuo renyuan chufen tiaoli [Disciplinary Regulations for People's Court Personnel], issued January 27, 2010.

[23] Ibid., Arts. 82–83.

Nonetheless, the SPC's formal bar against disciplining Chinese judges for simple legal error appears to endure, at least for the moment. The 1998 Experimental Responsibility Measures, and their protective language, is still in effect. And in other judicial regulations issued in 2010, the SPC has continued to directly cite the 1998 Experimental Responsibility Measures for the principle that judges may not be disciplined for appellate reversal resulting from unclear law or regulations or from errors in understanding of the law or facts.[24]

II. DISCIPLINARY SYSTEMS IN LOCAL CHINESE COURTS

Although the 1998 SPC directives established national judicial disciplinary standards, they do not accurately represent the myriad of systems actually adopted by local courts. In contrast to the SPC directives, some local court responsibility systems expressly sanction judges for accidental legal error. Other local responsibility systems adopt collective liability principles, sanctioning judges for errors they have not actually committed themselves. Local court responsibility systems are simply one specific example of party-led responsibility systems. These are administrative governance mechanisms on which higher-level Chinese officials commonly rely to manage a sprawling bureaucracy.

Generalizations regarding local Chinese court responsibility systems face significant practical problems, given the sensitivity of party-run management systems and their lack of systematic filing or publication. Given these limits, this chapter will simply sketch some of the similarities and differences of local court responsibility systems. It will do so based on an unscientific and non–statistically representative selection of three relevant provincial-level regulations and twelve different local basic people's court (BPC) and intermediate people's court (IPC) systems. At the same time, it is not completely lacking in probative value. These documents represent a range of Chinese courts drawn from different geographical jurisdictions and bureaucratic rank and aptly demonstrate some of the variations that exist in responsibility systems.[25]

[24] Zuigao renmin fayuan guanyu jin yi bu jiaqiang heyiting zhize de ruogan guiding [Relevant Decisions of the Supreme People's Court on Strengthening Work Responsibilities for Collective Tribunals], issued January 11, 2010, Art. 10.

[25] These include provincial-level rules from Guangdong, Hainan, and Jiangxi, and local rules from IPC and BPC courts in Shandong (2), Yunnan (2), Shaanxi (2), Sichuan (2), Beijing (1), Hebei (1), Hubei (1), and Ningxia (1). (Gaocheng Municipal People's Court, Hebei; Jingshan County People's Court, Hubei; Hainan District People's Court,

A. Judicial Responsibility Systems

Chinese Communist Party (CCP) authorities use responsibility systems (*mubiao guanli zeren zhi, zeren zhuijiu zhi*) to evaluate, reward, and discipline a wide range of officials. These systems set specific performance targets that local cadres must meet in different fields. These may include economic development goals, birth control targets, and social order statistics. Success in meeting these goals results in financial and career rewards. Failure leads to fines and career sanctions.[26]

As part of the bureaucratic apparatus, Chinese courts also adopt responsibility systems. These set out specific performance targets that individual judges and court tribunals are expected to meet. Precise targets vary from court to court but often include the number of cases to be handled each year, successful case closure ratios, and mediation rates. Some local courts include "incorrectly decided cases" (and corresponding sanctions) as part of comprehensive annual work targets, whereas other courts have established stand-alone "responsibility systems for incorrectly decided cases" (*cuo'an zeren zhuijiu zhi*). According to Chinese judges and academics, these systems originated in the late 1980s and early 1990s as a means to check judicial corruption and reduce errors on the part of lower courts.[27]

Chinese court authorities rely on a variety of information sources to evaluate judges and tribunals. These include internal court statistics regarding numbers of cases filed, reversal rates, and mediation rates. They also include external sources of information regarding particular cases. Some court systems direct adjudication committees to review a wide range of cases reversed or remanded on appeal; cases reversed through internal

Ningxia; Pengzhou Municipal People's Court, Sichuan; Guanghan Municipal People's Court, Sichuan; Zhenping County People's Court, Shaanxi; Xunyang County People's Court, Shaanxi; Tai'an Municipal Intermediate People's Court, Shandong; Kenli County People's Court, Shandong; Kunming Intermediate People's Court, Yunnan; Tonghai County People's Court, Yunnan; Beijing No. 1 Intermediate People's Court, Beijing.)

26 Maria Edin, "State Capacity and Local Agent Control in China: CCP Cadre Management from a Township Perspective," *The China Quarterly*, no. 173 (2003): 35, 38–40.

27 Mao Hongjuan, Cuo'an zeren zhuijiu zhi chutan (Preliminary Investigation into Responsibility Systems for Incorrectly Decided Cases), http://www.nxyclawyer.com/llyj/html/929.html (accessed September 22, 2008); Di Tianli, "Woguo xianxing shenpan yunxing jizhi ruogan wenti sikao" (Thoughts on Some Problems with the Operation of China's Existing Adjudication System), *Zhengfa luncong* (Commentary on Law and Politics), no. 3 (2002): 9–12.

court retrial processes (*zaishen*); cases selected by officials in the local people's congress (LPC), procuratorate, party committees, or other organs; and cases raised by citizen petitioners through the *xinfang* (letters and visits) system to determine whether disciplinary sanctions should apply.[28]

Party authorities play a key role in evaluating judges and tribunals. The 2006 Zhenping BPC system explicitly makes court party committees responsible for supervising the evaluation process.[29] Others establish an internal "evaluation leading group" to analyze and report on evaluation results[30] or specify that the court adjudication committee is responsible for determining what constitutes an "incorrectly decided case."[31] But court party committees enjoy extensive influence even under the latter systems. The 2002 Tonghai BPC evaluation measures, for example, provide that the court party secretary should chair the "evaluation leading group."[32] Other systems charge internal court party committees with the ultimate responsibility of reviewing the reports of adjudication

[28] Guangdong sheng gaoji renmin fayuan guanyu weifa shenpan zeren zhuijiu de zanxing banfa (Temporary Measures of the Guangdong Provincial HPC Regarding Responsibility for the Illegal [Behavior] of Court Personnel), issued August 30, 2000 (hereafter Guangdong Measures), Art 12; Hainan sheng gaoji renmin fayuan guanche zhixing "Renmin fayuan shenpan renyuan weifa shenpan zeren zhuijiu banfa (shixing)" he "Renmin fayuan shenpan jilü chufen banfa (shixing)" ruogan guiding (Relevant Decision of the Hainan Provincial HPC Regarding the Implementation of the "[Experimental] Responsibility Measures for the Illegal [Behavior] of Court Personnel" and the "[Experimental] Disciplinary Measures for Court Trials"), issued May 9, 2000 (hereafter Hainan Decision), Art. 4; Jingshan xian renmin fayuan cuo'an zeren zhuijiu banfa (Jingshan County People's Court Responsibility Measures for Incorrectly Decided Cases), Art 22(3) (hereafter Jingshan Measures).

[29] Zhenping xian renmin fayuan 2006 nian gangwei mubiao zeren zhi ji kaoping banfa (shixing) (Zhenping County People's Court 2006 Work Target Responsibility System and Assessment Measures [Provisional] (hereafter Zhenping System), issued February 15, 2006, Art 5(c).

[30] Kunming shi zhongji renmin fayuan shenpan ting, heyi ting gongzuo guize (shixing) (Kunming Municipal Intermediate People's Court Trial Tribunals, Collegiate Judicial Panels Work Principles [Provisional]) (hereafter Kunming Principles), issued April 27, 2001, Art 28.

[31] Pengzhou Municipal People's Court Responsibility System for Incorrectly Decided Cases (Pengzhou shi renmin fayuan cuo'an zeren zhuijiu banfa) (hereafter Pengzhou System), issued March 8, 2004, Art. 17. Some systems that charge the adjudication committee with general oversight responsibilities specify that other court organizations (such as the internal court oversight authorities) carry out operational management of the evaluation process. Guangdong Measures, Art. 5.

[32] Tonghai xian renmin fayuan gangwei mubiao guanli zeren zhi ban'an jiangcheng kaohe banfa (Tonghai County People's Court Punishment and Reward Assessment Measures for the Target Management Responsibility System (hereafter Tonghai Measures), issued November 25, 2002, Art. 3(1).

committees regarding incorrectly decided cases, approving the numerical evaluations of judges and tribunals, and making the final decision regarding the application of sanctions.[33]

Local Chinese court responsibility systems link career advancement (or sanctions) to judges' success (or failure) in avoiding incorrect decisions. Depending on the court system in question, sanctions can range from the deduction of points from a judge's annual performance evaluation (affecting the eligibility for and amount of annual financial bonuses) to more severe fines of several hundred yuan per incorrect case to negative personnel evaluations and other career sanctions to removal from office.[34] Specific sanctions depend on the seriousness and frequency of the infraction.

In practice, the definition of "incorrectly decided case" under these systems is highly unclear. As one judge on the Changzhou IPC noted:

> Judging from some court regulations on responsibility systems for incorrectly decided cases, there does not yet exist a common understanding as to the conceptual extent of "incorrectly decided case."
>
> Some define "incorrectly decided case" as cases in which adjudication personnel should bear responsibility as a result of violations of substantive or procedural law that result in clearly erroneous cases or cases that create a negative impression.
>
> Some include in the definition of "incorrectly decided case" situations such as errors in basic facts ... that create serious unfairness in the judicial decision, clear errors in the application of law that result in incorrect decisions, and serious violation of procedure that affect the substantive fairness of the case.
>
> Some take "incorrectly decided case" to mean all types of judgments with unclear factual determinations, insufficient evidence, errors in the application of law, or violations of legal procedures.
>
> Still others define "incorrectly decided case" as cases in which adjudication personnel and others involved in adjudication activities have violated

[33] Guangdong sheng gaoji renmin fayuan guanyu weifa shenpan zeren zhuijiu de caozuo xize (shixing) ([Experimental] Operational Details of the Guangdong Provincial HPC Regarding Responsibility for the Illegal [Behavior] of Court Personnel), issued December 26, 2003, Art. 12; Pengzhou System, Art. 17; Hainanqu renmin fayuan chacuo anjian zeren zhuijiu chufa shishi banfa (Hainan District People's Court Implementation Measures for the Erroneous or Incorrect Cases Responsibility System) (hereafter Hainan District [Ningxia] Measures), issued May 23, 2006, http://www.whhnfy.gov.cn/news.php?id=13, Art. 38 (accessed September 20, 2008); Zhenping System, Art. 5(d).

[34] Zhenping System, Art. 2(b); Hainan District (Ningxia) Measures, Arts. 18–36; Hainan Decision, Art. 7.

substantive and procedural law in the docketing, trial, or execution process, have been overturned or corrected on appeal (*er shen*) or rehearing (*zaishen*), and should bear responsibility as a result.

As one can see from the above, local courts have extremely different definitions of an "incorrectly decided case." This has led in practice to confusion as to the extent of the definition of "incorrectly decided cases" and the resulting responsibility.[35]

The 1998 SPC directives did not eliminate this lack of clarity. As one Chinese law professor has noted, the "effort [of the 1998 SPC notice] to institutionally regularize the unclear concept of 'incorrectly decided cases' has not had the practical effect that it should. In the face of the massive inertia of administrative management [habits], 'responsibility systems for incorrectly decided cases' still continue to be used, and continue to be the subject of debate."[36]

Periodic campaigns to improve judicial performance also place pressures on Chinese courts and judges to reduce the number of cases reversed on appeal. For example, in 2008, the Feidong county BPC in Hefei, Anhui Province, set a goal of "four highs, four lows," aiming to raise the number of cases disposed of through simplified procedures, disposed of through mediation, withdrawn by the parties, and closed out within one trial period, as well as to reduce the number of appeals, petitions, reversals on appeal, and reversals through adjudicatory supervisions. The court noted that it would expand the use of responsibility systems for incorrectly decided cases as a key means of reaching this goal.[37]

B. *Liability for Legal Error*

Some provincial and local court systems comply with the 1998 SPC directives that exempt judges from disciplinary sanctions arising from accidental legal error. Relevant 2000 Guangdong High People's Court

35 Shi Yongcai and Jiang Jiye, Xiandai sifa linian xia de cuo'an zeren zhuijiu (Responsibility for Incorrectly Decided Cases Under a Modern Concept of the Judiciary), posted August 23, 2007 on the Web site of the Changzhou Intermediate People's Court, http://www.jsczfy.gov.cn/plus/view.php?aid=15938 (accessed September 20, 2008).

36 Wang Lin, Quxiao cuo'an zhuijiu zhi yi huan yuan sifa lixing (Eliminate Responsibility Systems for Incorrectly Decided Cases in Order to Return to Judicial Ideals), 2006, http://www.rdyj.com.cn/2006/rdqk-04–17.html (accessed September 20, 2008). For similar comments from a Shandong HPC judge, see Di Tianli, supra note 27.

37 "Feidong fayuan 'sigao sidi' gongzuo yaoqiu xianqi xin yi lun xiaoneng geming" (Feidong Court "Four Highs, Four Lows" Work Requirement Initiates New Revolution in Efficiency), *Hefei wanbao* (Hefei Evening News), September 7, 2008, http://news.qq.com/a/20080907/001471.htm (accessed October 13, 2008).

(HPC) rules explicitly adopt the exculpatory clause present in the 1998 SPC directives.[38] Similarly, the Kunming IPC (in 2001) and the Beijing No. 1 IPC (in 1999) both adopted rules that specifically exclude those legal errors outlined in the 1998 SPC directives from disciplinary sanctions.[39] Still other local court systems incorporate the SPC exemptions without directly citing the 1998 directives.[40]

Yet other systems define "incorrectly decided cases" so broadly as to encompass simple legal error, openly violating the 1998 SPC directives. Jiangxi provincial regulations explicitly define "incorrectly decided case" to include any case reversed on appeal or retrial.[41] Local Hainan district BPC court rules provide that cases reversed on appeal, cases in which the judge has altered or tampered with evidence, and cases in which illegal judicial behavior has "caused a serious social impact" all constitute "incorrectly decided cases."[42]

Other local court systems contravene the 1998 SPC directives by mechanically including the number of cases reversed or sent back for retrial on appeal as part of the annual work targets linked to career and financial rewards and sanctions. The Xunyang BPC, for example, requires that civil and criminal tribunals have no more than 3 percent of appealed cases either reversed or sent back for retrial by the appellate court. Each judge must handle no fewer than thirty cases per year, and at least 95 percent of the cases filed during the year must be successfully

[38] The Guangdong Measures prohibit the application of disciplinary sanctions against judges where appellate reversal was the result of the lack of clarity of the laws or regulations in question or "errors caused by reasons other than the objective intent or negligence of the adjudication personnel." Guangdong Measures, Art. 8(1–3).

[39] Implementation Details for the Responsibility System for Illegal [Behavior] of Trial Officers of the Beijing City First Intermediate People's Court (Beijing shi di yi zhongji renmin fayuan shenpan renyuan weifa shenpan zeren zhuijiu shishi xize [shixing]) (hereafter Beijing Details), issued April 7, 1999, Art. 8; Kunming Principles, Art. 31.

[40] Pengzhou System, Art. 11; Jingshan Measures, Art. 17. Other systems are inconsistent. Relevant 2000 Hainan provincial HPC rules specify (consistent with the 1998 SPC directives) that sanctions should apply to cases where "intentional ignorance of the facts or law leads to an incorrect decision, or where negligence leads to errors in the decision that cause serious consequences." Confusingly, the Hainan system also delineates a range of disciplinary sanctions that may apply when negligent judicial error results in an incorrect case, but does *not* cause "serious consequences." Ibid., Art. 7. However, the Hainan rules lack the SPC language clearly protecting judges from sanction in cases of unintentional legal error. This appears to contradict the language not only of the SPC Measures, but also of the Hainan system itself.

[41] Jiangxi sheng sifa jiguan cuo'an zeren zhuijiu tiaoli (Jiangxi Provincial Responsibility Measures for Incorrectly Decided Cases), issued August 15, 1997, amended March 29, 2007, Art. 8(1).

[42] Hainan District (Ningxia) Measures, Art. 7.

closed out.[43] The 2007 Kenli BPC and 2006 Zhenping BPC rules include the number of cases reversed or sent back for retrial on appeal as part of a 100-point scale used to evaluate the work performance of individual tribunals and judges.[44] Points may be deducted or added for failure or success in meeting specific targets, such as case closures and successful mediation ratios, as well as number of required political study sessions and (in the case of the Zhenping BPC) office hygiene. Cases reversed or sent back on appeal count against a tribunal or judge's overall point total. For instance, the 2006 Zhenping system awards 20 points based on the "quality and efficiency" of cases handled and will deduct points for any of the following occurrences:

1) Handling an incorrect[ly] decided case, causing serious consequences and a negative impression. Deduct 10 points per case if done intentionally, 5 points per case if done unintentionally;
2) violations of procedural law or substantive unfairness in a case lead to repeated appeals, deduct 4 points per case. If caused by negligence, deduct 2 points per case.

Deduct 5 or 6 points for any of the following situations:

1) If it is discovered upon investigation or found by the court of second instance that the jurisdiction is clearly illegal;
2) incorrect decisions to not accept or to turn away cases;
3) violations of the recusal system by adjudication personnel;
4) failing to hear cases in open court that should be heard in open court;
5) failure of the adjudication body to comport with legal requirements regarding its composition;
6) failing to list, or incorrectly listing, the parties to litigation in civil, commercial, and administrative decisions;
7) conducting mediation in violation of the principles of voluntariness and legality;

43 Xunyang County People's Court Target Responsibility System (Xunyang xian renmin fayuan gangwei mubiao zeren zhi), Arts. 2(2)(4), 2(3)(5).

44 Kenli xian renmin fayuan 2007 nian gangwei mubiao zeren zhi kaohe jiangcheng banfa (Kenli County People's Court 2007 Measures for Assessment of the Target Work Responsibility System), issued March 15, 2007, Art. 2; Zhenping xian renmin fayuan 2006 nian gangwei mubiao zeren zhi ji kaoping banfa (shixing) (Zhenping County People's Court 2006 Work Target Responsibility System and Assessment Measures [Provisional]) (hereafter Zhenping System), issued February 15, 2006, Art. 5(c).

8) violating relevant requirements of the litigation laws, taking incomplete or improper measures to preserve property, causing serious consequences or a negative impression;
9) cases with incorrect factual determinations or unclear factual determinations with inadequate evidence;
10) failing to sentence a defendant in a criminal trial to additional punishment as required by law, or sentencing a defendant in a criminal trial to additional punishment when not required by law;
11) preparing official documents of court decisions lacking required content;
12) exceeding the legally required trial time limits without prior approval;
13) issuing official documents of court decisions with unclear description of facts, insufficient or vague presentation of evidence, incorrect or incomplete use of legal provisions, or requiring revisions or additions.

Deduct 3 or 4 points for any of the following circumstances:

1) Requiring the plaintiff to produce evidence in administrative cases, in violation of the requirements of the Administrative Litigation Law;
2) if the court of second instance finds that the civil portion of the decision in a criminal case with a joined civil suit has errors and makes large alterations to the liability for civil compensation;
3) verdicts where the factual determination is without errors, but the application of law is in error;
4) official documents of court decisions with unclear structure, confusing language, or incorrectly written Chinese characters;
5) violating relevant requirements of the litigation laws, taking incomplete or improper measures to preserve property;
6) although having conducted an open court hearing of a case, failing to issue the advance public notice required by law;
7) requesting or granting an extension of time limits for hearing cases when the reason requested, or the procedures for granting, do not respectively comport with the legal requirements;
8) cases determined to be inadequate during the internal court review and evaluation of cases (cases where points have already been deducted for exceeding time limits will not have points further deducted);
9) failure by adjudication tribunals to submit cases within the required monthly time period for review and archiving.

Deduct 1 or 2 points for any of the following circumstances:

1) If the court of second instance finds no fault with the original decision's determination of facts or use of law, but made relatively large alterations to the substance of the original decision;
2) failing to designate a lawyer to assume legal aid responsibilities, or other representative, for a blind, deaf, mute, or minor defendant in a criminal case who has not designated a representative;
3) official documents of a court decision with unclear explanation, insufficient presentation of evidence, lack analysis of the conflict between the parties, or are unconvincing;
4) if careless drafting or reviewing results in official documents of court decisions needing to be redrafted, corrected, or reprinted.[45]

Systems that sanction judges for cases resulting in "serious consequences" also risk punishing judges for unintentional legal errors. For example, the 2006 responsibility system adopted by the Tai'an IPC includes a broad exculpatory clause consistent with the 1998 SPC directives, barring judicial disciplinary sanctions for incorrectly decided cases that are caused by unclear laws or regulations or differences of opinion regarding the law or facts.[46] Yet the Tai'an system also provides that "negligent violations of law or regulations that result in . . . a) cases where state compensation is paid, b) leads to collective petitions by parties, suicides, or other evil incidents, or c) causes a negative social impression that harms the image of the court" are to be treated as exceptionally serious incidents of "incorrectly decided cases" and punished appropriately.[47] This, of course, raises the question of whether practical liability for judicial decisions hinges on the *consequences* of the decision (which may be out of the actual control of judges or the court) or on the original error itself. The Tai'an IPC responsibility system arguably violates the 1998 SPC directives (and itself) in rendering judges liable for cases that are reversed either for simple, non-negligent legal error or for correctly decided cases that simply incite public controversy.

[45] Ibid.

[46] Tai'an shi zhongji renmin fayuan weifa shenpan zeren zhuijiu banfa (shixing) (Tai'an Municipal Intermediate People's Court Illegal Trial Responsibility Measures [Provisional]), Art. 43, http://www.tacourt.gov.cn/html/gzzd/2006–11/gzzd04747304.shtml (accessed September 20, 2008) (hereafter Tai'an Measures).

[47] Ibid., Art. 8. See also Guangdong Measures, Art. 7(2) (providing that the "serious consequences" for which negligent judicial error should be disciplined includes cases resulting in "negative social influence, harming the image of the court").

Some trial courts review cases reversed or sent back on appeal before applying sanctions to the judges who drafted the original opinion. Some require court supervision tribunals to review such cases, as well as those reversed during internal rehearing procedures, and provide suggestions to court adjudication committees on whether sanctions should apply.[48] Chinese judges note that these processes of internal review can serve in practice as channels for reducing or eliminating potential sanctions their colleagues may face for incorrectly decided cases resulting from simple legal error.[49]

C. Collective Liability for Errors

Do local court responsibility systems comply with the 1998 SPC directives requiring judicial personnel to bear individualized liability for erroneous decisions? It depends. Some fully comply. Relevant 1999 Beijing rules incorporate the original SPC language word for word.[50] Others comport with the spirit of the 1998 directives. The 2000 Guangdong rules, for example, require all members of collegiate judicial panels and adjudication committees to bear collective liability for errors of law in incorrectly decided cases. But the rules expressly exempt from liability any individual members who firmly adhered to the "correct" answer during deliberation (but who presumably were outvoted).[51]

Other local court systems violate the 1998 SPC directives by incorporating principles of collective judicial liability whereby annual numerical work targets are set for tribunals that collectively sanction (or reward) the entire tribunal for failure (or success) in fulfilling the targets. Hainan district BPC measures provide that civil and criminal court tribunals should receive a financial sanction (or reward) of 100 yuan per person for each percentage point of reversed cases above (or below) the set annual target

[48] Tai'an Measures, Art. 6; Dongzhi fayuan shenpan weiyuanhui jizhong zhenzhi "wenti an" (Dongzhi Court Adjudication Committee Concentrates on Diagnosing and Curing "Problem Cases"), http://www.ahcourt.gov.cn/gb/ahgy_2004/fyxw/userobject1ai3253.html (accessed September 20, 2008). See also Guangdong Measures, Art. 13 (requiring the collegiate three-judge panel that handled the initial [i.e., reversed] case to analyze the appellate opinion and report on the reasons for their reversal to court authorities).

[49] Interview, IPC judge, on file with author.

[50] Beijing Details, Arts. 9–11.

[51] Guangdong Measures, Art. 10. See also Jingshan Measures, Arts. 8–9. Pengzhou sets a default responsibility ratio for three-person collegiate panels, requiring the tribunal head to bear 60 percent of the responsibility for incorrect cases and the other two members 20 percent apiece (if the tribunal head has assumed primary responsibility for the case). But it similarly allows exculpation for those members who adhered to the "correct" opinion during deliberations. Pengzhou System, Art. 13.

of 1.5 percent.[52] If the civil tribunal collectively experiences a 3.5 percent appellate reversal ratio, it is assessed a fine amounting to 200 yuan per tribunal member, regardless of whether the reversal rates of particular judges within the tribunal were below the set target.

Other local court systems require tribunal heads and court presidents to bear personal liability for the errors of their subordinates, in direct violation of the 1998 SPC directives. The 2002 Gaocheng court measures require that collective financial sanctions assessed against a tribunal be automatically deducted from the tribunal head personally, who then may assess sanctions against the responsible subordinate.[53] Still other local court responsibility systems designate a range of career sanctions against the heads of judicial tribunals and collegiate panels whose subordinates fail to meet designated target work ratios.[54]

Some local court rules even explicitly create mechanisms for judicial officials to "pass the buck" and limit their own responsibility for their subordinates' errors. Hainan provincial rules charge presiding judges and tribunal heads with default liability for incorrect decisions issuing from subordinate judicial panels if there were dissenting voices among the original trial judges. However, the rules offer presiding judges and tribunal heads an "out." They may reduce their liability by reporting cases "likely to result in incorrect decisions" to their immediate superiors in advance of allowing the case opinion to be issued. After this has happened, the responsibility for any resulting case opinion deemed to be incorrectly decided falls on the heads of higher-level authorities (such as tribunal heads and court vice presidents and presidents) to whom the case was referred.[55]

[52] Hainan District [Ningxia] Measures, Arts. 2–5, 13. For a similar principle, see Tonghai Measures, Art. 3. An alternative system involves competition between different tribunals, with financial rewards (or sanctions) accruing collectively to tribunals who exceed (or fail to meet) target ratios and additional bonuses accruing to individual tribunals and judges with the greatest success in meeting their targets. Zhenping System, Art. 4(b).

[53] Gaocheng shi renmin fayuan gongzuo mubiao guanli kaohe jiangli banfa shishi xize (Gaocheng Municipal People's Court Implementation Details for the Management of the Work Target Assessments and Rewards), issued August 14, 2002, Art. 3(6). Similarly, financial rewards for tribunal performance are directed to the tribunal head personally, who then may dispense them to the responsible subordinates.

[54] Ibid., Art. 22(1); Zhenping System, Art. 5(a); Guanghan fayuan 2004 niandu gangwei mubiao guanli kaohe banfa (Guanghan Court 2004 Evaluation System for the Management of Annual Work Targets), issued May 17, 2004, Art. 24.

[55] Hainan Decision, Art. 9. Under the Hainan system it is not entirely clear that this process of "reporting up" guarantees that lower-level authorities will entirely escape from resulting liability for any resulting incorrect decisions. If presiding judges report to

III. PRACTICAL EFFECTS OF RESPONSIBILITY SYSTEMS FOR INCORRECTLY DECIDED CASES

Court responsibility systems create incentives that affect the behavior of Chinese judges. A desire to avoid sanctions for incorrectly decided cases leads many lower court judges to rely on *qingshi* (requests for advisory opinions) from higher courts and judges regarding the disposition of particular cases. Chinese judges criticize existing local court *qingshi* practices. They assert that many are legally questionable and create a range of practical problems for the Chinese judiciary. In response to some of these concerns, Chinese judicial authorities have included *qingshi* reform in both the 2004–08 and 2009–13 plans for court reform.

Qingshi requests are a common element of administrative governance throughout the sprawling Chinese bureaucracy. Lower-level governments or administrative agencies make regular *qingshi* requests of their superior organs upon encountering a difficult or complex issue. These range from the banal (whether specific administrative fees are admissible under national regulations) to the exceptionally sensitive (how to respond to large-scale citizen protests).[56] Such requests enable lower-level officials to ensure that their decisions correspond with the views and aims of their superiors, simplify decision making in complex or unclear cases, and to "pass the buck" in resolving thorny issues.

tribunal heads on a case likely to result in an incorrect decision and "if their proposed course of action is correct," then the presiding judge does not bear liability. After a case has been reported, tribunal heads then bear "corresponding responsibility" for "incorrect actions" or "failure to act" that results in an incorrect decision. Ibid. "Reporting up" a case "likely to result in an incorrect decision" thus may allow lower-level judicial officials to simply "spread the responsibility around" rather than avoid sanctions entirely.

[56] For the former, see Guowuyuan fazhi bangongshi dui youguan tushu, baokan, yinxiang dianzi chubanwu shenpi fei wenti de qingshi de fuhan (State Council Legislative Affairs Office Response to the Advisory Request Regarding Examination and Approval Fees Regarding Books, Periodicals, and Electronic Publications), issued November 23, 2004, (responding to a provincial legislative affairs office [LAO] *qingshi* request as to whether the censorship costs involved in screening books and videos for publication constituted admissible administrative fees, and stating that such fees should be included in the annual budget rather than be charged to the author or the publisher). For the latter, see Daqing shi Datong qu renmin zhengfu bangongshi guanyu yinfa datong qu zhongda quntixing shijian yingji yu'an de tongzhi ([Daqing City]) Datong District Government Notice Regarding Distributing the Emergency Response Plan for Large-Scale Mass Incidents), issued September 4, 2007, Art. 2(2) (instructing local officials to issue requests for guidance to district party and government officials before taking "major" measures to resolve large-scale mass incidents).

Qingshi practices are also prevalent in the Chinese judiciary. In part, this reflects the fact that the Chinese judiciary historically has been quite undifferentiated from the rest of the centrally controlled administrative Chinese government apparatus. Chinese judges and scholars note that *qingshi* practices originated in the pre-1978 reform period as a means for higher-level court party committees to supervise the work of corresponding party committees in lower-level courts, and for the latter to seek advance guidance in difficult cases in which a wrong decision risks running afoul of policies set by higher-level party authorities.[57] The onset of legal reform in the 1980s and the rise of an increasingly professional judiciary have somewhat altered these functions. Lower courts continue to rely on *qingshi* channels to obtain direction from higher courts and officials in handling politically sensitive cases. But lower courts also depend on *qingshi* channels for guidance in deciding a range of issues that pose legal or practical difficulties.

Despite some efforts in the 1980s and 1990s by central judicial authorities to standardize *qingshi* procedures, actual *qingshi* practices of lower courts remain highly flexible and ill defined.[58] In more formal *qingshi* proceedings, the adjudication committee of a lower court may, after internal deliberation, identify a specific case as "difficult" to decide and submit a formal written report and request for guidance to the appellate court prior to deciding the case. Many higher court responses to such requests are openly filed and available on Chinese legal databases.[59] In less formal proceedings, lower court judges may simply contact the relevant trial division of the appellate court (which would be responsible for handling

[57] Chongqing HPC judge Zhang Qingguo, "Guanyu fayuan anjian qingshi de ruogan sikao" (Thoughts Regarding the Advisory Request System in Court Cases), *Yunnan faxue* (Yunnan Jurisprudence), no. 4 (1998): 76.

[58] For examples of SPC reform efforts, see Zuigao renmin fayuan guanyu baosong qingshi anjian ying zhuyi de wenti de tongzhi (SPC Notice Regarding Issues to Pay Attention to in Submitting Advisory Requests), issued March 24, 1986 (requiring provincial HPCs to include clear factual determinations in their *qingshi* requests), and Zuigao renmin fayuan guanyu sifa jieshi gongzuo de ruogan guiding (SPC Decision Regarding the Work of Judicial Interpretation), issued June 23, 1997 (standardizing the use of *pifu* (reply) as the correct term to refer to an SPC reply to a lower-court *qingshi* request regarding the application of law in a specific case [as opposed to the use of *jieshi* (interpretation) to refer to broad interpretations regarding the application of the law in a category of cases]).

[59] See, for example, the results of searching for *qingshi* and *fayuan*, http://www.law-lib.com/law/ (accessed September 20, 2008). Responses to *qingshi* requests by higher courts bear a range of different titles, such as *fuhan*, *pifu*, and *dafu*.

the case on appeal), orally explain the case, and solicit advice on how to decide the case.[60]

Chinese scholars identify a range of reasons motivating Chinese judges to resort to *qingshi* channels for guidance from higher courts. Some reasons reflect challenges linked to China's rapid economic development during the last thirty years. Social change generates many new issues for which existing law has no clear answer, and new laws and regulations create inconsistencies that must be resolved. Prevailing low levels of legal education exacerbate the difficulties lower-level Chinese trial judges face in applying new laws to specific situations. Other reasons reflect structural factors associated with China's legal system. Absent other mechanisms (such as a system of binding case precedent) to address issues of legal uniformity, all levels of the Chinese judiciary depend heavily on *qingshi* requests and responses. Lower courts rely on such requests to resolve unclear issues in specific cases. The SPC depends on *qingshi* requests from lower courts to identify important, unresolved issues of law on which it may be necessary to issue a binding SPC judicial interpretation (*sifa jieshi*) for the judiciary as a whole.[61]

Resort to *qingshi* channels also reflects Chinese political realities. In sensitive cases, it simply may be politically prudent for a lower court judge to solicit central views regarding how a case should be decided. Yet *qingshi* channels can also be tactically employed by Chinese judges who seek to defend themselves against external pressure to decide specific cases in accordance with powerful local or government interests. Under such circumstances, using *qingshi* channels to solicit higher-level support before issuing a decision may provide lower courts with a convenient excuse for issuing decisions that contravene local interests – allowing them to assert that as much as they would have liked to reach a different decision, their hands simply were tied by their superiors.[62]

60 Zhang Qingguo, supra note 57, p. 79. For a description by a Shandong HPC judge, see Di Tianli, supra note 27.

61 Wan Yi, "Lishi yu xianshi jiaokun zhong de anjian qingshi zhidu" (The History and Practical Difficulties of the System of Advisory Requests in Cases), *Faxue* (Jurisprudence), no. 2 (2005): 11–12. The SPC codified this role of *qingshi* requests in a 2007 decision. Zuigao renmin fayuan guanyu sifa jieshi gongzuo de guiding (SPC Decision Regarding the Work of Judicial Interpretation), issued March 23, 2007, Art. 10(3).

62 Zhao Shuping, "Woguo fayuan zai juti anjian shang shiyong falü de qingshi yu pifu de lixing sikao" (Thoughts Regarding China's Courts Advisory Requests and Responses Regarding the Application of Law in Specific Cases), *Hunan gongan gaodeng zhuanke xuexiao xuebao* (Journal of Hunan Public Security College) 16, no. 2 (1994): 36.

But Chinese judges themselves identify a more direct reason for lower court judges to resort to *qingshi* requests: to avoid potential sanctions for decisions that might be overturned or remanded on appeal or that otherwise might be deemed incorrect under court responsibility systems. Chinese judges note that such use is common.[63] As one Jiangsu BPC judge phrased it:

> Existing responsibility systems for incorrectly decided cases provide the soil for the continued existence of *qingshi* practices.... Regardless of how much a judge believes in the law, and regardless of how creative he may be in trial work, in order to avoid "incorrectly decided cases" from occurring, and in order to avoid a financial or a professional impact on himself, it is difficult to avoid certain "public relations" activities (with higher courts) from taking place.[64]

Faced with the incentives created by many existing local court responsibility systems, the extent of *qingshi* requests by lower courts can become extremely varied, broad, and murky in scope. As one Chongqing HPC judge noted:

> In order to decrease their numbers of reversed or remanded cases, some lower courts not only submit *qingshi* requests to higher courts regarding how to classify a case [i.e., whether criminal, civil, economic, or administrative] or how to apply the law, but what the factual determinations should be as well. The SPC, and some HPCs and IPCs, have issued rules aimed at addressing this, but their impact is not evident.[65]

Chinese judges identify a range of legal and practical problems stemming from existing *qingshi* practices. Legally, the basis for *qingshi* requests is highly unclear. Both the Chinese Constitution and the Organic Law of the Courts specify that higher courts are to "supervise" the trial work of

[63] See, for example, Zhu Zhijun, "Fayuan neibu qingshi feng bu ke chang" (Internal Court Advisory Request Practices Cannot Be Continued), *Faxue* (Jurisprudence), no. 4 (1999): 50 (Nanjing IPC judge); Ren Chengyu, "Shangxiaji fayuan jian anjian qingshi huibao de zuofa bi da yu li" (The Detriments of the Advisory Request and Reporting Practices Between Higher and Lower Courts Are Greater than the Benefits), *Renmin jiancha* (People's Procuratorate), no. 3 (1997): 48 (Henan BPC judge).

[64] Ping Jialin, "Quxiao ge'an qingshi ying yi gaige xianxing cuo'an zhuijiu zhi zhidu wei jichu" (Eliminating Qingshi Requests for Individual Cases Should Focus on Reform of Existing Responsibility Systems for Incorrect Cases), *Falü shiyong* (Legal Application), no. 9 (2006). For similar comments by a Chinese scholar, see Wang Lin, supra note 36.

[65] Zhang Qingguo, supra note 57, p. 79.

lower courts, but they provide no details as to how that is to be carried out in practice apart from ordinary appellate review of lower court cases.[66] No clear standards exist that set out the appropriate extent, content, or procedure for lower court *qingshi* requests, or how these should interact with ordinary trial and appellate procedures.

The unclear and somewhat secretive nature of many *qingshi* proceedings also creates concerns regarding judicial fairness and individual rights. In the words of one Chongqing HPC judge:

> Because the process of handling *qingshi* requests is secret, it is "black box manipulation." Parties do not know anything about the judges who are responding to the *qingshi* requests. They are thus unable to exercise their rights guaranteed by procedural laws with regard to the hearing that may decide their fate, such as the right to request recusal (of a judge with a conflict of interest), or the right to present a case or offer opinions.[67]

Excessive reliance on *qingshi* practices also raises classic problems regarding court advisory opinions. It may impact the quality of court decisions, particularly when the core facts have yet to be developed at trial. Higher courts generally rely on the oral and written reports of lower courts as the basis for responding to *qingshi* requests rather than independently collecting evidence or interviewing witnesses and parties. This can lead to higher courts issuing responses in which "their grasp of the case is not complete or deep, and the foundation for the response (to the *qingshi* request) is not solid, lacking in guarantees as to its accuracy."[68]

Chinese judges also point out that reliance on *qingshi* requests can undermine the value of appellate review. China's litigation procedure laws guarantee the parties' right to independent appellate review of trial court decisions.[69] Yet if higher and lower courts use *qingshi* channels to hammer out the content of a decision prior to actually issuing it, then appellate courts can be placed in the position of reviewing on

[66] Chinese Constitution, Art. 127; Organic Law, Arts. 17 and 30.
[67] Zhang Qingguo, supra note 57, p. 77. Parties may also experience difficulties even learning the underlying reasons for a higher-court reply to a *qingshi* request that decides their case. One Shandong HPC judge notes that "in practice, lower courts generally resolve cases in accordance with the opinion of the higher-level court and attach the opinion to the internal court file of the case, and do not publicly disclose it (to the parties)." Di Tianli, supra note 27, p. 12.
[68] Zhang Qingguo, supra note 57, p. 78.
[69] See, for example, PRC Civil Procedure Law, amended October 28, 2007, Arts. 147–59.

appeal a decision they already have instructed lower courts to make. In such a situation, "parties are deprived of their right of appeal, and the legally-established distinctions of trial and appeal are effectively abolished."[70]

Chinese judges also argue that the existence of the *qingshi* system contributes to passivity and dependency on the part of lower courts and inflates the workload of higher courts. The ready availability of *qingshi* channels breeds an inclination on the part of lower court judges to forgo careful analysis of legal issues with any degree of complexity in favor of simply referring them to higher authorities for decision. This in turn exacerbates the workload of higher court authorities, who must bear the burden of responding not only to the original *qingshi* requests but also to any resulting appeal of the underlying case.[71]

Existing *qingshi* practices also contribute to court difficulties in resolving cases in a timely manner. Chinese judges note that the internal processes of seeking higher-level approval or advice on particular cases can significantly lengthen the time it takes for the trial courts to issue their decisions.[72] This can contribute to violations of trial and sentencing time limits. Chinese judicial officials have attempted to address some of these problems. From 2003 to 2005, for example, Chinese courts and law enforcement officials pursued a nationwide campaign aimed at clearing up instances of "illegal extended detentions" of criminal suspects without formal charges or trial.[73] As part of the campaign, the SPC and provincial HPCs issued orders barring lower courts from resorting to *qingshi* requests except in "difficult cases involving the application of law" to

[70] Chai Jianguo and Wang Yanxia, "Duli shenpan yu sifa tizhi gaige" (Independent Trial and Judicial System Reforms), *Hebei faxue* (Hebei Jurisprudence) no. 23 (2005): 85, 87 (comments by the director of the research office of the Hebei HPC). For a similar point by a vice president of the Jiangsu HPC, see Liao Disheng, "Lun sifa gongzheng xiaolü de shixian tujing" (Discussion on Methods to Realizing Judicial Fairness and Efficiency) *Jinling falü pinglun* (Jinling Law Review), no. 2 (2002): 127, 130.

[71] Ping Jialin, supra note 64; Ren Chengyu, supra note 63.

[72] Zhu Zhijun, supra note 63, p. 51; Wang Yuming and Xie Shanjuan, "Minshi shenpan zhong de yinxing chaoshenxian xianxiang chutan" (A Preliminary Investigation into the Phenomena of Invisible Violations of Trial Time Limits in Civil Cases), http://www.lawbook.com.cn/lw/lw_view.asp?no=583 (accessed September 20, 2008).

[73] 2005 Annual Report of the Congressional-Executive Commission on China, http://www.cecc.gov/pages/annualRpt/annualRpt05/index.php (accessed September 20, 2008), p. 26; 2004 Annual Report of the Congressional-Executive Commission on China, http://www.cecc.gov/pages/annualRpt/annualRpt04/index.php (accessed September 20, 2008), p. 15.

"prevent extended detentions from arising as a result of repeated *qingshi* requests."[74]

Recognizing this problem, the SPC 2004–08 five-year court reform plan lists *qingshi* reform in "difficult cases involving the application of law" as a goal and states that lower courts may resort to *qingshi* in cases involving "common questions of the applicability of law," requesting that the higher court itself directly handle the case.[75] Naturally, this leaves open the question of whether and how to reform the use of *qingshi* in other circumstances. At least one provincial HPC has announced its intention to go even further. In 2006, the Shaanxi HPC issued an opinion regarding the implementation of the SPC's five-year plan in which it listed the "gradual elimination" of *qingshi* requests in individual cases as one of its long-term goals. *Qingshi* requests should be limited to questions regarding the use of the law and must come from the adjudication committees of lower courts (as opposed to individual judges).[76]

IV. ROOTS OF RESPONSIBILITY SYSTEMS FOR INCORRECTLY DECIDED CASES

Modern Chinese responsibility systems for incorrectly decided cases are deeply rooted in prior imperial practices. For centuries, Chinese emperors relied on fused administrative and judicial authority, the application of strict liability for judicial error, and use of collective responsibility for official mistakes as tools to govern the sprawling bureaucracy.

Imperial Chinese governance was marked by a fusion of administrative and judicial power. As one Chinese author has noted, "[u]ltimate judicial authority rested in the hands of the emperor, while all judicial organs were theoretically but consulting organs [to assist] the emperor in making

[74] Jiangxi sheng gaoji renmin fayuan guanyu jiuzheng he yufang chaoqi jiya qingkuang de huibao (Report of the Jiangxi HPC Regarding Addressing and Preventing Extended Detentions), issued July 29, 2004. For the relevant SPC order, see Zuigao renmin fayuan guanyu tuixing shi xiang zhidu qieshi fangzhi chansheng xin de chaoqi jiya de tongzhi (Opinion of the Supreme People's Court Regarding Promoting Ten Systems to Prevent the Emergence of New Cases of Extended Detention), issued December 1, 2005, Art. 4.

[75] 2004–2008 renmin fayuan dierge wunian gaige gangyao (2004–2008 Second Five-Year People's Court Reform Plan) (2005) (hereafter 2004–2008 Reform Plan). The Third Five-Year Plan also lists *qingshi* reform as a goal. 2009–2013 renmin fayuan disange wunian gaige gangyao (2009–2013 Third Five-Year People's Court Reform Plan) (2009).

[76] Shaanxi sheng fayuan guanche luoshi "Renmin fayuan di'erge wunian gaige gangyao" shishi yijian (Shaanxi Provincial Court Opinion Regarding the Implementation of the Second Five-Year People's Court Reform Plan) (2006).

the final decision."[77] Local district magistrates, the lowest-level officials of the Chinese bureaucracy, bore responsibility for applying the law in particular cases. Hearing civil and criminal cases was but one component of the magistrate's official responsibilities for administering the affairs of a given Chinese county, alongside the supervision of tax collection and corvée labor requirements.[78]

A complex and centralized personnel review system governed the careers of Chinese magistrates. Officials were subject to a range of disciplinary sanctions administered by an imperial civil service board, the Board of Civil Office, for specific infractions such as neglect of duty, corruption, and other malfeasances. Punishments included fines, demotion, or dismissal.[79] In addition, all officials were subject to regular performance assessments. Under the Qing dynasty (1644–1912), imperial authorities held a "great reckoning" every three years, which required immediate superiors to write performance evaluations of their subordinate officials. Progressively higher-level officials reviewed these evaluations in turn before submitting them to the Board of Civil Office. Magistrates with superior performance received promotions and audiences with the emperor himself. Magistrates found to be corrupt or incompetent or who failed to meet centrally designated targets, such as tax quotas, could be demoted or removed from office.[80]

Two principles broadly characterized the disciplinary liability of imperial officials from the Tang (618–907) to the Qing dynasties. First, "officials were liable if they made a wrong decision, the nature of the punishment depending on a variety of circumstances."[81] Officials received more severe sanctions for "private offenses" (*si zui*), such as those committed for personal gain, than for "public offenses" (*gong zui*), including those committed inadvertently in the course of administration.[82] Second, such liability was applied collectively to officials within the same administrative unit and within the bureaucratic chain of command in which

77 Guo Jian, Yao Rongtao, and Wang Zhiqiang, *Zhongguo fazhi shi* (A History of the Chinese Legal System) (Shanghai: Shanghai renmin chubanshe, 2000), pp. 428–429.

78 Derk Bodde and Clarence Morris, *Law in Imperial China* (Philadelphia: University of Pennsylvania Press, 1967), pp. 4–5, 114; John R. Watt, *The District Magistrate in Late Imperial China* (New York: Columbia University Press, 1972), pp. 11–21.

79 T'ung-tsu Ch'ü, *Local Government in China Under the Ch'ing* (Cambridge: Harvard University Press, 1962), pp. 32–33.

80 Ibid., pp. 34–35, 132–133.

81 Geoffrey MacCormack, *Traditional Chinese Penal Law* (Edinburgh: Edinburgh University Press, 1990), p. 91.

82 Ibid., pp. 91, 134–135.

the mistake was made. The Tang code and its successors drew upon the concept of principal-accessory liability for joint crimes such as murder or robbery to apply collegiate liability to officials for errors. "The principal is defined as the person from whom the mistake originated, whether or not he was aware he was doing something wrong, and the accessories are those who have joined in the mistaken decision, even though they do not know a mistake has occurred."[83] Such liability extended vertically through the bureaucracy as well. Imperial officials who committed an error were punished according to the offense committed. Superior officials who failed to uncover the error were disciplined in descending degrees of severity depending on their distance in the chain of command from the official who committed the error.[84]

As with modern judicial discipline practices in China today, such imperial disciplinary practices were not exempt from criticism. Imperial governors condemned the practice of holding officials responsible for actions beyond their control.[85] Early nineteenth-century writers on governance criticized imperial disciplinary regulations as responsible for reducing state effectiveness. Disciplinary regulations were faulted for reducing the independent initiative of local officials in addressing governance problems for fear of committing an error. Similarly, disciplinary rules were faulted for creating incentives that led them to focus excessively on pleasing their superiors instead of responding to bottom-up popular pressures.[86]

Nonetheless, as Thomas Metzger notes, the nature of Chinese disciplinary regulations responded to the practical concerns faced by imperial rulers. Central authorities lacked effective mechanisms to independently monitor the actions of local officials.[87] In part, this was the result of poor communications and bookkeeping. But central officials also faced a classic principal-agent problem. Because of the centralization of power and information in the hands of the local district magistrates, central officials lacked independent mechanisms to assess the veracity of, for example, a local magistrate's report that external factors, rather than his own failings, were responsible for his inability to meet his tax collection responsibilities. "Since [the central government] could hardly tailor his

[83] Ibid., pp. 138–139.

[84] Ibid., p. 139. Superior officials also bore liability for private offences of subordinates, including intentionally incorrect decisions that the originator of the error attempted to conceal.

[85] Thomas A. Metzger, *The Internal Organization of Ch'ing Bureaucracy* (Cambridge: Harvard University Press, 1973), p. 291.

[86] Ibid., p. 327.

[87] Ibid., pp. 288–289.

responsibilities to [the local magistrate's] unverifiable account of what was within his control, it has no choice but to define his responsibility according to some standard reasonable in its own eyes, whether or not the standard conformed to the actual situation."[88] Compelling officials to bear collective responsibility for the actions of their subordinates and assigning them broad responsibility for governance failures occurring on their watch was one solution for central officials to overcome these problems. It also (ideally) created a deterrent that encouraged local officials to do their utmost to avoid such failures.[89]

As in modern judicial responsibility systems, the general principles of disciplinary liability just described translated into sanctions for imperial magistrates who committed errors in the handling of judicial cases. Internal administrative regulations governing the bureaucracy specified sanctions for such errors.[90] Under Qing administrative regulations (*chufen zeli*), magistrates were subject to administrative disciplinary sanctions ranging from temporary loss of salary to demotion to dismissal for errors such as the failure to determine the facts of a case.[91] Similar sanctions applied to instances of unintentional legal error that led to appellate reversal.[92] Qing regulations also applied principles of collective responsibility in the sanctions regime, decreeing disciplinary sanctions for officials in the chain of command above the official who committed the error.[93]

Additionally, magistrates faced sanctions for errors in judicial verdicts under the imperial criminal codes. As with other errors, the imperial criminal codes distinguished between "public crimes" and "private crimes."

88 Ibid., p. 289.

89 Ibid., pp. 288–89; MacCormack, *Traditional Chinese Penal Law*, p. 142. The imperial Chinese system widely used collective responsibility for misdeeds as a tool of social and political control, regardless of whether or not the individual involved had been directly concerned, involved, or even aware of the wrongdoing in question. See, generally, Joanna Waley-Cohen, "Collective Responsibility in Qing Criminal Law." In *The Limits of the Rule of Law in China*, ed. Karen G. Turner, James V. Feinerman, and R. Kent Guy (Seattle University of Washington Press, 2000), pp. 112–131.

90 Regarding the imperial administrative disciplinary sanctions that governed the Chinese bureaucracy, see, generally, Metzger, *The Internal Organization of Ch'ing Bureaucracy*, pp. 235–417. Metzger notes that such sanctions have been overlooked in the operation of the imperial Chinese bureaucracy. Ibid., pp. 235–236. This parallels the neglect of this subject in the study of operations of the modern Chinese bureaucracy and judiciary.

91 Ch'ü, *Local Government in China Under the Ch'ing*, pp. 128–129.

92 Ibid.; Metzger, *The Internal Organization of Ch'ing Bureaucracy*, pp. 278–279. See, generally, *Qinding liu bu chufen zeli* (Disciplinary Regulations of the Six Bureaus) (1887), 48. In some cases, these left open the possibility of reducing sanctions if the magistrate subsequently corrected the error after appellate reversal.

93 Ch'ü, *Local Government in China Under the Ch'ing*, p. 128, footnotes 108–109.

Intentional errors committed for personal gain fell within the latter category. Under the Ming and Qing codes, magistrates who intentionally exonerated the guilty or convicted the innocent received the same punishment they had (improperly) decreed that the accused should receive. If the magistrate deliberately applied a lesser or heavier sentence than was warranted, such as fifty lashes rather than twenty, he himself would receive the difference between the sentence he had issued and what was merited.[94] The imperial codes, however, allowed magistrates to convert such corporal punishments into salary fines or reductions in rank.[95] Consequently, the actual sanctions faced by magistrates in practice for either public or private crimes (at least relatively minor crimes) were generally administrative in nature.

Inadvertent errors in judicial verdicts were not immune from imperial sanctions. Rather, they were viewed as a form of public crime. Article 433(3) of the Ming code stated:

> If, in judging cases [officials or functionaries] negligently implicate innocent persons or increase a lighter penalty to a heavier one, in each case their penalty shall be reduced three degrees [from that for the original criminal]. If they negligently exonerate guilty persons or reduce a heavier penalty to a lighter one, in each case their penalty shall be reduced five degrees [from that of the original criminal].[96]

The Qing code contained similar provisions, and – as in the Ming code[97] – magistrates received lesser punishments for inadvertent errors in their verdicts than for deliberate errors committed for private gain.

Under the imperial criminal codes, Chinese magistrates also faced collective responsibility for judicial errors. The Ming code applied collective criminal liability to two groups of people: 1) relatives of criminals who committed certain serious crimes, such as rebellion, sedition, or treason, and 2) officials or functionaries who worked in the same office as those who committed "public crimes," as well as their supervisors.[98]

94 See Art. 433 of the Ming code, in *The Great Ming Code*, trans. Jiang Yonglin (Seattle: University of Washington, 2005), pp. 233–234.

95 See, for example, Arts. 7 and 8 of the Qing code, in *The Great Qing Code*, trans. William Jones (New York: Oxford University Press, 1994), pp. 40–41.

96 *The Great Ming Code*, trans. Jiang Yonglin, p. 234. For the relevant Qing rules, see Art. 409 of the Qing code, in *The Great Qing Code*, trans. Jones, p. 381.

97 See Art. 409(3) of the Qing code, in *The Great Qing Code*, trans. Jones, p. 381 (translating the relevant term as "mistaken" rather than "negligent"); Ch'ü, *Local Government in China Under the Ch'ing*, p. 129.

98 *The Great Ming Code*, trans. Jiang Yonglin, pp. lxviii, 38 (Art. 27 of the Ming code) ("[I]f lower offices send up reports to higher offices, and the higher offices do not

The degree to which any individual official bore collective liability for the inadvertent errors of another depended on his status in the bureaucratic chain of command. For example, Article 433 of the Ming code applied graduated degrees of collective punishment to officials for the commission of inadvertent errors in judicial verdicts:

> [Functionaries who make the errors] shall be punished as principals; the staff supervisors shall have their penalty reduced one degree from that for the functionaries; the associate officials shall have their penalty reduced one degree from that for the staff supervisors; the head officials shall have their penalty reduced one degree from that for associate officials.[99]

A review of Chinese legal history reveals several key points. First, all of the components of modern Chinese responsibility systems for incorrectly decided cases identified earlier in this chapter – the fusion of administrative and judicial authority, strict liability for judicial error, and collective responsibility for official mistakes – have deep roots in prior imperial legal practice. Second, these elements are a subset of broader governance practices that extended beyond the Chinese judicial system. Last, Chinese authorities adopted these methods in part to respond to concrete problems, namely principal-agent problems, that limited the ability of central Chinese authorities to effectively monitor their local officials.

V. ANALYSIS OF JUDICIAL RESPONSIBILITY SYSTEMS

Why do local court responsibility systems violate the 1998 SPC directives curtailing their use? One answer: conflicting directives from different masters. Central party policy directives emphasize the need to adopt responsibility systems to strengthen party governance, respond to citizen discontent, and address official errors.[100] Local party committee orders implementing these directives explicitly call for the strengthening of judicial responsibility systems for incorrectly decided cases.[101] When

discover the mistakes or errors in them and allow them to be carried out, then officials and functionaries in the higher offices shall have their punishment successively reduced two degrees from that for the officials and functionaries in the lower offices. . . . ").

99 Art. 27 of the Ming code, in *The Great Ming Code*, trans. Jiang Yonglin, p. 38. Art. 28 is the corollary under the Qing code. *The Great Qing Code*, trans. Jones, p. 61.

100 See, for example, Zhonggong zhongyang guanyu jiaqiang dang de zhizheng nengli jianshe de jueding (Central Party Committee Decision Regarding Strengthening Party Governance Capacity), issued September 19, 2004.

101 Zhonggong Fujian shengwei guanche "Zhonggong zhongyang guanyu jiaqiang dang de zhizheng nengli jianshe de jueding" de shishi yijian (Fujian Communist Party Provincial

court party officials translate these instructions into the detailed systems employed within the courts to evaluate and grade judicial personnel, they do not always correspond to instructions from higher-level judicial institutions, such as the 1998 SPC measures.

Why might instructions issued by party authorities and the SPC differ? One reason is that their institutional aims do not necessarily coincide. The 1998 SPC directives attempt to ensure judicial fidelity to the written law. They recognize that the law may not always be clear and that judges should not bear liability for good-faith legal error. By contrast, central party directives may emphasize other issues – such as the paramount importance of social stability and the need for local authorities to prevent the emergence of large-scale citizen protests at all costs. When these differing sets of instructions trickle down through the bureaucracy, it is entirely possible for local court authorities to adopt responsibility systems that discipline judges for decisions resulting in large-scale citizen protests (consistent with party interests), even if the decisions actually are legally correct or are merely the result of a good-faith legal error (contrary to the SPC directives).

Other conflicts exist as well. Party-run court responsibility systems manage the Chinese judiciary in a manner entirely consistent with how the rest of the bureaucracy is run. Higher authorities set targets for officials to reach and evaluate their performance based on their ability to reach them. Easily quantifiable statistics are attractive to this end; qualitative statistics are less so. Creating standardized "grades" for all of the various conceivable shades of judicial error involved in appellate reversal is complicated. By contrast, statistics such as raw appellate reversal ratios are both simple and readily available. Using them as a direct proxy for judicial performance has a natural appeal for busy party and court administrators.[102] The interests of the party and the state bureaucratic

Party Committee Implementation Opinion Regarding the "Central Party Committee Decision Regarding Strengthening Party Governance Capacity"), issued December 19, 2004, Art. 4(4); Zhonggong Pingliang shiwei guanyu jin yi bu jiaqiang yifa zhi shi gongzuo de yijian (Pingliang Municipal Communist Party Committee Opinion Regarding Strengthening the Work of Managing the City According to Law), issued August 9, 2005, Art. 2(3); Zhonggong Shennongjia lin qu weiyuanhui guanyu xuexi guanche "Zhonggong zhongyang guanyu jiaqiang dang de zhizheng nengli jianshe de jueding" de yijian (Shennongjia Lin District Party Committee Implementation Opinion Regarding Studying and Carrying Out the "Central Party Committee Decision Regarding Strengthening Party Governance Capacity"), issued December 30, 2004.

102 This problem is not unlike the one facing academic faculties seeking to evaluate tenure-track professors. The difficulty of agreeing on applicable qualitative standards to evaluate academic work renders quantitative standards, such as strict numbers of publications, more attractive.

personnel system in streamlining administrative management thus can directly conflict with (and possibly trump) SPC efforts to ensure that judges can freely decide the legal merit of cases without risking sanctions for unintentional legal error.

Yet deeper philosophical tensions exist as well. Local court responsibility systems that mechanically sanction judges for legal error fundamentally differ from the 1998 SPC directives in their view of what the law is and what the process of judicial application of the law involves. For the former, the law is little different from, for example, widget production quotas. It is never unclear. Application involves little discretion on the part of an individual judge. For precisely this reason, it is entirely reasonable to sanction judges (just like widget production team leaders) for any failure to meet centrally mandated standards. Judicial failure to get the law right thus can be "endogenized" as a variable for evaluating official performance. By contrast, the 1998 SPC directives take a very different view. The law may be unclear. Judges may have to use their judgment to discern what the law "is" and apply it to the specific situation before them. Consequently, it is unreasonable to mechanically discipline judges for every occurrence of legal error. For the 1998 SPC directives (and those of local court responsibility systems that incorporate their norms), the law and its interpretation must be independent of the rest of the factors that are used to evaluate official performance.

Ultimately, party governance methods reflected in local court responsibility systems are not new. They are the modern incarnation of imperial Chinese measures developed to allow the emperor to wield absolute authority over a sprawling administrative apparatus and to address pervasive principal-agent problems within the Chinese bureaucracy. To achieve these goals, the Chinese imperial state fused administrative and judicial authority in the hands of the ruler, adopted extensive bureaucratic means to evaluate official performance, and applied strict liability for judicial error and collective responsibility for official mistakes.

The 1998 SPC directives challenge this governance model. They view judges and the law as different from the rest of the bureaucratic structure. They grant judges a degree of individual independent judgment in deciding cases. They regard the law and its application as outside the constraints of the ordinary personnel evaluation system. In doing so, they reflect the efforts of at least some of the post-1978 Chinese legal reformers to shift the underlying governance methods of the Chinese state.

Problematically, this conflict is a fissure extending throughout Chinese governance. During the past several decades, Chinese authorities have enacted a large number of laws directed at society at large. But in order to actually implement them, Chinese authorities rely on internal responsibility systems that "translate" these norms into specific target goals for lower-level officials to meet. The judicial responsibility systems discussed in this chapter are but one example. Many others exist as well.[103] Target goals do not necessarily correspond with the requirements of formal law or regulations, nor is there any clear institutional channel for resolving conflicts between them. This can affect broader rule-of-law norms. Aims and goals expressed in national law that have not been reduced to hard targets, or are not capable of being so reduced, may fade in importance for local authorities. Local officials may learn that satisfying the specific details of their target responsibility system is all that is required and that higher-level legal norms can be ignored.

Furthermore, in some cases, problematic official behavior that worries Chinese central authorities is directly attributable to the incentives created by the target responsibility systems that Chinese authorities use to control and manage lower-level officials. Court responsibility systems that apply sanctions for unintentional legal error lead judges to rely excessively on *qingshi* requests to decide cases, contrary to the wishes of higher-level judicial officials. Other examples include *xinfang* responsibility systems that discipline government officials based on the size and scale of citizen petitions from their jurisdiction to higher-level authorities. This prompts local authorities to rely on violence and repression to prevent petitioners from contacting central officials, despite explicit instructions from national authorities barring such practices.[104] These reflect the efforts of local officials to "game the system" by figuring out specific tactics to manipulate or circumvent the target incentives they face.

Addressing these problems requires looking at the underlying behavioral incentives that fuel them. Efforts by Chinese judicial officials to carry out *qingshi* reform are unlikely to be successful unless they can alter the standards by which Chinese judges are evaluated. Trial judges who face possible disciplinary sanctions for any and all cases reversed on appeal are likely to – in one way or another – aggressively seek advance input from appellate judges regarding how they should rule. If Chinese authorities

[103] "Operationalizing" of central-level directives through responsibility systems takes place in a wide range of other fields. For a discussion of central norms regarding citizen petitioning and the *xinfang* (letters and visits) system, as well as the local responsibility systems that implement these norms, see Carl F. Minzner, "*Xinfang*: An Alternative to Formal Chinese Legal Institutions," *Stanford Journal of International Law* 42 (2006): 103, 120–136, 151–158.

[104] Ibid., pp. 151–158.

want *qingshi* channels to be used more sparingly, requests phrased more carefully, and the workload of higher-level authorities reduced, then altering the pressures facing lower-level authorities is necessary. The 1998 SPC directives appear to be a concrete step in this direction.

It is unclear whether this will take place. Some judicial officials accept the need to adjust these incentives. But it is not clear whether all party officials accept this need. At least some party authorities may be locked into the bureaucratic authoritarian mechanisms that they and their imperial predecessors have used to manage China for generations. Mechanical top-down evaluations of lower-level officials using simple numerical measurements may be administratively attractive. Passive lower-level bureaucrats, trained to respond to targets set from above and heavily dependent on *qingshi* requests and responses for direction, may meet the interests of central state authorities seeking to uniformly guide and direct the country, as well as the interests of party authorities fearful of the emergence of independent sources of political authority. In short, the issues associated with court responsibility systems may reflect a fundamental conflict between party governance interests and practical needs of judicial reform.

Scholars vary in their assessments and predictions regarding the course of Chinese legal reform. Some assert that China will (or should) parallel the developmental track of the Western countries. According to this view, gradual development of the rule of law in China will be accompanied by political liberalization, or even outright democratization.[105] Others contest this. They assert that China will (or should) parallel the developmental track of other East Asian countries. They argue that China will (or should) avoid significant political reforms (at least in the near future) and concentrate instead on procedural or institutional rule-of-law reforms similar to those found in other East Asian societies such as Hong Kong, Singapore, and South Korea.[106]

This chapter calls these projections into question. It identifies modern party governance mechanisms that are direct descendants of imperial practices. At least some party authorities and institutions may be pursuing party governance strategies corresponding to a "rule of *fa*" that is entirely

[105] See, for example, Larry Diamond, "The Rule of Law as Transition to Democracy in China," in *Debating Political Reform in China: Rule of Law vs. Democratization*, ed. Suisheng Zhao (New York: M.E. Sharpe, 2006).

[106] Randall Peerenboom, *China Modernizes* (New York: Oxford University Press, 2007), pp. 228–232, 287–297; Pan Wei, "Toward a Consultative Rule of Law Regime in China," in *Debating Political Reform in China: Rule of Law vs. Democratization*, ed. Zhao, pp. 32–40.

consistent with China's own history and bureaucratic practices. China may not pursue an "East Asian" or a "Western" version of rule of law. It may pursue its own.

In emphasizing the influence of China's own historical legacy and bureaucratic practices on the development of its legal institutions, this chapter resonates with others in this volume. In Chapter 5, Landry suggests that pre-1949 Nationalist legal developments may have had lasting residual effects on post-1949 PRC institutions. In Chapter 9, Liebman analyzes the efforts of modern PRC judicial authorities to revive revolutionary judging practices rooted in the 1940s and 1950s. Collectively, these chapters suggest the extent to which China's past may continue to influence the future of its legal institutions, as Chinese authorities invoke or rely on models taken from their own past to resolve governance problems they face now.

However, these efforts are not uncontested. At least some forces are pushing for an alternative system of governance. It may be inaccurate to say that "China is pursuing..." or "China will...." It may be more accurate to say that different factions within the Chinese government and society have differing views regarding how China should be governed and what the role of law is in Chinese governance. The future track of Chinese legal reform depends on how that struggle plays itself out.

This is not simply an abstract, normative debate regarding what system of governance is "best" for China. Existing party practices are generating concrete governance difficulties. Chinese authorities themselves have identified these as significant problems they would like to address. Doing so, however, requires Chinese officials to address deep institutional issues at the core of how the Chinese state has been administered for centuries.

3

Legalizing the Local State: Administrative "Legality" at China's Grassroots

Douglas B. Grob

Assessing the development of law in China is a challenging proposition by any standard. One provincial government official I interviewed described current conditions with uncommon eloquence:

> Legal reform in the context of China's economic reform is an "overlay" (*fugaimiande*). The challenge we face is that the overlay contains many bare patches (*haiyou kongbai dian*). Legal development continues to expand the size and quality of that overlay. But so long as economic development moves faster than legal development, those bare patches only increase in size, number, or both. Economic development moves at the speed of money; legal development moves at the speed of changing minds.

He continued:

> The old system was one of administration according to policy, documents, and leaders (*yi zhengce xingzheng; yi wenjian xingzheng; yi lingdao xingzheng*). In the new system people are supposed to think in terms of administration according to law (*yi fa xingzheng*). That is what we strive for. But peasants have changed their minds more quickly than officials have changed their ways. Both are changing, but the pace is different.

To be sure, legal development does involve changing minds, and it does demand adjustment and adaptation both by officials and by citizens. Adaptation and adjustment are pressing concerns. But they are not the only, or necessarily even the most important reasons why legal development has not proceeded in the same way or at the same pace across

This chapter previously was presented at the China Law Center, Yale Law School, Workshop on Chinese Legal Reform, April 23, 2007, and at the Fairbank Center, Harvard University, Workshop on Reconfiguring the Party-State: The Shifting Locus of Power in Reform Era China, May 2006.

China, up and down the Chinese administrative hierarchy or across the state-society divide. One of the main reasons is that Chinese law, by design, explicitly prevents it from proceeding uniformly.

Chinese law establishes not one legal state, but explicitly carves out two. The local state as written into Chinese law is delineated somewhat more explicitly than it is as typically discussed in scholarly research on China. Under current Chinese law, governing bodies with formal legislative power exist at the center, the provincial level, and in forty-nine cities designated as "large cities" (*jiaoda de shi*) by the People's Republic of China (PRC) State Council.[1] By contrast, governing bodies – including local people's congresses, local people's governments, and administrative departments – in China's more than six hundred remaining cities, in all of its nearly three thousand county-level political divisions, and in its more than forty thousand township-level divisions have no *independent* formal legislative power.[2] Regulatory documents issued at these levels do not have binding legal effect in and of themselves and may acquire binding legal effect only with an official determination of legal consistency with higher-level measures.[3] Although a rule issued at the lowest levels may be imposed on citizens in any number of (just or unjust) ways, it becomes

[1] PRC Law on Legislation, Arts. 63–64, 69, 73, 80, 88, and 89. The "large city" designation is awarded by the State Council and, under Article 63 of the PRC Law on Legislation, is used in connection with the assignment of lawmaking power. It is not directly related to other designations the State Council applies to select cities for other purposes (e.g., *tequ chengshi* and *jihua danlie chengshi*) The forty-nine "large cities" include the twenty-seven provincial and autonomous region capitals, the four special economic zones, and eighteen other cities as follows (dates of designation by the State Council in parentheses): Tangshan, Datong, Baotou, Dalian, Anshan, Wushun, Jilin, Qiqihar, Qingdao, Wuyang, Huainan, and Luoyang (1984); Ningbo (1988); Zibo, Handan, and Benxi (1992); and Suzhou and Xuzhou (1993).

[2] PRC Law on Legislation, Arts. 63–77; PRC Administrative Litigation Law, Art. 53; Organic Law of Local People's Congresses and Local People's Governments, Arts. 7, 43, and 60; PRC Constitution, Arts. 58, 89–90, 100, and 105; State Council Implementation Outline for the Comprehensive Promotion of Administration According to Law (*Guowuyuan quanmian tuijin yifa xingzheng shishi gangyao*), 22 March 2004.

See also Xixin Wang, "Rule of Rules: An Inquiry into Administrative Rules in China's Rule of Law Context." In *The Rule of Law: Perspectives from the Pacific Rim* (Washington, D.C.: Mansfield Foundation, 2000); Peter Howard Corne, "Creation and Application of Law in the PRC," *The American Journal of Comparative Law* 50, no. 2 (2002): 369–443.

[3] Wang, "Rule of Rules"; Corne, "Creation and Application"; State Council Implementation Outline for the Comprehensive Promotion of Administration According to Law (*Guowuyuan quanmian tuijin yifa xingzheng shishi gangyao*), 22 March 2004; Randall Peerenboom, *China's Long March toward Rule of Law* (New York: Cambridge University Press, 2002).

"legal" (*hefa*) and legally enforceable only when explicitly linked, via a chain of consistency determinations made during the rule-making process, to an enactment or promulgation previously issued at or above the level of one of the forty-nine "large cities." Hence China has two legal states: the lawmaking state that includes the forty-nine "large cities" and levels of government above them, and the "legalized" local state below them.

In this local state, where "law" from above meets real conditions on the ground below, formal "legality" critically depends on those determinations of consistency. More to the point, it depends on the people who render them and on the institutions within which they operate. In China's vast local administrative realm, the government entity chiefly responsible for findings of legal consistency during the rule-making process, and hence for the "legality" of local administrative rules, is the local legal affairs office (*fazhi bangongshi* or *fazhiban*) (FZB) attached to the local people's government (*difang zhengfu*) at each level down to the county (*xian*) level. Although the Legal Affairs Office of the State Council has received some attention in the scholarly literature, FZBs beyond the center have received little notice. This chapter attempts to address that deficit.[4]

As Section 2 makes plain, the local FZBs' portfolio of formal duties appears modest – at least at first glance. But the research findings on which this chapter is based show that institutional dynamics permit the local FZBs greater de facto influence than their formal powers imply. This is manifest in three ways. First, as detailed below in Section 2, the structure of institutions affords local FZBs opportunities to exercise gatekeeping and agenda-setting influence over rule making. Second, the structure of institutions empowers local FZBs to preempt, mediate, and at times to resolve administrative conflicts that may arise between government organs during the post–rule-making stages. Third, local FZBs pursue and protect their bureaucratic missions and institutional interests by emphasizing, implementing, and enforcing procedure. As discussed below in

[4] In some localities, local legal affairs offices are formally called *fazhisi or fazhike*. For consistency, I use the abbreviation FZB throughout. Care should be taken not to confuse the FZB discussed here with the legal affairs departments of the standing committee of the local people's congresses (*renda fagui gongzuo shi* or *fagui chu*). These departments receive draft legislation from the specialized committees of the people's congresses to be considered for enactment by the local people's congress. I use the term "rules" herein to refer mainly to administrative measures (*guizhang and guifanxing wenjian*) adopted by the local government and local administrative departments, and not to measures enacted by the local people's congresses. Administrative rules are the main focus of this chapter.

Section 4, the development of legal institutions depends on increasing the importance and weight attached to procedure.[5] Legal development assigns increasing importance to the form of procedural legality that the FZBs are uniquely positioned both to proffer and protect. For this reason, the influence of local FZBs is self-reinforcing and likely only to grow with time.[6] Thus, it is imperative that observers of legal institutions and dispute resolution in China develop sufficient understanding of the structure and functions of the local FZB.

1. PUZZLES

Legal reform presents a number of puzzles in any context, and China is no exception. Examination of China's local FZBs enhances our understanding of at least three such puzzles. The first has to do with the role of strong and independent courts in legal development. Independent courts are necessary in any well-functioning legal system and must be the end goals of legal reform. Yet that does not necessarily imply that they must or should be the sole starting point of legal development and reform. In a state such as China, where courts are chronically weak and dependent, it also makes sense to focus attention on nonjudicial actors as possible loci of legal development. As described below in Section 3, by mediating the legality gap between administrative levels, the FZBs promote a form

[5] For scholarly treatment of the link between procedure and the development of the rule of law, see, for example, Martin Shapiro, *Courts: A Comparative and Political Analysis* (Chicago: University of Chicago Press, 1981); Philippe Nonet and Philip Selznick, *Law and Society in Transition: Toward Responsive Law* (New York: Harper & Row, 1978); Richard Posner, "Creating a Legal Framework for Economic Development," *World Bank Research Observer* 13, no. 1 (1998): 1–11. For discussion of the topic in the context of contemporary Asia, see, for example, Stanley B. Lubman, *Bird in a Cage: Legal Reform in China after Mao* (Stanford: Stanford University Press. 2000), and Tom Ginsburg, *Judicial Review in New Democracies: Constitutional Courts in Asian Cases* (New York: Cambridge University Press, 2003). See also State Council Implementation Outline for the Comprehensive Promotion of Administration According to Law (*Guowuyuan quanmian tuijin yifa xingzheng shishi gangyao*), 22 March 2004.

[6] Findings are based on field research and interviews I conducted with forty-eight provincial-, city-, and county-level FZB officials from Beijing, Anhui, Hubei, Sichuan, Shanghai, Shandong, Henan, and Guangzhou between 2002 and 2007. Field research also included interviews with thirty-four other local justice department officials, local judges, lawyers, local party officials, and administrative officials, and frequent discussions with Chinese law professors and lawyers. I conducted a portion of the interviews during the interviewees' visits to the United States.

of procedural legality that mitigates some of the risks and problems of judicial politicization.

The second puzzle relates to the mechanisms for resolution of administrative disputes. There are multiple avenues for resolution of administrative disputes in China. The literature on two of them – administrative litigation and the petition (*xinfang*) system – is vibrant and growing. We know far less, however, about the system of administrative reconsideration (*xingzheng fuyi*), in which the FZBs play a central role. This understanding is relevant in part because administrative reconsideration alters and helps to shape the universe of cases subject to administrative litigation in ways not sufficiently accounted for in extant research. This chapter explores the interaction between administrative litigation and administrative reconsideration and provides guideposts for future research.[7]

The third puzzle concerns bureaucratic competition. The question of whether bureaucratic redundancy leads to inefficiencies that hamper development or results in more effective rule of law has received increasing attention from researchers.[8] If loci of legal development exist outside the courts, then one must consider first how these loci are "selected"; second, whether they must be unique; and third, whether bureaucratic rivalry may be harnessed in ways that support legal development. My research has found that the institutional rivalry between the local FZBs and local justice departments (*sifa si* or *sifa ting*) (SFT) may, under some conditions, play a positive role in the development of legal institutions and the rule of law at the grassroots.

Section 2 provides a basic introduction to the structure and processes of the local FZBs. Section 3 explains the FZBs' mediating role in local administrative government. Section 4 describes the FZBs' role as purveyor of what this chapter describes as "didactic proceduralism." Section 5

[7] A fourth mechanism of administrative dispute resolution is provided under the Administrative Supervision Law and is the subject of a larger ongoing research project of which this chapter is one part.

[8] For a description of conditions under which bureaucratic redundancy may lead not to inefficiency but to more effective policy outcomes, see Andrew Mertha, "'Policy Enforcement Markets': How Bureaucratic Redundancy Contributes to Effective IPR Policy Implementation in China," *Comparative Politics* 38, no. 3 (2006): 295–316. Mertha argues that "the widespread assumption in which redundancy necessarily leads to inefficiency is incorrect, that there are different types of redundancies. In some cases, redundancy does produce inefficient results. But in others, parallel bureaucracies can contribute to efficient and effective policy outcomes, while their absence can lead to wasteful and ineffective policy implementation" (295).

describes the rivalry between the FZBs and the SFT as, under some conditions, supporting rather than undermining legal development. Section 6 is the conclusion.

II. A PRIMER ON LOCAL-LEVEL LEGAL AFFAIRS OFFICES

As the legal-affairs arm of the local government, the FZBs operate in an ostensibly procedural realm. Their legal status is that of an operational department (*bangong bumen*) of government at each level, not an administrative department (*zhineng bumen*). As such, they receive no delegation of substantive administrative power from either the local people's government or local people's congress and have no direct responsibility for substantive policy implementation (apart from administrative law reform). Their formal purpose is to assist government at all levels to promote legality in administration (*yifa xingzheng*). Nonetheless, amidst significant administrative law reform, especially during the last decade, the evolution of the FZBs provides an example of how a thin form of procedural legality can be both politically influential and politically insulating.

The FZBs' main activities fall into four categories:

- Planning of the local government-wide rule-making agenda;
- reviewing (or redrafting) of rules submitted by functional administrative departments for legal consistency with superior measures (*hefaxing shencha*);
- following up with administrative departments on problems brought to the government's attention – for example, through the petition system;
- conducting administrative reconsideration on behalf of the local government under the Administrative Reconsideration Law (*xingzheng fuyi fa*) (ARL); advising and supervising administrative reconsideration organs within local administrative departments.

Overview of Local-Level Rule Making in China

The following is an illustration of how the rule-making process generally begins in a typical city-level or county-level administrative department. Within the administrative department (e.g., the local city planning department, land bureau, water resources department, or technology supervision bureau, to name but a few), there is a legal affairs section (*fazhichu*), usually with three subsections: drafting; enforcement and supervision; and administrative reconsideration. A group within the legal affairs section is responsible for identifying areas in which new rules are needed. After identifying an area, the group proposes the idea of a new rule to the section head. With his or her approval, the idea goes to the department head.

If the department head approves the idea, a formal description, explanation, and preliminary draft are sent to the FZB at the same level. The FZB then decides whether or not to place the proposed rule on the annual rule-making plan. It is according to this plan that the local government (*zhengfu*) will formally promulgate administrative rules during the next year. The final decision of whether to give a department's proposal a place on the plan is made by the head (*zhuren*) of the local FZB. Though she is subject to oversight by the standing committee of the local people's government and to "supervision" by the local people's congress, as well as to supervision by the FZB at the next level up, the head of the local FZB is the first real gatekeeper of consequence in the local rule-making process.

The FZB head may refuse to place a proposal on the plan for any number of reasons, including:

- The proposed rule is explicitly contrary to or strongly implies inconsistency with a higher-level measure that has legal effect;
- the proposed rule is intended to protect bureaucratic turf or to enhance a department's revenue (e.g., through the levying of fees) with no clear public benefit or without serving a general policy goal;
- a higher-level measure that will accomplish the same end or will cause a conflict (the FZB often receives information about forthcoming measures before individual departments do) is under development;
- the proposed rule is deemed to be an inadequately or inappropriately designed measure based on the FZB's own analysis of current local circumstances (e.g., *gen shiji jingji qingkuang bu heshi*);
- the legislative plan already is too long.

Noninclusion on the plan does not kill a proposal, however. Especially if there are officials strongly advocating a measure, the FZB may recommend, and even assist with, further analysis, information gathering, and development of a revised proposal for future consideration.

If, however, the FZB does place a departmental proposal on the plan, the proposal is then sent back to the original administrative department's internal legal affairs section for drafting. Alternatively, the FZB at this juncture may become directly involved in the drafting. Or it may deem that the rule affects areas outside the purview of the proposing department and will mandate the involvement of other departments in the drafting. This is a second juncture at which the FZB may exert agenda-setting influence during rule making. In the last several years, some local governments have begun to solicit comments from interested parties or the public on some proposed rules. The State Council has encouraged local governments to solicit comments on proposed rules during local level rule making.[9] Practices and procedures for soliciting and incorporating comments vary across locales. In some locales, the local FZB advises functional administrative departments on the handling of comments. This is another juncture at which some FZB may exert influence during rule making.

Once completed, the draft rule is resubmitted to the FZB for final consistency review. At this point, the FZB has yet another opportunity to recommend or to make changes. After its review, including its review for legal consistency, is complete, the FZB reports the final draft to the local government working conference (*zhengfu bangong huiyi*), which consists mainly of the county or city head, deputies, and a few other top-ranking local officials. There is discussion, but no vote. The head (mayor or county head) (*shizhang* or *xianzhang*) decides whether or not to sign off. If she does not sign off, then the rule is dead. If she does sign off, the rule becomes "legal," but its "legality" remains vulnerable to challenge through administrative reconsideration (which, under the ARL, may be handled by the FZB) or *bei'an* review[10] at the next level up (often handled

[9] State Council Implementation Outline for the Comprehensive Promotion of Administration According to Law (*Guowuyuan quanmian tuijin yifa xingzheng shishi gangyao*), 22 March 2004.

[10] *Bei'an* refers to the system whereby an official entity files documents with the next-higher level. On the *Bei'an* system generally, see PRC Constitution, Arts. 100 and 110; PRC Law on Legislation, Arts. 55, 89, and 92; and State Council Regulation on Filing Rules and Regulations (*Fagui guizhang bei'an tiaoli*), issued 14 December 2001, effective 1 January 2002. As noted in Section 3 of this chapter, there appears to be great variance in the extent to which FZB at higher levels effectively or selectively use *bei'an* review to monitor and influence lower-level FZB behavior. In some places, the threat of effective *bei'an* review is real, whereas in others it seems hardly to exist. Research aimed at identifying the factors that explain this variance is still in process, but preliminary findings suggest that the variance generally tracks legal development. Officials who have experience or training in "open government information" (*zhengfu xinxi gongkai*) seem to have an awareness of oversight dynamics that prompts them to more effectively take advantage of *bei'an* as a mechanism to promote accountability at local levels.

by the FZB at the next level up).[11] Hence, the FZB continues to play a central role, even in the post–rule-making stages.

At the city level, the FZB always acts in the name of the mayor, and the FZB's approval is the mayor's seal. At the county level, the FZB acts in the name of the county head. Appointments to the FZB are made by the head of the local government, with the consent of the standing committee of the local people's congress. In addition, appointment to the FZB must be approved by the party Organization Department (*dang de zuzhibu*). At every point, the local-level Party Political and Legal Affairs Committee (*zhengfa wei*) may have input. But supervision of the FZB is a secondary priority for the Party Political and Legal Affairs Committee. The Political and Legal Affairs Committee's principal activities include, but are not limited to, conducting legal campaigns and the resolution of conflict among the courts, prosecutors, and the public security bureau (PSB). Except in unusual circumstances (e.g., a highly contentious administrative reconsideration case), therefore, the FZB has latitude to exercise discretion.

FZB posts are staffed by individuals who in some way can lay claim to being members of the local legal elite. In some places, this may mean simply "those with a better sense of the law" (*you fazhi yishi de guanyuan*). In counties close to "large cities," county-level FZBs are staffed by between two and five individuals, most with prior village-level legal experience, half or more with college degrees, and some of whom were law majors. Villages have no FZB, but they do have a legal affairs officer (*fazhiyuan*). The staffing of this office varies across locales, but in villages near "large cities," it is staffed by a village resident seconded on a nonpermanent basis from the village justice office (*sifasuo*) or the village's party political office (*dang zhengban*). Typically, it is not staffed by an individual sent down (*paichu*) from the county-level FZB.

Networks of FZB professionals have begun to crystallize across China, but mainly among provincial-level and large city-level FZB personnel. Some prominent law school faculty and administrative agency officials began their careers working in provincial or large-city FZBs. FZB officials at these levels convene interprovincial conferences and also travel

[11] Generally, the legality of the rule is not vulnerable to challenge through administrative litigation, because, under the Administrative Litigation Law (see especially Arts. 5, 12(2), and 54), the court has the authority to review only so-called "specific" administrative acts (*juti xingzheng xingwei*); the law does not give the courts an explicit grant of authority to review so-called "abstract" administrative acts (i.e., agency rule making). What limited ability they do have to review abstract acts is de facto and indirect.

abroad together for training. These relatively well-trained, law-oriented, networked officials provide a meaningful portion of the human capital for administrative law reform in China today. At nearly all local levels, FZB personnel consult and advise government officials across the policy spectrum.

It is important to appreciate, however, that the FZB community and the judicial community are quite separate, with less interaction than one might expect. FZB-initiated consultation with the courts is rare for two reasons. First, it can be seen as an admission by the FZBs of an inability to perform their official duties as adviser to the government on legal affairs. Second, in some locales, FZB officials have superior training and legal knowledge than some judges. FZB officials are routinely involved in legislative drafting, research, and analysis at a level of detail not usually included in judicial training. Although FZB officials are exposed to a broad array of issues across policy areas, they are still specialists in administrative law, whereas local judges often tend to lack the same opportunities to develop the kind of specialized expertise that FZB officials more routinely develop.

On technical issues outside the context of a specific case, judges from time to time do consult with the FZBs. The frequency of such consultations varied across the levels and across the locales I examined. When provincial and city-level FZBs perceived a general need for clarification on technical issues, they convened seminars (*yantaohui*) and invited professors, experts, and judges as participants. At the county level, overt consultation between the FZBs and the courts appeared to be far less frequent, even outside of the context of a specific case.

The office of legislative affairs of the local people's congresses (*renda fagui chu*) has formal supervisory authority over the FZBs, and consultation does occur between the two, particularly regarding matters of legislative planning. Yet, as discussed and elaborated below in Sections 3 and 4, important aspects of the FZBs' influence and importance derive from institutional dynamics quite insulated from conventional supervisory authority. Some early reformers envisioned the FZB as a transitional organ, expressing the hope that all government employees eventually would develop a "sense of the law" sufficiently strong to render the FZBs obsolete. Now, however, the role of the local FZB appears to have achieved permanence. As elaborated below in Sections 4 and 5, this is due in part to the division of labor imposed by China's system of administrative reconsideration and new forms of bureaucratic rivalry that support legal development. The FZBs' rather limited portfolio of formal duties understates the influence they have not only over "legality" per se, but also over the mediation of legal, economic, and political development more generally.

III. MEDIATING ROLE

The economic, social, and demographic diversity of locales that fall under the jurisdiction of China's forty-nine "large cities" varies across and even within provinces. Depending on the policy area, diversity within a city's jurisdiction may not be appreciably less than that of a region or the country as a whole. Under such circumstances, it is not unusual for a rule to be reasonable (*he li*) in one locale but unreasonable in another.

This frequently places local officials between a rock and a hard place. The official is required first to follow the law, and only then to take steps to address the clash between law and local reality – for instance, by reporting (*baogao qingkuang*) to the next-higher level, to the same-level government, or to the party leadership (e.g., through the party-controlled press, which is used to "supervise" administration). At the same time, however, the official is held accountable for citizen grievances caused by implementation of an unreasonable – though "legal" – rule. It is in this type of situation that the FZB at the next level up has the potential to play a mediating role between higher law and actual conditions on the ground. Put differently, the FZB mediates the "legality gap" between China's two legal states.

Faced with the obligation to implement an unreasonable, though legal, superior rule, a county official may be able to finesse a difficult situation by issuing an implementing rule or other normative document that alleviates the unreasonableness of the superior rule. The challenge for the official is to avoid having the FZB deem this document legally inconsistent with higher-level rules. The FZB, as an office of the local government, shares the incentive to avoid social discontent. But the FZB is constrained by review (*jiandu*) from the FZB above and held responsible for the enforcement of legal consistency. Accordingly, there was variance across the locales I examined in the extent to which FZB at higher levels used the *bei'an review* system either effectively or selectively to monitor lower-level FZBs. In some places, interviewees described the threat of effective *bei'an* review as hardly existing, whereas in others they reported that the threat was significant.[12]

[12] The Anhui Provincial FZB, for example, received 281 documents from the two "large cities" (Hefei and Huainan) under its jurisdiction in 2002 and reviewed every one of them. On the *Bei'an* system generally, see PRC Constitution, Arts. 100 and 110; PRC

The tendency of administrative law scholars to extol in their writings the importance of the spirit of the law opens a procedural loophole that broadens local discretion and variance instead of narrowing it.[13] Emphasizing consistency with the spirit over the letter of superior measures is a strategy departmental legal affairs sections and local FZBs use to mitigate the constraints of the FZB at the next level up and lessen the chances that a rule designed to cope with the diversity of local conditions will be invalidated upon review. This still leaves officials vulnerable to challenge through administrative reconsideration, but far less so than would their continued use today of strategies frequently employed in the 1990s, which included omitting reference to the higher-level rule or regulation altogether or making such references vague. These strategies are still employed today, but somewhat less so. Moreover, to the extent that strategies are employed to accommodate the needs of the local citizenry, on average they tend to mitigate, not increase, the risk of allegations of illegality or unreasonableness made through administrative reconsideration initiated from below.

Administrative law reform increasingly has formalized the FZBs' potential for influence. China's system of administrative reconsideration, initially set forth in an Administrative Reconsideration Regulation (ARR), was revised in 1999 and enacted by the National People's Congress (NPC) as the ARL. One difference between the ARL and the previous ARR is that the ARL specifically allows applicants to challenge the legality of some rules on which an administrative department had based an allegedly illegal or unreasonable administrative act, in addition to challenging the specific act itself.[14] Because the ARL specifies the FZB as an organ for administrative reconsideration (as did the ARR),[15] the FZB effectively, if indirectly, enjoys the authority to review some abstract administrative acts (*chouxiang xingzheng xingwei*). Courts, however, under the Administrative Litigation Law (ALL) do not have such an explicit grant of authority to review abstract acts.[16]

Law on Legislation, Arts. 55, 89, and 92; and State Council Regulation on Filing Rules and Regulations (*Fagui guizhang bei'an tiaoli*), issued 14 December 2001, effective 1 January 2002.

13 See, for example, Shen Kui, "Is it the Beginning of the Era of the Rule of the Constitution? Reinterpreting China's 'First Constitutional Case,'" *Pacific Rim Law & Policy Journal* 12, no. 1 (2003): 199–231.

14 PRC Administrative Reconsideration Law, Art. 7; Implementing Regulations for the Administrative Reconsideration Law [*Xingzheng Fuyi Fa Shishi Tiaoli*], Art. 26.

15 See Administrative Reconsideration Law, Arts. 3, 17, 22–23, 28, and 38.

16 See PRC Administrative Litigation Law, Arts. 2, 5, 11–12, 14, 17, 25–27, and 54.

The FZB also plays an important mediating role laterally among competing government departments. When two departments with overlapping portfolios both seek to promulgate a rule, the government at that level has the ultimate authority to resolve differences. In most cases, the government assigns the task of working out a compromise to the FZB. Draft rules and regulations originate in each department, are drafted and reviewed by the department's legal affairs section, and then sent to the FZB. Thus, it is the FZB that often first spots conflicting drafts among departments. In such cases, the FZB typically consults with each department to resolve conflicting issues and calls a joint meeting with the two (or more) departmental legal affairs sections to work out a compromise. It is not uncommon for such meetings to result in a draft jointly proposed by both departments and for a rule to be issued jointly in both departments' names. When no compromise solution can be found, the situation is referred to the local government leadership. At the county level, such disagreements usually are referred to the deputy county head (*fu xianzhang*) in charge of the policy area(s) in question. At the provincial level, appeal is made to the chairman or vice chairman of the standing committee of the government (*zhengfu changwei hui [fu]huizhang*) or to the standing committee of the local people's congress. The extent to which interdepartmental differences are resolved before that stage depends on factors including how well regarded the FZB is locally. A number of provincial governments in recent years have made the improvement of FZB staffing a priority. The State Council has encouraged this as a matter of national policy.[17] As a result, as the level of professionalism of local (city and county) FZBs has increased, government deferral to FZB judgment also has increased. To the extent that governments have become more inclined to follow cues in such matters from the FZBs, departments have fewer incentives to appeal FZB-brokered compromises to the government.

Joint issuance of rules by two or more administrative departments not only reflects the FZBs' mediating role during regulatory development but also results in the FZBs' increased influence during implementation and enforcement. Citizens may apply for administrative reconsideration of an allegedly illegal or unreasonable act by an agency. In some cases, the rule the agency uses to justify the act is issued jointly with another department. Should the citizen wish to apply for review of the rule in addition to

[17] State Council Implementation Outline for the Comprehensive Promotion of Administration According to Law (*Guowuyuan quanmian tuijin yifa xingzheng shishi gangyao*), 22 March 2004.

reconsideration of the specific action (as would be her right under the ARL), she has two options under the ARL: to apply to the administrative department at the next level up or to apply to the same-level FZB.[18] To the extent that the department at the next level up might be reluctant to review a rule issued in part by another administrative line, the citizen may be better off applying to the FZB. Thus, the legal framework within which the FZBs have become embedded results in individuals valuing the existence of the FZBs and creates incentives for behavior that enhances the FZBs' opportunities for influence.

The opportunity to review a jointly issued rule has another implication. When reviewing a jointly issued rule during administrative reconsideration, the FZB is in a position to make recommendations regarding not only future revision of the rule, but also the division of labor in revision and subsequent interpretation of the revision. Therefore, FZB-brokered compromise between rival departments represents an implicit mutual agreement between or among departments to surrender some future discretion to the FZB. Unresolved interdepartmental disputes create administrative inefficiency and other social costs. FZB-brokered compromise today lowers the social and economic costs of administration by providing a mechanism that enables administrative departments to credibly commit to constraints on their own exercise of discretion tomorrow.

IV. DIDACTIC PROCEDURALISM

Selection Effects

Judges I interviewed at the provincial and city levels reported that the number of plaintiffs who allege procedural errors as the basis for their claims has been on the rise. This may be attributable to improved understanding of the law and administrative process by citizens and their agents. Yet it may also be due to a selection effect produced by the administrative reconsideration system itself and by the FZBs' role in the system. Because administrative reconsideration tends to address questions of substantive fairness more so than does administrative litigation (where courts review mainly the legality of agency actions),[19] it is the more

[18] PRC Administrative Litigation Law, Art. 37; Implementing Regulations for the Administrative Reconsideration Law, Arts. 23–24.

[19] Except in the case of administrative penalties, in which case the ALL (Art. 54(4)) allows the court to make findings of "manifest unreasonableness."

procedurally based claims that tend to be left unresolved by administrative reconsideration or, put differently, "naturally selected" for litigation.

The salutary effect of an emphasis on procedure not only for the rule of law, but also for good governance in administration seems increasingly well appreciated in China, and reformers have encouraged a procedural orientation in many ways. According to the Regulations of the Supreme People's Court (SPC) on the Collection of Litigation Fees, for example, if an administrative department being sued for allegedly illegal behavior changes its behavior during the course of the case and the plaintiff subsequently withdraws the case, she is entitled to recoup half of her litigation fee.[20] This accomplishes several ends. First, it helps to ease caseloads for overburdened courts. Second, it provides a face-saving way for the department to correct manifest illegality prior to an adverse judicial decision. To the extent that the withdrawn cases reflect manifest illegality more so than the cases that remain in litigation, the difficulty of deciding the cases that remain creates incentives for sophistication in argument. Thus, third, it performs a didactic role by creating incentives for the litigants and the courts to focus attention on procedural matters and reasoning.

Although it might seem somewhat striking that the SPC would take the initiative to force lower courts to reopen their coffers to provide refunds when they already tend to be strapped for resources and beholden to local governments, there are reasons why the SPC nonetheless might find this economically advantageous. First, lightening the caseload also lightens the associated financial burdens. Second, interviewees reported that government departments, including local finance bureaus, tend to rally around one another when one of them is sued and that judicial rulings against a government department may be met with budgetary retribution against the court. As long as the amount of the fee refund is less, on average, than the expected costs of possible retribution and the added caseload, the guidelines would not necessarily be disadvantageous to courts. Third, removing the most egregious cases from the docket reduces the probability of politically contentious judicial rulings. Politically contentious rulings may trigger Party intervention or other forms of politicization that undermine the fledgling legitimacy of some courts. Their removal shrinks the domain of important social issues over which courts may attempt to exert authority, but within that smaller domain, courts may be freer to

[20] "Regulations of the Supreme People's Court on the Collection of Litigation Fees (*Zuigao fayuan susong shoufei banfa*), issued by the Supreme People's Court on July 12, 1989, and effective September 1, 1989, Art. 23.

render decisions that appear to the observer to be less politicized.[21] In other words, at the price of exercising political caution and not expanding their frontiers, courts may be able to purchase the opportunity to exercise less caution in rendering decisions in cases that are ex ante less contentious.

If the game ended there, the result would be a court system capable of producing streams of judicial decisions that appear less politicized on matters that were relatively uncontroversial to begin with and therefore not likely to be terribly consequential in terms of social impact. Although this would likely appeal especially to power holders outside the courts, it certainly would not merit description as a positive developmental outcome. But the game does not end there. Whether or not a system of "cautious courts" can grow into a system of "consequential courts" depends on whether the stream of decisions produced by cautious judges can provide a gradual accumulation of credibility or "judicial capital" sufficient for the court later to exercise less caution in expanding its frontiers. In the aggregate, judges will be cautious if it is most advantageous for them to be so. The operative question is whether judges, in their exercise of caution, nevertheless have ways to accumulate judicial capital.

Judges in China have some tools available that enable them to gradually accumulate judicial capital. Chinese courts, for example, are permitted by law to rule against an agency based on a procedural error committed by the agency even if the plaintiff does not sue on those grounds. Whether the reason is a lack of training or experience, part of a litigation strategy, or other factors, lawyers and plaintiffs do not always bring out all sides of an issue when building a case. As a practical matter, therefore, the judicial process allows judges to place procedural issues on the table when they may have been overlooked or ignored. Under what conditions judges are more or less likely to use this discretion, and whether they tend to use it in ways that systematically advantage or limit the state, are questions that are the subject of ongoing empirical research. Anecdotal data do not provide an adequate basis from which to draw general conclusions on these points but do suggest opportunities for further systematic research. For example, a legal expert who consults for city- and district-level governments in central China on matters concerning administrative litigation observed local governments prevailing less and less beginning

[21] See Tom Ginsburg's excellent discussion of "low" and "high" equilibria and "cautious courts." Tom Ginsburg, *Judicial Review in New Democracies: Constitutional Courts in Asian Case* (New York: Cambridge University Press, 2003).

in approximately 2002. At the same time, he observed an increase in the plaintiffs' alleging procedural errors as the basis of their arguments. He attributes this trend first to plaintiffs and their attorneys moving up the learning curve, and second to the political insulation that procedural arguments provide for judges. When judges can point to a procedural rule to justify their decisions, they may be able to more easily stick to their guns in the face of political pressure.

Sequence Matters: Reconsideration and Litigation

Administrative cases generally fall into three categories: those in which administrative reconsideration is a mandatory prerequisite to litigation; those in which a party may choose either to apply for administrative reconsideration or to go directly to litigation; and those in which administrative reconsideration is permitted, with no recourse to litigation. With respect to the first two categories, government pressure sometimes reduces the judges' inclination to go against administrative reconsideration decisions, in spite of institutional features designed to discourage such behavior (such as the requirement that judges must file their decisions both with the court at the next level up and with the procuratorate at the same level). Systematic data on the win rate for plaintiffs against the government in administrative litigation cases in which administrative reconsideration preceded litigation compared with cases that went directly to litigation were not available at the time of this writing. However, provincial-, city-, and county-level judges I interviewed in a number of locales noted they had the impression that the win rate for plaintiffs against the government was slightly higher in cases in which administrative reconsideration preceded litigation compared with that in cases that went directly to litigation. The judges speculated that this was likely due primarily to two factors: first, the plaintiffs' learning from the administrative reconsideration process, and second, the revelation of information during reconsideration that later helped the plaintiffs build stronger cases going into litigation. Plaintiffs surely learn from the reconsideration process, but that by itself is unlikely to provide a complete explanation of why the win rates for plaintiffs in litigation cases preceded by reconsideration may be higher than the win rates for plaintiffs in cases not preceded by reconsideration. A more robust explanation must take selection effects into account. Controlling for variance both in individual resources and litigation costs, cases in which the plaintiff goes on to (costly) litigation after losing in (less costly) reconsideration would tend on average to involve more egregious behavior on the part of public officials than cases in which the plaintiff loses at reconsideration and chooses not to go on to litigation. It follows, then, that the expected win rate for plaintiffs in cases preceded by administrative reconsideration would be higher than that in cases not preceded by administrative reconsideration. This logic is consistent with interviewees' impressions and, although it does not by itself constitute empirical proof, it does provide an empirically testable theoretical explanation ripe for further empirical research.

Hierarchical Effects

In some locales, manpower shortages and lack of qualified personnel weaken the integrity of reconsideration handled within administrative departments. In such locales, citizens have incentives to apply to the FZB rather than to administrative departments for reconsideration. Some counties now require that all county-level administrative reconsideration be handled by the county FZB rather than by individual functional departments. But there are exceptions. In some locales with such requirements, the county public security bureau (PSB) still conducts its own administrative reconsideration. The taxation (*guoshui* and *dishui*), industry and commerce (*gongshang*), and technical supervision (*jishu jiandu*) bureaus tend to have internal regulations that require all administrative reconsideration cases to be handled at the city level.

There are two possible interpretations for the mandated elevation of reconsideration to a higher level. One is that it represents an effort to wrest control over these critical policy areas from errant or abusive county-level officials and to relocate it higher up on the hierarchy, where officials tend to have better training, fewer ties to local interests, and thus, presumably, more insulation against local biases and political pressure. A second interpretation is that the higher up the hierarchy an individual must go to apply for administrative reconsideration, the higher the transaction costs are of doing so. Some county officials noted that one of the advantages of seeking relief through administrative reconsideration over seeking relief through the petition system is that administrative "reconsideration can solve many of the inconveniences of *xinfang*" (*fuyi keyi jiejue xinfang de bu fangbian*). Shifting reconsideration authority upward increases the transaction costs for the applicants. The relevant empirical question is whether the social benefit of any resultant increase in fairness outweighs the diminished access to justice resulting from the increase in the transaction costs.

There have been calls from both within the FZB community and without to reform the system of administrative reconsideration.[22] One proposal that has been implemented in some locales on a pilot basis is to place administrative reconsideration in the hands of Administrative Reconsideration Committees (*xingzheng fuyi weiyuanhui*).[23] The likely impact of such proposed reforms is the subject of ongoing research and debate within China, but the importance the central government attaches to administrative reconsideration is clear.[24]

Challenges

The FZBs' handling of administrative reconsideration, and their increasing influence in that realm, presents challenges. The FZBs' influence on legal development and implementation derives from their role in drafting and establishing the legality of local documents and then reasserting their claims over legality as interpreter and arbiter during reconsideration. Through reconsideration, the FZBs may be called upon to review their own prior consistency determinations. The question, therefore, is whether the FZBs can function neutrally as a reconsideration organ in a manner that preserves the integrity and objectives of the administrative reconsideration process. The risk of bias is reduced (though not eliminated) if the threat of litigation following administrative reconsideration is real and if the courts are not predisposed ex ante to uphold administrative reconsideration decisions.

Whether these conditions can be met remains unclear. Administrative reconsideration in China does not really take place "in the shadow of the courts" to the extent that analysts of other systems sometimes presume that it does. Generally, Chinese courts have authority to rule on the legality of specific administrative acts, but not on their reasonableness (except in the case of "manifest unreasonableness" [*xianshi gongsheng*] with respect to administrative fines, as explicitly provided in the Administrative

[22] See for example, Zhou Hanhua, *Trend Toward the Judiciary-Oriented Reform of Administrative Reconsideration (Xingzheng fuyi sifa hua: lilun, shizhan yu gaige)* (Beijing: Peking University Press, 2005).

[23] State Council Legal Affairs Office Notice Concerning the Establishment on a Pilot Basis of Administrative Reconsideration Committees in Select Provinces and Cities (*Guowuyuan fazhi bangongshi guanyu zai bufen sheng zhixiashi kaizhan xingzheng fuyi weiyuanhui shidian gongzuo de tongzhi*), issued 16 September 2008.

[24] State Council Implementation Outline for the Comprehensive Promotion of Administration According to Law (*Guowuyuan quanmian tuijin yifa xingzheng shishi gangyao*), 22 March 2004.

Litigation Law).[25] Administrative reconsideration, however, does function as a limited review for reasonableness and was established, in part, for that reason.

Administrative reconsideration organs also can review some abstract acts in ways that the courts cannot. But although the courts do not have de jure review authority over abstract acts, they do have de jure review authority over some reconsideration decisions.[26] This means that, because issues can be raised in administrative reconsideration that cannot be raised in litigation, administrative reconsideration may in some cases "judicialize" issues for the court that the court otherwise would not have an opportunity to address. In this way, the FZBs' role in legal development is not strictly extrajudicial. In tangible, identifiable ways, by carrying out its mandated nonjudicial responsibilities, the FZB may nevertheless create conditions that enhance the institutional capacity of the courts.

Because reconsideration takes place within administrative departments and the offices of the local people's government, by applying for administrative reconsideration at the next level up, citizens also may trigger *bei'an* supervision. Litigation typically would not directly trigger *bei'an* supervision because turning to the courts necessarily involves relying on a process that resides outside government administrative departments. To the extent that triggering *bei'an* review resolves disputes that otherwise would lead to litigation, the judicial caseload would be reduced (a consideration that motivated the central government to provide for administrative reconsideration in the first place). The nexus between litigation and reconsideration is complex, with the role of the FZB as an organ heavily involved in administrative reconsideration at its core.

V. INSTITUTIONAL RIVALRY AS A DRIVER OF LEGAL DEVELOPMENT

Much of Chinese administrative law in theory empowers citizens to sound alarms when they suffer the transgressions of local officials. By outsourcing the alarm-pulling function to people at a level below the officials over

[25] PRC Administrative Litigation Law, Art. 54(4).
[26] PRC Administrative Litigation Law, Arts. 25 and 38; see also Art. 17; Supreme People's Court Interpretation on Several Problems in Implementing the People's Republic of China Administrative Litigation Law [*Zui gao renmin fayuan guanyu zhixing Zhonghua renmin gongheguo xingzheng susong fa ruogan wenti de jieshi*], Art. 53, and Arts. 7, 13, 22, 31, 33, and 35.

which the center wishes to have control, the center alters the strategic incentives of local officials such that they find it advantageous to preempt alarm pulls. The remarks of one county-level industry and commerce official I interviewed illustrate the point. When asked to describe the typical new employee's first day on his staff, he responded:

> I tell every person on my staff on their first day here "every person you have contact with outside this office today may be the plaintiff we confront tomorrow. You must go about your duties with this clearly in mind."

The Ministry of Justice (MoJ) (*sifa bu*) and local justice departments, bureaus, and offices at all levels down to the village justice officer (*sifayuan*) have taken part in officially mandated efforts to promote legal awareness (*pu fa*) at the local level among citizens. The availability of administrative reconsideration as a lower-cost, simpler alternative to administrative litigation and one which people may take advantage without forfeiting their right to litigate later also has contributed to awareness of the law among citizens. As explained above in Section 4, the local FZB represents the government in administrative reconsideration at the same time that the SFT promotes awareness among citizens of their right to apply for administrative reconsideration.

Officials I interviewed spoke openly of the rivalry between the FZB and SFT. The current legal framework creates this rivalry but also harnesses it in a way that deepens the potential for lasting change. The MoJ's third Five-Year *Pu Fa* Plan (1995–2000) emphasized administrative law. It was during this period that the FZB system evolved. The SFT is responsible for mediation, provides legal aid and counsel for citizens, manages the bar, and administers prisons. The SFT often cites its administration of the bar to claim oversight or supervisory authority over FZB officials when they are acting in their capacity as counsel for the government.[27] Many FZB officials are credentialed as lawyers. That the rivalry between the two will continue is virtually assured. What remains to be seen is whether

[27] On this score, for example, the Anhui provincial SFT scored a victory in 2002 when the Anhui party leadership included in an official document, over the FZB's objection, explicit mention of the provincial government's (and, by implication, the SFT's) "active" involvement in promoting the legal adviser system. The effect was to imply that attorneys performing the role of legal adviser to the government at every level – that is, a role assigned to the FZB – must not be objectionable to the SFT (Anhui Province Program of Work for Governing the Province According to Law During the Period of the Ten Five-Year Plan [*Anhui sheng "shi wu" qijian yifa zhisheng gongzuo gangyao*], issued by the Anhui Provincial Party Committee of the Chinese Communist Party on April 9, 2002, Art. 32).

the tensions, which in theory under some conditions may be constructive, will in fact be so.

The SFT is a functional department (*zhineng bumen*). Functional departments generally act through the promulgation of administrative rules, subject to the gatekeeping functions that local FZBs perform as described in Section 2, and theoretically subject to review by the FZB during administrative reconsideration. Yet in Anhui, for example, at the time of this writing, only 25 percent of the provincial-level legal-aid provisions available online through government Web sites are in the form of administrative rules (*guizhang*) issued by the government. The other 75 percent are in the form of enactments of the provincial people's congress. This advantages the SFT, for it follows that it is the people's congress (and not the FZB acting on behalf of the government) that is responsible for oversight of implementation and interpretation of measures. In other words, enactment by the people's congress lessens the role of the FZB in SFT affairs. Rivalry with the FZB, then, provides additional incentives for the SFT to cast its support of legal aid in terms of fundamental rights that are more likely to require approval by the people's congress. For these reasons, the FZB has less leverage either to manipulate the SFT's place on the annual legislative agenda or to resist SFT proposals to initiate measures as legislative enactments rather than administrative rules.[28] Bureaucratic rivalry in other contexts has been noted as producing political instability. FZB-SFT rivalry appears to be a form of bureaucratic rivalry favorable to some aspects of legal development.

VI. CONCLUSION

To recall the words of the official quoted at the start of this chapter, local legal development depends on changing the minds of citizens and public officials alike, but that, in turn, depends on the mediating role of institutions. Certainly the courts play a critical role, but nonjudicial institutions are at least as important. When institutions create conditions that make it advantageous for people to think beyond substantive outcomes and place value on process, they support the development of law. It is a credible promise of a fair shake in the next round that makes it rational for people to consider not abandoning (or, in the language of game

[28] It is the distinctive nature of the SFT's portfolio that provides legal and constitutional justifications for pursuing measures through the people's congress instead of administratively through the government – justifications that may not exist to the same degree in other policy areas.

theory, not "defecting" from) the system even if they incur a substantive loss during this round. Procedural fairness today can support the promise of a fair shake tomorrow. When institutions make it advantageous for people to think in such sequential, and not just distributional, terms, conditions ripen for procedural legality to take hold. In the ideal case, today's substantive loser still may recognize a procedural win.

All development includes a temporal dynamic. It is neither reasonable nor logical, therefore, to expect to observe ex ante the developmental outcomes that are hoped for ex post. This applies as much to the development of strong, independent courts as it does to any other hoped-for outcome. Much legal development can take place outside of, and at least for now, quite independent of the courts. To students of legal culture, this is nothing new. But even students of legal development risk missing an important part of the action by remaining focused too squarely on the courts. Development of law in China is propelled by institutional dynamics that have emerged part and parcel in the way China's legal institutions have changed over a long season of cacophonic construction. The predicates of judicial power take shape in unexpected and unfamiliar ways. In China, these predicates include the development of local FZB as nonjudicial interpreters of legality. Shining a light on them reveals a clearer picture of "legality" at the grassroots, and in particular on the ways in which China goes about "legalizing" the local state.

4

Economic Development and the Development of the Legal Profession in China

Randall Peerenboom

The development of the legal profession in China since 1978 has been largely a modernization story of economic development. The transition to a market economy stimulated the demand for lawyers. Conversely, lawyers contributed to economic growth, both directly through their work on commercial transactions and protecting property rights, and indirectly by promoting, along with other legal professionals, legal reforms aimed at implementing rule of law and establishing the institutions necessary for a market economy.[1] As such, the development of the legal profession and its relationship to the market in China is broadly consistent with experiences in other countries.[2]

However, whereas China and other East Asian countries lend support to modernization theories, they have also diverged from the more classical straight-line versions whereby all states end up with Euro-American liberal democracy. Hong Kong, Singapore, Japan, South Korea, and Taiwan are all economically wealthy countries with legal systems that rank high on rule of law indices and protect both property and non-property rights reasonably well. Yet some of them continue to be nondemocratic, or somewhat dysfunctional democracies, and on the whole less liberal than

[1] This project was supported in part by an ARC Discovery grant, number DP0985927. Randall Peerenboom, *China's Long March toward Rule of Law* (Cambridge: Cambridge University Press, 2002); Donald C. Clarke, Peter Murrell, and Susan H. Whiting, "The Role of Law in China's Economic Development," 2006, http://ssrn.com/abstract=878672 (accessed March 15, 2008).

[2] Richard Sander and E. Douglass Williams, "Why Are There So Many Lawyers? Perspectives on a Turbulent Market," *Law & Social Inquiry* 14, no. 3 (1989): 431–479; Terence C. Halliday and Sida Liu, "Birth of a Liberal Moment? Looking Through a One-Way Mirror at Lawyers' Defence of Criminal Defendants in China." In *Fighting for Political Freedom: Comparative Studies of the Legal Complex and Political Change*, ed. Terence Halliday, Lucien Karpik, and Malcolm M. Feeley (Oxford: Hart Press, 2007).

their economically advanced Western counterparts.[3] Moreover, these East Asian states have not always followed the prescribed path with respect to political reforms, economic policy, or institutional development, including the development of the legal profession.[4]

Much of the concern of Western scholarship on the legal profession in China, and East Asia more broadly, has been on the role of the legal profession in political reforms.[5] East Asian countries have followed a two-track model of legal reforms, with rapid development of commercial law combined with tight restrictions on the exercise of civil and political rights when it was deemed to threaten sociopolitical stability.[6] While the role of the legal profession varied from country to country, the commercial bar in general did not serve as a force for political reforms, political liberalism, or liberal democracy.[7] Even in the commercial area, the legal profession in Japan, South Korea, and Taiwan was and remains extremely small,

[3] Randall Peerenboom, *China Modernizes: Threat to the West or Model for the Rest?* (Oxford: Oxford University Press, 2007); Randall Peerenboom, Carole J. Petersen, and Albert H. Y. Chen, eds., *Human Rights in Asia* (London: Routledge, 2006).

[4] Peerenboom, *China Modernizes*; Randall Peerenboom, "Searching for Political Liberalism in all the Wrong Places: The Legal Profession as the Leading Edge of Political Reform in China?" In *Lawyers and the Rule of Law in an Era of Globalization*, ed. Bryant Garth and Yves Dezalay eds. (New York: Routledge, 2011) Thomas Ginsburg, "Law and the Liberal Transformation of the Northeast Asian Legal Complex in Korea and Taiwan." In *Fighting for Political Freedom*, ed. Halliday et al.; William P. Alford, "Introduction." In *Raising the Bar: The Emerging Legal Profession in Asia*, ed. William P. Alford (Cambridge: East Asian Legal Studies, Harvard Law School, 2007); John K. M. Ohnesorge, "Developing Development Theory: Law and Development Orthodoxies and Northeast Asian Experience," 2006, http://ssrn.com/abstract=916781 (accessed October 13, 2008).

[5] William P. Alford, "Of Lawyers Lost and Found: Searching for Legal Professionalism in the People's Republic of China." In *Raising the Bar: The Emerging Legal Profession in Asia*, ed. Alford; Eva Pils, "Asking the Tiger for His Skin: Rights Activism in China," *Fordham International Law Journal* 30, no. 4 (2007): 1209–1287; Halliday and Liu, "Birth of a Liberal Moment?"; Hualing Fu and Richard Cullen, "Weiquan (Rights Protection) Lawyering in an Authoritarian State: Toward Critical Lawyering," 2008, http://ssrn.com/abstract=1083925 (accessed March 15, 2008); Ginsburg, "Law and the Liberal Transformation of the Northeast Asian Legal Complex"; Terence C. Halliday, Lucien Karpik, and Malcolm M. Feeley, "The Legal Complex and Struggles for Political Liberalism." In *Fighting for Political Freedom*, ed. Halliday et al.

[6] Peerenboom, *China Modernizes*; Randall Peerenboom and Weitseng Chen, "Developing the Rule of Law." In *Political Change in China: Comparisons with Taiwan*, ed. Bruce Gilley and Larry Diamond (Boulder, Colo.: Lynne Rienner, 2008).

[7] Alford, "Of Lawyers Lost and Found"; Ginsburg, "Law and the Liberal Transformation of the Northeast Asian Legal Complex"; Chang Hee Lee, "Law and Development: Korean Contemporary History in Retrospect." In *Law and Development at the Crossroads: Asian Alternatives to Universal Schemes?*, ed. Gerald P. McAlinn and Toshiyuki Kono (London: Routledge, 2009).

though there are now significant reforms occurring in all countries that will, among other things, increase the size of the bar and provide a larger role for law and lawyers in the economy.[8]

The result of the two-track system in China has been that Chinese citizens have been able to use the formal institutions (including courts, mediation, and arbitration services) to resolve civil and commercial disputes, but have been less successful in using formal institutions to resolve politically sensitive cases (e.g., those involving the Falun Gong, free speech issues, or the establishment of political parties or organizations) and socioeconomic cases.[9] The latter type of case includes pension and other welfare claims, labor disputes, land takings, and environmental issues. These cases present problems for developing countries everywhere because institutions are weak and the state lacks the financial resources to address what are in essence economic issues. They are also problematic, particularly in China, because they threaten social stability. Dispute resolution of socioeconomic cases has been characterized by: 1) notably less effective resolution than commercial cases; 2) a trend toward dejudicialization, in contrast to the judicialization of commercial disputes; that is, the government has steered socioeconomic disputes away from the courts toward other mechanisms such as administrative reconsideration, mediation, arbitration, public hearings, and the political process more generally when it became apparent that the courts lacked the resources, competence, and stature to provide effective relief in such cases; 3) a sharp rise in mass-plaintiff suits; 4) a dramatic increase in letters, petitions, and social protests in response to the inability of the courts and other mechanisms to address adequately citizen demands and expectations; 5) a reallocation of resources toward the least well-off members of society as part of a government effort to contain social instability and create a harmonious society, combined with a simultaneous increase in targeted repression of potential sources of instability, including political dissidents, nongovernmental organizations (NGOs), and activist lawyers.[10]

[8] Alford, "Introduction"; Kay-Wah Chan, "The Reform of the Profession of Lawyers in Japan: Impact on the Role of Law." In *Lawyers and the Construction of Rule of Law: National and Transnational Processes*, ed. Garth and Dezalay.

[9] Randall Peerenboom, "More Law, Less Courts: Legalized Governance, Judicialization and Dejudicialization in China." In *Administrative Law and Governance in Asia*, ed. Tom Ginsburg and Albert H. Y. Chen (London: Routledge, 2008).

[10] Randall Peerenboom and Xin He, "Dispute Resolution in China: Patterns, Causes and Prognosis." In *Dispute Resolution in China*, ed. Randall Peerenboom (Oxford: Oxford Foundation for Law, Justice and Society, 2008).

Even in the commercial area, how successfully cases are resolved depends on many factors, including regional differences and levels of wealth and the level of courts. In general, urban courts are better than rural courts, and higher-level courts are better than lower-level courts. Moreover, although the legal profession as a whole has promoted legal reforms and been a positive force for rule of law, lawyers have also sought to protect their own interests both collectively (vis-à-vis nonlicensed barefoot lawyers and foreign law firms) and individually, in some cases leading to ethical violations and corruption.

Section 1 demonstrates that the development of the legal profession and legal system as a whole has closely tracked economic growth patterns. Section 2 focuses on the business of law, examining various challenges confronting the legal profession, and in particular the commercial bar, as China modernizes.

1. ECONOMIC GROWTH AND THE DEVELOPMENT OF THE LEGAL PROFESSION: A TWO-WAY STREET

Development of the Legal Profession and Legal Complex

The number of law schools and law students has risen rapidly since China embarked on economic reforms in 1978. Law schools have increased from a mere 8 in 1976 to 62 in 1989, 183 in 1999, 389 in 2003, and 559 in 2005.[11] The number of law students has also shot up, from 25,000 in 1991 to 450,000 in 2005.[12] As a result, the number of lawyers has increased from a few thousand in the early 1980s to more than 130,000 today.

Given the dearth of lawyers in the early years of economic reform, the qualifications for becoming a lawyer initially were quite lax. Over time, the bar has been steadily raised. In 1997, only 33 percent of lawyers had college or graduate degrees. By 2004, two-thirds had such degrees: 11 percent had graduate degrees, 44 percent had bachelor of law degrees (LL.B.s), and 12 percent had undergraduate degrees in other subjects.[13] The percentage is sure to rise in the future, as the Lawyers Law now requires lawyers to have college degrees, although exceptions are made for poor areas where lawyers are few and far between. In 2006, 95 percent

[11] Zhu Jingwen, ed., *Zhongguo falü fazhan baogao (1979–2004)* (China Legal Development Report [1979–2004]) (Beijing: Zhongguo renmin daxue chubanshe, 2007).

[12] Ibid., p. 41.

[13] Ibid., p. 37.

of the candidates who took the judicial exam had a bachelor's degree or higher, whereas in 2004, 97.7 percent of the twenty thousand candidates who passed the unified judicial exam had such degrees.[14] Moreover, the percentage of lawyers with undergraduate or graduate degrees in law will continue to rise as increasing competition within the legal profession, particularly for the higher-paying jobs available in law firms, is rewarding those with more specialized training.

The increase in the size and professionalism of the legal profession is also reflected in other areas. There has been an explosion in lawmaking. Between 1979 and 2005, 805 laws, 4,156 State Council administrative regulations, 58,797 ministry-level rules, and 115,369 provincial people's congress regulations were passed.[15] Not surprisingly, the qualifications of members of the National People's Congress (NPC) have risen steadily. Approximately 90 percent of NPC Standing Committee members now have college or graduate degrees.[16] The number of NPC delegates and staff members with legal training has also risen dramatically. The number of legally trained people working in state agencies has grown as well. There are now high-ranking CCP members and government officials with a legal background, including Politburo member Li Keqiang.

By 2000, all judges had junior college degrees. The 2001 Judges Law then ratcheted up admissions standards, requiring a college degree except in certain poor areas. By 2004, 52 percent of judges were college graduates, up from 7 percent in 1995,[17] and 44 percent of prosecutors and 51 percent of notaries also had college or graduate degrees.[18]

Strong Correlation between Economic Development and Development of the Legal Profession and Legal System

Multiple-country empirical studies show that rule of law and good governance are highly correlated with wealth and that institutional development and growth are mutually reinforcing.[19] The correlation between

[14] "2006 nian guojia sifa kaoshi kaosheng goucheng xiangdui wending" (Composition of Exam-takers Relatively Stable for 2006 National Judicial Examination), http://www.legalinfo.gov.cn/misc/2006-09/17/content_411880.htm (accessed October 13, 2008).

[15] Zhu Jingwen, ed., *Zhongguo falü fazhan baogao*, p. 2.

[16] Ibid., p. 33.

[17] Ibid., p. 34.

[18] Ibid., p. 38.

[19] Using time series data, Alberto Chong and César Caldéron, "Causality and Feedback between Institutional Measures and Economic Growth," *Economics & Politics* 12, no. 1 (2000): 69–81, find that the causal relationship between institutions and economic growth runs in both directions, although the impact of growth on institutional development is stronger than the impact of institutions on growth. See also Roberto

GDP and the World Bank indicators for rule of law is $R = .82$; government effectiveness, $R = .77$; control of corruption, $R = .76$; and voice and accountability (i.e., civil and political rights), $R = .62$.[20]

Nevertheless, one of the problems confronting law and development scholars in sorting out the relationship between rule of law, good governance, and economic growth is that it is difficult to compare development patterns across countries because of differences in political systems, cultural differences, and other factors. China provides an enviable case study to test modernization theories in that there is remarkably wide regional diversity within a single country, allowing us to control in effect for the nature of the political system and cultural factors (although cultural differences between the dominant Han majority and minority groups may also be a factor in some areas). Whereas Shanghai's GDP per capita is RMB 55,000 (roughly U.S.$8,000), compared to RMB 37,058 (U.S.$5,200) for Beijing, and RMB 19,707 (U.S.$2,800) for Guangdong, the GDP per capita for Gansu is RMB 5,970 (U.S.$850) and just RMB 4,215 (U.S.$600) for Guizhou.[21] In short, although China overall is a lower middle-income country, some of China's provinces are as rich as the wealthier middle-income countries, others fall within the lower middle-income range, and still others are as poor as low-income countries like India, Indonesia, or Bangladesh.

Provincial-level comparisons in China demonstrate the same general relationship between wealth and institutional development as shown globally. There is a strong correlation between provincial GDP per capita

Rigobon and Dani Rodrik, "Rule of Law, Democracy, Openness, and Income: Estimating the Interrelationships," *Economics of Transition* 13 (2005): 533–564; D. Kaufmann, A. Kraay, and M. Mastruzzi, in "Governance Matters VI: Governance Indicators for 1996–2006" (Washington, D.C.: World Bank Policy Research Working Paper no. 4280, 2007), agree that wealth matters to some extent but claim that the causal impact of income on governance is small and that "most of the correlation between governance and per capita incomes reflects causation from the former to the latter." The policy implications are largely the same: Both wealth and institutional capacity building are necessary to achieve sustained economic growth and establish rule of law. The causal relationship between growth and the development of a specific legal institution such as the legal profession is less clear, though again, the relationship is bidirectional. No doubt lawyers and legally trained professionals have played a role in drafting rules and establishing the institutions necessary for a market economy, drafting contracts, advising clients, facilitating transactions, resolving disputes, and so on. However, the effect of wealth on the size and geographical distribution of the legal profession appears to be stronger than the effect of lawyers on growth. Lawyers follow the money.

20 The dependent variable is the natural log of GDP per capita, with $p < .01$ for all. Peerenboom, *China Modernizes*, p. 41, table 2.

21 Zhu Jingwen, ed., *Zhongguo falü fazhan baogao*, pp. 64–65.

and lawyers per capita (.98), legal education as measured by the number of law graduates per capita (.90), and litigation (.92).[22]

The general trend in the commercial area has been for an increase in litigation, with an expansion of the range of justiciable disputes, whereas mediation has decreased and arbitration has remained relatively stable and limited.[23] The number of first-instance economic cases increased from 44,080 in 1983 to 1,519,793 in 1996, whereas the number of first-instance civil cases increased from 300,787 in 1978 to 3,519,244 in 1999. Between 1983 and 2001, economic disputes increased by an average of 18.3 percent per year – twice the rate of civil disputes and four times the rate of criminal cases.[24]

Contract disputes are the major cause of litigation.[25] The number of first-instance purchase and sale contract cases increased from 23,482 in 1983 to 422,655 in 1996. The number of cases involving the contracting out of land in rural areas increased from 21,459 in 1983 to 87,503 in 1995. Money-lending cases increased from 1,264 in 1983 to 558,499 in 1996.[26]

Although non-litigation work accounts for 80 percent of legal work in developed countries, litigation work exceeds non-litigation work by 1.8 times.[27] Accordingly, there is a strong correlation between litigation per capita and lawyers per capita.[28] Most of the top law firms and most of China's lawyers are concentrated in a few large cities, whereas in some areas there are no firms or even no lawyers. The rate of litigation in Beijing, Shanghai, and Tianjin per 100,000 people is 1,307, 994, and 802, respectively, compared to between 177 and 230 in poorer provinces such as Hunan, Jiangxi, and Tibet. The number of lawyers per 100,000 people is 54.3 in Beijing, 32.3 in Shanghai, 17.1 in Tianjin, and 12.2 in Guangzhou, compared to just 6.4 in Hunan, 4.4 in Jiangxi, and 1.3 in Tibet.[29]

Looking at the legal system more broadly, one also sees a clear relationship between the quality of the judiciary and wealth. The education level of judges in upper-level courts in urban areas is often quite high. For

[22] Ibid., p. 60. [23] Ibid., pp. 21, 26.
[24] Clarke, Murrell, and Whiting, "The Role of Law in China's Economic Development."
[25] Xin He, "The Recent Decline in Chinese Economic Caseloads in Chinese Courts: Exploration of a Surprising Puzzle," *The China Quarterly*, no. 190 (2007): 352–374; Zhu Jingwen, ed., *Zhongguo falü fazhan baogao*, p. 221.
[26] He, "The Recent Decline in Chinese Economic Caseloads."
[27] Zhu Jingwen, ed., *Zhongguo falü fazhan baogao*, p. 351.
[28] Ibid., p. 90. [29] Ibid., pp. 51–52.

instance, one-third of High Court judges and nearly one-third of Intermediate Court judges in Shanghai have a master's or doctoral degree in law. Education levels also vary by division within the same courts. Among the thirteen judges in Civil Division No. 5 of Shanghai Intermediate Court No. 1, one has a doctorate, another is completing a doctorate, eight have master of law degrees, and the others are studying for their master's degrees.[30] By contrast, basic-level courts and even upper-level courts in rural areas tend to have less highly qualified judges.

Although enforcement of judicial decisions is often portrayed as difficult in China, it has improved overall.[31] In keeping with the general development pattern, recent studies have found significant improvements in wealthier urban areas, with continued problems in poorer rural areas.[32] The main reasons for the improvement in enforcement are changes in the nature of the economy, general judicial reforms aimed at institution building and increasing the professionalism of the judiciary, and specific measures to strengthen enforcement. The economy in many urban areas is now more diversified, with the private sector playing a dominant role. The fate of a single company is less important to the local government, which has a broader interest in protecting its reputation as an attractive investment environment. As a result, the incentive for governments to engage in local protectionism has diminished.[33] According to the World Bank's World Business Environment Survey, China has less legal corruption than countries at similar levels of per-capita income.[34] This is consistent with general corruption data from Transparency International and other surveys.[35] Nevertheless, corruption remains an issue in some cases.

The high correlation of wealth and corruption globally is also found within China. In rural areas where the courts lack adequate funding,

[30] Peerenboom and He, "Dispute Resolution in China."

[31] Zhu Jingwen, ed., *Zhongguo falü fazhan baogao*, pp. 243–247; World Bank, "Doing Business," 2008, http://www.doingbusiness.org/ExploreEconomies/?economyid=42 (accessed March 15, 2008).

[32] Xin He, "The Enforcement of Commercial Judgments in China." In *Dispute Resolution in China*, ed. Peerenboom.

[33] Mei Ying Gechlik, "Judicial Reform in China: Lessons from Shanghai," *Columbia Journal of Asian Law* 19, no. 1 (2005): 97–137; Peerenboom, *China's Long March toward Rule of Law*.

[34] Clarke, Murrell, and Whiting, "The Role of Law in China's Economic Development."

[35] China ranked 71 of 163 countries on the Corruption Perception Index. See Transparency International, "Global Corruption Report," 2007, http://www.transparency.org/publications/gcr/download_gcr#download (accessed March 15, 2008), p. 327. See also Dali L. Yang, *Remaking the Chinese Leviathan: Market Transition and the Politics of Governance in China* (Stanford: Stanford University Press, 2004).

there tends to be more systematic institutional corruption generated by the need to raise funds.[36]

Public attitudes also reflect differences consistent with general growth patterns. Although Chinese citizens overall express surprisingly high levels of trust in the judiciary, there are significant differences between rural and urban residents.[37] Urban residents are much likelier to litigate (even though rural residents have a higher incidence of grievances) and to be satisfied with their experience than are rural residents. Economic development in rural areas is likely to lead to fewer disputes, stronger institutions, and higher satisfaction levels, as has been the case in wealthier urban areas.[38]

II. THE LAW BUSINESS: CHALLENGES AND PROSPECTS

Oversupply of Lawyers?

A common if surprising complaint among lawyers and commentators about the legal profession is that there is an oversupply of lawyers in China. It is true that there has been a sharp increase in the number of law students and that each year, between two hundred thousand and two hundred sixty thousand people take the national judicial exam.[39]

It is also true that graduates are finding it increasingly difficult to find jobs, or at least to find jobs to their liking. Although more than one

[36] He Xin, "Zhongguo fayuan de caizheng buzu yu sifa fubai" (Insufficient Financial Resources and Judicial Corruption in Chinese Courts), *Ershiyi shiji* (21st Century), no. 105 (February 2008): 12–23.

[37] Peerenboom and He, "Dispute Resolution in China."

[38] Ethan Michelson, "Dispute Processing in Urban and Rural China: Findings from Two Surveys." In *Dispute Resolution in China*, ed. Peerenboom.

[39] The average pass rate is 13.8 percent. However, the pass rate has varied throughout the years: In 2007, 22.4 percent of the 258,000 who took the exam passed, compared to 14.8 percent of the 244,000 who took the exam in 2006 and 14.4 percent of the 219,000 who took the exam in 2005. "Sifa kaoshi kaikao 6 nian 19 wan ren shunli guoguan" (190,000 Pass Judicial Exam in Six Years), http://www.legalinfo.gov.cn/misc/2008–01/11/content_779488.htm (accessed October 13, 2008); "2006 nian guojia tongyi sifa kaoshi baoming kaosheng da 27.8 wanyu ren" (278,000 Register to Take 2006 National Judicial Exam), http://www.legalinfo.gov.cn/misc/2006–08/03/content_370145.htm (accessed October 13, 2008); "Jinnian sifa kaoshi 360 fen guoguan, fangkuan diqu fenshu xianwei 330 fen" (This Year's National Judicial Exam Passing Score Relaxed from 360 to 330 for Certain Areas), http://www.legalinfo.gov.cn/misc/2005–11/17/content_221756.htm (accessed October 13, 2008); "Cong yanzhi kao, riqing fuwu, renzhen zuohao diliuci guojia sifa kaoshi gongzuo" (Strictly Regulate, Warmly Serve, Earnestly Carry Out Work for the Sixth National Judicial Exam), 2007, http://www.legalinfo.gov.cn/misc/2007–08/29/content_689926.htm (accessed October 13, 2008).

hundred ninety thousand people have passed the exam since 2002, the total number of licensed practicing lawyers has only increased from approximately ninety thousand to one hundred fifty thousand. Jobs in law firms are difficult to come by for new graduates. In 2002, 26 percent of law graduates found jobs as lawyers in firms or as in-house counsel in companies, 23 percent took jobs in government agencies, 7 percent in other non-private agencies, and 21 percent went to graduate school, took jobs in academia, left the country, or joined the military. Another 23 percent were unable to find work. Of 214 majors, law ranks 187 in terms of students' ability to find jobs.[40]

The problem, however, is that lawyers are unwilling to relocate to rural areas or to accept the lower fees charged by "legal workers" (*falü fuwuzhe*). Clearly there is work available in rural areas. According to the Ministry of Justice (MoJ), there were more than two hundred counties that did not have a single lawyer in 2004. The need for lawyers, prosecutors, and judges in rural areas has required a relaxation of admission standards. In 2007, candidates without college degrees from twelve hundred counties were allowed to take the national judicial exam and were able to pass with a score of 320, compared to a normal score of 360. Candidates from Tibet, which has the lowest number of lawyers per capita (1.3/10,000 compared to the national average of 8.3/10,000), were able to pass with a score of only 290.[41]

Much of the legal work in rural areas is now being performed by legal workers who are decidedly less qualified than lawyers. Rather than a college degree, they are required to be high school or middle school graduates and to undergo six months' training. In practice, almost two-thirds have no more than a junior college degree (*dazhuan*), compared to the two-thirds of lawyers with a college degree. In 2003, legal workers provided more legal advice and drafted more documents on behalf of clients than did fully qualified lawyers.[42] They also regularly represent clients in civil litigation and occasionally in criminal cases, although they are technically prohibited from taking on criminal cases.

Legal workers are to be distinguished from so-called "barefoot lawyers" who have no formal legal qualifications. Because PRC law allows parties to represent themselves or to choose their own representative, barefoot lawyers are able to appear in court. They may also offer non-litigation services. One study in rural Henan in 2001 and 2004 found

[40] Zhu Jingwen, ed., *Zhongguo falü fazhan baogao*, p. 45.
[41] "Jinnian sifa kaoshi 360 fen guoguan, fangkuan diqu fenshu xianwei 330 fen."
[42] Ibid., p. 388.

that barefoot lawyers handled more cases than qualified lawyers.[43] Barefoot lawyers often take on controversial cases involving land takings, environmental disputes, local corruption, and government abuse of power. Many licensed lawyers are unwilling to take on these cases, as are legal workers, who often are closely aligned with local justice offices and frequently depend on them for referrals.

Lawyers often complain that these grassroots and barefoot lawyers are robbing them of business. But the reality is more that lawyers have turned their backs on this segment of the market. Although some legal offices exist in cities where lawyers ply their trade, most legal offices are established in rural areas or the outer regions of large metropolitan areas. Their clients are mainly farmers. Most cases involve family matters and minor property disputes. It is true that legal workers and barefoot lawyers have sought to blur the line between themselves and fully licensed lawyers.[44] To some extent, the strategy appears to be working in that some people do not seem to be aware of the differences. However, the decline in civil litigation representation by legal workers and the increase in representation by lawyers suggest that people are able to distinguish between them and would prefer a lawyer if one were available and affordable.[45]

Although the government has increased legal aid and expanded access to justice by providing fee waivers or reductions for the poor, many people are still unable to afford lawyers' fees and thus are forced to turn to cheaper legal workers. Even so, the rate of representation in civil cases is still extremely low; clients are represented by lawyers in only one of four civil cases.[46]

Qualified lawyers are increasingly concentrating on corporate clients rather than on low-paying individuals.[47] They also are increasingly focused on commercial law rather than criminal law. Higher profits are not the only reason for the focus on commercial law. Criminal law is a

[43] Ibid., pp. 412–413.

[44] Ethan Michelson, "The Practice of Law as an Obstacle to Justice: Chinese Lawyers at Work, *Law & Society Review* 40, no. 1 (2006): 1–38; William P. Alford, "'Second Lawyers,' First Principles: Lawyers, Rice-Roots Legal Workers, and the Battle Over Legal Professionalism in China." In *Prospects for Professionalism in China: Essays on Civic Vocations*, ed. William P. Alford, Kenneth Winston, and William C. Kirby (New York: Routledge, forthcoming 2009); Sida Liu, "Lawyers, State Officials, and Significant Others: An Ecological Analysis of the Chinese Legal Services Market," annual meeting of the American Sociological Association, Boston, August 1–4, 2008.

[45] Zhu Jingwen, ed., *Zhongguo falü fazhan baogao*, p. 387.

[46] Ibid., p. 351.

[47] Liu, "Lawyers, State Officials, and Significant Others."

notoriously difficult area. Lawyers face a number of obstacles, including access to clients and files, problems of collecting evidence and cross-examining witnesses, and the danger of prosecution on trumped-up charges of falsifying testimony or obstructing justice. Although most criminal defense lawyers make little money and are among the more marginalized members of the legal profession, some criminal lawyers are more established figures who make a lot of money handling high-profile cases, well-known academics or members of the national or local bar associations, or former judges or prosecutors. As such, they have better connections to the authorities and a better idea about which cases are too hot to handle. They are also less likely to be harassed or subject to trumped-up charges than their less-connected defense bar colleagues.[48] Not surprisingly, representation rates in criminal cases have declined in recent years. Whether the proposed changes to the Criminal Procedure Law to enhance the ability of criminal lawyers to provide an effective defense will reverse this trend remains to be seen.

Chinese law students are far from unique in facing an increasingly competitive market. In many countries, law school graduates find it difficult to find jobs, or at least to find the type of job they expected when they applied to law school. In the United States, for example, students attracted by the high starting salaries at elite firms have flocked to law schools, only to discover few such opportunities upon graduation. The U.S. Department of Labor has cautioned prospective students:

> As in the past, some graduates may have to accept positions outside of their field of interest or for which they feel overqualified. Some recent law school graduates who have been unable to find permanent positions are turning to the growing number of temporary staffing firms that place attorneys in short-term jobs. This service allows companies to hire lawyers on an as-needed basis and permits beginning lawyers to develop practical skills.... Because of the keen competition for jobs, geographic mobility and work experience assume greater importance.... In addition, employers increasingly seek graduates who have advanced law degrees and experience in a specialty, such as tax, patent, or admiralty law.[49]

[48] Ethan Michelson, "Lawyers, Political Embeddedness, and Institutional Continuity in China's Transition from Socialism," *American Journal of Sociology* 113, no. 2 (2007): 352–414.

[49] U.S. Department of Labor, Bureau of Labor Statistics, *Occupational Outlook Handbook, 2008–09 Edition*, http://www.bls.gov/oco/ocos053.htm (accessed October 17, 2008).

In China, some recent graduates have started their careers as legal-service workers, gaining experience until they can pass the exam and complete the mandatory on-the-job training required to be a lawyer.

Are Lawyers Paid Too Little?

Chinese lawyers often are portrayed in academic and popular articles as being in dire straits economically. As a whole, however, China's lawyers do fairly well. One recent survey found that the medium income of 1,300 lawyers in eight provinces was RMB 100,000, or approximately U.S.$13,700.[50] Another report calculated the average income to be about RMB 80,000 (U.S.$11,400) in 2005.[51]

We can make a rough comparison to U.S. lawyers by taking the median income of lawyers in China and the United States and then multiplying China's median income by twenty to adjust for differences in per capita income (U.S. per capita income being about U.S.$40,000 compared to just over U.S.$2000 in China). According to the Department of Labor, the median income for U.S. lawyers in 2006 was just over U.S.$100,000.[52] If one multiplies the median income in China of approximately U.S.$13,000 by twenty, the adjusted median income of China's lawyers would be equivalent to about U.S.$260,000.

Chinese lawyers also are doing well compared with other professionals. The average salary for someone in information technology is RMB 35,000, compared to RMB 27,000 in finance, RMB 19,000 in real estate, RMB 16,000 in education, and RMB 18,000 in government.[53]

As is true everywhere, legal salaries vary widely depending on the employer and the type, size, and location of the firm. Lawyers in law firms generally make more than in-house counsel, who make more than government lawyers, who make more than academics. Within firms, there is also an increasing differentiation in salaries. For example, twelve of more than one hundred thousand firms in Beijing had revenues in excess

[50] Ji Weidong, "Zhongguo falü fuwu shichang de shikuang fenxi: Cong 2007 nian wenjuan diaocha kan lüshi shiwusuo de jingji jichu he shehui zuoyong" (An Empirical Analysis of the Legal Service Market in China: Viewing the Economic Basis and Social Role of Law Firms from the 2007 Questionnaire Research), *Zhongguo lüshi* (Chinese Lawyer), no. 5(2008): 84–86 and no. 6 (2008): 67–71.

[51] Zhu Jingwen, ed., *Zhongguo falü fazhan baogao*, p. 363.

[52] *Occupational Outlook Handbook, 2008–2009 Edition*, http://www.bls.gov/oco/ocos053.htm (accessed October 13, 2008).

[53] Zhu Jingwen, ed., *Zhongguo falü fazhan baogao*, p. 363.

of RMB 100 million in 2007. And although the top 20 percent of Beijing firms account for almost 80 percent of the total revenue, the bottom third accounts for only 2 percent.[54]

Elite Firms

The legal profession is becoming increasingly stratified, with a handful of top firms concentrated in major cities, a second tier in major cities and secondary markets, and then the rest. Most elite firms, including Zhonglun, King & Wood, Junhe, Haiwen, and Commerce and Finance, are headquartered in Beijing.

Although the average size of PRC law firms is just twelve lawyers, a recent trend has been toward the creation of large firms, usually through mergers and acquisitions. King & Wood claims more than 600 lawyers and legal professionals, including 65 partners and 170 lawyers and legal assistants in Beijing and 27 partners and 150 lawyers and assistants in Shanghai. Zhonglun has more than 500 lawyers, including 40 partners in Beijing, 19 in Shanghai, and 19 in Shenzhen. Zhonglun has expanded rapidly by incorporating firms in Beijing and Shenzhen. Junhe has 300 lawyers, including 40 partners in Beijing and 15 in Shanghai. After the merger of three Shanghai firms, Albright has 200 lawyers, including 34 partners.

Among the second-tier firms, Guantao Law Firm has 200 lawyers. Jincheng & Tongda, another product of a merger, now has 57 partners. Grandall Legal Group has more than fifty partners and one hundred lawyers since the merger of firms in Beijing, Shanghai, and Shenzhen. Jingtian & Gongcheng now has more than 40 partners and 120 lawyers. Other recent mergers include Li Wen & Partners with Beijing Haotian Law Office and Junyi with Runbo to form Run Ming Law Firm.

Some of the top firms have remained relatively small. Commerce and Finance has one hundred lawyers, including twenty-seven partners. Haiwen has only twenty partners, plus another fifty lawyers and legal assistants. Fangda, a Shanghai-based firm, also has one hundred lawyers, including twenty-six partners, with small offices in Beijing and Shenzhen. In addition, there are a few other highly profitable niche firms in Beijing, such as the three-partner firm of Bokang, with average post-tax, pre-cost profits of more than RMB 3 million per partner, and Benghe,

[54] Interview, Beijing Bureau of Justice official, 2007.

with eighteen lawyers, including five partners, and average post-tax, pre-cost profits of more than RMB 2 million per partner. Although some of these firms generate revenue in special areas such as intellectual property registrations, others derive their income through non-legal work, including lobbying or introducing companies to investment zones, for which they are paid a commission based on the total value of the investment.

The top Chinese firms generally have multiple offices in the primary markets of Beijing, Shanghai, and Shenzhen. Several now have also established offices in second-tier cities. King & Wood has small offices in Tianjin, Guangzhou, Chongqing, Chengdu, Hangzhou, and Xi'an. Junhe has offices in Dalian and Haikou. Zhonglun has an office in Guangzhou. Guantao has offices in Xi'an and Dalian. Jincheng & Tongda has offices in Xi'an, Shenyang, and Chengdu.

Some firms also have attempted to create beachfronts outside China, often through associations with foreign law firms. Zhonglun has an office in Tokyo; Junhe in New York; Jincheng and Tongda in Los Angeles; and Zhonglun W&D in London. Tang Law Office cooperates with Daniel Arthur Lapres Cabinet d'avocats, whereas Xin Ji Yuan has a relationship with a New York firm.

The hiring practices at the top firms also reflect the increased stratification and professionalism of the legal profession. Zhonglun's Beijing office draws almost exclusively from the top students at Peking University, Zhengfa, Renda, and Tsinghua. Others also take students from Jingmao, which is known for specializing in commercial law and emphasizing foreign languages and common law training. Foreign law degrees, including a rising number of doctor of law (J.D.) degrees as well as LL.M.s, are increasingly common. As a result, firms are now attaching more importance to the quality of the foreign institution. Having a foreign LL.M. is no longer sufficient to secure a job at a top firm.

King & Wood, for example, requires a bachelor's degree or higher in law from a top-tier law school, with overseas education preferred; PRC or foreign bar qualification, with experience in a major law firm or multinational company preferred; and excellent command of both written and spoken English. Applicants must also be self-motivated, detail oriented, and stress tolerant! Zhonglun looks for graduates from prestigious Chinese or foreign law schools. Candidates with a J.D. or master's degree are preferred. Applicants must be licensed to practice in China or other countries. Non-litigation associates need at least two years of work experience in foreign-related legal services. Experience with leading domestic or international law firms is an advantage. Applicants must be able to speak at least one foreign language, although in practice, many lawyers who service Chinese clients or specialize in litigation may have limited foreign language ability at best.

Although the vast majority of lawyers in China are general practitioners, the legal practice in elite firms is increasingly specialized. Law firms now regularly recruit lawyers with experience in bankruptcy, venture capital, tax, insurance, foreign investment, securities, M&A, asset-backed securitization, or patents or with technical backgrounds in chemistry, medicine, or high-tech.

Elite firms generally do commercial work, including general corporate work, M&A, private equity, securities, banking, and financing (including project finance, structured finance, and aircraft and real-estate financing). With the increased involvement of private equity firms, the market for M&A work has become large. In 2006, 68 private equity funds invested more than U.S.$12 billion, whereas the U.S.$1.78 billion that was invested in 324 venture capital deals was a 50 percent increase from the previous year.[55]

Chinese firms also specialize in certain areas or at least have lawyers with a wide range of special expertise. Real estate, including acquisition and disposal, finance, leasing, and litigation, is a big area for some firms. Bankruptcy became a new practice area with the passing of the 2006 Enterprise Bankruptcy Law. Insurance is a growing area as well. Employment law is another area, including advice regarding compliance with labor laws and regulations, enforceability of noncompetition agreements, workplace harassment, anti-bribery, foreign corrupt practices act investigations, termination, confidentiality, wrongful dismissal, regulatory compliance, contracts, and incentives.

Some firms have extensive Internet protocol practices, including company, domain, and brand-name protection; anti-counterfeiting; copyright; trademark; and patent registration and prosecution (including administrative remedies and litigation).

Most of the top Chinese firms generate significant revenues from dispute resolution, mainly litigation, though lawyers also serve as arbitrators or represent clients at arbitration. Formal mediation is not popular.

[55] American Chamber of Commerce, "The Business Climate for U.S. Firms in China," *White Paper 2007*, http://www.amcham-china.org.cn/amcham/show/content.php?Id=2361&menuid=&submid=&PHPSESSID=11eade809492f6ad040c37af69cec8af (accessed October 17, 2008).

Chinese firms may also provide other services, including advising the government on commercial regulations or institutional developments.

Foreign Firms and Their Relationship with Domestic Firms

There are more than two hundred foreign firms in China, including more than fifty Hong Kong firms. Most have one office in China, although some have up to three. Most of the offices are small, with fewer than ten lawyers. Foreign law firms are generally headed by a foreign-national partner. Some will also have other foreign partners or associates. However, the vast majority of lawyers working in foreign law firms are PRC nationals who have studied PRC law and have LL.M.s or other degrees from foreign universities.

Foreign and PRC firms overlap in the main commercial areas of general corporate work, M&A, securities, and financing. Foreign firms have an advantage in large projects that involve transnational elements, including listings in New York, London, or Hong Kong; project financing involving foreign investors and loan agreements governed by foreign law; the establishment of offshore vehicles; and corporate restructuring that has offshore elements. However, foreign firms charge higher rates, often for relatively junior Chinese associates who have comparably less experience than the more senior lawyers and partners at Chinese firms, many of whom were originally trained at foreign firms before joining the elite PRC firms. Therefore, it is increasingly common for sophisticated clients to use foreign firms for the transnational aspects of a deal together with a Chinese firm for the onshore Chinese aspects, including corporate restructuring and due diligence. Foreign investors also have increasingly sought out Chinese firms for general corporate work. Moreover, given their size, foreign firms generally do not have as wide a range of specialized expertise, although some foreign firms have sought to carve out a market niche by specializing in a particular area. Thus, foreign investors have turned to the Chinese firms when they have more specific needs.

The dispute-resolution practice of foreign firms is limited given that they cannot litigate in Chinese courts. However, some do represent clients in arbitration in China, Hong Kong, or elsewhere. Some also provide foreign corrupt practice compliance advice and international litigation assistance and are involved in international trade disputes, antidumping actions, and anti-subsidy cases.

Foreign firms tend to represent mainly foreign clients, though some also increasingly represent large Chinese companies. The elite Chinese firms all represent foreign clients, including most of the Fortune 500 companies doing business in China, as well as Chinese clients, with the balance of foreign to Chinese clients varying from firm to firm.

Client demand for quality work is rising. At the same time, there is pressure to lower fees. Chinese companies in particular tend to be price sensitive, although large companies, including state-owned enterprises (SOEs), are beginning to accept that quality legal advice does not come cheaply.

Both foreign and Chinese firms have a problem finding, and retaining, qualified senior associates, particularly those with the legal skills, experience, stamina, and language ability to handle foreign clients. The pattern has been for foreign firms to make few new partners. As a result, senior associates often leave for Chinese firms, where they either become a partner immediately or within a few years, depending on their client base. The rush of foreign firms into the market in recent years has also resulted in the poaching of foreign partners and thus the instability of many foreign firms.

In the past, Chinese firms were also unstable, as founders and other key lawyers often left because of conflicts about management or compensation. Now, however, jumping ship to establish one's own firm is more difficult, as new firms lack the size and reputation to compete with the top firms. Nevertheless, some Chinese firms have had problems retaining associates because associates are paid relatively poorly, the firms often fail to provide adequate (and much-needed) training, and partners in the past have been reluctant to allow associates to deal directly with clients for fear of losing clients.

Although the top Chinese firms are better run today, overall, foreign firms tend to have an advantage in terms of management, client relations, and marketing. Most importantly, they are also perceived as a "safer" choice for risk-averse in-house counsel who are not familiar with the Chinese legal-services market. However, given the increased reliance of more experienced and sophisticated foreign clients on Chinese firms, perhaps the tipping point is approaching at which the conventional wisdom will be that local firms are deeper and cheaper and that more expensive foreign firms should be relied on only when the nature of the deal requires transnational expertise.

III. CONCLUSION

Discussions of the development of the legal profession tend to oscillate between two extremes. The first is to see China as complying with some simple, often very idealized universal or American model (e.g., the lawyer as noble statesmen,[56] the legal profession as the leading edge for political liberalism and liberal democracy,[57] or the much-vaunted globalization/Americanization of PRC law firms). The other extreme emphasizes difference – at least, commentators assume a rhetorical posture of difference even if in the fine print in the body of the article and in the footnotes they point out that what occurs in China is not that much different from what takes place anywhere else. For example, lawyers in China are portrayed as self-interested actors who screen clients based on their ability to pay and who use legal discourse as a way of enticing or avoiding clients – thus as an obstacle to justice.[58] Alternately, Chinese lawyers are portrayed as deeply embedded politically or dependent on social networks (invariably referred to as *guanxi* to exoticize an otherwise unremarkable feature of most lawyers' lives), thus preventing the emergence of a "rational-legal" system and the rule of law.[59] Both of these approaches suffer from adoption of an overly simple model as a baseline. The truth, as one would expect, lies somewhere in between, both with respect to China and the reality, compared to the idealized portrayal of legal systems and the legal profession in other countries.

The development of China's legal profession has been, by and large, similar to the development in many other countries. First and foremost, at the most general level, the development of the legal profession, and the legal system as a whole, has tracked economic development, with lawyers contributing to and benefiting from economic growth. The legal profession has also exhibited features found elsewhere,[60] such as greater stratification – especially between the elite firms and others but even among the elite firms – greater specialization, particularly at the top end, more corporate work, including from Chinese companies (SOEs and private firms), and more in-house lawyers.

Second, as is also true elsewhere, the "legal profession" is not a homogenous whole. Elite law firms, by definition, are not representative of the legal profession. They do more corporate work, they make more money, and they are more insulated from problems, especially those that do transactional work. By contrast, most of China's lawyers are in effect solo practitioners, even if they work in firms. They do less work for

[56] See Alford, "Of Lawyers Lost and Found," warning against this approach.
[57] Halliday and Liu, "Birth of a Liberal Moment?"
[58] Michelson, "The Practice of Law as an Obstacle to Justice."
[59] Liu, "Lawyers, State Officials, and Significant Others"; Michelson, "Lawyers, Political Embeddedness, and Institutional Continuity."
[60] Sander and Williams, "Why Are There So Many Lawyers?"

corporations and more work for individuals than do lawyers in top firms. They are also less specialized and often have to scramble to make ends meet. Many are forced to mobilize their connections to drum up business and survive economically. Those in criminal law also must rely on their connections to overcome the many obstacles erected by the police and prosecutors.[61]

Over time, economic growth will result in a larger economy able to support more lawyers. However, the recent trend for elite firms to expand into secondary markets suggests that the profession will remain highly stratified. Local firms will find it difficult to compete for the more profitable projects, and those that are successful will be merger targets for increasingly aggressive elite national firms.

Third, lawyers in China, like their counterparts elsewhere, seek to protect their own interests. They complain, frequently and loudly, about "unfair competition." Elite Chinese law firms worry about competition from foreign firms. Lower on the legal food chain, lawyers complain bitterly about legal workers and barefoot lawyers. Licensed lawyers and even non-licensed legal workers worry about lobbyists and fixers – former judges, prosecutors, and police – who rely on their connections rather than legal skills to address their clients' needs. Yet law firms continue to hire these fixers as consultants for particular transactions or even as members of firms – a venerable, and profitable, practice found in all countries.

On the positive side, increased competition is leading toward more professionalism at every level, as shown in the education rates, even for legal workers.[62] Furthermore, although competition is fierce, lawyers still are better off than most professionals, and there are ample opportunities for lawyers with the necessary analytical and legal skills, and the willingness to put in the hours, to rise up the legal hierarchy.

Of course, the legal profession and context in China also differ from those in other countries. First, China is still a relatively poor developing country, with huge regional differences. Many people are too poor to pay the prices charged by licensed lawyers, thus creating a market for other legal workers. The lack of resources and weak institutions also limit the opportunities for cause lawyering, as is generally true in low- and middle-income countries.[63]

61 Michelson, "Lawyers, Political Embeddedness, and Institutional Continuity."

62 Zhu Jingwen, ed., *Zhongguo falü fazhan baogao*, p. 58; Ji Weidong, "Legal Education in China: A Great Leap Forward in Professionalism," *Kobe University Law Review*, no. 39 (2004): 1–21.

63 Peerenboom, "Searching for Political Liberalism in all the Wrong Places."

Second, China's economy remains heavily regulated. This creates opportunities for lawyers who are able to keep up with the rapidly changing regulatory environment and have the connections and judgment to anticipate future changes and the consequences for their clients. Lawyers themselves often need special licenses to practice certain types of law, such as securities, patent registration, or bankruptcy. Government agencies still exercise influence over access to these often lucrative practice areas, creating opportunities for rent seeking and incentives for some lawyers to maintain close relations with government officials. However, although some lawyers may be awarded licenses based on their connections to some extent, increasingly lawyers in these fields also must possess the requisite legal skills. If not, the license is of little value, as clients are increasingly demanding.

Third, the legal profession, and the market for legal services, is relatively new. Individual consumers are less sophisticated than those in other countries. Many individuals do not appreciate the differences between lawyers, legal workers, and unlicensed barefoot lawyers. Many people also have unrealistic demands about what lawyers, courts, and the legal system can do. Some clients refuse to pay if they lose in court, and sometimes even when they win.

The newness of the profession, the lack of an understanding about the role of lawyers, the relatively high levels of corruption typically found in middle-income countries, and the dire economic straits of some lawyers have led to numerous violations of legal ethics and sharp practices. In 2004, the MoJ sanctioned 719 lawyers and 213 law firms for inappropriate interactions with judges, overcharging and improper billing, failure to diligently work on a matter, unfair competition, and deceptive advertising.[64] The Beijing Bureau of Justice reported 207 complaints, resulting in sanctions for 25 firms and 32 lawyers.[65]

A fourth difference is that China is not a liberal democracy. The professed goal is to establish a socialist rule of law state. In practice, this means limited space for "political lawyering" and for the legal profession in political reforms.[66]

[64] "719 ming lüshi he 213 jia lüshisuo weifa weiji shoudao chengchu: Quanguo lüshi duiwu jizhong jiaoyu zhengdun huodong bu zuoguo chang" (719 Lawyers and 213 Law Firms that Violate Disciplinary Rules Are Sanctioned), http://www.legalinfo.gov.cn/misc/2005–05/17/content_134159.htm (accessed October 13, 2008).

[65] "Beijing lüshi jiaoyu zhengdunzhong you 25 jia lüshisuo shou chufen" (Twenty-five Law Firms Sanctioned during Education and Rectification of Beijing Lawyers), http://www.legalinfo.gov.cn/misc/2005–05/17/content_134168.htm (accessed October 13, 2008).

[66] Peerenboom, "Searching for Political Liberalism in all the Wrong Places."

Although the basic story to date is largely consistent with the general modernization story of economic growth fueling legal reforms and vice versa, the development process will take a long time. As in other middle-income countries, numerous obstacles must be overcome. Many of the obstacles reflect conflicts of interest among lawyers and other legal-service providers, between elite and non-elite lawyers, and between lawyers and citizens and other legal complex actors, including judges, the police, and the procuracy. The resolution of these conflicts will lead to some variation in institutions and practices from other countries and to different varieties of capitalism and rule of law. There will always be differences between the practice of elite commercial lawyers in Beijing and Shanghai and that of general practitioners in Gansu and Yunnan. However, there will be continued convergence as well, as different parts of China catch up with the more developed eastern coast and as China continues to become integrated into the global economy. Whether one chooses to emphasize convergence or divergence is largely a matter of rhetorical posture, the academic market, the journals in which one publishes, and the author's own social and professional networks and political orientation.

PART II

Pu fa and the Dissemination of Law in the Chinese Context

5

The Impact of Nationalist and Maoist Legacies on Popular Trust in Legal Institutions

Pierre F. Landry

After thirty years of reform in China, one can legitimately wonder whether individual or local experiences with the Maoist state are still relevant to the lives of ordinary Chinese. The shift to a market economy; the radical transformation of the workplace, housing, consumptions patterns; and countless other aspects of daily life leave few observational clues about the long-term consequences of three decades of Maoism. Few would question the historical importance of the Chinese revolution, but it is incumbent on students of contemporary issues to demonstrate empirically whether nearly one generation after the regime's break from Maoism, individual decisions and beliefs are still decisively linked to these historical events.

As the People's Republic of China (PRC) approaches its seventh decade, we may be even less willing to explore the relevance of the 1949 divide between the so-called "old" and "new" Chinas. Social scientists who conduct survey research in the PRC no longer can interview respondents with living memories of the Nationalist regime. Furthermore, the regime's long standing emphasis on sharply demarcating the post-1949 political and social landscape from China's historical experience has further weakened interest in exploring whether and how antecedent regimes have had any impact on contemporary mass opinion and behavior. Yet several aspects of China's reform era compel observers to look back in search of explanations that cannot be easily rooted in contemporary

I am most grateful to Huang Xian and Zuo Cai for their invaluable help with the coding of the gazetteers that were available at the Peking University Library and the National Library of China. I also thank the Universities Service Centre for China Studies – particularly Dr. Li Yonggang – at The Chinese University of Hong Kong for their support in quickly acquiring the county-level gazetteers that were still missing from the Centre's outstanding collection. I also thank the East Asia Library at Yale University for assistance.

institutional or cultural settings. Among those, the legal reforms of the past twenty years have been far ranging, and – as Phillip Huang[1] has repeatedly noted – historians have indeed uncovered intriguing parallels between the modern Chinese legal system and its predecessors under the Nationalist regime and even the Qing empire.

Recent research in comparative politics shows that the divide between socialist and nonsocialist regimes is an intellectual construction that can be transcended on the ground. Wittenberg's account of electoral continuity in Hungary or Darden's explanations for enduring national loyalties[2] show that even long-deceased political regimes can have a profound influence on contemporary behavior, provided that the right set of institutional and historical conditions are preserved. Enduring patterns are even more likely in the Chinese case because deep reforms occurred comparatively early in the history of the Communist regime: The socialization of the urban and rural economies was not completed until 1956, whereas the Chinese Communist Party (CCP) launched its wave of reform and opening in 1978. The consequences of the early reforms cannot be underestimated, because the reforms reintroduced principles and practices – including legal ones, such as contracts – to a generation that personally had experienced them under the Guomindang (KMT). Thus, the attitudes and behavior of many middle-aged and older Chinese in the late 1970s and 1980s may be traced directly to their personal experiences before the foundation of the PRC. The transmission of "legal" memory also can occur across generations through socialization in the household or the community where historical experiences are retained.

In this chapter, I explore how the variety of historical experiences at the local level still shapes mass public opinion in contemporary China. I do so by linking survey data collected from a national sample of Chinese adults collected in 2003–04 to historical evidence gleaned from nearly one hundred county (or district) gazetteers and related sources. Using the benchmark of trust in the courts, I show that even when individual-level characteristics are accounted for, variables that capture the

[1] Philip C. C. Huang, *Civil Justice in China: Representation and Practice in the Qing* (Stanford: Stanford University Press, 1996); Philip C. Huang, *Code, Custom, and Legal Practice in China: The Qing and the Republic Compared* (Stanford: Stanford University Press, 2001).

[2] Jason Wittenberg, *Crucibles of Political Loyalty: Church Institutions and Electoral Continuity in Hungary* (New York: Cambridge University Press, 2006); Keith Darden, "The Causes and Consequences of Enduring National Loyalties," unpublished manuscript.

institutional evolution of counties have a substantial (and statistically significant) impact on the contemporary level of popular trust in the courts.

HISTORICAL LEGACIES

Nationalist Legacies

The historical experiences of Chinese counties vary greatly because the reach of the state has been highly uneven across time and space. The competing visions of the Beiyang, Guangzhou, and Nanjing regimes in the early twentieth century were not fully reconciled even after 1927, when much of China's territory remained beyond the effective reach of the Nationalist government. However, some regions experienced extensive modernization efforts, including ambitious legal reforms.[3] As Zhao Jinkang notes, the KMT established as many as 115 high (*gaodeng fayuan*) or divisional courts (*gaodeng fayuan fenyuan*) between 1934 and 1937, which supplemented the courts that had been created in the earlier years of the regime.[4] To be sure, the courts of the Republican era were fraught with the problems of limited autonomy from the KMT and a lack of financial and human resources.[5] They also were constrained in their actions in criminal cases, as both the army and county administrators leaders relied on special provisional rules for rebels and bandits, including the CCP guerrillas.[6] The weakness of the courts in criminal matters only enhanced their relative importance in civil and business cases, where they tended to be more effective. Nevertheless, the most important aspect of these reforms was the institutionalization of the separation of powers between county administrators and judges, which historically had been fused. Although the Organic Law on Courts of 1932 resulted in the creation of judicial districts that were somewhat larger than counties, many county seats did witness the creation of a local court. This effort continued in the KMT-controlled areas, even during World War II. For

[3] Xiaoqun Xu, "The Fate of Judicial Independence in Republican China, 1912–37," *The China Quarterly*, no. 149 (March 1997): 1–28.

[4] Zhao Jinkang, *Nanjing minguo zhengfu fazhi lilun sheji jiqi yunzuo (1927–1937)* (The Legal Basis and Operation of the Nanjing Republican Government [1927–1937]) (Beijing: Renmin chubanshe, 2006), pp. 202–203.

[5] Ibid.

[6] Xiaoqun Xu, "The Rule of Law Without Due Process: Punishing Robbers and Bandits in Early-Twentieth-Century China," *Modern China* 33, no. 2 (2007): 230–257.

instance, in Sichuan in May 1941, the Renshou local court was set up, along with a distinct prosecutor's office.[7]

Because the distribution of KMT power was not random, one therefore must guard against the possibility that indicators of KMT strength (or CCP weakness) may be capturing only deeper underlying factors that are correlated with a stronger legal culture and societal demand for effective legal institutions. Urbanization is likely to affect both: The CCP was notoriously weak in urban areas where the guerrilla tactics favored by Mao Zedong were inappropriate. At the same time, the stronger urban economies and the presence of better-educated social actors with higher stakes in property rights created a stronger demand for functional legal institutions, as well as substantial support for the Nationalist Party. Based on KMT membership data compiled at the provincial level by Cui Zhiqing,[8] Figure 5.1 illustrates the weak correlation between urbanization and KMT support by the end of the "Nanjing decade." Membership was especially dense in the special cities of Guangzhou, Nanjing, Hankou, Shanghai, Tianjin, and Beiping, yet, as the figure shows, the party was also relatively strong in regions with low degrees of urbanization, such as Gansu, Ningxia, Shanxi, and Suiyuan.

We cannot know for sure how memories of the Nationalist era were transmitted at the popular level during periods of intense social change and strong propaganda that generally vilified the KMT regime. However, the speed with which the non-state sector was able to take advantage of the opportunities that the regime offered after 1978 suggests that just as the principles of a market economy remained entrenched among the population, the core legal principles that underpin functioning markets are just as likely to have endured in areas where a functioning legal system existed prior to the CCP takeover.

Maoist Legacies

Because both the Nationalist and the Communist regimes were led by Leninist parties modeled on Soviet and Comintern advice, the legal system that was created on the mainland after 1949 bore a strong institutional resemblance to its Nationalist predecessor. Both ruling parties

[7] *Renshou xianzhi* (Gazetteer of Renshou) (Chengdu: Sichuan renmin chubanshe, 1990), p. 378.

[8] Cui Zhiqing, *Guomindang zhengzhi yu shehui jiegou zhi yanbian: 1905–1949* (The Evolution of the Kuomintang's Political and Social Structures: 1905–1949), 3 vols. (Beijing: Shehui kexue wenxian chubanshe, 2007).

FIGURE 5.1. Distribution of KMT membership by province, 1937. *Note:* Gray dashes denote Republic of China (ROC) provinces not under formal KMT control. *Source:* Cui Zhiqing, *Guomindang zhengzhi yu shehui jiegou zhi yanbian: 1905–1949* (The Evolution of the Guomindang's Political and Social Structures: 1905–1949) (Beijing: Shehui kexue wenxian chubanshe, 3 vols., 2007).

sought to tightly control the courts by directly appointing judges who were party members and who took orders from local party organizations. After 1949, the regime encouraged mid- and lower-ranking Nationalist officials to remain at their posts, and many in fact were absorbed into the bureaucracy, at least in the short run.[9] It is likely that this decision facilitated the persistence of some degree of "institutional memory" within the bureaucracies of the new regime, including the courts.

There were, of course, obvious differences, and these differences grew sharper as the Maoist regime transitioned to more radical policies in the 1950s. The nationalization of industry and commerce in 1956, quickly followed by the antirightist campaign in 1957, marked the end of the last remnants of an independent legal profession. The counties that had operated legal advisory offices (albeit under close government

[9] Harry Harding, *Organizing China: The Problem of Bureaucracy 1949–1976* (Stanford: Stanford University Press, 1981), p. 36.

control) were forced to close them. They would not reappear until the 1980s.

Yet the pattern of Chinese legal reforms since 1978 suggests that the legacies of the Mao period are more likely to endure in the legal reforms than in other aspects of ordinary life. Unlike economic reforms in which policy change was concomitant with unambiguous institutional change, the reforms affecting the Chinese legal system have not formally altered the key institutions in a manner that ordinary citizens can easily comprehend. When rural collectives ended and the household responsibility system was introduced in the countryside, the institutions that had dominated rural life since 1958 also came to an end: People's communes were reorganized into townships, brigades became village committees, and teams were turned into natural villages. Not only were these institutions given new names, but the boundaries of many townships and villages also evolved along with the economic reform. In contrast, contemporary residents of virtually every Chinese county can point to a people's court, the offices of the procuracy, a local mediation committee, or the office of "letters and visits" (*xinfang*) where complaints can be lodged, namely institutions whose presence in the county almost always predates the era of "reform and opening." Scholars and legal practitioners have produced a substantial literature that details how and why the Chinese legal system is being reformed. Yet it is not entirely clear how public opinion perceives the extent to which long-standing legal institutions have changed and whether ordinary Chinese are willing to trust institutions that originally were introduced in the Mao period because the recent reforms make them more appealing to resolve legal matters, or whether they place their trust in seemingly enduring institutions that have spanned several decades in many localities.

MASS PERCEPTIONS OF LEGAL INSTITUTIONS IN CHINA

Although the study of public opinion in China has made considerable progress, it has been extraordinarily difficult to establish historical benchmarks or to understand trends over time in the absence of comparable survey research during the Mao era. Thanks to China's participation in cross-national research projects, paradoxically we know far more about the attitudes of Chinese citizens in comparison to those abroad than we do about changes over time within the Chinese public. In this chapter, I attempt to use both contemporary public opinion data – the survey on the Institutionalization of Legal Reforms in China (ILCR) conducted by Peking University in 2003–04 – and externally obtained information about the counties where the survey was conducted to gain some understanding about the long-term effect of historical processes that have not been measured directly at the individual level.

Even though the ILRC data provide only a snapshot of the attitudes and behavior of more than seven thousand respondents located in one hundred county units, we can uncover explanations for their answers by linking individual-level data to the specific historical context of the communities in which these respondents live. The Chinese terrain is particularly rich if one wishes to test multilevel explanations, because local historical data are unusually disaggregated. Since the 1980s, all counties of the PRC have been expected to produce a gazetteer (*xianzhi*) documenting the evolution of their locality from 1949 to the late 1980s. In particular, the structure of the formal institutions of the party, the government, and the legal system are articulated in considerable detail. By linking the institutional evolution of each county to the survey data collected in 2003, we can test explicitly whether the pattern of historical development of legal institutions at the local level still affects how these institutions are perceived today and whether their past performance has a detectable impact on the trust that ordinary citizens are willing to put in them.

The ILRC Survey

The ILRC survey is the first nationally representative sample specifically designed to understand popular attitudes toward legal institutions. This equal-probability sample of all Chinese adults (including internal migrants) is also spatially representative, as it draws from all Chinese provinces. Thus, the survey provides a solid foundation for making point predictions and reaching generalizable conclusions about the behavior of ordinary citizens.

The survey draws on a multistage stratified sample in which each province, municipality, or autonomous region was taken as a stratum. Within each stratum, counties (or urban districts) were selected at random by probability proportional to size (PPS) proportionally to the magnitude of each stratum. Within each county, two townships (or their street committee counterparts in urban areas) were also randomly selected. Below the township level, a spatial sampling design was used to avoid the problem of coverage errors caused by imprecise household registration lists that exclude internal migrants and temporary residents.[10] In short, the sample conforms to the principle of equal probability selection and is spatially representative of China's varied demographic, social, and economic environments.

Local Histories since 1949: Using County Gazetteers

Because the ILCR questionnaire was administered to respondents drawn from one hundred randomly distributed county-level units, it is impractical to recount the extensive details of this multitude of local legal and political histories in a single chapter. Instead, I link individual survey data with benchmarks of the evolution of legal institutions in each of the respondent's county of residence. These data were primarily collected and coded from the gazetteer of each primary sampling unit. The gazetteers corresponding to three primary sampling units (PSUs) remain unavailable, and in four other cases at least one of the variables used in the econometric model presented here is missing because the sources are unclear.[11]

The publication of post-1949 gazetteers in the early 1980s generated considerable interest among scholars who sought to ask questions about the structure of the Chinese state at a level that heretofore had been relatively untouched.[12] More recently, students of Chinese legal institutions have published important narratives based at least in part on local

[10] Pierre F. Landry and Mingming Shen, "Reaching Migrants in Survey Research: The Use of the Global Positioning System to Reduce Coverage Bias in China," *Political Analysis* 13, no. 1 (2005): 1–22.

[11] Units completely missing are PSU 213 (urban district under Fuxin municipality, Liaoning province, affecting eighty-three respondents), PSU 363 (county under Shangrao municipality, Jiangxi province, affecting ninety respondents), and PSU 551 (county under Lhasa municipality in Tibet affecting seventy-nine respondents). The three counties combined account for 3.3 percent of the survey's respondents. The entire missing data pattern affecting four additional counties in Shandong, Henan, Hunan, and Guangdong implies that 551 (or 7.1 percent of the same) individual respondents are excluded from the analysis.

[12] Stig Thogersen and Soren Clausen, "New Reflections in the Mirror: Local Chinese Gazetteers (*Difangzhi*) in the 1980s," *Australian Journal of Chinese Affairs*, no. 27 (January 1992): 161–184; Elizabeth J. Perry, "Trends in the Study of Chinese Politics: State-Society Relations," *The China Quarterly*, no. 139 (September 1994): 704–713. A. Doak Barnett's famous study of "county X" relied exclusively on face-to-face interviews with a handful of respondents who had to recall every detail from memory. A. Doak Barnett, *Cadres, Bureaucracy, and Political Power in Communist China* (New York: Columbia University Press, 1967).

gazetteers (*difangzhi*) that contradict the view that the Maoist state was uniformly centralized, even in the 1950s.[13] Bachman has highlighted the importance of the court system before the Cultural Revolution, finding that – even after 1958 – courts were used to a far greater extent than had been assumed and that the proportion of guilty verdicts and conviction rates was surprisingly lower than that of criminal cases handled by U.S. federal courts.[14]

The research strategy in this chapter builds on this fledgling literature but adds two distinctive components. First, I explicitly eschew the risk of selection bias by relying on a random sample of one hundred counties drawn not from a preexisting list of published gazetteers, but instead from the total population of county-level units of the PRC, namely the set of PSUs drawn for the ILRC project in 2003–04.[15] Matching each PSU to its relevant gazetteer was straightforward in most cases. When the unit name had changed, I verified the name and delineation of the locality at the time of the 1949 "liberation" and matched it to the proper source. In a handful of instances when county-level boundaries had been redrawn extensively, the current PSU could be mapped to multiple county-level "ancestors." In these cases, I used the county gazetteers (*xian zhi*) that could be matched to the physical area(s) of the townships (i.e., secondary sampling units) that were drawn in the contemporary county. In short, the guiding principle was to organize the county-level information in such a way that it could be linked to individual survey respondents based on their current physical location.

The second distinctive strategy is to link county-level institutional data with survey results in an effort to test the hypothesis that the institutional features of the Nationalist and Maoist eras are still relevant to the attitudes of contemporary residents of the same localities. We can thus measure explicitly the extent of institutional variation at the local level as well as its impact on the key dependent variable of interest: popular trust in the courts. This strategy is related to recent developments in hierarchal

[13] Neil J. Diamant, "Re-Examining the Impact of the 1950 Marriage Law: State Improvisation, Local Initiative and Rural Family Change," *The China Quarterly*, no. 161 (March 2000): 171–198; Laura M. Luehrmann, "Facing Citizen Complaints in China, 1951–1996," *Asian Survey* 43, no. 5 (2003): 845–866.

[14] David Bachman, "Aspects of an Institutionalizing Political System: China, 1958–1965," *The China Quarterly*, no. 188 (2006): 933–958.

[15] The master list was based on the administrative divisions of 2000, when the latest census was compiled. The counties were drawn by PPS, using a stratification scheme that ensured drawing from all provinces. The raw number of PSUs from each stratum (province) was proportional to the population size of the province in 2000.

linear modeling (HLM) in which observations nested in higher-order units are organized in multilevel structures of varying complexity.[16] However, the multivariate models presented here are not formal multilevel models because the current econometric technology of HLM cannot incorporate the sampling weights that are required to properly analyze ordinal survey data. Thus, "county-effects" are used simply as right-hand side variables that can take no more than ninety-three distinct values, namely the number of counties included in the study.

The gazetteers follow the guidelines set by the State Council, although the details of their content and presentation are handled at the local levels.[17] Most sources include specific chapters on legal affairs, usually titled "public security and justice" (*gongan sifa*), as well as accounts of the evolution of the county's administrative and political affairs since 1949. Although these sources are extremely valuable for tracking the institutional evolution of Chinese counties over time, they also present difficult empirical challenges. The historical end point of the volumes varies because the dates of publication of the gazetteers range from 1981 to 2005.[18] With an average publication date of 1995 and coverage of events until 1990 in most cases, the gazetteers thus provide a substantial description of each county's history during the Mao and Deng eras. Furthermore, the level of precision in these accounts varies, ranging from general descriptions of each issue area to detailed annual statistical information on virtually every subject matter. Therefore, any effort to capture usable data across both time and space must focus on a somewhat stylized "common denominator."

Based on data from eighty-seven counties, county-level cities, or urban districts, the gazetteer data set was subsequently merged with the ILRC survey data. This is a one-to-many match, because all respondents from a given county share the same institutional features compiled in the gazetteer data.

16 Stephen W. Raudenbush and Anthony S. Bryk, *Hierarchical Linear Models: Applications and Data Analysis Methods* (Newbury Park, Calif.: Sage, 2001); Douglas A. Luke, *Multilevel Modeling* (Thousand Oaks, Calif.: Sage, 2004); Andrew Gelman and Jennifer Hill, *Data Analysis Using Regression and Multilevel/Hierarchical Models* (New York: Cambridge University Press, 2007).

17 "Zhonghua renmin gongheguo guowuyuan ling di 467 hao" (Order No. 467 of the State Council of the People's Republic of China), http://www.gov.cn/ziliao/flfg/2006-05/29/content_294229.htm (accessed October 13, 2008).

18 However, several of the initial gazetteers are complemented by follow-up publications in the form of supplemental gazetteers or yearbooks.

CONTEMPORARY TRUST IN LEGAL INSTITUTIONS

A considerable scholarship in political science focuses on how citizens trust "institutions," the "system," or the "regime" where they live, and much intellectual energy is devoted to understanding the variability of this trustworthiness among citizens or voters.[19] In stable democracies, the architecture of governing institutions changes relatively slowly, and the core functions of institutions tend to be taken as given. In this context, it is reasonable to ascribe changes in the level of institutional trust to changes affecting the underlying population. However, in regimes where the functions of legal institutions evolve rapidly, observations on increases or decreases in "trust in institutions" say less about changes in public opinion per se than they do about the impact of institutional reform on public opinion. It is therefore necessary to explicitly account for institutional variability.

Numerous surveys conducted in China concur that the stated level of trust in government institutions is remarkably high.[20] These levels are higher not only than those in other culturally Chinese societies for which we have data (Taiwan, Hong Kong, and Singapore), but also than those in most other authoritarian regimes where identical surveys have been conducted.[21] Fear among respondents or the desire to provide politically correct answers cannot be the explanation for China's unusually high ratings, because respondents from regimes that are at least as repressive as the PRC express far lower levels of trust in their institutions than respondents from mainland China.

[19] Marc J. Hetherington, "The Political Relevance of Political Trust," *American Political Science Review* 92, no. 4 (1998): 791–808; Margaret Levi, "A State of Trust." In *Trust and Governance*, ed. Valerie A. Braithwaite and Margaret Levi (New York: Russell Sage Foundation, 1998), pp. 77–101; Margaret Levi and Laura Stoker, "Political Trust and Trustworthiness," *Annual Review of Political Science* 3, no. 1 (2000): 475–507; Stacey G. Ulbig, "Policies, Procedures, and People: Sources of Support for Government?" *Social Science Quarterly* 83, no. 3 (2002): 789–809; Russell Hardin, *Trust and Trustworthiness* (New York: Russell Sage Foundation, 2002); Russell Hardin, *Trust* (Cambridge, U.K.: Polity, 2006); Charles Tilly, *Trust and Rule* (New York: Cambridge University Press, 2005).

[20] Wenfang Tang and William L. Parish, *Chinese Urban Life under Reform: The Changing Social Contract* (New York: Cambridge University Press, 2000); Tianjian Shi, "Cultural Values and Political Trust: A Comparison of the People's Republic of China and Taiwan," *Comparative Politics* 33, no. 4 (2001): 401–418.

[21] Ronald Inglehart, *Modernization and Postmodernization: Cultural, Economic, and Political Change in 43 Societies* (Princeton, N.J.: Princeton University Press, 1997).

However, some features of the regime are likely to shape popular perceptions of the country's institutions systematically: The educational system is closely supervised and emphasizes the Marxian historical inevitability of the political system, including legal institutions. Beyond the school system, state-controlled media routinely report on legal matters in ways that are likely to reinforce the feeling of legitimacy of the political and legal systems among press readers or television viewers. Furthermore, some of the most politically active members of society – CCP members – are likely to further trust institutions that are closely controlled by the CCP. These factors were incorporated into the survey instrument and are included as control variables. We expect positive correlations between trust in courts and education, media exposure, and CCP membership.

Just as public opinion research has identified high levels of trust in government institutions, the ILRC survey items that focused on legal institutions specifically indicate similar results. So far, the literature on public opinion research offers causal explanations of the level of trust centered on individual attributes.[22] Although these explanations have merit, they often fail to take into account the diversity of the experiences of the specific communities where the respondents live. Public opinion research often is conducted in countries characterized by institutional homomorphism, and most public opinion research is conducted on samples drawn in a single country, with little precision about the specific geographical and historical characteristics of the sampled clusters.[23] The lack of focus on contextual variables is particularly problematic when

[22] See, inter alia, Paul R. Abramson and Ada W. Finifter, "On the Meaning of Political Trust: New Evidence from Items Introduced in 1978," *American Journal of Political Science* 25, no. 2 (1981): 297–307; John Ambler, "Trust in Political and Nonpolitical Authorities in France," *Comparative Politics* 8, no. 1 (1975): 31–58; John Brehm and Wendy Rahn, "Individual-Level Evidence for the Causes and Consequences of Social Capital," *American Journal of Political Science* 41, no. 3 (1997): 999–1023; Virginia A. Chanley, Thomas J. Rudolph, and Wendy M. Rahn, "The Origins and Consequences of Public Trust in Government: A Time Series Analysis," *Public Opinion Quarterly* 64, no. 3 (2000): 239–256; David B. Hill, "Attitude Generalization and the Measurement of Trust in American Leadership," *Political Behavior* 3, no. 3 (1981): 257–270; Lawrence R. Jacobs and Robert Y. Shapiro, "Studying Substantive Democracy," *PS: Political Science and Politics* 27, no. 1 (1994): 9–17; Eric M. Uslaner, "Producing and Consuming Trust," *Political Science Quarterly* 115, no. 4 (2000–2001): 569–590.

[23] Rare cases of natural experiments allow researchers to test their hypotheses on a single population divided along a state boundary, but such circumstances are rare. Daniel N. Posner, "The Political Salience of Cultural Difference: Why Chewas and Tumbukas Are Allies in Zambia and Adversaries in Malawi," *American Political Science Review* 98, no. 4 (2004): 529–545.

individual trust in government institutions can be highly differentiated.[24] Li Lianjiang finds that rural Chinese exhibit highly differentiated levels of trust regarding central and local institutions.[25]

The ILRC survey asked all respondents to rate the trustworthiness of a series of political and legal institutions on a four-point scale. Although the mean scores are generally high and only a small minority of the respondents was willing to assign the lowest ratings, the results demonstrate that the broad findings on high levels of institutional trust also hold with respect to legal institutions. Trust is institution specific: Organizations that are frequently involved in dispute resolution (such as village committees) received the lowest rankings, whereas the courts and the procuracy are held in relatively high regard. Furthermore, most respondents trust institutions that are closely associated with the state to a far greater extent than they do nonbureaucratic actors: Legal professionals are less trusted than courts or public security organs. We also find a great deal of geographical heterogeneity. Figure 5.2 displays the scatterplots of the average values by county of the mean values of trust in courts versus lawyers in the top quadrant and the letters and visits offices (*xinfang jigou*) versus public security organs in the bottom quadrant. For each variable, the gap between counties with the lowest and highest ratings is approximately 1 point on a 1 to 4 scale.

Measuring the Importance of County-Level Effects

A very simple hierarchical linear model with no independent variables and only two random intercepts at the province and county levels can easily decompose the variance of popular trust in courts, lawyers, *xinfang*, and public-security organs (see Table 5.1). Although the results show that much of the variance originates at the respondent level, they also indicate that the provincial – and more importantly – the county-level intercepts vary systematically. It is also clear that the relative impact of each level is nearly identical regardless of the specific aspect of institutional trust under consideration. The empirical Bayes predictions of the random intercepts for the provinces and counties show that popular trust varies much more across counties that it does across provinces: The graphs drawing county

[24] M. Kent Jennings, "Political Trust and the Roots of Devolution." In *Trust and Governance*, ed. Valerie A. Braithwaite and Margaret Levi (New York: Russell Sage Foundation, 1998), pp. 218–244; Levi, "A State of Trust."

[25] Lianjiang Li, "Political Trust in Rural China," *Modern China* 30, no. 2 (2004): 228–258.

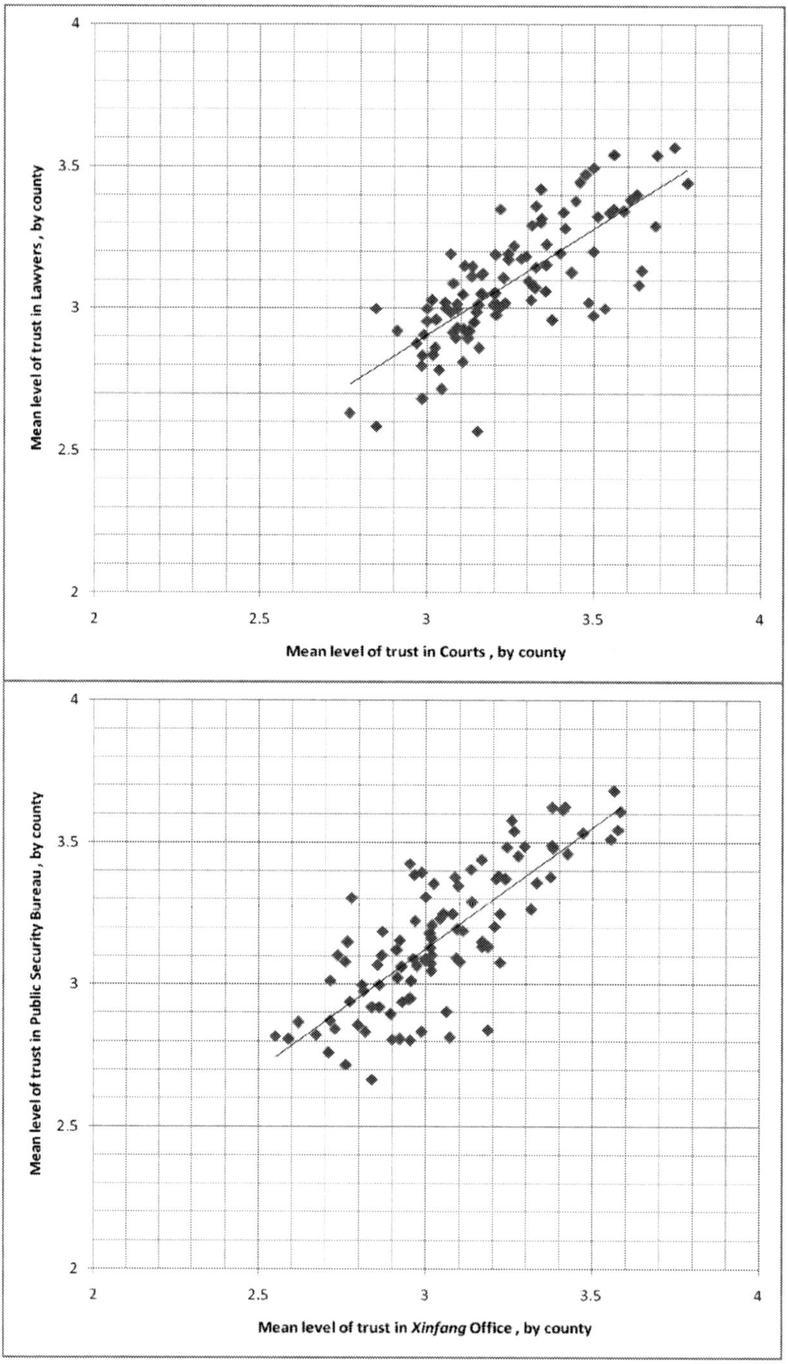

FIGURE 5.2. Scatterplots of Trust in Legal Institutions, Aggregated by County (1–4 scale). *Source:* ILRC.

TABLE 5.1. *Multilevel variance of trust in legal institutions*

Mixed-effects REML regression								
xtmixed TRUST COURT II PROVINCE: II COUNTY:								
	Court		Lawyers		Xinfang		Pub. Sec.	
Coef.	3.260		3.108		3.051		3.168	
Std. Err.	0.027		0.029		0.033		0.030	
Random-effects Parameters								
PROVINCE: Identity sd(_cons)								
Estimate	0.091		0.112		0.132		0.095	
Std. Err.	0.040		0.031		0.035		0.046	
[95% Conf. Interval]	0.039	0.214	0.066	0.191	0.079	0.223	0.037	0.246
COUNTY: Identity sd(_cons)								
Estimate	0.184		0.163		0.177		0.216	
Std. Err.	0.019		0.017		0.019		0.022	
[95% Conf. Interval]	0.150	0.226	0.133	0.201	0.143	0.218	0.177	0.263
sd(Residual)								
Estimate	0.646		0.642		0.661		0.683	
Std. Err.	0.005		0.006		0.006		0.006	
[95% Conf. Interval]	0.636	0.657	0.632	0.653	0.650	0.673	0.672	0.694
LR test vs. linear regression:	0.0000		0.0000		0.0000		0.0000	
Number of Observations	7259		6682		6048		7246	
Number of Provinces	31		31		31		31	
Number of Counties	100		100		100		100	

effects horizontally and provincial effects vertically show "wide" rather than "tall" scatterplots, particularly with respect to the courts and public security organs (Figure 5.3). This is not surprising given the rich history of Chinese counties, particularly because counties have remained the most stable level of local government since the imperial era. In the remainder of this chapter, I unpack the specific county-level characteristics that underlie this variability at the local level.

Measuring Institutional Diversity at the County Level

I measured the timing of the introduction of the key legal institutions in the county's contemporary history as well as several important political variables. Three variables capture how committed a county was to the Nationalist regime: Later dates of the creation of the first Communist Party branch in the locality and the date of "liberation" – measured in months deviating from October 1949, which is coded zero – are both markers of counties that were more supportive of the Nationalists. In addition to these timing variables, I also approximate the local strength of the KMT by counting the number of Nationalist officials whose native place (*jiguan*) is identified as the sampling unit, using an extensive biographical encyclopedia of KMT personages.[26] Here, too, larger numbers denote greater likelihoods of KMT support in the county.

The other county-level variables capture the development of legal institutions since the founding of the PRC. By averaging the value over the range of the sampling units for which data were available, we can paint an approximate picture of the evolution of a "typical" Chinese county. Consider the mean values for CCP variables across counties in Table 5.2. We observe that the first CCP branches typically were created in 1932, that the party seized power in early 1948, and that the Political and Legal Affairs Committee of the CCP (*zhengfa wei*) typically was created in 1976. Because the normal operations of most government institutions were severely affected by the Cultural Revolution, it is useful to capture both the initial creation of an institution (regardless of the period when it was introduced) and its reintroduction following the most disruptive phase of the Cultural Revolution. Thus, most county people's courts were

[26] Liu Guoming and Huang Jinming, *Zhongguo guomindang bainian renwu quanshu* (A Comprehensive Volume on Personages during One Hundred Years of the Chinese Kuomintang) (Beijing: Tuanjie chubanshe, 2 vols., 2005), pp. 2532–2587.

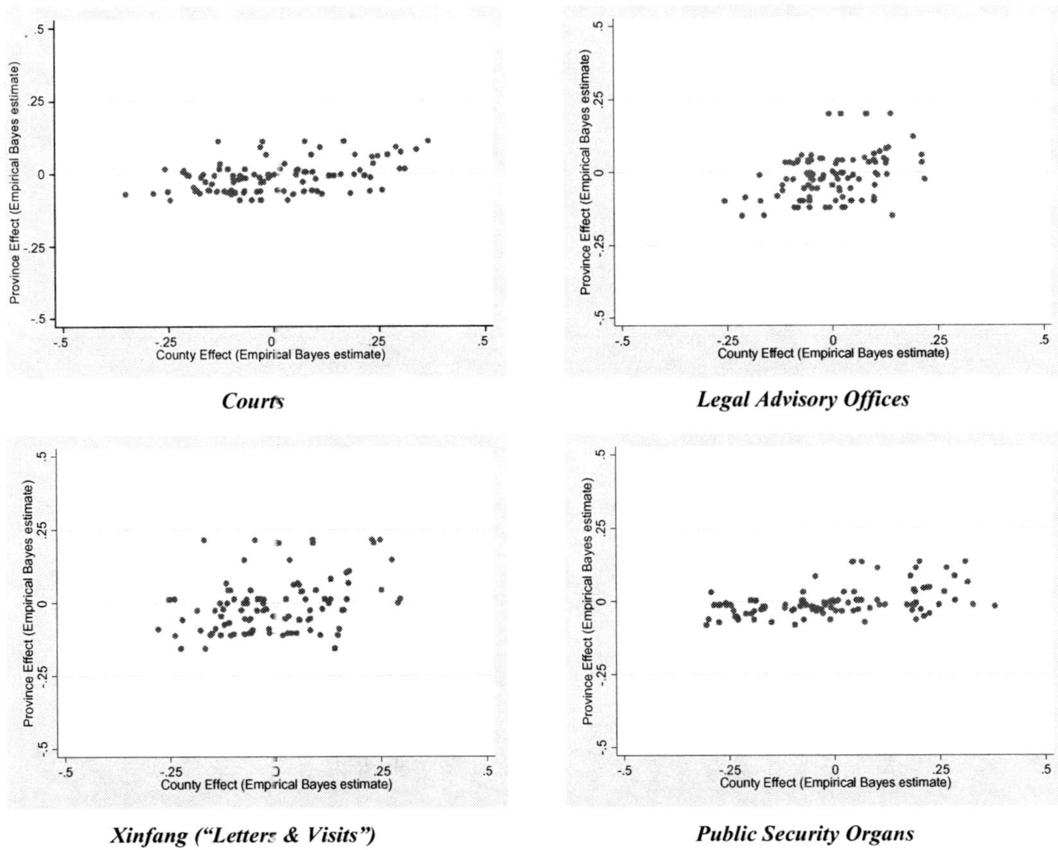

FIGURE 5.3. Comparison of Random Effects at the Province and County Levels (each dot represents a PSU).

TABLE 5.2. *Summary of the evolution of legal institutions in 87 ILRC counties*

Variable	Min.	Mean	Std. Dev.	Max.
Number of KMT officials from the locality	0	12.8	22.5	167
End of KMT rule (measured in months relative to October 1949)	−147	−12.2	22.6	19
End of KMT rule (year)	1937	1948.2	1.86	1951
First CCP branch was founded in the county	1921	1932.1	8.4	1951
Foundation of the County People's government	1940	1949.1	2.8	1960
Party political and legal affairs committee/group established	1954	1977.4	10	1990
County (basic) people's court established	1934	1950.9	2.4	1961
People's court reestablished (post–cultural revolution)	1972	1973	1.1	1981
County Judicial division/bureau established	1948	1978	8.8	1984
Legal advisory office first established	1954	1972.3	12.77	1991
Legal advisory office (re-)established after cultural revolution	1966–76	1981.2	3.56	1991
Criminal tribunals established	1940	1959.2	11.7	1988
Civil tribunals established	1940	1960.7	12.2	1988
Economic tribunals established	1978	1981.5	1.5	1988
Administrative tribunals established	1984	1987.8	1.4	1990
People's Mediation Committees established	1931	1956.4	10	1982
Letters and Visits bureau/office established	1950	1968.4	11.8	1987
Notary established	1935	1974	13.6	1987
Contract-management office established (within ind. and commercial administration or association)	1956	1980	7	1987
Contract arbitration committee established	1979	1983.8	1.5	1987

created in 1950 (though some outliers do exist) and were reestablished in 1973.

Although these mean values provide a convenient summary of the sequence of institution creation in a typical county, the average values can be misleading when the distributions are not unimodal. We find such an instance with the creation of legal advisory offices (*falü guwen chu*), for which the computed mean is implausibly 1973.[27] In fact, we can clearly distinguish two sets of counties: in twenty-seven cases, legal advisory offices were introduced between 1956 and 1958 but closed quickly thereafter.[28] In most counties, they were created in the early 1980s.

Table 5.1 also reveals the extent of institutional variation across counties, which is captured by the standard deviation. A small standard deviation implies that the institution in question was introduced concurrently across counties. These concern primarily innovations of the reform era, such as the formation of economic contract arbitration committees (*jingji hetong zhongcai weiyuanhui*) in approximately 1983 or administrative tribunals (*xingzheng shenpan tingcheng*) in 1987. By contrast, the standard deviations for many variables exceed ten years, which indicates that a wide variety of institutional arrangements at the county level existed before 1978. For instance, many county party organizations did not create political and legal committees until the 1980s, but in sixteen cases – concentrated in Guangdong and Guizhou – they were introduced between 1954 and 1966.[29] We see a similar pattern for legal advisory offices as well as for specialized civil and criminal tribunals within the courts. Here again, the greatest extent of local variation occurred during the Maoist period, not the reform era.

CAUSAL MECHANISMS AT THE INDIVIDUAL LEVEL

Is this institutional diversity consequential? The skeptics can point to the extent of institutional, economic, and social change since 1978 – let

[27] The value 1972.3 implies April 1972 because 3 is the decimal value, not the month of observation.

[28] Among those, eleven gazetteers mention that the legal advisory offices were closed by 1957–58, which coincides with the end of the antirightist campaign and the launch of the great leap forward. The sources are silent about the exact date of closure of the legal advisory offices in twelve counties (especially in Anhui, Jiangxi, and Guangdong). Anhui gazetteers do not specify the date of reintroduction after the Cultural Revolution, perhaps because it did not occur until after their publication.

[29] In county 533 (Guizhou), the term used was *zhengzhi zu* between 1953 and 1955 and again from 1959 to 1966.

alone the shrinking share of the Chinese population brought up or socialized during the Mao era – to dismiss the contemporary relevance of these past differences. If we ignored the timing of their introduction and only checked for their contemporary existence, we would be hard-pressed to find any variation in the organization of county-level institutions today. Trust levels are more likely to shift when policy changes are matched with radical institutional change and when reforms are not concurrent across geographical units, as was the case with many of the economic reforms. However, legal reforms differ significantly from economic reforms because most formal legal institutions of the Maoist state have nominally survived the 1978 divide, even though they may now function quite differently than they did in the past. In most localities, county people's courts, the procuracy, or the *xinfang* system all have been part of the legal landscape since the 1950s. From the perspective of ordinary residents, the simple fact that they often bear the same name as they did under Mao suggests that the degree of popular trust or distrust in these institutions accumulated before the reforms is likely to affect how citizens evaluate them today. The longer the presence of an institution in a county, the more likely it is that its past performance still shapes its trustworthiness in the eyes of county residents.

Attitude versus Experience

When gauging the level of trust that respondents have in legal institutions, it is necessary to delineate the subpopulation that actually experienced disputes from the group of respondents whose opinion is entirely based on perceptions. Respondents who confronted a civil, economic, or administrative dispute had the opportunity to "test" the institutions we enquired about in the questionnaire. Resolving disputes is costly, and outcomes are uncertain. Unfavorable outcomes or disputes left unresolved are likely to undermine trust in institutions that fail to meet the respondents' expectations, whether realistic or not. Thus, the multivariate models of trust in legal institutions control for individual dispute experience.

Respondents' Exposure to the County

Although it is easy to establish the existence of geographical heterogeneity, it is more difficult to prove that the cause of this variation is linked to the characteristics of local institutions independently of the characteristics of the residents who happen to migrate into the same localities. As internal migration intensifies, an ever-increasing proportion of the population no longer lives in the county where they grew up. If trust in institutions is based on socialization in a specific locality, one must account for the geographical mobility of the population and control for in-migrants who may carry over attitudes based on life experiences in their home communities. Gender also affects the exposure to one's county of current residence because women are more likely than men to cross county boundaries upon marriage. I computed this "exposure" by calculating the proportion of each respondent's life spent outside the county. Respondents who had moved to the county less than one month before they were interviewed are assigned the value 1, whereas those who were born in the same PSU where they were interviewed in 2003 are coded 0. Though it is still the case that the majority of the population is still not mobile in this sense, histograms by age and gender confirm that mobility rates are higher among women, particularly younger women. The weighted mean among men is 0.10, suggesting that a typical male respondent has spent 10 percent of his life outside the county. By contrast, the mean value among women is 0.15 (see Figure 5.4).

If the hypothesis that trust is acquired over repeated opportunities to engage local institutions directly is correct, exposure to one's county of residence should matter as long as residents assume that the characteristics of the county's legal institutions do not vary systematically across localities. However, if trust is not "portable" in the sense that residents believe that whatever lessons were drawn outside the county do not apply in their current place of residence, exposure to the county should have little impact on trust: In-migrants behave as Baysian updaters when they cross county boundaries. The more heteromorphic institutions are, the more likely residents are to behave in this way.

In contrast to the impact of the life history of the local residents, a more direct causal explanation for the level of trust falls squarely on the characteristics of the legal institutions themselves. If they are heteromorphic, the range and quality of services that are available locally are likely to vary across counties, and this variation should in turn affect their trustworthiness. The mechanism for this mode of diffusion of trust is geographic, not demographic. When information about past institutional performance is easily transmitted, all residents – whether or not they are newcomers – will take it into account when they evaluate the legal institutions. If information flows are restricted, we may observe differences in the level of trust between newcomers and old-timers.

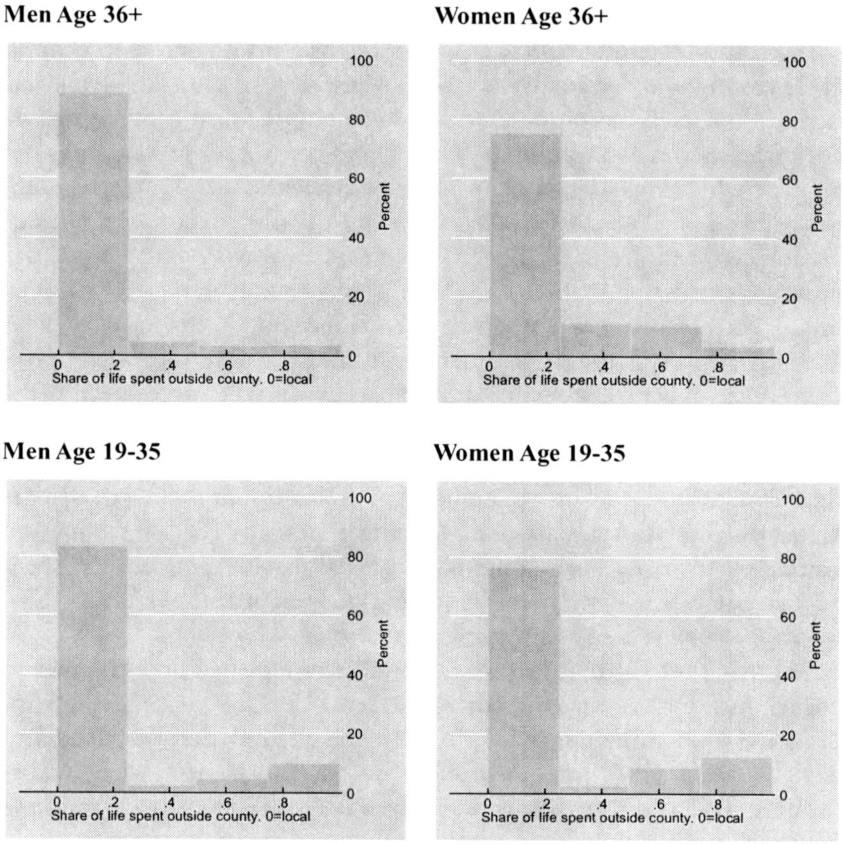

FIGURE 5.4. Respondents' Exposure to Their County of Residence.

Media Exposure

A firsthand encounter with a legal institutional may be decisive in shaping one's views about its performance and one's subsequent degree of trust in it. However, only a minority of citizens reported having such direct experiences. The views of the majority are likely to be shaped in part by their exposure to the media (particularly when the regime's propaganda efforts were as intensive as they were in the 1950s and 1960s) as well as by information gleaned from kin and neighbors who may have had direct encounters.

Chinese media messages about the law have not been uniform over time: The content of propaganda changed along with the evolving goals of the regime that at times strongly promoted the role of institutions, like the people's courts, but could suddenly compel its media outlets to vilify or ignore them altogether. In the long run, erratic media content may produce a heterogeneous public opinion, stratified along the waves of the messages the regime sought to infuse to the public during each period.

Although direct public opinion data dating back to the Mao era are not available, we can at least measure the effort the state has exerted and capture the different themes that populated the Chinese media after 1949. I did this through content analysis of the full-text archive of the *People's Daily* electronic edition.[30] Because of the newspaper's status as the official mouthpiece of the CCP, its contents mirror the goals of the regime and changes in the party line. I queried the database by counting how many times per year various legal institutions were mentioned at least once in any article, searching for "people's court," "people's procurary," "people's mediation," and "legal advice" (*falü guwen*).The long-term trends plotted in Figure 5.5 clearly show that the post-1978 era is distinctive, but not novel. After we control for the size of the newspaper, it appears that people's courts were mentioned with greater frequency during the campaigns of the early 1950s than during the contemporary period of legal reforms. The data for the people's procuracy follow the same pattern, though it is mentioned less frequently. Legal advice offices were established in most localities in the 1980s, but they existed in some areas before the Cultural Revolution, a pattern that is indeed captured in the data. The pattern for people's mediation committees is more surprising. Although mediation committees were created early in the Mao era, paradoxically, the *People's Daily* mentioned them more frequently after 1990, when the use of mediation committees declined noticeably.

The time series indicate that if the propaganda machine has been effective, the Chinese public can be divided into three groups (Figure 5.5). The generation that lived or grew up during the 1950s was made aware of legal institutions at a time of considerable political repression, but there were frequent discussions of legal issues in the press. The second group consists of those for whom the media's discussions of legal institutions declined dramatically, between the great leap forward and the end of the Cultural Revolution. The third group was exposed to the "reform" message after 1981, although one must distinguish between the older segments of the population who experienced the pre–great leap forward

[30] *People's Daily Newspaper Electronic Edition*, http://www.twinbridge.com/Peoples Daily, *On-Line Edition* (Beijing: Online database by TwinBridge Software Corporation, Monterey Park, Calif., 1946–2006).

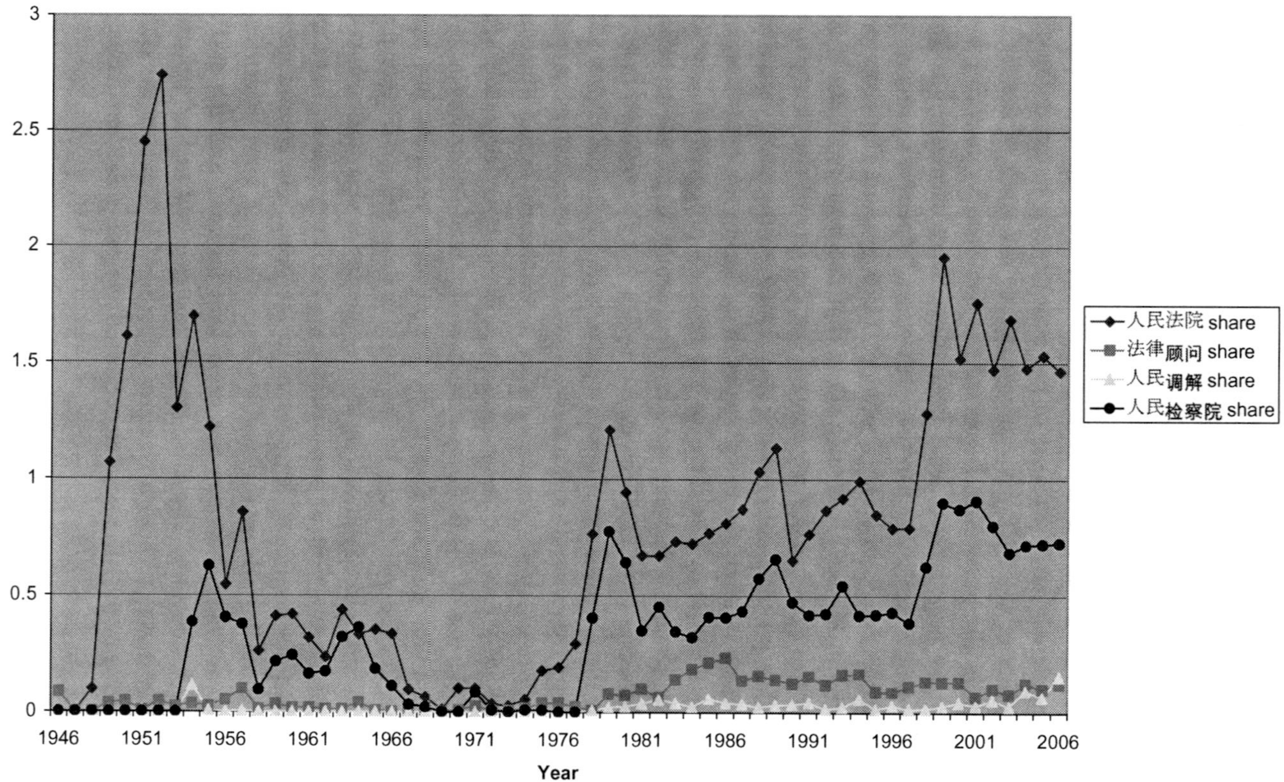

FIGURE 5.5. Mentions of Legal Institutions in the *People's Daily* (1946–2006).

propaganda (born before 1940), the quasisilence of the media until 1976 (born between 1952 and 1960), or both. They must be contrasted with the cohorts born after 1960 who only have been primed directly by the message of reform.

To some extent, the contemporary relevance of Maoist institutions is generational: Its effects are likely to be more pronounced among citizens who were socialized before the 1980s. The repression of the Maoist years is likely to have eroded the trustworthiness of legal institutions among those who witnessed how they operated before the reform era. Current surveys such as the ILRC can capture only a few members of the dwindling cohorts who were exposed to early Maoist propaganda and were still reachable in 2003. However, these impacts do not mechanically dissipate with age, because reputational effects can cross generational boundaries. The impact of Maoism is also felt through socialization in the family: Parental trust or distrust in legal institutions also can be internalized by their children's generation, particularly if these experiences were noteworthy or traumatic. A teenager brought up in the reform era by parents who were affected by an institution (or event) is likely to inherit similar preferences for or against the same institution. The countervailing influence of peers, the media, or schoolteachers can mitigate these views, but family encounters with the Maoist legal system still are likely to have a measurable impact on the attitudes and behavior of the post-Mao generation.

The ILRC survey also directly measured media consumption. Prior analysis of patterns of media consumption revealed that the frequency of television viewing captured much of the variation within the sample. Television is also a key medium in the regime's effort to propagate its message on the rule of law, in the form of both news broadcasts and in entertainment programs aimed at conveying "proper" and concordant views about legal institutions. The hypothesis here is straightforward: The more individuals watch television programs, the more they are likely to trust legal institutions.

MULTIVARIATE ANALYSIS OF TRUST IN COURTS

I estimate ordered-probit models to test the relative impact of both individual-level attributes and institutional diversity across counties on the level of trust the respondents express about courts. These are most appropriate given the nature of the dependent variable: The respondents had to choose among four ordered levels while evaluating how much they trusted each institution: trust a great deal (*feichang xinren*), basically trust (*bijiao xinren*), rather distrust (*butai xinren*), and completely distrust (*wanquan buxinren*). The question did not distinguish between the local courts and other courts, although as a follow-up, the respondents were asked whether or not they trusted local courts more than the Supreme People's Court. Variance estimates also account for the sampling weights.[31]

I include two sets of independent variables. Individual-level variables control for the heterogeneity in human capital, political resources, and life experiences that are likely to impact institutional trust. In addition to age, education, television consumption, exposure to the county, and past experiences with disputes that are discussed above, individual-level variables also control for membership in the CCP (presumably positively associated with trust in legal institutions) and whether or not the respondent holds an urban registration (*feinongye hukou*).

The second set of predictors captures the development of county-level political and legal institutions. Two variables account for the county's commitment to the Maoist regime: the date of creation of the first party branch (*dang zhibu*) and the time of the county's "liberation." The latter variable is measured in months away from October 1949 to better capture localities that were historical revolutionary bases (e.g., counties already under CCP control during the war against Japan), counties where the CCP won power before the official founding of the regime, and counties that were taken over after the PRC was proclaimed and the KMT had effectively evacuated the mainland.

The hypothesis is that in counties where the CCP failed to establish an early institutional presence or were "liberated" at the tail end of the civil war, the legacies of the KMT's efforts in favor of legal reforms still endure today. In the 1980s, the CCP's emphasis on law, along with the enhanced role of the courts in civil and administrative cases, was likely to be appealing in communities where courts historically had performed useful social functions, and these communities paradoxically map to regions where the KMT was strong. Of course, I do not argue that respondents surveyed in 2004 had personal experiences with KMT institutions, because only a handful of the respondents had even reached adulthood by 1949. The transmission mechanism is rooted instead in family and community traditions, not unlike those that Jason Wittenberg identifies in his

[31] It is not possible to fully account for the design effects at this point, because the lack of institutional data for three counties causes the problem of strata with singular PSUs.

work on Hungarian politics. In the Chinese case, the process is simpler because of the shorter duration of the period of high socialism. The Maoist regime did not immediately dismantle all extant institutions; in fact, middle- and low-ranking officials of the KMT bureaucracy were actively retained after 1949, and many legal institutions, although duly renamed and closely supervised by the CCP, lingered until 1957. In south and southwest China, as well as in large urban areas, lawyers and legal offices were allowed to operate until 1957 (and in a few instances, 1958). These regions saw their return in the early 1980s, albeit in the form of legal advisory offices under the close supervision of county courts, and today these areas are seeing a marked rise in the availability of private lawyers. In these counties, the era of high legal Maoism thus was relatively short, allowing popular perceptions of the role and social utility of these legal actors to endure.

Measures of urbanization during the Nationalist era are difficult to compile at the county level because no census was undertaken in China between the fall of the Qing dynasty in 1911 and 1953. As a control variable, I rely instead on the census count of 1953, supplemented in a few cases with demographic information from local gazetteers as a control variable for the degree of urbanization during the transition from KMT to CCP rule.

Finally, two variables account for the timing of the creation of the institutions in each county at key junctions in the regime's history: in the early Mao era, the creation of the people's court – which usually (but not always) closely followed the formation of the county (and district) people's government. The variable that measures the creation of legal advisory offices that effectively mark the introduction of lawyers in the county is bimodal: In many counties, it occurred in the early 1980s. However, a substantial minority of counties had functioning legal offices in the 1950s, though all were closed by 1958. Here, too, I hypothesize that institutions created early in the Mao area are most likely to be trusted because their persistence in the county confers them greater legitimacy.

The results based on 5,688 respondents located in ninety-three counties strongly support the hypothesis that institutional developments that predate the reform era still have a powerful impact on contemporary levels of trust in legal institutions (Table 5.3). Given that county-level institutional variables are measured in years (except for the liberation of the county), their impact on the dependent variable is substantial. The estimates confirm the independent impact of all variables that capture the historical strength of the Guomindang in the locality. Residence in a

TABLE 5.3. *Ordered probit model of trust in legal institutions*

Dependent variable: Trust in courts (ordered from very little to a great deal)	
Number of observations	5688
Wald chi-square (16)	117.78
Prob > chi-square	0
Log pseudo-likelihood	−5509.26
County-level effects	
Number of KMT officials from the county	.001[a]
	(0.001)
County population in 1953	.000[b]
	(0.000)
Date of liberation	.003[b]
	(0.001)
First CCP branch in the county	.009[b]
	(0.003)
Court creation year	−.032[c]
	(0.014)
Legal advisory office creation	.004[b]
	(0.001)
Individual-Level Effects	
Age	−.010
	(0.010)
Age^2	.000
	(0.000)
Female	0.054
	(0.036)
Education	0.011[a]
	(0.006)
CCP member	0.234[b]
	(0.073)
Urban *hukou*	−0.180[b]
	(0.051)
Exposure to the county	0.022
	(0.072)
Gov. Dispute	−0.266[b]
	(0.077)
Econ. Dispute	−0.041
	(0.073)
Civil Dispute	−0.139[c]
	(0.071)
Ancillary parameters	
/cut1	−39.576
	(27.543)
/cut2	−38.552
	(27.540)
/cut3	−36.964
	(27.541)

Standard errors (using sampling weights) in parentheses.
[a], [b], and [c] denote probability levels of .1, .05, and .01, respectively.

county where the CCP was established late, where the KMT was defeated late in the civil war, or where the Nationalists drew greater numbers of their elite all predict substantially higher levels of popular trust in contemporary courts. The result is particularly interesting given the opposite and unexpected impact of urbanization in the early 1950s, which is associated with lower levels of trust.

We also note the independent impact of institutional change during the Mao era. In counties that introduced courts early in the history of the regime, the level of trust in the people's courts is higher than in localities where courts were introduced more recently. In order to see this, consider the difference between a county where the court was created in June 1948 (one standard deviation below the mean) and a county that was late by about one standard deviation (September 1952). Taking all other continuous variables at their sample mean and assuming that the respondent is a woman who is not a party member, holds a rural *hukou*, has always lived in her county of residence, and was never engaged in a civil, administrative, or economic dispute, her probability of trusting courts is "a great deal," namely .403 in an "early" county. By contrast, the probability for an otherwise identical resident of a county that created its people's court in September 1952 drops to .360. These findings suggest that institutions that we typically associate with the Maoist state did not have a negative impact on popular trust.

CONCLUSIONS

Although the results regarding long-standing county courts may be interpreted as a case of Maoist nostalgia, the variables that capture the county's commitment to the regime in the 1950s suggest that if there is residual trust in institutions created long before the reform era, this trust is related specifically to the longevity of the courts and not to the longevity of the Communist Party in the county. Paradoxically, positive and significant coefficients suggest that trust in legal institutions is higher in counties that committed to the revolution late, whether measured by the benchmark of the establishment of the first CCP branch or the departure of the KMT.

Where are such counties located? Confidentiality rules of survey research prevent us from naming them specifically, but it is widely known from accounts of CCP history that the party established a powerful base in northern China, did not effectively penetrate urban areas until 1949, and only entered former KMT strongholds of south and southwest China in late 1949 and early 1950. Why would the residents of such areas place more trust in courts established by the CCP than residents of more "revolutionary" counties? One explanation may be that courts and lawyers were weak, or nonexistent, in regions where the CCP was able to establish an early presence. Because the party controlled these regions first, it was able to create a formal state apparatus early (including people's courts), but these courts would have had little cultural meaning in regions where war and revolution – and not even the most minimalist conceptions of the rule of law – defined ordinary life. By contrast, when the CCP took over the rest of China in the late 1940s, it "inherited" regions where the KMT's project of state building and modernization during the Nanjing decade had been relatively more successful and where the courts had already been established as a useful component of proper local governance.

We can rule out the argument that KMT strength is merely another proxy for the more advanced economic condition in territories that happened to be under KMT control for a longer period time. The variable "county population in 1953" is significant but negative. Yet even when we control for urbanization at the early stage of the regime, we still find that counties that experienced a weaker CCP presence and a longer length of KMT rule are the localities where the respondents are relatively more trusting of the courts.

These conclusions do not imply that contemporary Chinese citizens are the prisoners of their history. History matters, but so does individual heterogeneity. Many respondent-level variables have a powerful and significant impact on institutional trust, independently of the historical characteristics of the counties in which they live. The findings do suggest, however, that a more careful analysis of the local context applied to survey data can reveal significant variations across space as well as historical continuities at the county level.

6

Public Attitudes toward Official Justice in Beijing and Rural China

Ethan Michelson and Benjamin L. Read

Gruesome media accounts from both China and abroad on the performance of Chinese legal institutions, perhaps best exemplified by the Pulitzer Prize–winning series on "ragged justice,"[1] are consistent with scholarly reports of pervasive travesties of justice in the court system[2] and abuses of power in the police system.[3] Notwithstanding this conventional

[1] Joseph Kahn, "Deep Flaws, and Little Justice, in China's Court System," *New York Times*, September 21, 2005, A1; Joseph Kahn, "Dispute Leaves U.S. Executive in Chinese Legal Netherworld," *New York Times*, November 1, 2005, A1; Joseph Kahn, "Legal Gadfly Bites Hard, and Beijing Slaps Him," *New York Times*, December 13, 2005, A1; Joseph Kahn, "When Chinese Sue the State, Cases Are Often Smothered," *New York Times*, December 28, 2005, A1; Jim Yardley, "A Judge Tests China's Courts, Making History," *New York Times*, November 28, 2005, A1; Jim Yardley, "Desperate Search for Justice: One Man vs. China," *New York Times*, November 12, 2005, A1; Jim Yardley, "Seeking a Public Voice on China's 'Angry River,'" *New York Times*, December 26, 2005, A1; Jim Yardley, "In Worker's Death, View of China's Harsh Justice," *New York Times*, December 31, 2005, A1.

[2] Ting Gong, "Dependent Judiciary and Unaccountable Judges: Judicial Corruption in Contemporary China," *The China Review* 4, no. 2 (2004): 33–54; Mary E. Gallagher, "Mobilizing the Law in China: 'Informed Disenchantment' and the Development of Legal Consciousness," *Law & Society Review* 40, no. 4 (2006): 783–816; Ethan Michelson, "Unhooking from the State: Chinese Lawyers in Transition" (Ph.D. diss., Dept. of Sociology, University of Chicago, 2003), chap. 9; Jerome A. Cohen, "A Slow March to Legal Reform," *Far Eastern Economic Review* 170, no. 8 (October 2007): 20–24.

[3] Kam C. Wong, "The Police Legitimacy Crisis and Police Law Reform in China: Part I," *International Journal of Police Science and Management* 6, no. 4 (2004): 199–218; Murray Scot Tanner, "Campaign-Style Policing in China and Its Critics." In *Crime, Punishment, and Policing in China*, ed. Børge Bakken (Lanham, Md.: Rowman & Littlefield, 2005), pp. 171–188; Hualing Fu, "Zhou Yongkang and the Recent Police Reform in China," *The Australian and New Zealand Journal of Criminology* 38, no. 2 (2005): 241–253.

We are grateful to Tom Tyler for making available his 1984 Chicago survey data. The Chinese survey data analyzed in this chapter were collected with generous funding from the Ford Foundation (Beijing) and the Lewis Mumford Center for Comparative Urban and Regional Research. Write-up support was provided by the Obermann Center for Advanced Studies, University of Iowa.

story of endemic failures in China's legal system, survey evidence tells the opposite story: highly positive popular perceptions of – and an overwhelming popular willingness to mobilize – both the courts[4] and the police.[5] Which of these two seemingly contradictory stories is correct? In this chapter, we use survey data from Beijing and rural China on popular perceptions of official justice and on firsthand assessments of encounters with official justice to argue that the story of upbeat perceptions and the story of downbeat encounters paradoxically are both correct.

Our analysis is divided into two steps. First, we analyze general perceptions of the performance of the legal system. Here we consider public attitudes toward, popular confidence in, and popular support for official justice – defined in this chapter as the courts and the police. Second, we analyze personal assessments of direct encounters with official justice. Whereas the first analytical step encompasses all individuals regardless of whether or not they reported prior experience in the legal system, the second is limited to aggrieved individuals who brought their grievances to some part of the legal system. Our essential puzzle is the glaring incongruity between upbeat general perceptions and downbeat experience-based assessments of official justice. We argue that the key to explaining this puzzle is the small proportion of people with personal experience: Intensely negative assessments of personal encounters failed to contaminate otherwise sanguine public perceptions of official justice because – borrowing terminology from Chapter 7 in this volume – the ratio of "users" to "non-users" was so miniscule. In the low-user context of China, negative experience-based assessments had only limited influence on general perceptions of official justice.

4 Gao Hongjun, "Zhongguo gongmin quanli yishi de yanjin" (The Evolution of Chinese Citizen Rights Consciousness). In *Zou xiang quanli de shidai: Zhongguo gongmin quanli fazhan yanjiu, xiuding ban* (Toward an Age of Rights: Research on the Development of Chinese Citizen Rights, Revised Edition), ed. Xia Yong (Beijing: Zhongguo zhengfa daxue chubanshe, 1999), pp. 43–106; Xueyi Chen and Tianjian Shi, "Media Effects on Political Confidence and Trust in the People's Republic of China in the Post-Tiananmen Period," *East Asia* 19, no. 3 (2001): 84–118; Pierre Landry, "The Institutional Diffusion of Courts in China: Evidence from Survey Data." In *Rule By Law: The Politics of Courts in Authoritarian Regimes*, ed. Tom Ginsburg and Tamir Moustafa (New York: Cambridge University Press, 2008), pp. 207–234.

5 Liqun Cao and Charles Hou, "A Comparison of Confidence in the Police in China and in the United States," *Journal of Criminal Justice* 29, no. 2 (2001): 87–99; Jiangsu Bureau of Statistics, "'Renmin qunzhong dui gongan gongzuo manyidu' wenjuan diaocha jieguo fenxi baogao" (Report of Analysis of Results of Questionnaire Survey on "People's Satisfaction with the Public Security"), December 1, 2004, http://www.yxtj.gov.cn/tjfx/20041211105237.asp (accessed on August 5, 2008).

Because our China surveys borrowed questions directly from Tom Tyler's 1984 Chicago survey,[6] we are in a unique position to compare general perceptions and experience-based assessments of official justice between the *low-user* context of China and the *high-user* context of Chicago. Consistent with our argument, in the Chicago survey, in which the ratio of users to non-users was high, there was no incongruity between general perceptions and experience-based assessments. Borrowing questions from the earlier Chicago survey affords us the additional opportunity to assess the extent to which the distinction between distributive justice (fairness of outcome) and procedural justice (fairness of process) applies to the Chinese context.[7] Decades of research suggest that people clearly distinguish between distributive justice and procedural justice, that people privilege the latter over the former, and that these patterns are universal.[8] Our survey data, however, fail to support any expectation that the salience of this distinction extends to China. On the contrary, respondents in our surveys conflated procedural justice and distributive justice.

We conclude from these findings that, if institutional performance and popular expectations remain constant, the gap between general perceptions and experience-based assessments of official justice will narrow as legal popularization continues to expand the legal system and swell the ranks of its users. Because the perceptions of users were so much more negative than the perceptions of non-users, growth in the population of users could serve to erode overall popular perceptions of official justice. At the same time, our findings also suggest that economic development may exert a contravening effect, serving to improve popular perceptions of official justice. Ultimately, however, only when people attach greater importance to procedural justice than to distributive justice will improvements in the objective delivery of official justice translate into more sanguine experience-based assessments of official justice. As long as they conflate procedural justice and distributive justice, people will continue to be disappointed by – and continue to assess negatively – undesirable substantive outcomes, regardless of the fairness of the procedures by which they were produced.

[6] Tom R. Tyler, *Why People Obey the Law* (New Haven, Conn.: Yale University Press, 1990).

[7] Ibid.

[8] See Robert J. MacCoun, "Voice, Control, and Belonging: The Double-Edged Sword of Procedural Fairness," *Annual Review of Law and Social Science* 1 (December 2005): 171–201, and for reviews, Rebecca L. Sandefur, "Access to Civil Justice and Race, Class, and Gender Inequality," *Annual Review of Sociology* 34 (2008): 339–358.

THE SURVEYS

Along with sociologists at Renmin University of China, we helped design and organize the first large-scale surveys in China on real-life grievances and real-life disputing behavior. The first survey was carried out in Beijing in 2001. In 2002, the rural counterpart was completed in six provinces.

In summer 2001, our survey team completed usable interviews of 1,124 households in twenty-six residents' committees in seven urban districts. In January and early February 2002, our survey team completed usable interviews of 2,902 rural households in one county in each of five provinces (Shaanxi, Henan, Jiangsu, Hunan, and Shandong) and one centrally administered city (Chongqing). Although they were not selected randomly, the six counties in which the rural survey was carried out capture enormous socioeconomic and regional diversity. They include relatively prosperous coastal areas. Indeed, one survey site is in the heart of the spectacularly developed Sunan region of southern Jiangsu Province, not far from Shanghai, where average household income approaches that of Beijing. At the other end of the spectrum are relatively poor, interior areas in Henan and Hunan.

Within the survey sites, interviewers were instructed to select households randomly and to select individual respondents randomly within households using a Kish grid. In the Beijing survey, household size and gender and age distributions are virtually identical to official information for the same year published by the Beijing Statistical Bureau. The only notable differences are with respect to income and education; our sample appears to have lower-than-average income and lower-than-average levels of education. Similarly, in the rural survey, age, education, income, and occupation distributions in the sample closely match the official statistics and published findings from nationally representative samples.

Consistent with several well-known surveys on "legal needs" and "access to justice" conducted in the United States and Europe,[9] our Chinese survey respondents were presented with lists of problem types. On the Beijing and rural survey questionnaires, the list included seventeen and

[9] American Bar Association, *Legal Needs and Civil Justice: A Survey of Americans: Major Findings from the Comprehensive Legal Needs Study* (Chicago: American Bar Association, 1994); Barbara A. Curran, *The Legal Needs of the Public: The Final Report of a National Survey* (Chicago: The Foundation, 1977); Hazel Genn, *Paths to Justice: What People Do and Think About Going to Law* (Portland, Ore.: Hart Publishing, 1999); Hazel Genn and Alan Paterson, *Paths to Justice Scotland: What People in Scotland Do and Think About Going to Law* (Portland, Ore.: Hart Publishing, 2001).

sixteen problem types, respectively, plus an "other dispute" category. The contents of the lists were tailored to each context. For example, only the Beijing survey questionnaire asked about housing rental problems, traffic citations, and home renovation disputes, and only the rural survey questionnaire asked about agricultural tax problems and family planning disputes. For each problem type, the survey respondent was asked whether she (or anyone else in the household) experienced the problem in question during the past five years.

The information collected from the questionnaires has permitted us to estimate the incidence of grievances, or potentially "justiciable events," and to estimate the relative popularity of different parts of the justice system. If a survey respondent reported having experienced a problem, she was then asked two additional pieces of information: where (or with whom) help was sought (including failure to seek help), and whether the source(s) of reported help exceeded, met, or failed to meet initial expectations.[10]

An obvious limitation of using a sample of the general population to measure assessments of personal encounters with official justice is that such encounters are few and far between. Only a small subset of any population anywhere has "justiciable problems" amenable to legal solutions, and only an even smaller subset chooses to pursue legal solutions. For this reason, the surveys also measured popular perceptions of the performance of the legal system among all respondents, even those lacking concrete experience with the legal system.[11] That is, in addition to these questions on real-life encounters, the questionnaires also asked all respondents to evaluate the performance of the police and the courts, even if they lacked real experience with the institutions they were being asked to evaluate. We borrowed questions on court and police performance from Tom Tyler's 1984 Chicago survey.[12]

[10] Although the questionnaire only asked for information about a single third party, many respondents indicated seeking multiple sources of help. See Ethan Michelson, "Justice from Above or Below? Popular Strategies for Resolving Grievances in Rural China," *The China Quarterly*, no. 93 (2008): 52, n. 25, for how we treat assessments of multiple third parties.

[11] Also see Landry, "The Institutional Diffusion of Courts in China," for a similar research design.

[12] In this chapter we limit our analysis to data from the first wave of this two-wave Chicago panel study. In 1985, one year after the first wave, 804 of the original respondents were reinterviewed. Of these, 18 with no reported legal encounters in the first wave reported a court experience and 112 reported a police experience (tabulated by the authors using data supplied by Tom Tyler). Tyler, *Why People Obey the Law*.

In this chapter we analyze nine questions about perceptions of court performance and seven questions about perceptions of police performance. All sixteen public opinion questions are presented in the Appendix. Because it would not be efficient to analyze all sixteen questions separately, we combined them into three aggregate measures. The first is calculated as the proportion of all answers that are negative, where "negative" answers are defined as response categories 4 or 5 for all questions except questions 8 and 16, for which response category 2 is "negative." Likewise, the second is calculated as the proportion of all answers that are positive, where "positive" answers are defined as response categories 1 or 2 for all questions except questions 8 and 16, for which response category 1 is "positive." The third aggregate measure is calculated as the average score of all items: questions 1 to 9 for courts (Appendix, Table A6.1) and questions 10 to 16 for police (Appendix, Table A6.2). The Cronbach alpha scores ranging from .77 to .87 indicate that these items can be combined (with high internal consistency) into aggregate scales of positive and negative attitudes toward the legal system.

In addition to borrowing attitudinal questions from Tyler's 1984 Chicago survey, we borrowed one of his methods of measuring people's assessments of their personal experiences in the legal system. Just as Tyler did, we separated satisfaction with the outcome from satisfaction with the process. Our goal was to test whether Chinese respondents, like their American counterparts, distinguished distributive justice (the desirability of the result) from procedural justice (the fairness of the process).

Despite the many similarities between the Chicago and China surveys, there also are important differences. Whereas our survey includes assessments of encounters with all kinds of third parties sought for help with all kinds of grievances, Tyler's Chicago survey is limited to assessments of experiences with the courts and police, and information about the precise event that precipitated the contact is not elicited. In Tyler's survey, personal experience with the police is defined as having called the police or having been stopped by the police in the past year. Personal experience with the court system is measured as having been part of or having observed a court case in the past year. In instances of multiple experiences (where both police and court experience were reported), respondents had to choose one or the other: They answered questions about "the experience you had with the police or courts during the past year that was *most important* to you in shaping your views about the legal system."[13] For

[13] Ibid., emphasis in original.

this reason, and because we cannot distinguish encounters precipitated by disputes from more mundane encounters, we must be cautious about using Tyler's Chicago data to estimate the frequency of legal mobilization. On the one hand, they may overestimate legal encounters insofar as they include non-disputes. On the other hand, they may underestimate legal encounters insofar as the survey instrument precluded multiple encounters.

In our presentation of findings, we alternate between aggregate and household levels of analysis. At the aggregate level, we combine the Beijing and rural samples to consider regional variations. Although our evidence is presented as simple univariate descriptions and bivariate differences, all patterns we report are robust to controls in multivariate models, details of which are omitted to simplify the presentation of evidence.

UPBEAT GENERAL PERCEPTIONS OF OFFICIAL JUSTICE

Prior research on popular perceptions of official justice in China shows generally high levels of public confidence and trust in the courts and police. Landry, analyzing data from a nationally representative Chinese survey conducted in 2003–04, reports that respondents ranked their trust in the procuracy and the courts third and fourth, respectively (behind only the CCP and the NPC), from a list of thirteen public and legal institutions.[14] In a 1993 survey, slightly more than half of the almost 5,500 respondents expressed confidence that a court would handle their case against an administrative agency lawfully and fairly.[15] In the same survey, respondents expressed an overwhelming inclination to mobilize courts and lawyers in the event of a hypothetical physical assault.[16] In a survey of more than three thousand people conducted at the same time, the average response value of 1.1 to a question about confidence in the courts was well above the midpoint of 0.0 (response categories ranged from −2.5 to 2.5 and were scaled in a positive direction).[17] Surveys reveal similarly positive public perceptions of the police. According to data from the Chinese sample in the 1991 World Values Survey, the average response value of 2.8 to a question about confidence in the police was 0.3 points higher than the midpoint of 2.5 (response categories ranged

[14] Landry, "The Institutional Diffusion of Courts in China," p. 211.

[15] Xia Yong, ed., *Zou xiang quanli de shidai*, p. 765.

[16] Ibid., pp. 866–868.

[17] Chen and Shi, "Media Effects on Political Confidence and Trust in the People's Republic of China," 94.

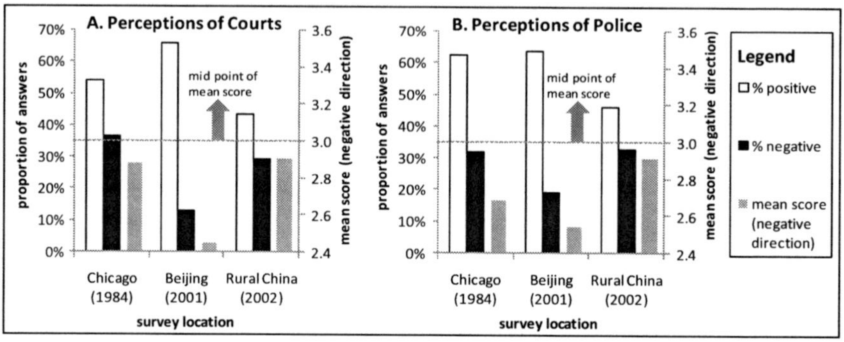

FIGURE 6.1. General Perceptions of Official Justice, Chicago (1984), Beijing (2001), and Rural China (2002). *Note:* Figure A: Chicago: N = 1,567 respondents; Beijing: N = 1,090 respondents; rural survey: N = 2,828 respondents. Figure B: Chicago: N = 1,575 respondents; Beijing: N = 1,120 respondents; rural survey: N = 2,866 respondents. *Sources:* 1984 Chicago survey data supplied by Tom Tyler; Authors' China surveys.

from 1 to 4 and were scaled in a positive direction).[18] Finally, a survey conducted in fifty-three county-level administrative units across Jiangsu Province in 2004 found overwhelmingly positive perceptions of police performance and an overwhelming willingness to seek police help.[19]

Our survey data, too, suggest that, even if China's legal system is "ragged," many people are either unaware of – or unwilling to acknowledge – this state of affairs. Figure 6.1 depicts the finding that evaluations of the police and courts were relatively sanguine in all three surveys. Moreover, of all survey samples, Beijing stands out as having the most positive perceptions of official justice. Although rural China exhibited the least positive perceptions of official justice, it does not appear to lag markedly behind Chicago. In all three samples, positive assessments always outnumbered negative assessments. Likewise, in all three samples, average scores (the gray bars) were considerably lower than the perfect midpoints, the point at which assessments would be equally positive and negative.[20]

18 Cao and Hou, "A Comparison of Confidence in the Police in China and in the United States," 91–92.

19 Jiangsu Bureau of Statistics, "'Renmin qunzhong dui gongan gongzuo manyidu' wenjuan diaocha jieguo fenxi baogao."

20 In all three surveys, response values are scaled in a negative direction; they range from 1 (most positive) to 5 (most negative). Thus, the midpoint of the scale is 3.0; an average score of 3.0 means that respondents were just as negative as they were positive.

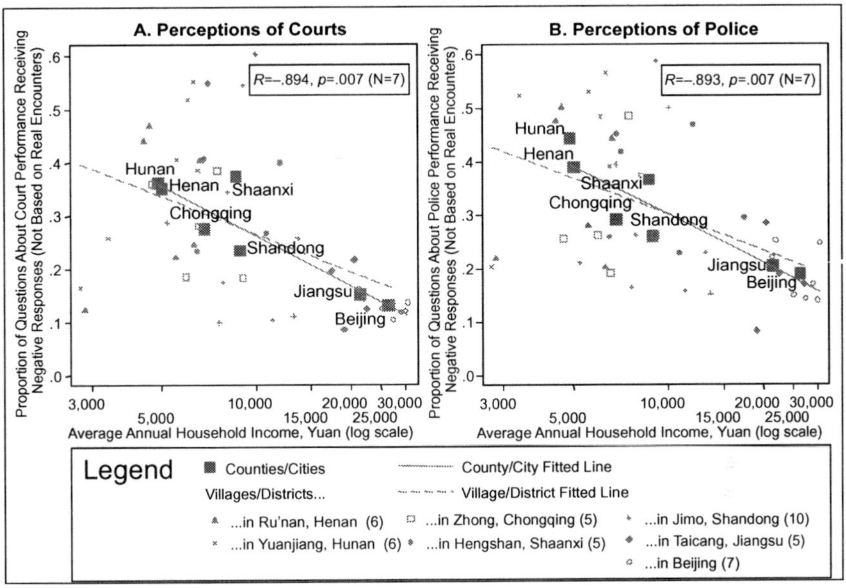

FIGURE 6.2. General Perceptions of the Performance of Courts and Police by Economic Development, Beijing (2001) and Rural China (2002). *Source:* Authors' China surveys.

The conspicuous perception gap in Figure 6.1 between respondents in rural China and Beijing appears to be a function of economic development. Figure 6.2 shows that economic development systematically reduced negative general assessments of the performance of the courts and police.

DOWNBEAT ENCOUNTERS WITH OFFICIAL JUSTICE

We just saw that Chinese respondents were more or less as upbeat as their Chicago counterparts with respect to general perceptions, supplying far more positive than negative answers. Now we turn to the issue of how positively and negatively people rated their direct, concrete experiences in the legal system. Although they reported similarly sanguine general perceptions, respondents in the Chinese and Chicago samples reported vastly different assessments of their concrete experiences. In prior research, Chinese users of official justice are shown to lament the apparent ease with which their adversaries with deeper pockets and insider connections exploit procedural loopholes and corruptly influence outcomes.[21] When court users describe their experiences, their vocabulary "shows a very low level of confidence in the fairness of judicial institutions: 'taking bribes' (*tanzang*), 'perverting justice' (*wangfa*), 'unjust treatment' (*yuanwang*), and 'releasing anger' (*chu zhe kou qi*) are recurring words *dangshiren* [users] use to describe their experiences."[22] Prior research on the police system, too, paints a picture of endemic corruption, negligence, and abuse, and of officers' "hostility to the public they are expected to serve."[23] Lawyers – in some ways the ultimate "users" of official justice – also complain bitterly about both judicial corruption and police abuse.[24]

As we see in Table 6.1, Chinese users of official justice in both of our surveys reported exceedingly negative experiences. Experiences with the courts were assessed far more negatively in rural China than in Beijing. But the sharpest contrast was between the Chinese samples and the Chicago sample. In Chicago, experience-based assessments, on the whole, remained more positive than negative. Chinese respondents were between two and three times more likely than their Chicago counterparts to report that an experience "failed to meet expectations." However, differences in evaluations across samples may not be wholly attributable to objective differences in the quality of experiences or in institutional performance. Differences could be explained in part by the fact that some Chicago respondents were evaluating their mundane, noncontentious experiences, whereas Chinese respondents were evaluating their disputing experiences. Nonetheless, the finding that negative assessments outweighed positive assessments in both Chinese samples stands in stark contrast to Landry's finding in his nationally representative sample that court users were far more positive than negative about their experiences.[25]

Consistent with the oft-replicated finding that people differentiate distributive and procedural justice,[26] Table 6.2 shows that in Chicago, experience-based assessments of outcome and process were equivalent about two-thirds of the time with respect to the courts and only about

[21] Gallagher, "Mobilizing the Law in China."
[22] Michelson, "Unhooking from the State: Chinese Lawyers in Transition," 267.
[23] Fu, "Zhou Yongkang and the Recent Police Reform in China," 245; also see Wong, "The Police Legitimacy Crisis and Police Law Reform in China."
[24] Ethan Michelson, "Lawyers, Political Embeddedness, and Institutional Continuity in China's Transition from Socialism," *American Journal of Sociology* 113, no. 2 (2007): 352–414.
[25] Landry, "The Institutional Diffusion of Courts in China," pp. 218–219.
[26] MacCoun, "Voice, Control, and Belonging"; Sandefur, "Access to Civil Justice and Race, Class, and Gender Inequality."

TABLE 6.1. *Experience-based assessments of official justice, Chicago (1984), Beijing (2001), and Rural China (2002)*

	Outcome			Process		
Evaluation	Chicago	Beijing	Rural China	Chicago	Beijing	Rural China
A. Courts						
exceeded expectations	32%	0%	4%	28%	0%	6%
met expectations	47%	64%	33%	50%	64%	37%
failed to meet expectations	21%	36%	61%	21%	36%	57%
TOTAL	100%	100%	98%	99%	100%	100%
N	121	11	84	137	11	82
B. Police						
exceeded expectations	32%	5%	2%	33%	5%	7%
met expectations	40%	19%	36%	44%	19%	39%
failed to meet expectations	27%	76%	62%	22%	76%	54%
TOTAL	99%	100%	100%	99%	100%	100%
N	381	42	47	447	42	46

Note: Not all totals equal 100 percent because of rounding errors.
Sources: 1984 Chicago survey data supplied by Tom Tyler; Authors' China surveys.

TABLE 6.2. *Overlap between experience-based assessments of official justice outcomes and procedures, Chicago (1984), Beijing (2001), and Rural China (2002)*

	Chicago (1984)	Beijing (2001)	Rural China (2002)
Encounters with courts			
% Encounters in which outcome and process assessed identically	67%	100%	92%
Correlation between outcome and process (Pearson's *r*)	0.61	1.00	0.84
N	119	11	44
Encounters with police			
% Encounters in which outcome and process assessed identically	54%	100%	86%
Correlation between outcome and process (Pearson's *r*)	0.43	1.00	0.62
N	344	41	78

Sources: Chicago survey data supplied by Tom Tyler; Authors' China surveys.

half of the time with respect to the police. In the Chinese samples, by contrast, the two assessments were equivalent about 90 percent of the time. In other words, whereas distributive justice and procedural justice were only moderately correlated in Chicago, they were almost perfectly correlated in China. Perhaps Chicago respondents were better able to separate a negative outcome (a speeding ticket) from a positive process (a courteous police officer) because they were often evaluating undisputed, low-stakes events such as routine traffic citations. Although measures of the association between distributive justice and procedural justice contained in Table 6.2 are limited to encounters with the courts and the police, the association is even stronger when all sources of help are considered. In Beijing, evaluations of outcome and process were identical in 91 percent of all 172 reported disputes and were correlated at $R = .89$. In the rural survey, evaluations of outcome and process were identical in 81 percent of all 910 reported disputes and were correlated at $R = .72$. This pattern is at odds with Gallagher's finding that plaintiffs in Shanghai possessed the "ability to distinguish between the legal process and outcome. . . . "[27] Elsewhere in the world, where people distinguish

[27] Gallagher, "Mobilizing the Law in China," 804.

process and outcome, fair procedures provide a "cushion of support" against undesirable outcomes.[28] An important implication of the conflation of procedural justice and distributive justice in China, therefore, is the inability of positive procedures to foster popular tolerance for negative outcomes.

Because the Chicago survey limited assessments to experiences with the courts and police, we are unable to see how official justice stacked up against alternative sources of help. The China surveys, by contrast, were designed to do just this. Because distributive justice and procedural justice were virtually synonymous and therefore redundant in China, we combined the two measures into a binary measure of dissatisfaction: An assessment is defined as "negative" if either the outcome "failed to meet expectations" or the process "failed to meet expectations." Generally, the closer to the legal system people brought their disputes, the less positive and the more negative they assessed their experiences. Bilateral negotiations and informal relations were the most positively rated sources of help. The next most popularly rated sources of help were local community leaders (neighborhood and workplace leaders in Beijing and village leaders in the rural areas). Higher-level government agencies followed next in the satisfaction ratings. At the bottom of the rankings were the police, lawyers, and courts. In both surveys, lawyers were rated more negatively than any other source of help (see Figure 6.3). To be sure, differences in satisfaction to some degree reflect differences in problems: Problems that were less serious and easier to resolve were overrepresented at local levels, and problems that were more intractable and difficult to resolve were overrepresented at higher levels. However, this pattern persists even when the nature of the problem is held constant.[29] It also stands in stark contrast to Landry's finding that village leaders received the lowest levels of public trust and the procuracy and courts received among the highest levels of public trust.[30] As we are about to see, in our surveys people rated their informed personal experiences and their uninformed perceptions very differently.

Experience-based assessments of the performance of the courts exhibited enormous regional variation. Figure 6.3 shows that Beijing residents rated the performance of courts quite favorably (even though they rated the performance of lawyers very negatively). In fact, Beijing may merely

[28] Tyler, *Why People Obey the Law*, pp. 98–101.
[29] Michelson, "Justice from Above or Below?"
[30] Landry, "The Institutional Diffusion of Courts in China."

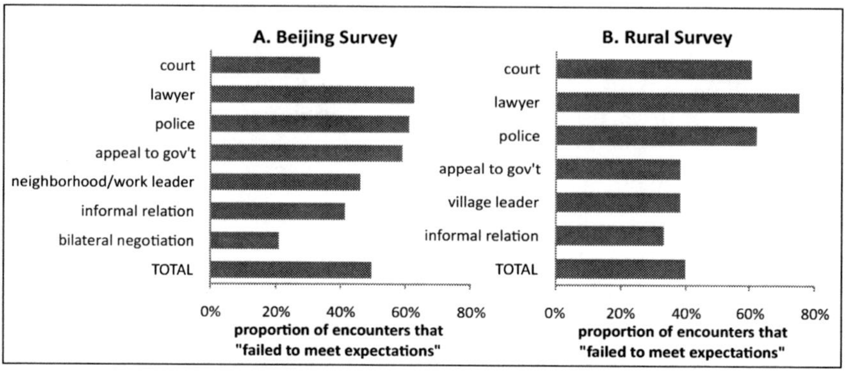

FIGURE 6.3. Experience-Based Assessments by Competing Sources of Help, Beijing (2001) and Rural China (2002). *Note:* Beijing: N = 199 encounters; rural survey: N = 956 encounters. In the Beijing survey, "bilateral negotiation" was inferred from information on the sources of help. The rural survey questionnaire included "bilateral negotiation" as a response category but did not ask respondents to assess its effectiveness or fairness. *Source:* Authors' China surveys.

represent the more general effect of economic development: Figure 6.4 shows that the probability of a negative experience in court diminished with economic development. Indeed, although the courts were evaluated far more negatively in rural China than in Beijing, we can see that economic development completely eliminated the gap.

EXPLAINING THE INCONGRUITY OF UPBEAT PERCEPTIONS AND DOWNBEAT ENCOUNTERS

In the Chicago survey, general perceptions and experience-based assessments were essentially congruent. Chicago respondents were upbeat both in their responses to a large battery of questions framed without reference to personal encounters with the institutions they were asked to evaluate and to questions about their actual experiences (reporting that they "exceeded expectations" about one-third of the time). That is, their assessments based on actual experiences were congruous with their assessments based on general perceptions. Although respondents in the Chinese samples were more or less as upbeat as their Chicago counterparts in terms of general perceptions, they evaluated their actual experiences far more negatively (almost never reporting that they "exceeded expectations"). We were surprised by this apparent ungluing of popular perceptions from

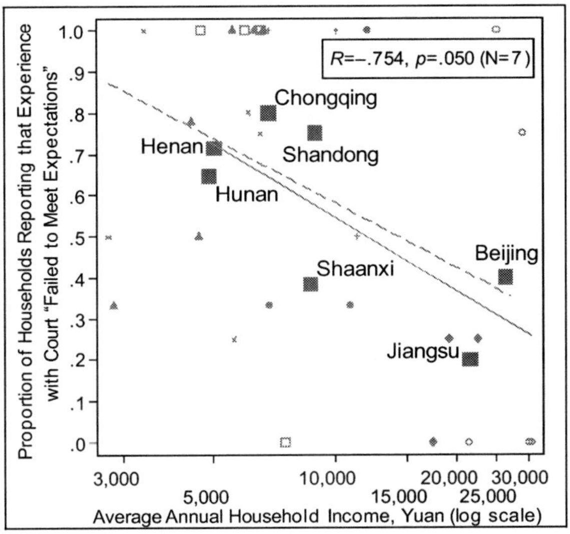

FIGURE 6.4. Incidence of Negative Experience-Based Assessments of Court Performance by Locality, Beijing (2001) and Rural China (2002). *Note:* See Figure 6.2 for legend. N = 25 rural villages and N = 5 Beijing districts rather than the full N = 44 because of the large numbers of respondents lacking court experience. *Source:* Authors' China surveys.

actual experience in the Chinese samples – the dramatic disconnect or incongruity between resoundingly negative assessments of personal experience with official justice and resoundingly positive general perceptions of and popular attitudes toward official justice. Explaining this puzzling incongruity in the Chinese samples is one of our tasks in this chapter.

One possible explanation is a sampling bias. Perhaps, given our less than perfectly random samples, the "users" in our samples are disproportionately disgruntled. Another possible explanation is a "political desirability bias": a reluctance to disclose politically illegitimate or deviant practices or beliefs. According to Rosen, "There is little basis in Chinese traditional political culture to suggest that citizens will reveal their true feelings on a questionnaire, even one in which respondents may omit their names."[31] Rosen argues that political pressure to conform to state goals exaggerates the sanguinity of public opinion toward state institutions and

[31] Stanley Rosen, "Survey Research in the People's Republic of China: Some Methodological Problems," *Canadian and International Education* 16, no. 1 (1987): 191.

policies: In China, "many surveys are seemingly conducted in support of a political agenda, to affirm a conclusion already predetermined.... It is important to confirm broad support for a given state policy.... [S]imilarly, it is important to show that one's charges are being properly socialized."[32] However, recent evidence of "an increased sense of personal autonomy coupled with a reduction in anxieties about offending authorities" suggests that a political desirability bias in Chinese surveys may have diminished over time.[33] Although some sort of bias may help account for the puzzling incongruity in the Chinese samples between upbeat perceptions and downbeat encounters, our explanation centers on the effect and prevalence of direct experience in the legal system.

Prior research has established that direct experience greatly influences attitudes toward legal institutions. (See Chapter 7 in this volume for a review of some of the literature on this relationship.)[34] Gallagher encountered "informed disenchantment" among users of a Shanghai legal-aid center: disillusionment and disappointment with the legal system fostered by concrete, first-hand experience.[35] In Russia, Gerber and Mendelson found that negative personal experience with police significantly eroded general perceptions of both the police and the courts.[36] As we now see, our survey results support these findings and are consistent with its flipside: uninformed enchantment among non-users and a naïve confidence in institutions with which informants have no concrete experience. Absent direct experience, perceptions are based on second-hand information and abstract expectations. Respondents in all three surveys had high expectations of the performance of their respective official justice systems. In China, initial expectations may have been further boosted by success stories in the media that provide a plethora of "good news" about official justice.[37] Yet, in most instances, reality fell short of expectations. As we

[32] Ibid., 193.

[33] Donald J. Treiman, William M. Mason, Yao Lu, Pan Yi, Qi Yaqiang, and Song Shige, "Observations on the Design and Implementation of Sample Surveys in China." In *Social Transformation in Chinese Societies*, ed. Bian Yan-jie, Chan Kwok-bun, and Cheung Tak-sing (Leiden: Brill), no. 1 (2006): 81–112.

[34] Also see Theodore P. Gerber and Sarah E. Mendelson, "Public Experiences of Police Violence and Corruption in Contemporary Russia: A Case of Predatory Policing?" *Law & Society Review* 42, no. 1 (2008): 1–43.

[35] Gallagher, "Mobilizing the Law in China."

[36] Gerber and Mendelson, "Public Experiences of Police Violence and Corruption in Contemporary Russia."

[37] Ibid.; Daniela Stockmann and Mary Gallagher, "Mass Media Mobilization as a Means of Legal Reform in China." Paper Prepared for the annual meeting of the American

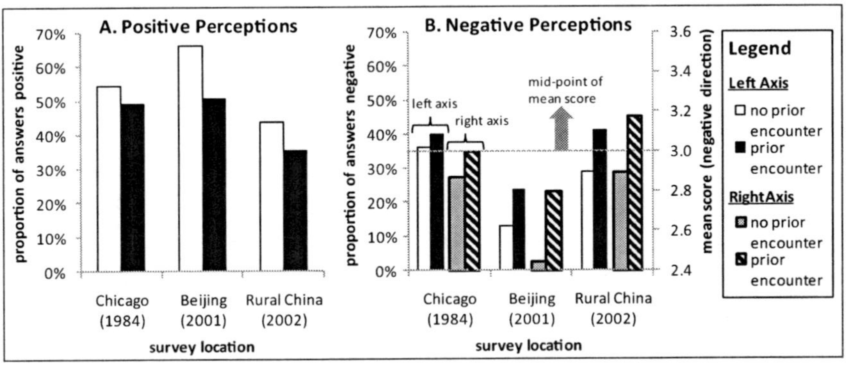

FIGURE 6.5. General Perceptions of Courts, by Personal Experience, Chicago (1984), Beijing (2001), and Rural China (2002). *Note:* Chicago: N = 1,567 respondents; Beijing: N = 1,090 respondents; rural survey: N = 2,828 respondents. In Figure A, all *t*-tests of differences are statistically significant at $p < .05$ (two-tailed). In Figure B, "proportion of answers negative" (left axis) *t*-tests of differences in Chicago, Beijing, and rural China are statistically significant at $p = .12$, $p = .003$, and $p < .001$, respectively (two-tailed); "mean score" (right axis) differences in Chicago, Beijing, and rural China are statistically significant at $p = .059$, $p = .003$, and $p < .001$, respectively (two-tailed). *Sources:* 1984 Chicago survey data supplied by Tom Tyler; Authors' China surveys.

see in Figures 6.5 and 6.6, in all three surveys, experience in the legal system reduced confidence in and support for official justice. Personal experience was associated with negative perceptions of official justice.

Beyond the *quantity* of experience (i.e., some experience versus no experience), however, the *quality* of experience also matters. In all three surveys, respondents with no prior experience were equally or similarly confident in and supportive of official justice, as people who were satisfied with their prior experience with official justice. Respondents with negative personal experiences, by contrast, had far less confidence in and support for official justice than those with positive personal experiences. Figure 6.7 depicts the effect of evaluations of personal experience on general perceptions in Chicago. In Chicago, compared with respondents with positive personal experience, respondents with negative personal experience reported significantly more negative perceptions of courts and police.

Political Science Association, Chicago, August 30–September 2, 2007. (But see Chen and Shi, "Media Effects on Political Confidence and Trust in the People's Republic of China," for precisely the opposite argument.)

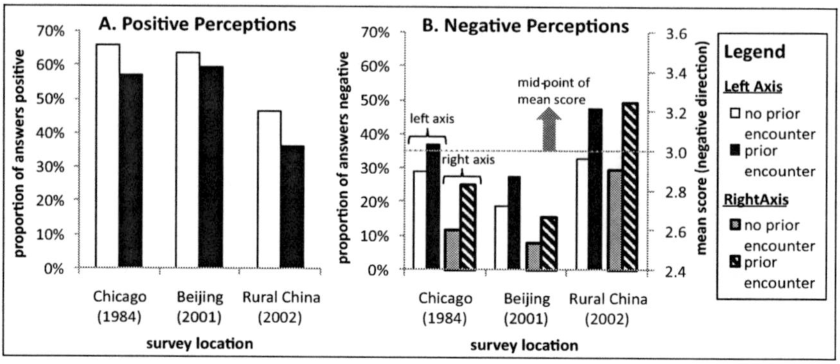

FIGURE 6.6. General Perceptions of Police by Personal Experience, Chicago (1984), Beijing (2001), and Rural China (2002). *Note:* Chicago: N = 1,575 respondents; Beijing: N = 1,120 respondents; rural survey: N = 2,866 respondents. In Figure A, *t*-tests of differences in Chicago, Beijing, and rural China are statistically significant at $p = .001$, $p = .32$, and $p = .03$, respectively (two-tailed). In Figure B, all *t*-tests of "proportion of answers negative" (left axis) differences are statistically significant at $p = .01$ (two-tailed); all *t*-tests of "mean score" (right axis) differences in Chicago, Beijing, and rural China are statistically significant at $p = .001$, $p = .17$, and $p = .01$, respectively (two-tailed). *Sources:* 1984 Chicago survey data supplied by Tom Tyler; Authors' China surveys.

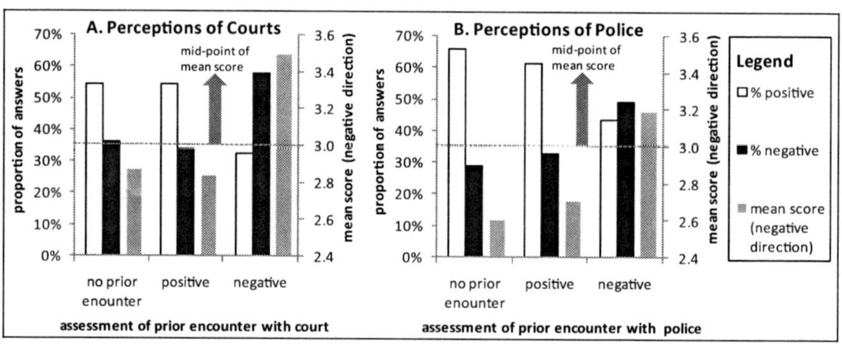

FIGURE 6.7. General Perceptions of Official Justice, by Personal Experience, Disaggregated by Evaluations of Personal Experience, Chicago (1984). *Note:* Figure A: N = 1,567 respondents; Figure B: N = 1,575. In both figures, all *t*-tests of differences between respondents with negative and positive prior experiences are statistically significant at $p < .001$ (two-tailed). *Source:* 1984 Chicago survey data supplied by Tom Tyler.

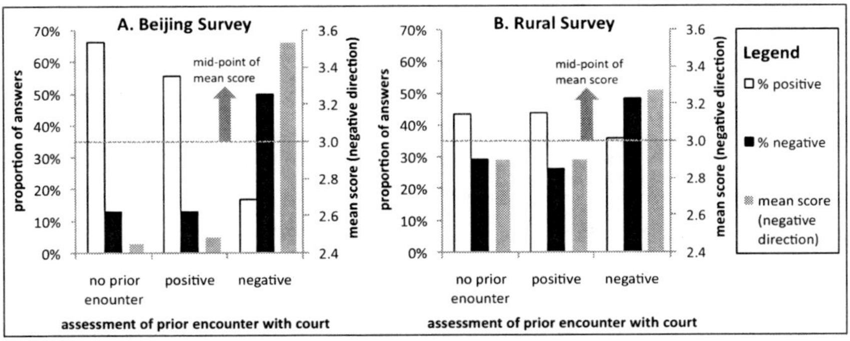

FIGURE 6.8. General Perceptions of Courts by Personal Experience, Disaggregated by Experience-Based Assessments, Beijing (2001) and Rural China (2002). *Note:* Beijing: N = 1,090 respondents; rural survey: N = 2,828 respondents. In Figure A, all *t*-tests of differences between respondents with negative and positive prior experiences are statistically significant at $p < .05$ (two-tailed). In Figure B, with the exception of "% positive assessments," all remaining *t*-tests of differences between respondents with negative and positive prior experiences are statistically significant at $p < .05$ (two-tailed). *Source:* Authors' China surveys.

Although the negative personal experience dramatically eroded perceptions of official justice, positive personal experience did not enhance perceptions of court performance and only modestly enhanced perceptions of police performance. It is for this reason that, when personal experience is not disaggregated into negative and positive personal experience, any experience appears to erode perceptions of official justice. In other words, the effect of positive personal experience was too small to countervail the effect of negative personal experience.

The results of the China surveys follow the Chicago pattern. As we see in Figures 6.8 and 6.9, in both Beijing and rural China, negative personal experience eroded general perceptions of the performance of courts and police. Moreover, respondents with positive personal experience were no more confident in and supportive of official justice than were respondents without personal experience.

Now that we have established the corrosive effect of experience in general and negative experience in particular on general perceptions of courts and police, we come to the crux of our explanation: The overall incidence of seeking help in the legal system in general and the overall incidence of disappointing experiences in the legal system in particular are critical determinants of a population's overall perceptions of

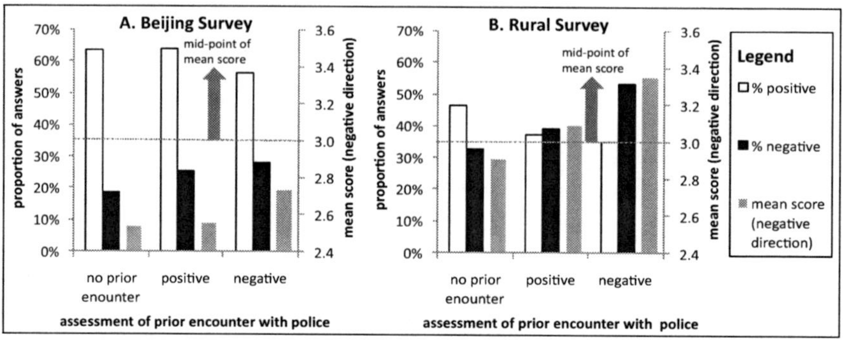

FIGURE 6.9. General Perceptions of Police by Personal Experience, Disaggregated by Experience-Based Assessments, Beijing (2001) and Rural China (2002). *Note:* Beijing: N = 1,120 respondents; rural survey: N = 2,866 respondents. In Figure B, *t*-tests of differences between respondents with negative and positive prior experiences are statistically significant at $p < .10$ for "% negative assessments" and "mean score" (one-tailed). *Source:* Authors' China surveys.

official justice. Where a population has more experience with official justice, public perceptions will be more heavily influenced by personal experience. Conversely, where a population has less experience with official justice, public perceptions will be less influenced by personal experience. The relative proportions of the population with positive and negative experiences influence the overall mix of public perceptions. Consider the metaphor of adding drops of ink to a pool of water. The extent to which ink drops color the water is a function of both quality and quantity. In tiny quantities, even the darkest ink will have a negligible effect on the color of a pool of water. But as its quantity increases, its effect on the color of the pool of water as a whole will grow.

To be sure, non-users elsewhere in the world are afflicted by uninformed enchantment. Americans, too, have misguided impressions and unrealistic expectations of their legal system.[38] But in the United States, the high ratio of users to non-users darkens the sanguinity of uninformed enchantment. In China, by contrast, because of the very small number of people with personal experience in the legal system, the intensely negative evaluations of personal experience reflected in Table 6.1 exerted only a trivial impact on public perceptions of the performance of the legal system.

[38] William M. O'Barr and John M. Conley, "Lay Expectations of the Civil Justice System," *Law & Society Review* 22, no. 1 (1988): 137–161.

Table 6.3 contains estimates of the prevalence of direct experience with official justice. The Chinese estimates are calculated from information on experiences with pursuing help to redress concrete grievances.[39] The Chicago estimates, however, are calculated from information on encounters regardless of whether or not they were in the context of a dispute. Thus, the Chinese and Chicago estimates are not perfectly comparable. Moreover, many respondents in the Chicago survey assessed their more superficial, mundane experiences with the police and the court system. For example, whereas some respondents assessed their own court cases, others assessed their experience observing a trial.[40] If the potentially more inclusive definition of legal experience inflated our Chicago prevalence estimates, this effect is surely offset both by the respondents' inability to report more than one encounter and by the shorter time frame in which the encounter occurred. Whereas reported encounters (often multiple encounters) in the China surveys occurred during the previous five years, in the Chicago survey the respondents' single encounters occurred within the previous year.

As we see in Table 6.3, only approximately one in twenty respondents in the Chinese samples reported direct encounters with the courts or police. In China, a low incidence of appeals to the official justice system in part reflects enduring bottom-up popular demand for informal local alternatives. Indeed, this is the general case around the world, even in the United States.[41] At the same time, a growing body of research shows that political forces at play in China discourage the use of the legal

[39] Chinese survey respondents were asked additional questions about their experience in court unrelated to concrete grievances. "Have you ever appeared in court as a defendant in a criminal case?" "Have you ever appeared in court as a defendant in a non-criminal case?" "Have you ever appeared in court as a plaintiff?" Adding these additional sources of information to the data on grievances increases the estimated court utilization rates in Table 3 from 0.9 percent to 2.6 percent in Beijing and from 2.7 percent to 4.9 percent in rural China.

[40] Tyler, *Why People Obey the Law*, pp. 190–191.

[41] Robert C. Ellickson, *Order Without Law: How Neighbors Settle Disputes* (Cambridge: Harvard University Press, 1994); David M. Engel, "The Oven Bird's Song: Insiders, Outsiders, and Personal Injuries in an American Community," *Law & Society Review* 18, no. 4 (1984): 551–582; Marc Galanter, "Reading the Landscape of Disputes: What We Know and Don't Know (and Think We Know) About Our Allegedly Contentious and Litigious Society," *UCLA Law Review* 31, no. 1 (1983): 4–71; Carol J. Greenhouse, *Praying for Justice: Faith, Order, and Community in an American Town* (Ithaca: Cornell University Press, 1986); Carol J. Greenhouse, Barbara Yngvesson, and David M. Engel, *Law and Community in Three American Towns* (Ithaca: Cornell University Press, 1994).

TABLE 6.3. *Prevalence of direct experience with official justice, Chicago (1984), Beijing (2001), and Rural China (2002)*

	Courts			Police			Either		
	Chicago (1984)	Beijing (2001)	Rural China (2002)	Chicago (1984)	Beijing (2001)	Rural China (2002)	Chicago (1984)	Beijing (2001)	Rural China (2002)
yes	9.3%	0.9%	2.7%	37.2%	4.4%	1.6%	46.5%	5.2%	4.1%
no	90.7%	99.1%	97.3%	62.8%	95.6%	98.4%	53.5%	94.8%	95.9%
TOTAL	100.0%	100.0%	100.0%	100.0%	100.0%	100.0%	100.0%	100.0%	100.0%
N	1,575	1,124	2,902	1,575	1,124	2,902	1,575	1,124	2,902

Sources: 1984 Chicago survey data supplied by Tom Tyler; Authors' China surveys.

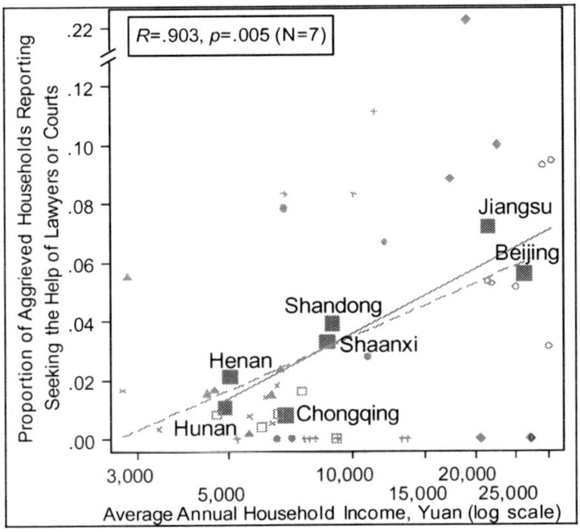

FIGURE 6.10. Incidence of Escalating Grievances to Lawyers and Courts, by Locality, Beijing (2001) and Rural China (2002). *Note:* See Figure 6.2 for legend. Because they are part of the official justice system, judicial (*sifa*) offices are included in the definition of courts. *Source:* Authors' China surveys.

system above and beyond the general case. State policies, in the service of the larger, overriding priority to preserve social and political stability, function to deflect disputes away from the courts – for example, by returning them to the localities from which they emerged or by channeling them through government complaints offices.[42] We should not be surprised, therefore, to find that the legal system is mobilized infrequently relative to the large menu of options outside the legal system.

Although legal mobilization was relatively rare in the Chinese samples, it exhibited tremendous regional variations. Figure 6.10 shows that the legal utilization rates were strongly and positively related to the level of economic development. Part of the reason for this relationship surely lies in differences in the nature of the disputes. First, in Beijing and prosperous parts of rural China, higher economic stakes may push more disputes to

[42] Yongshun Cai, "Managed Participation in China," *Political Science Quarterly* 119, no. 3 (2004): 425–451; Christopher Heurlin and Susan Whiting, "Villagers Against the State: The Politics of Land Disputes." Paper prepared for the American Political Science Association annual meeting, Chicago, August 30, 2007; Carl Minzner, "*Xinfang*: An Alternative to Formal Chinese Legal Institutions," *Stanford Journal of International Law* 42, no. 1 (2006): 103–179.

the courts. Second, insofar as criminal matters and other problems that activate top-down state intervention and that demand court adjudication are relatively common in urban areas, we should not be surprised to find a greater probability of litigation in Beijing than in rural China. However, two additional reasons unrelated to the nature of the disputes help explain the regional variations in the utilization of courts and lawyers. First, wealthier areas enjoy greater geographical proximity to the courts, which are concentrated in cities. Second, court fees and other related expenses represent financial barriers to official justice. Because localities that are more remote also tend to be poorer, low levels of economic development represent a "double whammy" against the utilization of lawyers and courts in rural China. Indeed, when the nature of the dispute is held constant, the positive effect of economic development persists. In other words, all else being equal, including the nature of the dispute, economic development facilitates access to official justice.[43]

But even compared to the parts of China with the greatest prevalence of experience, legal mobilization in Chicago was clearly of an entirely different order of magnitude – even if the gap is discounted because of the measurement differences discussed previously. Almost half of all respondents providing their general opinions had had some kind of contact with the legal system in the previous year. Because the Chicago respondents with informed opinions of the performance of the legal system were almost as numerous as their counterparts with uninformed opinions, those with prior experience in the legal system heavily influenced the overall mix of perceptions of the legal system. Even though users of the legal system in China were far more intensely negative about their experiences than their counterparts in Chicago, they were so greatly outnumbered by non-users of the legal system that their informed voices of disenchantment were drowned out by the far more numerous uninformed voices of enchantment. Likewise, relatively negative general perceptions of the legal system in Russia could, at least in part, be a function of a higher incidence of negative experiences with police. Whereas fewer than 5 percent of respondents in our Chinese samples reported *any* experience

[43] Ethan Michelson, "Climbing the Dispute Pagoda: Grievances and Appeals to the Official Justice System in Rural China," *American Sociological Review* 72, no. 3 (2007): 459–485; Benjamin L. Read and Ethan Michelson, "Mediating the Mediation Debate: Conflict Resolution and the Local State in China," *Journal of Conflict Resolution* 52, no. 5 (2008): 737–764.

with the police in the previous five years (Table 6.3), in Russia 14 percent of respondents reported a (direct or indirect) *negative* experience with the police (i.e., police misconduct) in the previous two or three years.[44] In other words, the impact of overwhelmingly negative assessments of personal experience in China was diluted by the vast majority of the population without personal experience.

IMPLICATIONS AND CONCLUSIONS

According to our survey data, the Chinese legal system played a relatively marginal role in 2001 and 2002. Not only were utilization rates low, but its performance also was rated relatively negatively by those who utilized it. Relative to how they assessed their experiences elsewhere in the justice system, people rated their experiences in the legal system unfavorably. Aggrieved individuals not only more frequently sought local help from informal relations and community and workplace leaders, but they also evaluated their experiences with these sources of help far more favorably than they evaluated their experiences with formal legal institutions.

At the same time, however, the survey data reflect a remarkably high degree of public confidence in and support for official justice in China. The Chinese public is by no means wholly insulated from news of police brutality and callousness. Occasionally, negative stories receive widespread coverage and stir popular sympathy. Examples include the vociferous public outcry over the beating death of Sun Zhigang in 2003 while in police custody; national outrage about the death of three-year-old Li Siyi, who starved at home after police arrested her mother and allegedly ignored her pleas to rescue the young girl; a riot at a police station in Guizhou Province involving thousands of people angered by allegations of police efforts to cover up the rape and murder of a teenaged girl to protect two suspects who happened to be relatives of local police officers; and the case of Yang Jia, who won some degree of support from "netizens" following his arrest for murdering six police officers allegedly in response to being viciously beaten by police.[45] Nonetheless,

[44] Gerber and Mendelson, "Public Experiences of Police Violence and Corruption in Contemporary Russia," p. 17.

[45] Keith J. Hand, "Using Law for a Righteous Purpose: The Sun Zhigang Incident and Evolving Forms of Citizen Action in the People's Republic of China," *Columbia Journal*

our survey data suggest that such popular reactions to occasionally publicized instances of police abuse have not turned the tide of public sentiment shaped by a larger and steadier stream of media reports of heroism and professional integrity in the police force. General perceptions of police in Beijing and rural China remained, on balance, favorable in 2001 and 2002. In light of the dramatic incongruity in our surveys between upbeat general perceptions of official justice and downbeat encounters with official justice, our first conclusion is that uninformed, non–experience-based perceptions are poor measures of institutional performance. The disjuncture in the Chinese samples between upbeat general perceptions and downbeat experience-based assessments suggests the methodological problem of information asymmetry and the perils of inferring institutional performance from questions asked in the abstract without reference to concrete encounters with the institutions in question.

Our second conclusion is that familiarity breeds contempt. This is markedly different from Landry's conclusion that Chinese court users, on the whole, are satisfied with their experiences and that these happy experiences are conveyed to non-users, resulting in widespread support for litigation.[46] As we saw, positive popular sentiment is concentrated among people either with no experience or with positive experiences in the legal system. Consistent with the concept of "informed disenchantment,"[47] personal experience in the legal system eroded confidence in and support for official justice. At the same time, the vast majority of people with no personal experience in the legal system exhibited "uninformed enchantment" with official justice. Because our survey respondents assessed their personal experiences so overwhelmingly negatively, and because negative personal experiences fostered negative general assessments of the performance of the legal system, more widespread popular experience in the legal system should translate into more negative public opinions of the legal system, assuming that nothing else changes. Consistent with previous research showing that court users often become "little experts" who

of Transnational Law 45 (2006): 14–94; Jill Drew, "Anger Over Rape-Murder Case Sparks Riot in China." *The Washington Post*, June 29, 2008, p. A7, 2008; Malcolm Moore, "Police 'Killer' is Chinese Hero," *The Daily Telegraph*, August 27, 2008, p. 17; John Pomfret, "Child's Death Highlights Problems in Chinese Justice," *The Washington Post*, July 3, 2003, p. A1.

46 Landry, "The Institutional Diffusion of Courts in China."

47 Gallagher, "Mobilizing the Law in China."

spread information about their disappointing experiences,[48] our findings suggest that, all else being equal, greater aggregate utilization of the legal system should compromise popular support for and confidence in the legal system.

However, the survey findings also suggest that not all else is equal. Economic development exerted an enormously powerful positive influence on the legal system. Economic development positively promoted utilization of the legal system (among similarly aggrieved households), assessments of the performance of the legal system, and popular perceptions of the legal system. Thus, our third conclusion is that the best medicine for treating China's ailing legal system is economic development, even though our survey data do not allow us to identify concrete mechanisms behind this association. Economic development may help to solve the problem of limited access to and the unsatisfactory performance of the court system. In the meantime, however, as we wait for the benefits of economic development to spread to the poor and remote parts of rural China, the survey findings also suggest that aggrieved villagers will benefit from continued access to local, informal solutions that appear to work relatively effectively.

To reiterate our conclusions thus far, general perceptions of official justice were very favorable to an important degree because so few people experienced it. Thus, until the performance of the court system in China improves, policy measures that increase its popular utilization may have the counterintuitive and paradoxical effect of compromising the popular confidence and support it currently enjoys. But, once again, our survey findings also show that the courts deliver the most satisfaction in the most developed parts of China. To the extent that real-life experiences in the legal system are the least favorable in the least developed parts of rural China, and to the extent that real-life encounters with official justice tend to reduce confidence in and support for official justice, policies that encourage the popular mobilization of the law could backfire by fostering "informed disenchantment"[49] on a massive scale. Our fourth conclusion, therefore, is that policy efforts to leverage local solutions with proven records of success outside the legal system should be complemented by policy efforts to improve the performance of the court system. All else being equal, better experiences in the legal system

[48] Ibid., 807–808.

[49] Ibid.

should improve public perceptions of the performance of the legal system.

At the same time, however, even if the objective performance of the legal system does not improve, more widespread utilization and greater public awareness of its services may serve to enhance satisfaction with personal efforts to utilize it by lowering expectations of its performance. Intensely negative assessments of encounters with official justice reflected in our surveys may have been, at least in part, a function of excessively high expectations fostered by state propaganda.[50] On the one hand, as we already concluded, further legal popularization may have the effect of negatively impacting public confidence in and support for the legal system. On the other hand, however, it may also have the effect of lowering expectations and improving experience-based assessments of official justice. If continued legal popularization in China serves to enhance public awareness of the fallibility and imperfection of the legal system, it may also serve to lower expectations of its performance, to increase satisfaction with personal experience using it, and, thus, to enhance its overall health. Thus, our fifth conclusion is that, just as general perceptions may decline in the direction of experience-based assessments, experience-based assessments also may rise in the direction of general perceptions. Ewick and Silbey argue that, in the American context, law's strength and durability is in part a function of contradictory popular perceptions of law both as imperfect and subject to exploitation (a "game") and as the flawless realization of an ideal ("god").[51] Unrealistically positive perceptions of any legal system, they contend, are unhealthy and dangerous insofar as public expectations of infallibility breed intolerance of failure. Thus, a modest dose of distrust may promote the health and well-being of rule of law systems. Rather than viewing the gap between the law in action and the law on the books as a problem, they view it as a source of institutional strength – within limits.[52]

> It is precisely because people believe that there is equality under law but also understand that sometimes the "haves" come out ahead that legality

[50] Ibid.

[51] Patricia Ewick and Susan S. Silbey, *The Common Place of Law: Stories from Everyday Life* (Chicago: University of Chicago Press, 1998), pp. 228, 232–233, 247–249.

[52] Ibid., p. 248.

> is sustained as a powerful structure of social action.... This contradictory embrace of law – a god and gimmick – is not a weakness nor flaw in the public culture. Nor is it a mark of confusion or naiveté. Legality, and the rule of law, is durable and powerful because it is cherished as both sacred and profane.[53]

Although the foregoing conclusions identify mechanisms by which experience-based assessments of official justice and general perceptions of its performance may become more closely aligned over time, our sixth and final conclusion identifies a reason why this gap may persist. As we have seen, people in China assess distributive justice (satisfaction with the outcome) and procedural justice (satisfaction with the fairness of the process) virtually identically. People's low tolerance for outcomes that go against them, even if they were reached through objectively fair procedures, are consistent with portraits of substantive justice trumping procedural fairness both in traditional Chinese legal culture and in socialist legality.[54] Regardless of its origins, however, the popular conflation of fairness with winning precludes greater congruity between assessments of personal experience in the legal system and general perceptions of the legal system. Litigation is a zero-sum game; parties to litigation lose half the time. For this reason, as long as people assess their personal experiences in terms of substantive outcomes, on average experience-based assessments will be more downbeat than general perceptions. Moreover, the unchecked persistence of a popular conflation of procedural justice and distributive justice may neutralize the benefits of procedural reforms. Only when people define the quality of their experiences in terms of their perceptions of fairness will objective improvements in procedures positively improve experience-based assessments of official justice in China.

[53] Susan S. Silbey and Patricia Ewick, "The Rule of Law – Sacred and Profane," *Society* 37, no. 6 (2000): 56.

[54] W. Yuen and D. Roebuck, "The Influence of Traditional Morality on the Enforcement of Foreign Arbitral Awards." In *Yearbook Law & Legal Practice in East Asia 1996*, vol. 2, ed. A. J. de Roo and R. W. Jagtenberg (The Hague: Kluwer Law International, 1996), pp. 47, 51; Stanley B. Lubman, *Bird in a Cage: Legal Reform in China after Mao* (Stanford: Stanford University Press, 1999), p. 23; Jerome A. Cohen, "Reforming China's Civil Procedure: Judging the Courts," *The American Journal of Comparative Law* 45, no. 4 (1997): 793–804; Bin Liang, *The Changing Chinese Legal System, 1978-Present: Centralization of Power and Rationalization of the Legal System* (New York: Routledge, 2008), pp. 166–167.

APPENDIX

TABLE A6.1. *Perceptions of the courts*

	Chicago, 1984	Beijing, 2001	Rural China, 2002
1. The courts generally guarantee everyone a fair trial. (Q21g)			
1. agree strongly	6%	7%	5%
2. agree	53%	66%	52%
3. neutral	–	17%	15%
4. disagree	35%	9%	26%
5. disagree strongly	6%	1%	2%
TOTAL	100%	100%	100%
N	1,497	1,029	2,603
Beijing vs. Rural China	$\chi^2 = 51.496$ (d.f. = 4), $p < .001$		
2. The basic rights of citizens are well protected in the courts. (Q21i)			
1. agree strongly	4%	8%	6%
2. agree	53%	69%	50%
3. neutral	–	17%	17%
4. disagree	37%	6%	25%
5. disagree strongly	6%	1%	2%
TOTAL	100%	101%	100%
N	1,472	1,036	2,574
Beijing vs. Rural China	$\chi^2 = 200.364$ (d.f. = 4), $p < .001$		
3. On the whole, judges are honest. (Q21k)			
1. agree strongly	4%	7%	4%
2. agree	53%	68%	51%
3. neutral	–	17%	15%
4. disagree	34%	7%	26%
5. disagree strongly	9%	0%	3%
TOTAL	100%	99%	99%
N	1,453	976	2,570
Beijing vs. Rural China	$\chi^2 = 194.560$ (d.f. = 4), $p < .001$		
4. Court decisions are almost always fair. (Q21l)			
1. agree strongly	3%	6%	4%
2. agree	53%	60%	39%
3. neutral	–	18%	18%
4. disagree	39%	14%	35%
5. disagree strongly	5%	1%	4%
TOTAL	100%	99%	100%
N	1,470	1,001	2,527
Beijing vs. Rural China	$\chi^2 = 201.738$ (d.f. = 4), $p < .001$		

	Chicago, 1984	Beijing, 2001	Rural China, 2002
5. Overall, how good a job are the courts doing? Are they doing... (Q12)			
1. ...a very good job	4%	5%	3%
2. ...a good job	22%	43%	23%
3. ...neutral (in Chicago, "fair")	47%	49%	59%
4. ...a poor job	18%	3%	13%
5. ...a very poor job	9%	1%	2%
TOTAL	100%	101%	100%
N	1,400	926	2,594
Chicago vs. Beijing	$\chi^2 = 253.74$ (d.f. = 4), $p < .001$		
Chicago vs. Rural China	$\chi^2 = 155.818$ (d.f. = 4), $p < .001$		
Beijing vs. Rural China	$\chi^2 = 196.003$ (d.f. = 4), $p < .001$		
6. In general, how satisfied are you with how well the courts solve its cases? Are you... (Q13)			
1. ...very satisfied	7%	5%	3%
2. ...somewhat satisfied	48%	73%	45%
3. ...neutral (in Chicago, volunteered)	1%	16%	36%
4. ...somewhat dissatisfied	32%	6%	15%
5. ...very dissatisfied	13%	1%	2%
TOTAL	101%	101%	101%
N	1,464	916	2,574
Chicago vs. Beijing	$\chi^2 = 532.03$ (d.f. = 4), $p < .001$		
Chicago vs. Rural China	$\chi^2 = 875.72$ (d.f. = 4), $p < .001$		
Beijing vs. Rural China	$\chi^2 = 232.520$ (d.f. = 4), $p < .001$		
7. How satisfied are you with the fairness of the decisions made by the courts? Are you... (Q14)			
1. ...very satisfied	7%	5%	3%
2. ...somewhat satisfied	49%	72%	42%
3. ...neutral (in Chicago, volunteered)	1%	17%	36%
4. ...somewhat dissatisfied	30%	5%	17%
5. ...very dissatisfied	12%	1%	2%
TOTAL	99%	100%	100%
N	1,475	910	2,570
Chicago vs. Beijing	$\chi^2 = 497.53$ (d.f. = 4), $p < .001$		
Chicago vs. Rural China	$\chi^2 = 771.569$ (d.f. = 4), $p < .001$		
Beijing vs. Rural China	$\chi^2 = 287.798$ (d.f. = 4), $p < .001$		

(continued)

TABLE A6.1 *(continued)*

	Chicago, 1984	Beijing, 2001	Rural China, 2002
8. Some people say that the courts treat everyone fairly, others that they favor some people over others. How about you? Do you think that the courts... (Q15)			
1. treat everyone equally,	28%	37%	24%
5. or that they favor some people over others?	72%	63%	76%
TOTAL	100%	100%	100%
N	1,465	849	2,423
Chicago vs. Beijing	$\chi^2 = 16.741$ (d.f. = 1), $p < .001$		
Chicago vs. Rural China	$\chi^2 = 7.536$ (d.f. = 1), $p = .006$		
Beijing vs. Rural China	$\chi^2 = 46.649$ (d.f. = 1), $p < .001$		
9. How fair do you think the outcome you receive from the court would be? Would it be... (Q32)			
1. very fair,	16%	6%	4%
2. somewhat fair,	70%	73%	44%
3. neutral	–	16%	32%
4. somewhat unfair, or	11%	3%	18%
5. very unfair?	3%	1%	1%
TOTAL	100%	99%	99%
N	1,413	847	2,227
Beijing vs. Rural China	$\chi^2 = 262.551$ (d.f. = 4), $p < .001$		
average score (negative assessment)	2.88	2.45	2.91
Cronbach's alpha	.838	.846	.870
average number of non-missing answers	8.32	7.55	7.81
average number of negative answers	3.10	1.03	2.39
average number of positive answers	4.47	5.30	3.59
average proportion of negative answers	.364	.131	.294
average proportion of positive answers	.540	.659	.434

Notes: Codes beginning with "Q" following survey questions indicate question numbers on the original questionnaire presented in Tyler, *Why People Obey the Law*, pp. 179–219. Not all totals equal 100 percent because of rounding errors. "d.f." stands for "degrees of freedom, a number which helps determine statistical significance.

Sources: Tyler, *Why People Obey the Law*, pp. 48–55; Authors' China surveys.

TABLE A6.2. *Perceptions of the police*

	Chicago, 1984	Beijing, 2001	Rural China, 2002
1. I have a great deal of respect for the police. (Q21a)			
1. agree strongly	19%	13%	12%
2. agree	57%	63%	51%
3. neutral	–	12%	10%
4. disagree	20%	12%	24%
5. disagree strongly	4%	1%	2%
TOTAL	100%	101%	99%
N	1,564	1,113	2,804
Beijing vs. Rural China	$\chi^2 = 85.705$ (d.f. = 4), $p < .001$		
2. On the whole, police officers are honest. (Q21b)			
1. agree strongly	7%	8%	5%
2. agree	51%	67%	50%
3. neutral	–	14%	13%
4. disagree	34%	11%	30%
5. disagree strongly	8%	1%	2%
TOTAL	100%	101%	100%
N	1,515	1,095	2,730
Beijing vs. Rural China	$\chi^2 = 188.124$ (d.f. = 4), $p < .001$		
3. I feel proud of the police. (Q21c)			
1. agree strongly	12%	8%	5%
2. agree	54%	52%	35%
3. neutral	–	20%	19%
4. disagree	29%	18%	36%
5. disagree strongly	5%	1%	5%
TOTAL	100%	99%	100%
N	1,530	1,103	2,747
Beijing vs. Rural China	$\chi^2 = 191.795$ (d.f. = 4), $p < .001$		
4. I feel that I should support the police. (Q21d)			
1. agree strongly	20%	18%	15%
2. agree	68%	75%	65%
3. neutral	–	5%	8%
4. disagree	10%	2%	11%
5. disagree strongly	3%	0%	1%
TOTAL	101%	100%	100%
N	1,549	1,112	2,785
Beijing vs. Rural China	$\chi^2 = 117.049$ (d.f. = 4), $p < .001$		

(continued)

TABLE A6.2 *(continued)*

	Chicago, 1984	Beijing, 2001	Rural China, 2002
5. Overall, how would you assess the work of the police? Are they doing... (Q1)			
1. ... a very good job	10%	5%	2%
2. ... a good job	44%	37%	24%
3. ... neutral (in Chicago, "fair")	38%	53%	56%
4. ... a poor job	6%	5%	16%
5. ... a very poor job	2%	1%	2%
TOTAL	100%	101%	100%
N	1,542	1,096	2,763
Chicago vs. Beijing	$\chi^2 = 72.871$ (d.f. = 4), $p < .001$		
Chicago vs. Rural China	$\chi^2 = 406.911$ (d.f. = 4), $p < .001$		
Beijing vs. Rural China	$\chi^2 = 158.747$ (d.f. = 4), $p < .001$		
6. How satisfied are you with the fairness of the outcomes when the police handle problems? Are you... (Q3)			
1. ... very satisfied	13%	4%	2%
2. ... somewhat satisfied	52%	67%	38%
3. ... neutral (in Chicago, volunteered)	2%	15%	34%
4. ... somewhat dissatisfied	26%	12%	23%
5. ... very dissatisfied	8%	2%	3%
TOTAL	101%	100%	100%
N	1,491	1,074	2,733
Chicago vs. Beijing	$\chi^2 = 340.378$ (d.f. = 4), $p < .001$		
Chicago vs. Rural China	$\chi^2 = 746.794$ (d.f. = 4), $p < .001$		
Beijing vs. Rural China	$\chi^2 = 304.652$ (d.f. = 4), $p < .001$		
7. Some people say that the police treat everyone fairly, others that they favor some people over others. How about you? Do you think that the police... (Q4)			
1. treat everyone equally,	26%	27%	19%
5. or that they favor some people over others?	74%	73%	81%
TOTAL	100%	100%	100%
N	1,465	1,030	2,557
Chicago vs. Beijing	$\chi^2 = .989$ (d.f. = 1), $p = .320$		
Chicago vs. Rural China	$\chi^2 = 26.240$ (d.f. = 1), $p < .001$		
Beijing vs. Rural China	$\chi^2 = 32.836$ (d.f. = 1), $p < .001$		
average score (negative assessment)	2.69	2.54	2.91

	Chicago, 1984	Beijing, 2001	Rural China, 2002
Cronbach's alpha	.816	.774	.819
average number of non-missing answers	6.77	6.78	6.59
average number of negative answers	2.18	1.30	2.23
average number of positive answers	4.20	4.34	3.10
average proportion of negative answers	.319	.189	.328
average proportion of positive answers	.624	.635	.462

Notes: Codes beginning with "Q" following survey questions indicate question numbers on the original questionnaire presented in Tyler, *Why People Obey the Law*, pp. 179–219. Not all totals equal 100 percent because of rounding errors.

Sources: Tyler, *Why People Obey the Law*, pp. 48–55; Authors' China surveys.

7

Users and Non-Users: Legal Experience and Its Effect on Legal Consciousness

Mary E. Gallagher and Yuhua Wang

A major question in the law and society literature is the effect of legal experience on individual attitudes toward legal institutions, in particular the court system. Positive attitudes and confidence in the legal system are important for generating citizen trust and confidence in government generally and also for inculcating citizen values and behavior that support the rule of law and encourage legal (and peaceful) resolution of disputes and grievances more specifically. Thus, these values are important for sustaining democracy. For a country like China, in transition from state socialism, in which legal modes of governance and social control were less common than administrative edicts, Communist Party campaigns, and state repression, attempts to build an effective legal system are also linked to limited political reform. Rule of law building is the Chinese Communist Party's (CCP) attempt to build more effective and efficient governance, while making an end run around democratization and the sharing of political power. In this case, creating positive citizen attitudes toward the legal system is part of a strategy to avoid democracy.

In this chapter, we examine how experience with the legal system affects Chinese citizens' evaluation of the courts through a series of comparisons between those who have used the law to resolve an employment dispute and those who have not as well as comparisons between disputants who remained positive and confident in the legal system and disputants who were fully disillusioned and negative. We find that legal experience leads to higher levels of disillusionment and more negative perceptions of the legal system's effectiveness and fairness. Whereas non-users tend to have vague but benevolent notions of the legal system and its effectiveness, actual disputants have less confidence in the effectiveness of the legal system.

Through in-depth interviews with disputants, however, we find that disillusionment is mitigated by increased feelings of personal efficacy and a sense that one has become educated about the law. These feelings are most evident among legal aid plaintiffs whose legal experiences were improved by constant contact with legal aid staff and a supportive social network built around the legal aid center.[1] Among disputants without the benefits of legal aid, however, we also find that disillusionment can be mitigated by increased feelings of personal efficacy and a perception that one is knowledgeable about the law, in effect, that one has become better at using the law, even if the law is more flawed than first believed. But why are some plaintiffs likelier to feel emboldened and encouraged by their legal experience whereas others fall into despondency, frustration, and anger? We argue that an individual's evaluation of her legal experience is strongly affected by her political identity. By political identity, we mean citizenship status, the nature (and timing) of political socialization, and whether the state's role in the dispute is fused as employer and political/legal authority. Older, urban disputants employed in the state sector are more prone to feelings of disillusionment, feelings of powerlessness, and inefficacy. Younger, rural disputants employed in the non-state sectors are likelier to have positive evaluations of their legal experience and to embrace the legal system as a potential space for rights protection. The construction of rule of law in China has attenuated the previously strong bonds between the party-state and urban workers in the public sectors but also has created new constituents from groups that previously were ignored or actively discriminated against in the old socialist order.

LABOR CONFLICT AND THE DISPUTE "PYRAMID"

The arguments presented here are based on research examining the legal mobilization of Chinese workers. Our findings and explanations may help us understand the broader legal context and the nature of dispute resolution in China today; however, we cannot be sure that labor disputes are representative of disputes more generally or are even similar to other types of common disputes. For example, given the high risks of unemployment in China, a large proportion of aggrieved employees "lump" their disputes in exchange for keeping their jobs. Second, Chinese lawyers

[1] Mary E. Gallagher, "'Hope for Protection and Hopeless Choices': Labor Legal Aid in the PRC." In *Grassroots Political Reform in Contemporary China*, ed. Elizabeth J. Perry and Merle Goldman (Cambridge: Harvard University Press, 2007).

often decline to represent workers in labor disputes because compensation is often very low or nonexistent.[2] Third, the procedures for labor dispute resolution can be onerous and time-consuming. Many employees prefer to "vote with their feet" and find new employment rather than lodge a formal complaint.

To comprehend how legal mobilization around workplace rights is shaped by the institutional environment, it is important to understand some aspects of the labor dispute resolution procedures. First, this system is a three-step process of voluntary mediation, compulsory but not binding arbitration, and finally civil-court litigation. The government continues to rely on mediation as a main channel for resolution despite the rapid decline of firm-based mediation after the 1994 National Labor Law. Whereas most workers reject firm-based mediation as too closely associated with firm management to be fair, local labor arbitrators and civil-court judges are encouraged through salary and career incentives to push mediated resolutions at every level. Therefore, arbitration cases can result in an arbitrated mediation or an arbitral award. Judges may also resolve their cases through judicial mediation. The 2008 Labor Dispute Mediation and Arbitration Law strengthened the role of non–firm-based mediation, but also reduced some of the barriers to arbitration and litigation by lowering fees and lengthening the statute of limitations on most disputes from sixty days to one year.

Second, the important and compulsory arbitration stage has been beset by a number of problems, including weak institutional capacity, lack of professionalism and training, political interference from powerful local actors, lack of legitimacy because of the committee's strong dependence on local labor bureaus, and lack of finality given the court-appeal option. Most arbitral awards are now appealed in civil court, making the arbitration process simply a stepping-stone to final resolution in court. This has added to the burden of the civil-court system, undermined the authority and legitimacy of labor arbitration, and complicated and lengthened an already difficult and expensive process for workers. Finally, labor disputes continue to rise on an annual basis at a fast rate. Despite the problems and frustrations of the formal resolution system, workers continue to make use of these institutions in increasing numbers. In 1995, arbitrated labor disputes reached 33,000; in 2006, this number increased to 447,000 disputes, with an annual average increase of more than 25 percent. In the

[2] Ethan Michelson, "The Practice of Law as an Obstacle to Justice: Chinese Lawyers at Work," *Law & Society Review* 40, no. 1 (2006): 1–38.

wake of the global financial crisis and the passage of a tougher Labor Contract Law in 2008, total labor disputes in China rose to more than eight hundred thousand in that year. These large increases reflect the growing awareness among Chinese workers of their legal rights and the continuing problem of rampant violations of labor laws and regulations by many firms.

Some of these characteristics account for the pattern of legal mobilization that we see among the survey respondents. By constructing a dispute "pyramid" following the idea of Miller and Sarat[3] and Michelson,[4] we can see that a large proportion of the respondents with work-related problems did not escalate the problems into disputes. Among the 3,699 respondents (the overall number of cases was 4,112) who answered this question, 319 (8.6 percent) reported that they had labor problems during the last ten years. These problems include contract issues, working time, wage, injury, social security, and training problems. Only about one of four of these respondents reported that the problem became a dispute. Our return interviews in summer 2007 targeted these eighty-two subjects and completed twenty-eight cases (34.1 percent). Among the eighty-two disputants, fifty-six (68.3 percent) took actions to solve the disputes. These fifty-six actors employed various methods to solve their disputes (mainly mediation, arbitration, administrative methods, and litigation), and most of them used multiple methods. Among the ninety-one responses, mediation had thirty-six counts (39.6 percent), administrative methods twenty-four counts (26.4 percent), arbitration twenty-one counts (23.1 percent), and litigation ten counts (11.0 percent). The ten litigators (3.1 percent of the 319 cases with problems) are at the peak of the pyramid, but they are hard to see because of their small numbers, although we highlight them in black. This use of multiple methods is in part a result of the institutional framework set out by the 1994 and 2008 labor laws, which require a multistep process and encourage mediated resolutions. It also reflects the strategies of many aggrieved persons to use as many options as possible to increase the chances of success.

In the first part of this chapter we compare users with non-users. Users refer to the eighty-two disputants, non-users include those who never have had labor disputes and those who had labor problems that did not

[3] Richard E. Miller and Austin Sarat, "Grievances, Claims, and Disputes: Assessing the Adversary Culture," *Law & Society Review* 15, no. 3/4 (1980–1981): 525–566.

[4] Ethan Michelson, "Climbing the Dispute Pagoda: Grievances and Appeals to the Official Justice System in Rural China," *American Sociological Review* 72, no. 3 (2007): 459–485.

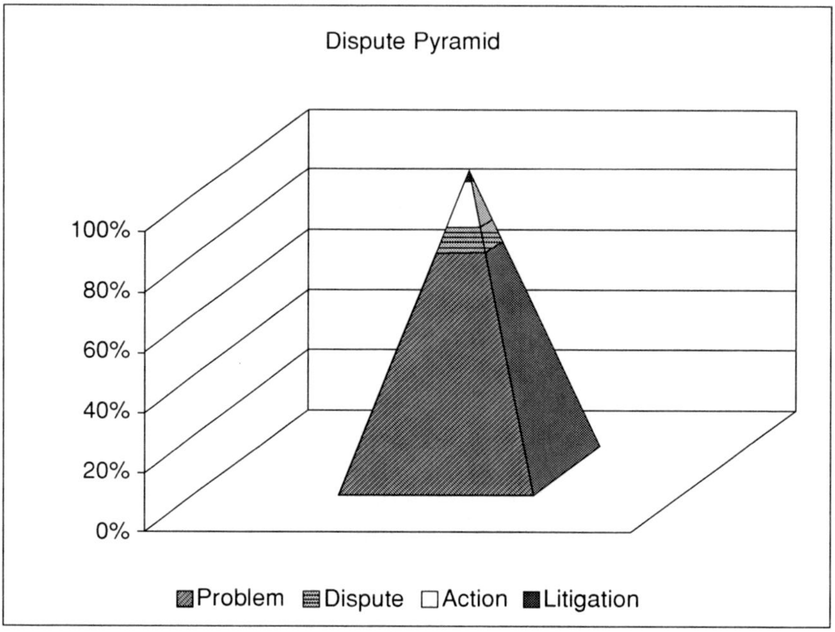

FIGURE 7.1. Dispute "Pyramid." *Source:* 2005 Labor Law Survey.

escalate to disputes. The second part of the chapter compares the people living at the top of the "pyramid," that is, the eighty-two disputants, with added evidence from an earlier interview project with legal-aid recipients in Shanghai (see Figure 7.1).

COMPARING USERS AND NON-USERS

One perplexing question that has puzzled generations of social scientists is the circulative relations between behavior and attitudes. Students of political participation have been haunted by the "reciprocal effects of participation and efficacy."[5] Political scientists find it necessary to distinguish between internal political efficacy and external political efficacy, because they usually have distinctive effects and causes.[6] Internal

[5] Steven E. Finkel, "Reciprocal Effects of Participation and Political Efficacy: A Panel Analysis," *American Journal of Political Science* 29, no. 4 (1985): 891–913.

[6] Robert E. Lane, *Political Life: Why and How People Get Involved in Politics* (New York: Free Press, 1965); George I. Balch, "Multiple Indicators in Survey Research: The Concept of 'Sense of Political Efficacy,'" *Political Methodology* 1, no. 2 (1974): 1–43; Stephen C. Craig, "Efficacy, Trust, and Political Behavior: An Attempt to Resolve a

political efficacy "indicates individuals' self-perceptions that they are capable of understanding politics and competent enough to participate in political acts such as voting." External efficacy, by contrast, "measures expressed beliefs about political institutions.... The lack of external efficacy... indicates the belief that the public cannot influence political outcomes because government leaders and institutions are unresponsive."[7] One of the main conclusions of the political efficacy literature is that participation, both its forms and results, have great but various impacts on internal and external efficacy. Mode of political participation matters. For example, it is found that involvement in campaign activities often enhances the feelings of political efficacy, yet peaceful protest has little effect.[8] Results matter as well. Madsen[9] finds that successful petitioners come to enjoy a somewhat enhanced sense of internal efficacy but do not view government as particularly responsive (external efficacy); unsuccessful petitioners do not see themselves as inefficacious (internal efficacy) but do see government responsiveness in distinctly negative terms (external efficacy). Participation behavior also has an indirect impact on efficacy through information seeking. Low participation usually leads to political inattentiveness, which contributes to low internal efficacy; high participation, by contrast, makes people more interested in political information and therefore contributes to enhanced efficacy.[10]

The law and society literature also finds the same pattern in people's judicial behavior. Legal experience is often found to influence people's confidence and their opinions of the legal system. Kritzer and Voelker,[11] in their Wisconsin study, find that those who have been to court recently have more favorable opinions about the courts than those who have not. Experience matters, but type of experience also is important. Benesh and

Lingering Conceptual Dilemma," *American Politics Research* 7, no. 2 (1979): 225–239; Stephen C. Craig and Michael A. Maggiotto, "Measuring Political Efficacy," *Political Methodology* 8, no. 3 (1982): 85–109.

[7] Warren E. Miller, Arthur H. Miller, and Edward J. Schneider, *American National Election Studies Data Sourcebook 1952–1978* (Cambridge: Harvard University Press, 1980), p. 253.

[8] Steven E. Finkel, "The Effects of Participation on Political Efficacy and Political Support: Evidence from a West German Panel," *Journal of Politics* 49, no. 2 (1987): 441–464.

[9] Douglas Madsen, "Political Self-Efficacy Tested," *American Political Science Review* 81, no. 2 (1987): 571–581.

[10] Bruce E. Pinkleton, Erica Weintraub Austin, and Kristine K. J. Fortman, "Relationships of Media Use and Political Disaffection to Political Efficacy and Voting Behavior," *Journal of Broadcasting and Electronic Media* 42, no. 1 (1998): 34–49.

[11] Herbert M. Kritzer and John Voelker, "Familiarity Breeds Respect: How Wisconsin Citizens View Their Courts," *Judicature* 82, no. 2 (1998): 59–64.

Howell[12] find that those with more stake in the outcome of the court case and less control over it are least confident (e.g., defendants and plaintiffs), whereas those with little stake and substantial control are most confident (jurors).

We find this to be a very interesting perspective for viewing the dynamic of dispute experience and disputants' attitudes and beliefs in the Chinese context. We adopt the quasiexperimental idea and assume that involvement in, and experience of solving, a dispute will cause some changes in people's attitudes – here, efficacy and knowledge in particular – and distinguish users from non-users. Much work has been done on showing the flaws of the Chinese legal system and legal profession,[13] whereas little effort has been made to investigate the impact of these flaws on individual end-users' attitudes and beliefs.[14] We found the theoretical framework of participation and efficacy to be a very useful tool in explaining the relationship between legal experience and legal consciousness and knowledge in China. Zemans[15] argues that legal mobilization also should be seen as a form of political participation in the United States. Although modes of political participation are quite different in an authoritarian regime where campaign activity, voting in competitive elections, legal protest and demonstration, and so forth are constrained or forbidden entirely, the invocation of legal norms and use of the legal system (legal mobilization) are even more intrinsically political in an authoritarian regime than in an established democracy. For instance, invoking the law for rights protection (*weiquan*) has become an important kind of political

[12] Sara C. Benesh and Susan E. Howell, "Confidence in the Courts: A Comparison of Users and Non-users," *Behaviorial Sciences and the Law* 19, no. 2 (2001): 199–214.

[13] Hungdah Chiu, "Institutionalizing a New Legal System in Deng's China" (Baltimore: School of Law University of Maryland, Occasional Papers/Reprints Series in Contemporary Asian Studies, no. 3, 1994); Ronald C. Keith, *China's Struggle for the Rule of Law* (New York: St. Martin's Press, 1994); Stanley B. Lubman, *Bird in a Cage: Legal Reform in China after Mao* (Stanford: Stanford University Press, 1999); Melanie Manion, "Corruption and Corruption Control: More of the Same in 1996." In *China Review, 1997*, ed. Maurice Brosseau, Kuan Hsin-chi, and Y. Y. Kueh (Hong Kong: The Chinese University Press, 1997), pp. 33–56; Pitman B. Potter, *Economic Contract Law of China: Legitimation and Contract Autonomy in the PRC* (Seattle: University of Washington Press, 1992); Randall Peerenboom, *China's Long March toward Rule of Law* (New York: Cambridge University Press, 2002); Michelson, "The Practice of Law as an Obstacle to Justice."

[14] Mary E. Gallagher, "Mobilizing the Law in China: 'Informed Disenchantment' and the Development of Legal Consciousness," *Law & Society Review* 40, no. 4 (2006): 783–816.

[15] Frances Kahn Zemans, "Legal Mobilization: The Neglected Role of Law in the Political System," *American Political Science Review* 77, no. 3 (1983): 690–703.

participation in contemporary China.[16] Although some of the *weiquan* activity is overtly political, involving administrative suits against powerful local governments and firms (i.e., the work of *weiquan* lawyers), even the self-interested and small-scale legal mobilization of individual workers involves engagement with the political authority and demands on the state to take action against important local actors.

Contrary to mass participation in democracies, legal mobilization in China has some distinctive characteristics. First, people are almost always involuntarily involved in disputes. To solve disputes, they have to resort to the dispute-settlement mechanisms, including mediation, arbitration, administrative intervention, and litigation. There are very few cases in which people deliberately become involved in disputes and seek settlement, though they may receive much media attention such as the consumer protection activist, Wang Hai. Second, instead of fulfilling one's "democratic creed" through voting, the process of dispute resolution in China almost always is associated with bad experiences and sad stories. This is partly a result of the unfairness and ineffectiveness of the legal system and legal profession, which are well documented by scholars.[17] In addition, most disputants, according to our survey and interviews, are not satisfied with the results. Some gave up because of time and financial constraints; some took actions but soon found them powerless; and some, even when they won the case, did not achieve implementation of court decisions. These distinctive factors all contribute to a negative view of the resolution mechanisms, which have an impact on what we call the external efficacy of disputants.

We also expect some positive consequences of dispute involvement. Unlike routine political participation, like voting, dispute resolution is a sort of ad hoc activity in which few people have opportunities to become involved. Before their involvement, people usually have very little prior knowledge about the resolution system. Many have noticed the rise of "legal consciousness" among Chinese citizens,[18] but "low legal

[16] Kevin J. O'Brien and Lianjiang Li, *Rightful Resistance in Rural China* (New York: Cambridge University Press, 2006).

[17] Peerenboom, *China's Long March toward Rule of Law*; Michelson, "The Practice of Law as an Obstacle to Justice.."

[18] Minxin Pei, "Citizens v. Mandarins: Administrative Litigation in China," *The China Quarterly*, no. 152 (1997): 832–862; Philip Pan, "In China, Turning the Law Into the People's Protector," *The Washington Post*, December 28, 2004, p. A01; Willy Wo-Lap Lam, "On the Wave of Political Reform," *South China Morning Post*, June 21, 2000, p. 18; Hugo Restall, "Chinese Farmers Learn Their Rights," *Asian Wall Street Journal*, November 27, 2000, p. A31.

consciousness" is still a major barrier to an effective and robust rule of law,[19] and people come to the legal process often with only vague and imprecise knowledge of legal procedure and their actual codified rights.[20] Thus, we expect to see that disputants learn from the process. Involvement in disputes and the incentive to win can completely change the calculation of cost and benefit; as a result, it is no longer rational to remain ignorant, and information seeking becomes worthwhile. Information seeking also results from increased interest in legal knowledge. Whereas for average people, legal codes, regulations, the hierarchy of the courts, and complicated litigation procedures are too mysterious and useless to have any real-life application, they are extremely interesting to disputants for practical reasons. Disputants pay more attention to law-related news and information in the media; actively find legal information from books, magazines, television, and the Internet; and become interested in conversations with other people regarding the law and the legal system.[21] A better understanding of the law and legal procedures will lead to higher self-confidence in solving a dispute. "Knowledge is power," and disputants feel empowered by the legal knowledge they attain through the resolution process. In addition, dispute-solving experience and practical knowledge help disputants find more efficient solutions, clearer targets, and more effective strategies. Because a successful campaign enhances a person's confidence in participating in politics,[22] we expect to see a raised internal efficacy of disputants. We also anticipate that confident disputants, as some studies have shown,[23] will become "little experts," diffusing legal information and helping other people with similar problems.

To summarize, we expect the effects of legal experience to be 1) a raised level of legal knowledge; 2) a higher internal efficacy (i.e., an enhanced confidence in dispute solving); and 3) a lowered external efficacy (i.e., a

[19] Peerenboom, *China's Long March toward Rule of Law.*

[20] Gallagher, "Mobilizing the Law in China."

[21] Daniela Stockmann and Mary E. Gallagher, "Mass Media Mobilization as a Means of Legal Reform in China." Paper presented at the annual meeting of the American Political Science Association, Chicago, August 30–September 1, 2007, http://www.allacademic.com//meta/p_mla_apa_research_citation/2/0/9/2/7/pages209272/p209272-1.php (accessed September 27, 2008).

[22] Finkel, "The Effects of Participation on Political Efficacy and Political Support."

[23] Pierre F. Landry, "Using Clustered Spatial Data to Study Diffusion: The Case of Legal Institutions in China." Paper presented at Sources and Methods in Chinese Politics: A Workshop on Methodology, Research Design and Fieldwork Strategies, University of Michigan, November 3–4, 2006; Gallagher, "Mobilizing the Law in China."

negative view of the dispute-resolution mechanisms). We will elaborate on these effects in the following paragraphs.

Legal Knowledge: How Well Do I Know the Law?

In Gallagher's 2006 study of legal-aid plaintiffs, she found that many of her respondents acquired strategic knowledge through legal mobilization at the legal-aid center. The most important aspects of their new knowledge were "understanding laws and regulations, understanding legal procedure, and understanding how to attain and use evidence."[24] We found the same effects in the 2005 survey and the return in-depth interviews. Most of our respondents expressed feelings of a better grasp of the law, both in text and in practice, and some regretted that they had not kept evidence that would have allowed them to win the case.

Liu, a forty-four-year-old female worker, was employed in a collective textile enterprise in Wuxi. She was laid off after the enterprise was sold to a private owner. Liu had a big fight with her boss about her months of wages, medical care, and pension in arrears. The conflict resulted in Liu being paid one month of medical care and pension, but she was not paid any wages in arrears. In retrospect, Liu told the researcher, now that she knew more about the labor law and related laws, she realized that she should have resorted to the labor arbitration committee to ask for the unpaid wages, and the result would have been much better. But at the time, she had no idea that the city had a labor arbitration committee and did not even realize that what the enterprise did to her was illegal and that she could sue. She said that although now she understood, it was too late; otherwise, she would have sued the enterprise.[25] Liu's failure to negotiate a satisfactory settlement with her boss makes her more confident that the legal system is a better option for future disputes now that she knows the range of options available to her.

Zhang, a thirty-eight-year old migrant worker in a Taiwanese chemical industry enterprise in Wuxi, was going to lead a strike to ask for overtime wages. Before he decided to lead the strike, Zhang spent hundreds of yuan buying law books; after careful homework, he assured himself that the enterprise's overtime policy was illegal. He persuaded more than one hundred workers in the enterprise to follow him to strike, yet the employers soon found out about the plan and bought off the workers.

[24] Gallagher, "Mobilizing the Law in China," 800.
[25] CASE: Wuxi#9.

In the interview, Zhang told the researcher that he should have found a lawyer to take care of the dispute. "[T]he enterprise should strictly follow the labor regulations, even if it must be shut down I don't have any sympathy for it."[26]

Many of our respondents learned the importance of evidence through the dispute resolution process. Li, a fifty-year-old woman worker in a collective enterprise in Chongqing, was laid off and paid 20,000 RMB at a rate of 850 RMB per year in compensation (she had worked for the enterprise for twenty-nine years). She told the researcher that she should be paid much more than this, but because the employers were corrupt and diverted the money, there was no money left. Several of Li's co-workers went to court to sue their employers for corruption, but they lost the case because they could not provide enough evidence. Li said the accountant in the enterprise had two versions of accounts, "one is real, the other fake; if we had had the real one, we would have won."[27]

Zhou, a sixty-two-year-old trade union chairwoman in a Shenyang state-owned enterprise (SOE), led other workers to sue their former boss. She rented out some of their factory houses and used the money for the litigation fee and then was arrested for embezzlement. She was beaten up by police officers, yet the police could not prove her guilty. After her son bribed the policemen and paid 5,000 RMB, she was released. Afterward, she went to the local police department and asked that the money be returned, but the police refused. One of the police officers said to her, "It is true that your son gave me money, cigarettes, and bought us dinner, so what? Can you get them back?!" Zhou was angry, and she told the researcher that she really should have brought a tape recorder to tape the conversation and sue the police officer.[28]

Not only did our respondents learn from the process itself, but many also became interested in and actively sought out legal knowledge. Respondents report paying more attention to law-related news and law programs on television; some became interested in the legal case accounts and analysis in the newspapers; and some went to law firms and consulted with lawyers. A general feeling of our respondents is that at the beginning, they merely had a vague sense that something had gone wrong with the employers and policies, but they had no idea why it was wrong or whom they should blame. After they delved into law books, they felt

[26] CASE: Wuxi#5.
[27] CASE: Chongqing#4.
[28] CASE: Shenyang#4.

TABLE 7.1. *Judgment of a Vignette: Work-unit actions legal or not*

		Frequency	Percent
Non-Disputants	Yes	112	3.1
	No	3,500	96.8
	DK	5	0.1
	Total	3,617	100
Disputants	Yes	1	1.2
	No	81	98.8
	Total	82	100

Source: 2005 Labor Law Survey.

that they were armed with the law and had become powerful. They could then fight confidently against their employers.

This point is also supported by our survey data. When asked to judge whether and why the employer's conduct is legal in a vignette,[29] disputants have a clearer view and a more accurate judgment about the case (see Tables 7.1 and 7.2). Disputants are likelier to give a correct answer (the company's actions are illegal) and also to understand the reasons for the illegality (contracts cannot be terminated without compensation).

Internal Efficacy: How Well Can I Work the Law?

As soon as the disputants understand the rules of the game, many want to play it again. Gallagher also found this "law-affirming behavior" in her 2006 study.[30] We attribute this sort of behavior to an appreciation for the knowledge and information they have learned from the dispute process and also to an enhanced sense of confidence and a belief that "I can work the law better now." They have a sense that if they played it again, they would adopt more strategic methods.

Zhang, the would-be strike leader, left the Taiwanese enterprise after the failure of his plan to organize a strike. He still felt hatred toward his

[29] Because of the relatively small number of people in the general population with actual dispute experience, we use a hypothetical vignette to elicit people's attitudes and expected behavior in the dispute-resolution process. The vignette states, "Old Chen works at a company and has signed a five-year contract. Three-and-a-half years into his contract, the company management decided to terminate the employment contract, citing financial difficulties. In addition, the company refused to provide termination compensation. If you were Old Chen, what would you do?"

[30] Gallagher, "Mobilizing the Law in China," 805.

TABLE 7.2. *Reasons provided for illegality of employer's action*

		Frequency	Percent
Non-Disputants	Cannot articulate reason	210	6
	Work-unit cannot terminate contracts	1,131	32.3
	Work-unit cannot terminate contracts without compensation	2,097	59.8
	Other	67	1.9
	Total	3,505	100
Disputants	Cannot articulate reason	1	1.2
	Work-unit cannot terminate contracts	24	29.6
	Work-unit cannot terminate contracts without compensation	53	65.4
	Other	3	3.7
	Total	81	100

Source: 2005 Labor Law Survey.

former boss even several years later when the interview was conducted. Because most of the workers he had mobilized to join the suit had been bought off by the employer, he had had to negotiate with the boss in a peaceful way. The dispute was resolved, but the workers had not gotten what they deserved (higher pay, overtime wages, and more labor protection). Zhang felt sorry for his co-workers and admitted that he had been too soft and the compromise was wrong. If he could do it again, he believes that he would be more strategic.

Liu, the textile factory worker, felt that she had already missed the chance to have a better position to negotiate with the employer. "We didn't know there was an arbitration committee in the city," Liu said. "[O]therwise, we should have gone there and ask[ed] for help. We could have gotten more.... We didn't have the sense at the time." Obviously, Liu had learned from the case: "[N]ow I know what the employer did was illegal. In retrospect, we should have used a legal method!"

Both Zhang and Liu thereafter became "little experts," thus reconfirming Gallagher's finding in her plaintiff study.[31] Liu told her friends with labor problems to go to the arbitration committee for consultancy. "We have already missed the chance," Liu said. "I wouldn't let my friends make the same mistake." One of her friends went to court after listening to her advice. "She will win," said Liu very confidently. Zhang was helping his brother-in-law on a similar labor case, and he suggested that his

[31] Ibid., 807.

TABLE 7.3. *If you were Mr. Chen, what would you do?*

		Frequency	Percent
Non-Disputants	Take action	3,091	88.2
	Do nothing	414	11.8
	Total	3,505	100
Disputants	Take action	71	87.7
	Do nothing	10	12.3
	Total	81	100

Source: 2005 Labor Law Survey.

brother-in-law consult a good lawyer. "A lot of friends came to me for help." Zhang was quite proud. "Every time they came, I told them to go find lawyers – not just one. I suggested that they find several lawyers and then compare them."

External Efficacy: How Well Does the Law Work?

Although the disputants attained higher internal efficacy through legal mobilization and learned new legal knowledge, most of them also had a negative view of the resolution mechanisms and felt disenchanted. This disenchantment resulted from their high expectations of the legal system.[32] To draw evidence from the survey and the return interviews, we can overcome some of the shortcomings of the legal-aid interviews, which was a nonrepresentative group.[33] In the survey, we interviewed a wide spectrum of disputants with experience in various dispute resolution methods. The results confirm that disenchantment is not limited to the legal-aid plaintiffs, but rather is associated with various kinds of disputants.

In Table 7.3, we cannot see any difference between the disputants and non-disputants as to whether they would take action; however, when we look at specific resolution methods, we find a more accurate picture whereby people who have had disputes also have less confidence in the resolution mechanisms, especially litigation (Tables 7.4–7.8). Nearly 78 percent of the non-disputants report that they would have used litigation to solve Mr. Chen's problem, but only 63 percent of the disputants select litigation as a method. On the one hand, the non-disputants have vague confidence in these mechanisms, even though they have never used them. On the other hand, the disputants, when asked about the relative

[32] Ibid., 791.

[33] Ibid.

TABLE 7.4. *Use mediation?*

		Frequency	Percent
Non-Disputants	Yes	2,944	95.2
	No	147	4.8
	Total	3,091	100
Disputants	Yes	64	90.1
	No	7	9.9
	Total	71	100

Source: 2005 Labor Law Survey.

TABLE 7.5. *Use administrative methods?*

		Frequency	Percent
Non-Disputants	Yes	2,521	81.6
	No	570	18.4
	Total	3,091	100
Disputants	Yes	52	73.2
	No	19	26.8
	Total	71	100

Source: 2005 Labor Law Survey.

effectiveness of the different methods of resolution, are far more likely to feel that none of the options is effective or useful (Table 7.9).

The return interviews strengthen these findings. Many of our respondents doubt the idea that the government institutions and legal systems can serve the interests of the common people, and they felt powerless because of the nonresponsiveness of the legal system. Zhou, the union chair, gave up after going to court more than twenty times and never receiving a response. Zhao, a thirty-nine-year-old woman worker in a township enterprise, sued the township government for not paying for her medical care. The local court never opened sessions to inquire into her case, and a lawyer who originally promised to help her disappeared.[34]

Interestingly, although almost all of the disputants felt somewhat disenchanted with their legal experiences, the reasons they provided and the party they blamed were quite different. We elaborate on this comparison next.

[34] CASE: Wuxi#4.

TABLE 7.6. *Use arbitration?*

		Frequency	Percent
Non-Disputants	Yes	2,585	83.6
	No	506	16.4
	Total	3,091	100
Disputants	Yes	54	76.1
	No	17	23.9
	Total	71	100

Source: 2005 Labor Law Survey.

TABLE 7.7. *Use litigation?*

		Frequency	Valid percent
Non-Disputants	Yes	2,406	77.8
	No	685	22.2
	Total	3,091	100
Disputants	Yes	45	63.4
	No	26	36.6
	Total	71	100

Source: 2005 Labor Law Survey.

TABLE 7.8. *Which method would you use first?*

		Frequency	Percent
Non-Disputants	Mediation	2,691	89.2
	Administrative methods	95	3.1
	Arbitration	146	4.8
	Litigation	84	2.8
	Total	3,016	100.0
Disputants	Mediation	60	87.0
	Administrative methods	2	2.9
	Arbitration	5	7.2
	Litigation	2	2.9
	Total	69	100.0

Source: 2005 Labor Law Survey.

TABLE 7.9. *Which method is most effective?*

		Frequency	Valid percent
Non-Disputants	Mediation	554	19.8
	Administrative methods	252	9.0
	Arbitration	535	19.1
	Litigation	1,378	49.3
	None is useful/effective	78	2.8
	Total	2,797	100.0
Disputants	Mediation	9	14.3
	Administrative methods	6	9.5
	Arbitration	20	31.7
	Litigation	18	28.6
	None is useful/effective	10	15.9
	Total	63	100.0

Source: 2005 Labor Law Survey.

COMPARING DISPUTANTS

In Gallagher's 2006 study of the effects of legal mobilization on legal-aid plaintiffs in Shanghai, she finds that disputants exhibit an interesting combination of disenchantment with the law and increased knowledge, confidence, and propensity to use the law. A large majority of the plaintiffs reported that they would use the law again to resolve future employment disputes, and three-quarters of the plaintiffs reported postdispute activities like helping friends, colleagues, and neighbors with their own workplace grievances. Although a propensity to sue is often used as evidence for a "rising legal consciousness" in China and other places where the rule of law is new or revived, Gallagher argues that legal consciousness does not develop linearly but should at least be conceptualized as dual, encompassing not only an individual's evaluation of the legal system but also including a separate evaluation of the individual's ability to use the legal system. A propensity to sue (measured by behavior) might be likelier, but it will coexist with higher levels of dissatisfaction with legal institutions (measured by attitudes).

In this chapter we extend this concept of legal consciousness to include these two components – how well does the law work (external efficacy) and how well can I work the law (internal efficacy) – while also paying attention to changes in legal knowledge. As the term "informed disenchantment" conveys, plaintiffs put much emphasize on the educative effects of the legal experience. Although increased legal knowledge can increase internal efficacy and give the disputants more confidence in their ability to work the legal system, it also can contribute to declines in external efficacy, especially when a disputant discovers that the law in reality is different from the law on the books. The most important aspect of this concept is that the two separate dimensions (external and internal efficacy) do not necessarily move in concert. How these attributes are affected by legal experience is potentially related to many different variables, including the type of dispute, the individual's role in the dispute, the region, the type of firm, individual-level attributes such as education level and gender, the presence or absence of legal assistance, and so forth.

Unlike in the United States, where race, gender, and other ascriptive labels are often most important in mediating people's experiences with the law,[35] we find that in China a plaintiff's political identity is important in determining how legality is experienced and how legal experiences can change how people think about and use the law. In this section, we explore the possibility that differences in disenchantment are related to the political identity of the plaintiffs in labor disputes. The concept of political identity encompasses the plaintiff's citizenship (whether rural or urban), the nature and timing of political socialization (pre- or postenterprise reform), and the plaintiff's relationship to the state (whether the state is both employer and the legal authority or only the legal authority). It is not the case that the most privileged groups under socialism are more likely to feel empowered and confident in their legal institutions. Groups privileged under socialism invoke their hierarchical status within the old system that granted urban workers much higher levels of benefits and employment security than others, especially rural citizens. However, the legal system is built on the notion of equality before the law, fairness, and equal treatment. On the one hand, this "rule of law" framework takes away the entitlements of socialism. On the other hand, young rural workers employed in the private sector are emboldened by discourses of equality, fairness, and nondiscrimination. These disputants are more likely to feel efficacious, seeking out legal knowledge and assistance and learning to use the law to press for their rights.[36]

[35] Ivan Y. Sun and Yuning Wu, "Citizens' Perceptions of the Courts: The Impact of Race, Gender, and Recent Experience," *Journal of Criminal Justice* 34, no. 5 (2006): 457–467; Laura Beth Nielsen, "Situating Legal Consciousness: Experiences and Attitudes of Ordinary Citizens about Law and Street Harassment," *Law & Society Review* 34, no. 4 (2000): 1055–1090.

[36] Neil J. Diamant, "Pursuing Rights and Getting Justice on China's Ethnic Frontier, 1949–1966," *Law & Society Review* 35, no. 4 (2001): 799–840, on research in southwestern China, and Frank K. Upham, "Litigation and Moral Consciousness in Japan: An Interpretative Analysis of Four Japanese Pollution Suits," *Law & Society Review*

It should be noted here that we are not attempting to explain variation in terms of who decides to invoke the legal system or, in other words, "to climb the dispute pyramid." Gallagher and colleagues find that a propensity to sue is related most consistently to levels of media exposure (higher levels of exposure are associated with escalation), residential status (local residents are more likely to escalate), and employment status (employed workers are more likely to escalate).[37] However, a considerable amount of city variation and contextual variables also is important. For example, the presence of a trade union at the workplace is associated with escalation among respondents in Wuxi and Shenyang, but not in Foshan or Chongqing. Our investigation here examines how different disputants experience and make sense of their attempts to resolve the conflict.[38]

Disputant Differences: The Role of Political Identity

The argument developed here was developed inductively and unexpectedly while conducting the first set of in-depth interviews with legal-aid plaintiffs in Shanghai. Some of the conclusions and arguments presented here contradict the original hypotheses and expectations developed while planning the process and applying for grants. Before the research began, we fully expected that a positive experience with the law and confidence in legal institutions would be associated with urban household status, higher levels of education and skills, and employment in firms with better working conditions and standards. When interviewing about fifty plaintiffs involved in labor disputes at a legal-aid center in Shanghai, we found that some of these expectations were borne out. For example, workers with higher levels of education and skills were more satisfied with their court experiences. However, we also noticed new and unexpected differences among disputants. Informants from outside Shanghai were more

10, no. 4 (1976): 579–619, on pollution victims in Japan, also find evidence that rural citizens can be more prone to legal mobilization than the supposed main beneficiaries of legal reform – urban, middle-class citizens. Whereas Mary E. Gallagher, Juan Chen, and Lyric Chen, "Losers and Lumpers: Determinants of Litigious Behavior Among Chinese Workers," paper in progress, do not find that migrant workers are more likely to use the law, we do find that they experience the law more positively. Michelson, "Climbing the Dispute Pagoda," also finds evidence questioning the link between legal mobilization and economic development.

37 Gallagher, Chen, and Chen, "Losers and Lumpers."

38 Because we examine only involvement in employment disputes, we do not explore how the type of dispute affects these variables. We also do not explore regional variation. The four-city survey does indicate, however, considerable regional variation in levels of dispute activity and some differences in individual outcomes.

satisfied with the legal system than we expected, given the importance of residential status in determining levels of citizenship and treatment by the local government. Young workers were almost complacent about the disputing process, often content that procedurally, things worked out, even if their substantive demands were not met or were much reduced by the court or arbitral decision. Older workers, often employed in the state sector, were the most frustrated and disenchanted of all, vowing to inflict personal violence on corrupt managers and wayward court officials. Some older plaintiffs turned their employment disputes into drawn-out personal battles against the state and the economic restructuring that had ruined their lives.

Given the qualitative and inductive nature of this research, it is impossible to ascertain the relative importance of the different variables that might help to account for these differences. Given the problem of multicollinearity, this problem might occur even if we could approach the problem statistically. Some of these differences track age (older workers are employed largely in public firms); others might be related to one's workplace (workers in the non-state sector may have greater confidence that the courts are impartial). The role of residential status (urban vs. rural, local vs. nonlocal) is complicated by that fact that most migrants, including highly skilled urban migrants, are young and employed in the non-state sectors. These problems are compounded by the fact that all of these potentially important variables are in motion. Restructuring and corporatization of state firms is changing the way even state enterprises interact with and treat their workforce. The reform of the system of residence permits (*hukou*) is breaking down some of the differences between residents and migrants. Finally, older workers imbued with the moral economy of state socialism are passing into retirement. These methodological problems encourage us to think more conceptually about the relationship between an individual plaintiff's relationship to the state and the effects of his/her legal experience. Although some basic characteristics might be important now (and we note them below), we remain sensitive to the reality that the relationship of the Chinese state to individual citizens is constantly in flux.

The notion of political identity relates to three different aspects of the state-citizen relationship. It includes citizenship (rural vs. urban), workplace socialization (pre- or postreform), and the role of the state in a legal dispute (legal authority or legal authority/employer). Citizenship is a critical factor in political identity because citizenship in China is tightly related to one's residential status, in particular whether one is a rural or an urban citizen. Social benefits, life chances, educational resources, formal employment opportunities, and access to key public goods all are closely tied to an individual's status as defined by citizenship.[39] Expectations and demands on the state are shaped by the *hukou* institution. Urban citizens in China have received much higher benefits and entitlements than their rural counterparts, and this continues to inform their expectations today.

The nature and timing of political socialization are important factors in understanding how people make sense of politics and government policies. We limit ourselves here to workplace socialization, in particular to whether a person was socialized into the workplace before or after enterprise reform. Workers who entered the workplace prior to the 1990s were more likely to be socialized into a socialist moral economy, enjoying a high level of benefits and a secure position in exchange for relatively low wages and mobility. Workers' identities were shaped by an ideology that exalted their status in society, and their relationship to the enterprise was noncontractual.

Workers who entered the workplace after enterprise reform (or who went directly into the small non-state sector in the 1980s) were more likely to be socialized into a workplace defined by contractual relations between firm and workers, fewer social benefits tied to the workplace, and a greater degree of mobility and insecurity. The workers' position in the workplace is established by their position, skills, and education rather than by their being part of a larger class. The political role of enterprises under socialism is underemphasized, whereas efficiency concerns are elevated. Firms in the non-state sectors exemplify this type of workplace socialization, but even some SOEs pursued these changes through the restructuring process.

Finally, the political identity of disputants is strongly affected by their perception of the state's role in the dispute. For workers employed at public firms, the role of the state is fused as both employer and the political/legal authority tasked with resolving the dispute. The plaintiffs' relationship to the legal system is powerfully affected by the notion that they are "suing the government," or "suing the party" and that by doing so, they are challenging the most powerful institutions by invoking its own institutions and organizations. There is a strong sense of disbelief that one can win against the state if the state itself is invested in the outcome, but this sense of disbelief is matched by a sense of anger that

[39] Dorothy J. Solinger, *Contesting Citizenship in Urban China: Peasant Migrants, the State, and the Logic of the Market* (Berkeley: University of California Press, 1999); Lianjiang Li, "The Empowering Effect of Village Elections in China," *Asian Survey* 43, no. 4 (2003): 648–662.

TABLE 7.10. *Political identity and mobilization*

	"Socialist" political identity	"Post-Socialist" political identity
Target	STATE and EMPLOYER	EMPLOYER
Pattern of Mobilization	*Petition* before, during, and after legal process	Seldom petition (*shangfang*)
Goal	"*Yao yige shuofa*" Tendency to pursue case for non-material goals	Cost-benefit analysis of legal battle
Strategy	Emphasis on particularistic social relations "workers' rights"	Emphasis on universal application of rules "citizen rights"
Evaluation	Emphasis on substantive justice	Emphasis on procedural justice

winning such disputes is impossible because the state will always protect itself.

The four cases presented next illustrate some of the basic differences among disputants. We then discuss these differences more generally, as presented in Table 7.10. Because the differences among disputants is observable as an age or generational effect, we use this language to differentiate between two ideal groups: a "socialist generation" of older, urban workers employed in the public sector and a "post-socialist generation" of younger workers employed in the non-state sector. This helps us understand how differences in political identity may be distributed across Chinese society.

Jiang's Experience at the Shanghai Aircraft Factory

Jiang was born in 1948 and is a typical representative of China's "lost generation" of the Cultural Revolution. His formal education ended with middle school, and in 1968 he was "sent down," as were many Shanghai youth, to the border area near the Soviet Union in Heilongjiang Province. He returned to Shanghai in 1979, and in 1985 he was allocated a job by the state in a local SOE producing airplane parts. In 1999, he was laid off by this enterprise. In 2002, he was formally given the status of laid off (*xiagang*) and given 10,000 RMB in severance compensation. His wife is also laid off and his son is still in school. Jiang and his family live on his meager income earned by odd jobs – for instance, delivering water and selling his paintings on the street. He worries about illness now that his medical care from the enterprise has stopped. Jiang sued for reinstatement, arguing that he should be treated as a retired worker and given a pension and other benefits. His claims were denied by the labor arbitration committee that heard his case. But his severance pay was raised from 10,000 to 21,000 RMB. Jiang became ill after arbitration and decided not to pursue the case in a court appeal.

Like many older workers, Jiang began the dispute resolution process by mobilizing outside the legal system through petitioning state offices directly. Jiang petitioned the Shanghai Municipal Trade Union, the Shanghai Bureau of Labor and Social Security, the Shanghai Mayor's Office, and the controlling corporation of his own company. During the petitioning process, Jiang invoked his identity as a state worker and a patriotic citizen who had helped China protect its borders during the Cultural Revolution. His engagement with the legal system was a long but ultimately unsuccessful struggle to retrieve some perquisites of the socialist era. Such cases are often unsuccessful because the legal system (as part of a general trend toward contractual social relationships) does not protect these long-held benefits. Jiang's perceptions of the legal system, market reform, and access to justice are shaped by his memories of the past and the loss of that past through the switch from lifetime employment to contract labor. Jiang noted in the interview that "the common people are very angry. I have been unfairly treated in comparison with treatment in other companies and even treatment in workshops in my own company. The leaders are corrupt whereas my wife and I have worked hard our whole life and have suffered much bitterness.... My company asked me to make a sacrifice because I am older and an old comrade; they promised to take care of me, but they didn't care at all. I could be dead on the street...."

Jiang's disappointment with the legal process goes far beyond his case and the individual circumstances that led to his job loss. He easily connects his hardships with his past identity as a patriotic student, then as a state sector worker, and finally as an "old comrade." Despite the legality of the enterprise's behavior, in his eyes it is unjust and immoral. His workplace dispute is linked to broader issues: corruption, government malfeasance, and the weak political position of Chinese workers.

Trade-Union Chairwoman Zhou's Disappointment

Zhou is the older female worker who was employed in the large state enterprise in Shenyang. Her case is also previously discussed. She was trade-union chairwoman until she retired in 1993. When her company was privatized, retired workers no longer received pensions, so Zhou began to mobilize the retired workers. She estimates that she filed more than twenty lawsuits, but ultimately she was unsuccessful. In the end, the local government restored her pension but not the pensions of sixty other retirees. Zhou feels that the law and the courts are completely useless. Although she tried many times to use connections with the local and provincial governments, she is disappointed that no official intervention in the case yielded better outcomes for her and her co-workers. She reports that she does not understand the law, that the labor law is not useful, and that she should have accepted long ago the statements of local officials that there is no way to win a case against the Communist Party. Unlike more efficacious disputants like Zhang and Li above, Zhou advises her friends and former co-workers to give up on lawsuits.

Wei's Experience at the Foreign Supermarket

Wei, a Shanghai local, was born in 1969 and has a high-school education. He was represented by the legal-aid center in his Shanghai labor dispute. Employed by a large, foreign supermarket, Wei worked on a year-to-year contract. He averaged about sixty hours in his six-day work week. After he inquired about some irregularities in how he was being compensated for overtime work, Wei was suddenly informed that his contract would not be renewed. Upon learning of his imminent dismissal, Wei sued the company for overtime compensation and holiday pay. The company negotiated some payment for holiday time but refused to pay any overtime. Wei lost the case in arbitration based on insufficient evidence. His appeal in civil court also was unsuccessful. After his loss, the company posted the court decision in the supermarket break room so that other workers would absorb the lesson of his loss. He now works as a cook in a hotel.

Wei's case was no more successful than Jiang's. But this reform-era loser experienced the legal system and the dispute resolution system very differently. He did not connect his problem at work with politics or the state. Like most disputants his age, he avoided petitioning or did not even consider it. He faced the typical difficulties of the "have-nots" in any legal system,[40] but these difficulties were not translated into a condemnation

[40] Marc Galanter, "Why the 'Haves' Come Out Ahead: Speculations on the Limits of Legal Change," *Law & Society Review* 9, no. 1 (1974): 95–160.

of reform, labor markets, or contract employment. Wei does not identify with the demands of the socialist generation, such as lifetime employment or increased benefits, because he has not experienced these institutions during his time in the labor market. Although disappointed in the ability of the legal system to deliver just outcomes, his evaluative process differed from that of Jiang and Zhou. Wei focused on the procedural difficulties of a successful case, in particular his inability to retrieve crucial evidence. Attempts to record his manager making incriminating statements were unsuccessful, as were requests to fellow colleagues to assist him in his case by serving as witnesses. Wei made many attempts to educate himself about the legal process through newspapers, the labor bureau's hotline, and the staff at the legal-aid center. He focused on his own mistakes and on the ability of the employer to manipulate the legal system more successfully.

Liao's Experience in a Japanese Company

Liao is a young, college-educated woman from rural Jiangxi Province. She moved to Shanghai from Jiangxi after graduation and was hired by a wholly owned Japanese company that offered to change her residential status by issuing her a Shanghai residence permit. When an explosion occurred in her home village, she received oral consent from her manager to leave work for one week. After returning to work, she found that she had been demoted from her office position to a production line worker job in the factory. When she tried to quit, the company fined her 20,000 RMB for breaking her service agreement. Liao then began a long process of arbitration and litigation against the company. She noted that her outsider status precluded other options like petitioning or using connections. "No one would have given me the time of day." Feeling that there were no other options and that she didn't know anyone in Shanghai, Liao began to research the labor law in newspapers. After finding information about legal aid in a local paper, she began to feel more confident and determined. She lost in arbitration and then went through two more court appeals to get a successful decision fully implemented. Compared to arbitration, Liao found that the court was more logical, with greater procedural regularities. The court asked for more evidence. She reports that she would use legal channels again and that she believes in the law. At her new place of employment, she works on a one-year contract, which she examined carefully when she received it. Her status as an outsider in Shanghai led her to believe that the law is the only option and is more effective for someone with her background. Although she cried intermittently during the interview, she remarked that the experience has strengthened her personality. She claims that she will not give up and that she has learned a lot and has greater confidence.

Migrant Worker Zhang's Dispute in Wuxi

Migrant worker Zhang was employed for many years in a Taiwanese company in Wuxi. He knew that the working conditions were poor and that the Taiwanese manager was not acting according to the law. To strengthen his case, Zhang took time off to go to a bookstore, where he purchased an expensive book on labor law. He then organized more than one hundred local and migrant workers to strike for better conditions. He promised the local workers that he could get the company to pay social insurance and promised the migrants that he could get the company to pay overtime. Before the strike, Zhang tried to entice support from the local safety bureau and the local trade union. The local safety bureau refused to help without more evidence, but a cadre at the trade union supported and encouraged him. Zhang reported that the trade-union cadre said, "[Y]ou have the ability to organize, you know how to use legal weapons to protect yourself, so you have the unconditional support of the trade union!" In the end, the company was successful in limiting the impact of the strike. Workers who pledged to strike were bought off, and the salaries of all the workers were raised slightly. Not long after the strike, Zhang left the company for new employment.

As was the case for Liao in her experience in Shanghai, Zhang did not believe that petitioning or government connections would have helped him with his dispute. Because he is a migrant worker, it is a waste of time to pursue these options. Yet Zhang also regrets not going further with his legal options. He concludes that next time he should try to find a good lawyer. This is the recommendation he makes to his friends when they seek him out for help with their own disputes.

These four cases show how different disputants dealt with the frustrations and difficulties of the dispute process. The disputants' patterns of mobilization were strongly affected by their own understandings of their identity in relationship to state institutions, policies, and ideologies. Older SOE workers like Zhou and Jiang unsuccessfully invoked their former identities as part of the vanguard class, whereas migrant workers like Zhang and Liao strategized according to their perception that as outsiders, legal options offered better chances than government connections. Whereas older workers judged the legal system for its inability to produce satisfactory outcomes, younger plaintiffs felt empowered by the procedures, regardless of the less-than-satisfactory outcomes. We summarize these differences next and in Table 7.10.

PATTERN OF MOBILIZATION: LAW VERSUS PETITIONING

The differences between the two approaches were apparent in the paths taken to legal mobilization, specifically whether or not the decision to use the legal system was prefaced by any petitioning activity. Younger, non-state workers tended to take their cases directly to the legal system after direct negotiations with management failed. If these disputants wanted to attract outside attention to their cases, they went to the media. They barely even contemplated going to the government's petitioning offices.

For those coming from a long history of employment in SOEs or in the public sector more generally, legal mobilization often was the last resort. A decision was made either after long periods of petitioning activity had failed or after the petition office itself had redirected the case to arbitration. Law was the last resort and a path often opened by the state as these petitioners were reoriented away from Letters and Visits Offices and toward arbitration and the courts. In many cases, their pattern of mobilization reflected a three-pronged assault on the state for not caring enough about the plight of SOE workers: Mobilization would start with petitioning, move to the media, and often be pushed to the legal system after failures in the other realms.

For many within this older generation, "resolving disputes through law" is the state's strategy to avoid the moral obligations of socialist employment. Legal options are suspect and unreliable because the legal system tends to minimize the workers' relationship with their work-unit and to attenuate the moral claims they want to make on their employer and, by extension, on the state itself. For these reasons, workers from state companies almost never start with the law. In fact, their recourse to the law most often is a result of redirection by state officials who instruct them that they must "*yifa banshi*" (do things according to law) or use the legal system only as a result of a complete failure with the *shangfang, jingzuo* (petitioning and sitting outside government offices) pattern of moral remonstration.

Goal of Mobilization: Strategic versus Expressive

This pattern of socialist mobilization (a long process of petitioning or, as one plaintiff stated, "I petitioned until my shoes broke," followed by a lengthy process of arbitration and court appeals, often ending in either complete failure, a paltry settlement, or an unimplemented court order) was pursued long after it was apparent that the relative gains were far outweighed by the lost time, expense, mental and physical energy expended, and damage to one's mental health. The most common explanation was the need or desire for a *shuofa* (an explanation).

For those in the post-socialist generation, however, decisions to pursue or give up, to mediate or settle, often were made with less regard to proving the point and with much greater regard for the opportunity costs of a lengthy court process. Post-socialist workers, with less invested in one particular workplace and also concerned that possible media coverage or co-worker gossip would affect their employment chances elsewhere, were far more likely to give up, settle, "lump" the dispute, or move on if their chances of winning dimmed.

This difference is partly the result of the relative importance of any one particular job. Older SOE workers know that they potentially face a long period of unemployment and falling living standards, whereas those in the post-socialist generation can, indeed must, quickly move on. But we argue that there is more to the differences between these two groups than material interests.

For those in the older generation, standing up to an injustice on the job (very often associated with restructuring and ownership changes) and getting an explanation from the state (through the courts) is a moral condemnation not only of a single leader or a mismanaged firm, but also of what they believe to be an unjust reform process. By contrast, post-socialist younger workers are defined in part by the disconnect between economics and politics. Their problems on the job are merely part of this disconnect. There is little ability or inclination to attach political meaning to their grievances at work.

Mobilization Discourse: Universalism versus Particularism

One of the reasons older plaintiffs look first to petitioning and only second or third to the law is the difficulty that they have in invoking particularistic social relations as a strategy to win support for their cases. Their (sometimes former) identities as state workers are not respected or honored in the courts.[41] What matters is their labor contract. Long

[41] Mary E. Gallagher, "'Use the Law as Your Weapon!' Institutional Change and Legal Mobilization in China." In *Engaging the Law in China: State, Society, and Possibilities for Justice*, ed. Neil J. Diamant, Stanley B. Lubman, and Kevin J. O'Brien (Stanford: Stanford University Press, 2005).

tenure at one work-unit will get you a bigger settlement, but it won't save your job. The universal application of laws rarely benefits those whose social welfare and employment security were for so long guaranteed not through the law but through a particularistic relationship with the state through the SOE.

For younger plaintiffs, especially those with an "outsider" status, the most important criterion is that the laws be applied fairly, for both locals and non-locals alike. The universalism of the law, if it is applied correctly, grants them protections that they did not enjoy previously. And, not surprisingly, suspicions of discrimination or corruption are common sore points for this post-socialist generation.

Evaluation: Procedural Fairness versus Substantive Outcomes

Plaintiffs of both generations were often dissatisfied with the results of their cases. In the postdispute period, many reflected on the problems within the system and the mistakes and missteps that they had made along the way. But the younger plaintiffs tended to be more realistic about the process, often judging the experience by how the institutions worked and whether or not procedurally they were treated fairly and respectfully by the state and the involved court officials. They often had criticisms: too-close ties between labor bureaus and companies, weak courts, and badly trained and ill-prepared labor arbitrators. They wanted the procedures to be improved. For those of the socialist generation, there was a tendency to judge the experience based on distributive outcomes. Procedural issues that block a desired outcome, even when applied correctly and fairly, arc illegitimate. Procedural technicalities that keep their issues out of the courts are seen as unfair amendments to a long-standing relationship that was not based on a legal contract. The rules of the game have been changed midstream. Therefore, the rules themselves are illegitimate and unfair.

CONCLUSION

The role of legal experience in changing people's attitudes and behavior vis-à-vis the legal system remains an understudied topic. In this chapter, we set out some basic arguments about the nature of legal mobilization in China. We find that legal experience can have contradictory effects on a "legal consciousness." Borrowing concepts from the study of political participation more broadly, we find that internal efficacy (how well one works the law) can be strengthened through engagement with the legal system. Respondents with and without legal assistance reported increased confidence, better understanding of procedures, and optimism that they had improved enough to have a better chance the next time around. External efficacy (how well the law works), however, is adversely affected by contacts with the legal system as plaintiffs find legal institutions to be less effective and less responsive than they initially expected.

Although disputants of all stripes and colors report negative experiences and difficulties, our comparison of "users" finds that patterns of mobilization and evaluations of the legal system are strongly shaped by a plaintiff's political identity. Disenchantment is most profound among those who were relatively well-off and protected by the socialist system of employment, whereas those who remained on the outside by virtue of age or birthplace are more sanguine about their chances with the law. Despite all the problems with the Chinese legal system, the very fact that it exists and is being increasingly used by workers seeking redress is an indication of the state's success in building new institutions that can demobilize a formally powerful sector of society while mobilizing new actors and constituents.

8

With or without the Law: The Changing Meaning of Ordinary Legal Work in China, 1979–2003

Sida Liu

Until 1979, China had never been a country with a highly differentiated legal system. From the *Law Classics* (*Fa jing*) in the Warring State period (480–221 B.C.) to the *Great Qing Criminal Code* (*Da Qing lü li*, effective during 1740–1910), the two-millennium history of codification in imperial China had always been characterized by a strong emphasis on criminal law; most noncriminal disputes were adjudicated according to the Confucian ethics (*li*) and social customs, without referring to any legal code.[1] Meanwhile, in the Chinese political system there was no separate judiciary from the government, and the local magistrate was both the administrative leader and the judge for crimes and social disputes.[2] Accordingly, no formal legal profession was found in imperial China. In certain periods, there were "litigation masters" (*song shi*) who provided help to the people in litigation, but they were neither organized into a legal profession in the Western sense nor recognized by the state.[3] Ordinary social order largely was maintained in a harmonious and unified way through non-legal means. However, in the twentieth century, this social order was almost completely broken down because of the incessant revolutions, culminating in the Cultural Revolution during 1966–76.

[1] T'ung-tsu Ch'u, *Law and Society in Traditional China* (Paris: Mouton, 1961).

[2] He Weifang, "Quanneng xing yamen: Chuantong yu yingxiang" (Omnipotent Government: Tradition and Effect), *Nanfang zhoumo* (Southern Weekend), January 16, 1998, reprinted in He Weifang, *Sifa de linian yu zhidu* (The Concepts and Systems of Judicature) (Beijing: Zhongguo zhengfa daxue chubanshe, 1998), pp. 244–246.

[3] Melissa Macauley, *Social Power and Legal Culture: Litigation Masters in Late Imperial China* (Stanford: Stanford University Press, 1998); Dang Jiangzhou, *Zhongguo songshi wenhua: Gudai lüshi xianxiang jiedu* (The Culture of Litigation Masters in China: Interpretations on the Phenomenon of Ancient Lawyers) (Beijing: Beijing daxue chubanshe, 2005).

An abridged Chinese version of this chapter was published as "Dangdai Zhongguo richang falü gongzuo de yihan bianqian (1979–2003)," *Zhongguo shehui kexue* (Social Sciences in China), no. 2 (2007): 90–105.

Since the late 1970s, the Chinese legal system has experienced a series of fundamental changes. Tens of thousands of laws, regulations, judicial interpretations, ministry regulations, and local regulations have been promulgated, starting with the Criminal Law and Criminal Procedure Law in 1979.[4] This grand process of codification has been coupled with the privatization of the legal profession, the proliferation of legal-service providers, and symbolic and substantive reforms of the judiciary.[5] Originating from the central leaders' reflections on the social and political turmoil during the Cultural Revolution, all of these reform efforts constitute a state-led "rule-of-law" project that aims to build a legal system capable of maintaining social stability and promoting economic development.

Nonetheless, this ongoing project largely failed to change the ways ordinary disputes were resolved in China. Although the Chinese now seem to be more litigious and have a stronger legal consciousness, the results of their encounters with lawyers and courts often are quite disappointing.[6] In rural areas, disputes and grievances are more likely to be resolved through non-legal means than through formal procedures,[7] and judges and lawyers often are caught in a dilemma of "bringing law to the countryside."[8] Basically, after more than twenty-five years, the Chinese

[4] From 1979 to 1997, the National People's Congress and its Standing Committee passed 328 laws, amended laws, or decisions; the State Council issued about 770 administrative regulations; and the provincial and local governments formulated more than 5,200 provincial regulations. In recent years, these numbers have continued to increase rapidly. See Cai Dingjian, "Development of the Chinese Legal System Since 1979 and its Current Crisis and Transformation," *Cultural Dynamic* 11, no. 2 (1999): 136.

[5] Ethan Michelson, *Unhooking from the State: Chinese Lawyers in Transition* (Ph.D. diss., Department of Sociology, University of Chicago, 2003); Sida Liu, "Beyond Global Convergence: Conflicts of Legitimacy in a Chinese Lower Court," *Law & Social Inquiry* 31, no. 1 (2006): 75–106; Sida Liu, "Lawyers, State Officials, and Significant Others: Symbiotic Exchange in the Chinese Legal Services Market," *The China Quarterly*, forthcoming.

[6] Ethan Michelson, "The Practice of Law as an Obstacle to Justice: Chinese Lawyers at Work," *Law & Society Review* 40, no. 1 (2006): 1–38; Mary E. Gallagher, "Mobilizing the Law in China: 'Informed Disenchantment' and the Development of Legal Consciousness," *Law & Society Review* 40, no. 4 (2006): 783–816; He Xin, "Yunzuo buliang de jiceng fayuan" (Dysfunctional Courts), *Falü he shehui kexue* (Law and Social Science), vol. 1, ed. Su Li (Beijing: Falü chubanshe, 2006), pp. 30–65.

[7] Kevin J. O'Brien and Lianjiang Li, *Rightful Resistance in Rural China* (New York: Cambridge University Press, 2006); Ethan Michelson, "Justice from Above or Justice from Below? Popular Strategies for Resolving Grievances in Rural China," *The China Quarterly*, no. 193 (2008): 43–64.

[8] Su Li, *Song fa xiaxiang: Zhongguo jiceng sifa zhidu yanjiu* (Bringing Law to the Countryside: Research on the Grassroots Judicial System of China) (Beijing: Zhongguo zhengfa

state's "rule-of-law" project has not reached its initial objectives, and there is a growing considerable gap between Chinese society and the legal system the state has built to change the society.

At the pivot of this historical transformation lies lawyers' legal advice to ordinary Chinese citizens. The legal reform has changed the case types of ordinary legal work, the statutes lawyers use, the styles of their legal reasoning, and, ultimately, the meaning of legal advice per se. To trace this transformation of ordinary legal work in China, this chapter analyzes 2,077 cases from the legal-advice column in the journal *Democracy and the Legal System* (*Minzhu yu fazhi*, hereinafter DALS) from 1979 to 2003. As the first and best-known popular political and legal magazine in China after the Cultural Revolution, DALS has borne witness to China's "long march to the rule of law."[9] It provides a unique and valuable playground for the interactions among popular legal demands, state legal policies, and lawyers' professional work.

Using this data source, I examine the decoupling process between the legal system and ordinary social disputes in contemporary China during the first twenty-five years of its legal reform. I argue that, somewhat ironically, the codification of law and the professionalization of lawyers increased the gap between law and society in China and made communication between citizens and legal professionals more difficult. Over time, lawyers have cited more statutes and adopted more technical language in their advice to readers of the column, yet the types of cases they handle largely have remained the same. Citing and interpreting statutes makes the lawyers' explanations clearer, more logical, and more precise; but, at the same time, it also makes it more difficult for the readers to fully understand and make use of the legal advice. This increasing difficulty in communication between the legal system and the daily life of the citizens partially explains why China's legal reform has fallen short of fulfilling its promises.

THE LEGAL SYSTEM AND EVERYDAY LIFE: THEORETICAL PERSPECTIVES

The legal reform in China since the late 1970s presents an appropriate contemporary case to examine the potential rapprochement of two

daxue chubanshe, 2000); Frank K. Upham, "Who Will Find the Defendant if He Stays with His Sheep? Justice in Rural China," *Yale Law Journal* 114, no. 7 (2005): 1675–1718.

[9] Randall Peerenboom, *China's Long March toward Rule of Law* (Cambridge: Cambridge University Press, 2002).

distinct traditions in the sociology of law: 1) the European sociolegal tradition on the formal rationalization of a modern legal system, which dates back to the seminal writings of Max Weber; and 2) the American law and society tradition on the construction of meanings of law in everyday life, which is best illustrated by the work of the Amherst School authors.

Much of our understanding of law in modern society is derived from Max Weber's thesis on the formal rationalization of law. Based on a theory of rationalization and a typology of legal thought, Weber argues that, along with the rise of the capitalist economic system, legal systems in modern Western countries became increasingly formal and rational. In the ideal type of the formal, rational legal system, decisions are based exclusively on the logical application of rational rules and legal principles.[10] The formal rationalization of law leads to an inevitable gap between the legal system and social life. Weber's extreme example of this process is the modern judge in continental Europe who becomes a "vending machine" into which one inserts the facts and a fee in order to have it spew out the judicial decision and its reasoning.[11]

With the differentiation of formally rational law from its social roots, the legal system gradually develops a series of self-sustaining mechanisms that protect its autonomy from external influence.[12] Consequently, the legal system is decoupled from the life-world in which communicative actions among ordinary citizens take place.[13] In such a highly differentiated and self-sustaining legal system, the language and logic that lawyers use within the system are qualitatively different from the language and logic that people use in ordinary social life. Thus, lawyers in one society might share more common beliefs and ways of thinking with lawyers from other societies rather than with citizens in their own society.[14] This is precisely what Anthony Giddens calls the "disembedding" effect of modernity – that is, the "lifting out" of expert knowledge from its local contexts.[15]

[10] Max Weber, *Economy and Society*, ed. G. Roth and C. Wittich (Berkeley: University of California Press, 1978), pp. 654–658.

[11] Max Weber, *Max Weber on Law in Economy and Society*, ed. Max Rheinstein (Cambridge: Harvard University Press, 1954), p. 354.

[12] For example, coding and programming in Luhmann's social system. Niklas Luhmann, *Law as a Social System* (New York: Oxford University Press, 2004).

[13] Jürgen Habermas, *Theory of Communicative Action*, trans. T. McCarthy (Boston: Beacon Press, 2 vols., 1984, 1987).

[14] Brian Z. Tamanaha, *A General Jurisprudence of Law and Society* (New York: Oxford University Press, 2001).

[15] Anthony Giddens, *The Consequences of Modernity* (Cambridge, U.K.: Polity Press, 1990), p. 21.

Accordingly, trust in abstract systems, or "faceless commitments,"[16] becomes essential for the working of modern legal institutions. In everyday legal practice, however, an inevitable gap exists between the lawyers' professional legal logic and the particular expectations of the lay parties.[17] This gap can only be mitigated at "access points" where representatives of the system (i.e., professionals) and lay individuals interact under specific circumstances. These access points are "places of vulnerability for abstract systems, but also junctions at which trust can be maintained or built up."[18] Therefore, what happens in the interactions between lawyers and lay individuals at such access points is crucial for understanding the operation of a modern legal system and its relationship with the social world in which it is embedded. Popular legal-advice columns, similar to consultation in law firms and mediation in lower courts, are one of these access points where communications between the legal system and ordinary social life take place.

The Weberian sociolegal theories are nevertheless too grand to shed sufficient light on micro-level interactions. Here I turn to the Amherst School in the American law and society literature.[19] A fundamental insight of this tradition is that the meaning of law is established not only in formal legal institutions like statutes, courts, or law enforcement agencies but, more importantly, constructed also through social interactions in everyday life. The encounters between law and everyday life produce people's legal consciousness, or what Ewick and Silbey call the "commonplace legality." People's participation in legality in everyday life takes multiple forms: 1) before the law: conceiving of the law as a separate sphere from ordinary social life but having faith in its authority and predictability; 2) with the law: treating the law as a game in which rules are deployed and invented to serve certain interests and values; and 3) against the law: exploiting the interstices of law to be up against it and to retain a sense of honor and dignity.[20] At the same time, the lawyers'

[16] Ibid, p. 80.

[17] Weber, *Max Weber on Law in Economy and Society*, pp. 307–308.

[18] Giddens, *The Consequences of Modernity*, p. 88.

[19] See, for example, Patricia Ewick and Susan S. Silbey, *The Common Place of Law: Stories from Everyday Life* (Chicago: University of Chicago Press, 1998); Austin Sarat and Thomas R. Kearns, *Law in Everyday Life* (Ann Arbor: University of Michigan Press, 1993); Sally E. Merry, *Getting Justice and Getting Even: Legal Consciousness among Working-Class Americans* (Chicago: University of Chicago Press, 1990); Barbara Yngvesson, *Virtuous Citizens, Disruptive Subjects: Order and Complaint in a New England Court* (New York: Routledge, 1993).

[20] Ewick and Silbey, *The Common Place of Law*, pp. 45–49.

diagnosis, inference, and treatment of legal problems in their work are also constructed by their daily interactions with ordinary people.[21]

Language has important symbolic power[22] in the interactions between law and social life. Legal discourse requires extensive training and often is considered difficult for common people to understand.[23] Nevertheless, the Amherst School authors focus precisely on how the law itself is made socially meaningful in everyday moral and relational contexts and examine the language that lawyers and judges use to explain the law and legal process to citizens. For instance, in her study of a New England lower court, Sally E. Merry distinguishes three types of discourse in the legal process, namely, the legal discourse, the moral discourse, and the therapeutic discourse. Whereas the legal discourse emphasizes notions of rights and formal legal concepts, the moral discourse relies on the morality and responsibilities contained in kinship and social relationships, and the therapeutic discourse attributes problems to individual or psychological weaknesses and offers therapy as recourse.[24]

Therefore, by focusing on the micro-level interactions between the legal system and everyday life, the Amherst School authors provide a rich repertoire of analytical tools for understanding the various meanings of law constructed in ordinary social life. On the surface, there seems to be a sharp contrast between this Foucauldian approach and the European sociolegal theories that treat the meanings of modern law as being increasingly produced in a legal system autonomous from everyday life. However, in my view, the two approaches are in fact complementary. First, although the European theories lay out the macro-level dual structures of system and life-world in modern society, the Amherst School studies demonstrate the complexity of micro-level interactions between the system and life-world. Second, they share an emphasis on the encounter between law and social life at "access points" of the legal system, as well as the social construction of legal meanings in the communication between legal professionals and ordinary people. Finally, the Amherst School presents ample evidence for the Weberian formal rationalization of the modern legal system, in which the meaning of law becomes Janus faced – as both

[21] Austin D. Sarat and William L. F. Felstiner, *Divorce Lawyers and Their Clients: Power and Meaning in the Legal Process* (New York: Oxford University Press, 1995).

[22] Pierre Bourdieu, *Language and Symbolic Power* (Cambridge: Harvard University Press, 1991).

[23] Elizabeth Mertz, *The Language of Law School: Learning to "Think Like a Lawyer"* (New York: Oxford University Press, 2007); John M. Conley and William M. O'Barr, *Just Words: Law, Language, and Power* (Chicago: University of Chicago Press, 1998).

[24] Merry, *Getting Justice and Getting Even.*

abstract rules standing outside people's lives (formal law) and cultural tool kits shaping and being shaped by ordinary social life (substantive law).

The theoretical relevance of the DALS legal-advice column lies precisely in the overlap of these two traditions. The evolution of this column over twenty-five years witnessed not only the formal rationalization of Chinese law and its gradual detachment from society after 1979, but also the interactions between legal professionals and ordinary citizens and the changing meaning of law as constructed through these public correspondences. In his groundbreaking study of the legal-advice column "Lawyer Bao" in *Beijing Evening News*, Michelson applies Merry's typology of discourses to China and emphasizes Lawyer Bao's "boundary work" in legitimizing state interests and delegitimizing certain types of social grievances.[25] However, the period of his data (1989–98) is not extensive enough to analyze the change of legal meanings over time, which is precisely the focus of the present chapter.

During the twenty-five-year period of the DALS column, lawyers' prescriptions for the problems of column readers became increasingly rational, which led to two consequences: On the one hand, the meaning of ordinary legal work in China changed from an organic part of social life to a logical, authoritative, but sometimes incoherent system; on the other hand, this seemingly rational system of legal work widened the gap between the readers' expectations and the lawyers' interpretations of the law and often left the substantive problems unresolved.

THE LEGAL-ADVICE COLUMN: A TWENTY-FIVE-YEAR OVERVIEW

DALS was established in August 1979 as the first popular political and legal (*zhengfa*) magazine after the Cultural Revolution. It was based in Shanghai during its first fifteen years and then moved to Beijing in the early 1990s under the guidance of the China Law Society (*Zhongguo faxuehui*), the official association of the legal academy in China. The main task of the magazine was to promote the legal consciousness of citizens by explaining new statutes, reporting on important or interesting cases (both domestic and foreign), commenting on issues in legal practice, and providing legal advice to readers.

[25] Ethan Michelson, "Dear Lawyer Bao: Everyday Problems, Legal Advice, and State Power in China," *Social Problems* 55, no. 1 (February 2008): 43–71.

An analysis of the geographical distribution of the DALS magazine readership suggests that, in its first fifteen years (1979–93) in Shanghai, it was a regional magazine that served mainly readers in Shanghai, Jiangsu, and Zhejiang, but also provided legal advice to readers in most other provinces, plus occasional cases in Hong Kong and abroad; in the following ten years (1994–2003) in Beijing, it became a national magazine with a more even geographical distribution that served readers from all provinces of China, including remote areas such as Qinghai and Tibet. During the twenty-five years, readers of the DALS column hailed from an extensive geographic range, from metropolises like Beijing and Shanghai to small villages in rural areas across the country.

In spite of its seemingly regional readership, DALS and its legal-advice column in fact were more popular in the 1980s than in the later years. It was a monthly magazine from 1979 to 1994, and in 1995 it became biweekly. In its first ten years, however, the column published 970 cases, or 46.7 percent of the 2,077 cases it published during the twenty-five years. Figure 8.1 shows the changes in the average number of cases per issue during the twenty-five years of the column. In the early 1980s, every issue consisted of usually nine to twelve cases, but the numbers dropped quickly in the late 1980s and stayed at about four cases per issue after 1990. This decrease in number of cases suggests that the column as a legal institution had become quite formalized by the early 1990s.

The early popularity of DALS was partly a result of the lack of alternative legal magazines in China at the time. Purportedly the only national political-legal magazine in the early 1980s, the per-issue circulation of DALS was as high as several million. Although the majority of cases in the column came from provinces adjacent to Shanghai, the distribution of the magazine enabled it from the very beginning to reach most provinces of the country. For instance, a distinguished Chinese law professor who was a law student at Southwest University of Political Science and Law in the early 1980s informed me that DALS was very popular among his college students at the time. In the May 1980 issue, Liang Huixing, then a graduate law student at the Chinese Academy of Social Sciences (CASS) who later would become a prominent scholar on civil law, wrote a reply to the column to correct a mistake in an earlier issue. In the April 1980 issue, there was even a letter from a Harvard law professor visiting Peking University who had consulted the column on some issues related to the Criminal Procedure Law in China. There were also a number of judges, lawyers, prosecutors, and local officials who wrote to the column for

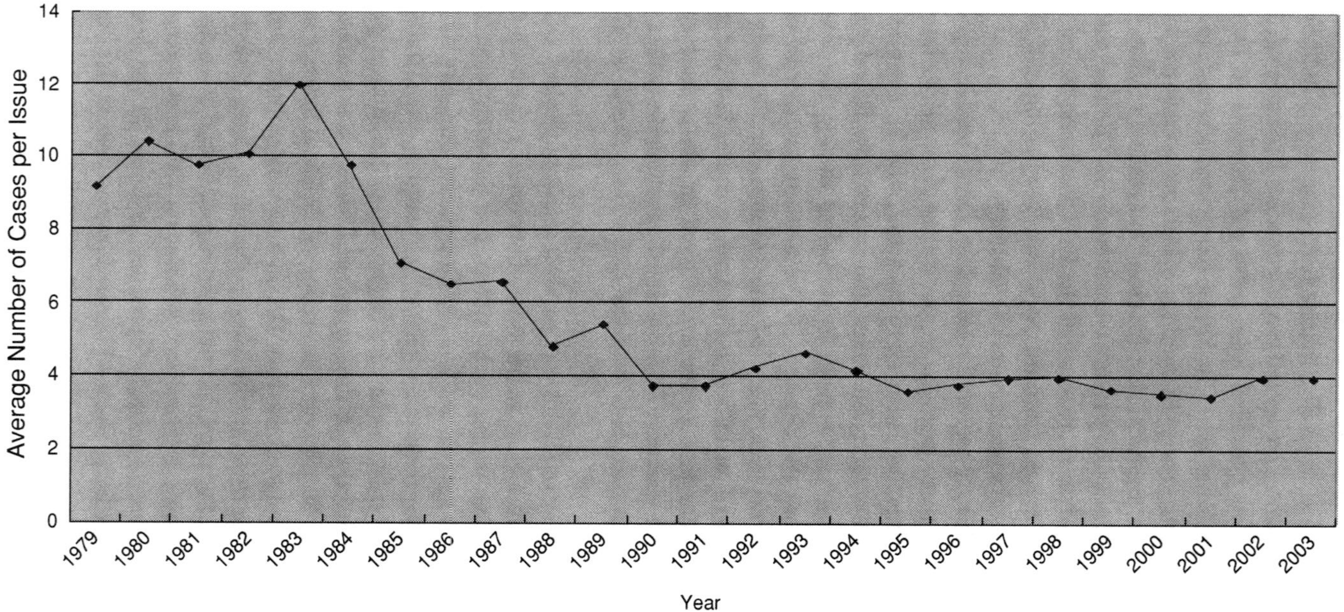

FIGURE 8.1. Changes in the Average Number of Cases per Issue, 1979–2003.

advice on the administration of justice. In a sense, in the early 1980s, the DALS legal-advice column became a nationwide authority in promoting and interpreting Chinese law and resolving social disputes.

Two types of legal professionals penned opinions for the column during the twenty-five years. For the majority of the time, the legal-advice column was outsourced to a law firm based in either Shanghai or Beijing. However, during its first several years, DALS had its own legal personnel to handle the cases presented in the column. Given the fact that Chinese lawyers were still working in state-owned legal advisory divisions in the early 1980s, it is likely that the internal legal professionals who handled the column at the time either were licensed lawyers or highly educated professionals – otherwise, they would not have been regarded as legal authorities by law students or scholars. Therefore, regardless of whether the legal professionals for the DALS column were in-house staff or outside lawyers, they were highly qualified representatives of the Chinese legal profession. For analytical convenience, in the following text I uniformly refer to them as "the column lawyer."

Table 8.1 presents the changing percentages of each type of cases in the DALS column during the twenty-five years. I divide the twenty-five-year period into five five-year intervals, that is, 1979–83, 1984–88, 1989–93, 1994–98, and 1999–2003. Incidentally, these periods coincided with the five terms of the National People's Congress (NPC) (i.e., the Sixth to the Tenth NPCs) from 1979 to 2003. Hence, using this table we are also able to explore some associations between national lawmaking activities and a diversification of case types during the first twenty-five years of China's legal reform.

In general, although the average number of cases per issue dropped significantly (Figure 8.1), the percentages of case types demonstrate notable stability over time. Most significant changes in case types occurred between 1979 and 1983 and between 1984 and 1988, the first ten years of legal reform. For example, the percentage of criminal cases decreased from 33.45 percent to 15.83 percent, while civil cases increased from 64.54 percent to 75.07 percent. Among the civil cases, the percentages of family and inheritance cases decreased from 39.06 percent to 19.18 percent; contract and tort cases increased from 1.81 percent to 15.11 percent and from 3.25 percent to 9.11 percent, respectively; and labor cases increased from 1.99 percent to 5.52 percent. Meanwhile, the percentage of administrative cases increased from 0.36 percent to 8.63 percent. All of these changes suggest that in the early 1980s, the Chinese legal system experienced a rapid diversification of case types. As a result, the

TABLE 8.1. *Distribution of case types (percentage), DALS legal-advice column, 1979–2003*

Case Type	1979–83	1984–88	1989–93	1994–98	1999–2003	1979–2003
Total no. of cases	553	417	262	397	448	2077
	%	%	%	%	%	%
Public security	3.62	2.16	1.53	3.78	3.79	3.13
Personal injury	7.41	3.60	2.29	1.26	1.79	3.61
Economic crime	4.70	3.60	2.29	6.05	3.79	4.24
Criminal procedure	17.72	6.47	4.20	11.08	6.70	10.11
Criminal total	33.45	15.83	10.31	22.17	16.07	21.09
Contract	1.81	15.11	11.45	4.03	10.04	7.90
Debt and loan	2.17	3.60	4.96	8.06	7.37	5.06
Tort	3.25	9.11	7.63	8.56	11.83	7.85
Family and inheritance	39.06	19.18	19.47	18.64	17.19	23.98
Land and real estate	7.41	6.71	7.63	7.05	6.47	7.03
Consumer rights	0	0.72	0.76	3.02	2.46	1.35
Corporation	0.18	2.88	2.67	1.76	2.46	1.83
Tax	0	0.96	0.38	0.25	0.22	0.34
Banking	0.54	1.20	1.53	2.02	1.34	1.25
Intellectual property	0.18	2.88	1.91	2.27	1.56	1.64
Labor	1.99	5.52	7.25	7.05	6.25	5.25
Insurance	0	0.72	0.76	0.76	0.67	0.53
Environmental law	0.54	0.96	0	1.01	0.22	0.58
Civil procedure	6.87	2.64	13.36	6.55	8.48	7.13
Other civil	0.54	2.88	1.91	0.25	2.01	1.43
Civil total	64.54	75.07	81.67	71.28	78.57	73.15
Constitutional law	0.36	0.24	0.38	0.25	0	0.24
Administrative law	0.36	8.63	6.87	5.79	5.13	4.91
Administrative total	0.72	8.87	7.25	6.04	5.13	5.15
Lawyer representation	0.54	0.24	0.38	0.50	0.22	0.39
Judicial system	0.72	0	0.38	0	0	0.24
Judicial tTotal	1.26	0.24	0.76	0.50	0.22	0.63

proportion of criminal cases and family and inheritance cases decreased, whereas cases related to contract, labor, and administrative law became important.

By contrast, from the second period (1984–88) to the last period (1999–2003), the percentages of most case types remained very stable. Family and inheritance cases always accounted for about 18 to 19 percent of all column cases throughout the twenty-year span (i.e., 1984–2003). The percentages of land and real-estate cases were also extremely stable, at about 7 percent. Other examples include labor cases, accounting for 5 to 7 percent, tort cases, accounting for 8 to 11 percent; and intellectual property cases, mostly copyright issues, accounting for about 2 percent. One obvious reason for this stability was the institutionalization of the legal-advice column since the late 1980s, but considering that the cases were sent in by readers from all over China, it also suggests that there was no fundamental change in the demands for different types of cases during this twenty-year period.

Nevertheless, not every category remained stable after the second period. Both debt and loan and consumer rights cases significantly increased in the 1994–98 and 1999–2003 periods compared with the pre-1993 period. These significant increases apparently were associated with the promulgation of two major statutes in these two areas of law: the Guarantee Law in 1995 and the Consumer Protection Law in 1993. Moreover, they may also indicate that economic activities, such as bank loans and purchases, played a more important role in the life of ordinary Chinese citizens after the mid-1990s, especially after Deng Xiaoping's 1992 Southern Tour that generated the rapid market economy reform in China. In addition to these two categories, the percentage of economic crimes also increased significantly in the 1994–98 period. Many of these cases involved white-collar crimes such as bribery and embezzlement, which had become prevalent among Chinese government officials by the 1990s. Furthermore, there were more cases on criminal procedure in the 1994–98 period than in any other period, which probably is related to the 1996 revision of the Criminal Procedure Law.

Although rapid codification did not change the distribution of case types to a large extent, it did change the manner in which the lawyers responded to the readers. Figure 8.2 presents the average number of statutes cited in the column each year. It is evident that in their replies to readers, lawyers cited more and more statutes from 1979 to 2003. Among the 2,077 cases, 384 cases cited no statute at all, 1,138 cases cited one statute, 443 cases cited two statutes, 91 cases cited three, 21 cases cited four, and no case cited five or more statutes. The average number of statutes cited during the twenty-five years is 1.15. Note that during the 1979–85 period, every year the average number of statutes cited was less than one, with the lowest (0.78) in 1983, whereas it increased to more than 1.30 statutes after 1993, with the highest (1.63) in 2002. Clearly, rapid codification armed the lawyers with many more "legal weapons" in their legal advice to the readers of the column.

Yet the scope of the statutes cited was highly limited. Altogether, only 419 distinct laws, administrative regulations, judicial interpretations and opinions, provincial regulations, party documents, and other statutes were cited for the 2,077 cases. Table 8.2 presents the twenty-six statutes that were cited ten or more times during the twenty-five years. These twenty-six statutes were cited 1,748 times, or 73.41 percent of the 2,381

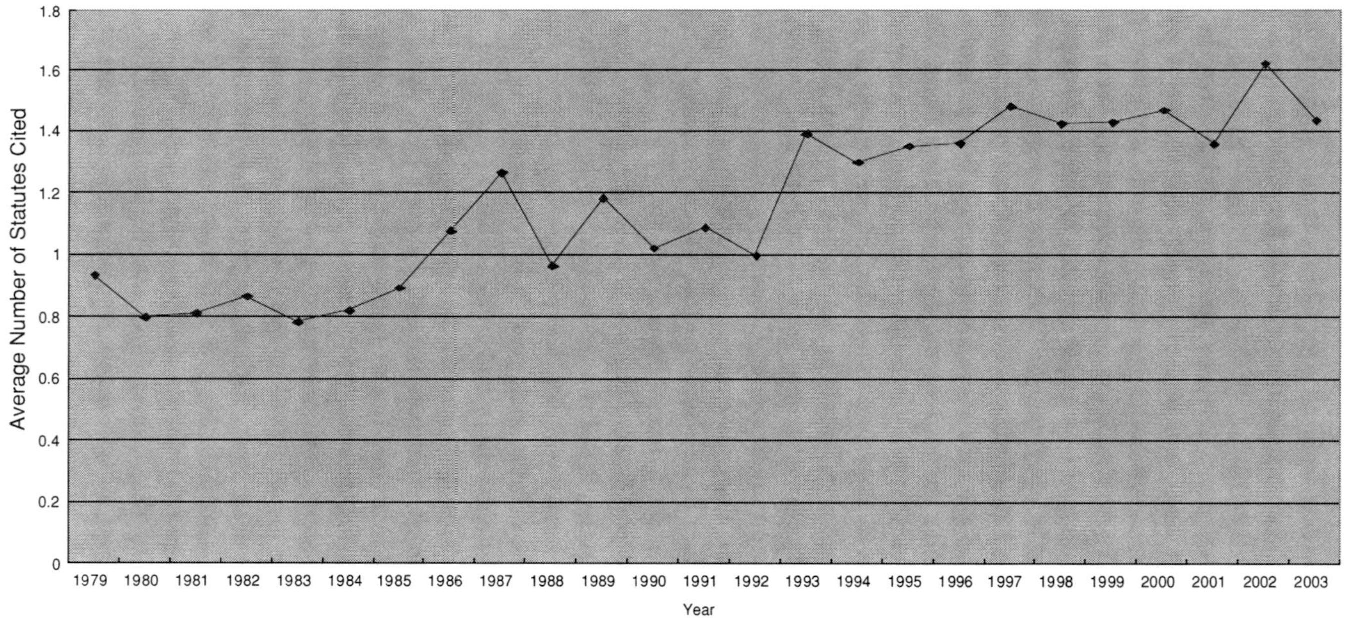

FIGURE 8.2. Average Number of Statutes Cited per Year, 1979–2003.

TABLE 8.2. *Statutes cited more than ten times in the DALS column, 1979–2003*

Title	Issuing dates	Total	Per year
Marriage law	1950.04; 1980.09; 2001.04	312	12.48
Criminal law	1979.07; 1997.03	275	11.00
General principles of civil law	1986.04	236	13.88
Civil procedure law	1982.03 (interim); 1991.04	175	8.33
Criminal procedure law	1979.07; 1996.03	132	5.28
Constitutional law	1954.09; 1975.01; 1978.03; 1982.12	75	3.00
Inheritance law	1985.04	71	3.94
Opinions on several issues in the implementation of the general principles of civil law	1988.04 (interim); 1990.12	58	3.87
Contract law	1999.03	57	14.25
Public security administration and punishment regulation	1986.09; 1994.05	57	3.35
	2005.08 (expired)		
Economic contract law	1981.12; 1993.09	48	2.67
	1999.03 (expired)		
Labor law	1994.07	37	4.11
Opinions on several issues in the application of the civil procedure law	1992.07	30	2.73
Guarantee law	1995.06	27	3.38
Interim regulation on lawyers	1980.08	18	0.75
Administrative procedure law	1989.04	17	1.21
Road traffic accident control method	1991.09; 2003.10 (expired)	15	1.15
State compensation law	1994.05	15	1.67
Opinions on issues related to the implementation of the inheritance law	1985.09	14	0.78
Consumer rights protection law	1993.10	13	1.30
Opinions on the people's courts' trial of cohabitation in the name of husband and wife without marriage registration cases	1989.11	12	0.86
Copyright law	1990.09; 2001.10	12	0.92
People's court organization law	1954.09; 1983.09	11	0.44
Land management law	1986.06; 1988.12; 1998.08; 2004.08	11	0.65
Urban private housing management regulation	1983.12	10	0.50
People's court litigation charging method	1989.07	10	0.71

times any statutes were cited. Moreover, the ten-most- cited statutes were cited 1,448 times, or 60.81 percent of the 2,381 citations. In other words, for more than 60 percent of the time during the twenty-five years, the column lawyers used only ten statutes in their legal advice to the readers. Both the low average number of statutes cited and the high concentration of statute use suggest that ordinary legal advice does not necessarily require extensive use of formal law – this contradicts the beliefs of many lawmakers and legal scholars in China.

The most widely cited statute is the Marriage Law – it was cited 312 times in the twenty-five years. However, if we take into account the issuance dates of the statutes, both the General Principles of Civil Law (13.88 times per year) and the Contract Law (14.25 times per year) were more frequently cited than the Marriage Law (12.48 times per year). The Criminal Law, the Criminal Procedure Law, and the Civil Procedure Law also were frequently cited. Despite the popular belief that constitutional law in China merely serves a symbolic function, the Constitutional Law was the sixth most cited in the DALS column. In the early years of the column, when there were not many formal statutes available, the Constitutional Law was particularly crucial for the work of lawyers. Therefore, although there had been no judicial review of constitutional issues in China, the Constitutional Law still played an important role in popular legal advice and in shaping the legal consciousness of citizens. This also partly reflects the legal propaganda function of the DALS column.

Overall, in the twenty-five-year development of the DALS legal-advice column, readership spread all over the country, the number and types of cases were institutionalized and became quite stable over time, and lawyers used an increasing number of statutes in their legal advice. These general trends closely correspond to the rationalization of Chinese law since 1979. However, although the legal system demonstrated many characteristics of rationalization, there was no fundamental change in the social problems that lawyers handled. Although the frequency of lawyers' citations of statutes significantly increased, the scope of the citations remained limited, and the percentages of different case types remained quite stable.

Nevertheless, the quantitative descriptions presented in this section are too general to allow us to observe how the content of the column cases changed over time. To further explore the extent to which the Chinese legal system became detached from ordinary social life, in the following section I analyze the changes in the lawyers' legal advice for three major types of cases, namely, family and inheritance, debt and loan, and labor cases. Because of space constraints, for each case type I focus on only one or two most frequently appearing issues for illustration.

THE CHANGING MEANING OF POPULAR LEGAL ADVICE: EXAMPLES FROM THREE CASE TYPES

Family and Inheritance

Family and inheritance cases represent the family life of ordinary Chinese people. This case type had the largest number of cases among all case types (Table 8.1). Almost a quarter of all the DALS column cases (498 of 2,077 cases) dealt with family and inheritance issues. In the first five years (1979–83), this case type alone accounted for 39.06 percent of all cases in the column. An obvious reason for this high concentration of family problems is that the Marriage Law was the only major statute in civil law during this period, and most other areas of civil law were still undeveloped. After the mid-1980s, the percentage of family and inheritance cases stabilized at about 18 to 19 percent (Table 8.1), remaining the largest of all case types. Major issues in family and inheritance cases include marriage, cohabitation, divorce, adoption, parental support, inheritance, and other family problems, as well as related housing and property issues. In this section I focus on two salient issues that frequently appeared in the column: 1) the inheritance of a widowed daughter-in-law and 2) cohabitation and de facto marriage.

The inheritance right of a widowed daughter-in-law is a sticky issue in China's family-law practice. Many families would deny their daughter-in-law's right of inheritance, especially if she remarried after her husband's death. In a March 1982 issue, for example, a reader named Yu Baozhen from Nantong City, Jiangsu Province, wrote to the column regarding an inheritance dispute with her brother-in-law that began after her mother-in-law passed away in 1979 (#19820302).[26] Although she had already been remarried for more than twenty years, Yu continued to support her former parents-in-law during their lives and fulfilled her filial duties when they passed away. However, her elder brother-in-law argued that she had

[26] All of the column cases cited or quoted in this chapter are coded in the form of "#19820302," in which "1982" is the year that the column was published, "03" is the issue number in that year, and "02" is the case number of the column in that issue.

no right to inherit the property of his parents after she remarried. The following is the reply of the column lawyer:

> Although you are a widowed daughter-in-law and have remarried to another husband, after your former husband died, you, together with your brother-in-law, fulfilled your obligations to the parents-in-law by supporting them when they were alive and burying them when they passed away. Therefore, you have the right to inherit the bequest of your parents-in-law. Your brother-in-law thinks because you have remarried you do not have the right to inherit, but this is groundless. With regard to how much you and your brother-in-law should inherit respectively, it should be resolved through coordination and negotiation. According to the judicial practice of our country, considering that your brother-in-law lived in the same house with your parents-in-law and fulfilled more duties of support while they were alive, plus the fact that the living condition of his own family was relatively difficult, you should promote mutual-helping and self-effacement and provide your brother-in-law with some benefits. If your brother-in-law insists on his own opinion, you can file a case with the local court, and the court would protect your proper rights according to the law. (#19820302)

When this reply was published (March 1982), there was no formal law on inheritance in China, with the exception of some relevant articles in the Marriage Law. Consequently, the lawyer did not cite any statute in the reply. Instead, she emphasized the "judicial practice of our country" and the "mutual-helping and self-effacement." As we will see later, this kind of moral discourse appeared repeatedly in the early years of the column. In addition, she recommended that the reader first attempt to negotiate the dispute and give her brother-in-law some benefits; filing the case in court was considered to be the last resort. There are two implications of this reply: First, where formal law was lacking, lawyers tended to adopt moral norms and social customs to deal with legal problems; second, in the early years of the legal reform, lawyers preferred conciliation within the family and community to going to court to resolve disputes.

In April 1985, the Inheritance Law was promulgated by the NPC. This formal statute quickly changed the way lawyers handled inheritance cases, including the issue of the right of inheritance of widowed daughters-in-law. A very similar case from Zhejiang Province titled "Can a Remarried Daughter-in-Law Inherit the Bequest of Her Parents-in-Law?" appeared in the March 1986 issue. In this case, the widowed daughter-in-law (Wang) remarried on the advice of her parents-in-law, but she continued to support and take care of them until their passing. As in the previous case, her uncle-in-law (Uncle Zhang) maintained that she could not inherit the family bequest after she remarried. The column lawyer offered advice very different from that in the previous case:

> Article 12 of the Inheritance Law prescribes: "A widowed daughter-in-law or son-in-law who fulfills the major supporting obligations to the parents-in-law is a first-order heir." As we can see, first, a widowed daughter-in-law or son-in-law must fulfill the major obligations of support to the parents-in-law in order to inherit their bequest, otherwise she or he cannot inherit; second, a widowed daughter-in-law or son-in-law who fulfills the major obligations of support is a first-order heir, not a second-order heir; third, as long as the widowed daughter-in-law or son-in-law fulfils the major obligations of support, whether or not there is a remarriage does not affect the inheritance.
>
> According to her letter, Wang always had a smooth relationship with her parents-in-law when she was married to Zhang, and after Zhang died, even though she remarried, she continued to support her parents-in-law and fulfill her major obligations to them, so she should be the first-order heir. Uncle Zhang is the brother of her father-in-law so he should be a second-order heir. According to Item I of Article 10 of the Inheritance Law, "After inheritance begins, first-order heirs should inherit, and second-order heirs do not inherit." Hence the bequest should be inherited by Wang. However, because Uncle Zhang fulfilled some obligations, he could receive some of the bequest. (#19860304)

The manner in which the column lawyer replied to the reader in this case is in sharp contrast to that in the previous case. In the first paragraph, the statute was cited and then elaborated upon in detail; in the second paragraph, the statute was applied to the specific case and a conclusion was drawn. This is a very typical way of legal reasoning in the civil law tradition. There is no mention at all of social custom, "judicial practice," or "spirit." This contrast signals the power of formal law in changing the lawyers' work – the formal law provides a clear and logical framework for the lawyer's legal reasoning and excludes the extralegal elements from his reasoning. Considering that this dramatic change occurred within merely four years (March 1982 to March 1986), the effect of the formal statute is particularly evident.

In addition, the formal statute cited in this case emphasizes the equal legal rights of a widowed daughter-in-law and a widowed son-in-law with regard to inheritance. However, in the twenty-five-year history of the DALS column, all such inheritance cases dealt with the interests of widowed daughters-in-law (e.g., #19801003, #19810503, #19810905, #19820302, #19831002, #19850906, #19860304, #19871004,

#19930505, and #20011902). No widowed son-in-law had written to the column for advice on inheritance matters. In other words, in reality, widowed daughters-in-law were more likely to be denied the right of inheritance than widowed sons-in-law, but equality in formal law does not reflect this gender inequality in social life.

Another common issue appearing in family and inheritance cases was cohabitation and de facto marriage. According to Article 5 of the 1980 Marriage Law, the legal marriage ages for Chinese citizens are twenty-two for males and twenty for females, one of the highest in the world. Moreover, because of the one-child policy, most local authorities set even higher marriage ages (e.g., twenty-five for males and twenty-three for females) to control birthrates. Nonetheless, in reality, many couples marry much earlier without formally registering the marriage – this is the so-called de facto marriage. Both the 1950 and 1980 Marriage Laws required marriage registration (Article 6) but did not provide any specific regulation on how to deal with de facto marriage. In a case in the January 1980 issue, the column lawyer explained de facto marriage in the following way:

> According to the situation described in your letter, we consider that you are in fact already married, and only lack a registration. Because we consider that, if a man and a woman without spouses cohabit and live together as husband and wife without a marriage registration, and the people in the community consider their relationship to be a marriage, then it constitutes a "de facto marriage." (#19800107)

Yet not all cohabitations are defined as de facto marriage. In the early 1980s, the concept of "illegal cohabitation" (*feifa tongju*) was not yet firmly established; thus, all column cases on this issue were interpreted as de facto marriage. Since the mid-1980s, however, cohabitation gradually has become a salient problem among young people. Accordingly, lawyers began to make an effort to distinguish between illegal cohabitation and de facto marriage. In a case in the February 1986 issue, for instance, the column lawyer stated that cohabitation without marriage registration is a problem "worthy of serious attention" and "representative in some areas," and it is "not considered a legal marriage relationship and cannot be protected by the law" (#19860206). Note that this statement contradicts the previous statement about de facto marriage because it defines all cohabitation without a marriage registration as illegal.

This confusion between illegal cohabitation and de facto marriage in practice aroused the attention of the Supreme People's Court (SPC) in the late 1980s. In its 1989 Opinion on the People's Courts' Trial of Cohabitation in the Name of Husband and Wife without Marriage Registration Cases, the SPC attempted to define the boundary between illegal cohabitation and de facto marriage: If both parties had already reached the marriage age when they began to cohabit and the relationship is considered to be a marriage by the people in the community, then it constitutes a de facto marriage; if one or both of the parties had not reached the marriage age when they began to cohabit, then it constitutes an illegal cohabitation (Article 2).

In appearance, this judicial interpretation seems to have resolved the confusion, but in practice, problems persisted. Throughout the 1990s, cases on cohabitation and de facto marriage frequently appeared in the DALS column, and the column lawyers struggled to define the two concepts. For example, in a March 1996 case, the column lawyer defined a case in which the couple had a small-scale wedding and even a child but did not register as a de facto marriage (#19960502). In a June 2000 case in Shandong Province, the reply was even more startling (#20001103). In this case, Wu (male) and Li (female) had a wedding ceremony according to the local custom without registering their marriage in July 1989, and then she gave birth to a child in March 1993. In July 1997, Wu registered to marry a woman he had met in school without revealing his former relationship with Li. When the case reached the court, there were differing opinions regarding how to define Wu and Li's former relationship. On the one hand, the couple had lived together for eight years and had had a child; on the other hand, when they started to cohabit, Wu was still two months short of the legal marriage age. The column lawyer offered the following reply:

> How to differentiate between de facto marriage and illegal cohabitation is indeed a very difficult problem. Because many citizens in our country have a relatively low level of legal consciousness, in practice there are many cases in which the performance of a wedding ceremony according to local customs without a marriage registration is considered to be marriage. Given this practical condition, the Supreme People's Court promulgated the Opinion of the People's Courts' Trial of Cohabitation in the Name of Husband and Wife without Marriage Registration Cases on November 21, 1989, which provided several different means for handling marriage disputes.... Wu and Li cohabited as husband and wife without registering their marriage after the Marriage Registration Method went into effect, so the above judicial interpretation should be applied. When Wu and Li cohabited in July 1989, Wu had not reached the legal marriage age of 22,

> which is not in accordance with the legal condition of marriage. Hence, the relationship between Wu and Li was illegal cohabitation, not de facto marriage. (#20001103)

This eight-year relationship is defined by the column lawyer as illegal cohabitation rather than de facto marriage merely because the "husband" was two months short of the legal marriage age prescribed in the law when the relationship began in 1989. In other words, "when cohabited" in the SPC Opinion is interpreted in the reply as "when the cohabitation started." This strict interpretation of the law may have appeared counter-intuitive to ordinary people in the community, but it also clearly showed the autonomous and self-sustaining character of the formal statutes as separate from social life. However, the irony here is that the self-perfection of the legal system generated confusion in the administration of justice in society. It suggests that formal law is not only a clarifying tool for lawyers as the inheritance examples suggest, but it can also be a potential source of disorder in social life.

Debts and Loans

Whereas family and inheritance cases represent the family life of ordinary Chinese people, debt and loan cases, together with other types of contract cases, represent their economic activities. During the twenty-five years, 105 debt and loan cases appeared in the DALS column, accounting for 5.06 percent of all cases in the column (Table 8.1). Note that the percentage of debt and loan cases increased significantly from 1979–83 to 1999–2003, indicating that this type of case had become increasingly important in Chinese people's daily lives. The most frequently appearing debt and loan cases were loan contracts related to guarantees (*dan bao*).[27] The discussion in this section focuses on this type of case to examine the changes in the column lawyers' language and legal reasoning when dealing with very similar cases during the twenty-five-year period.

In 1979, when the DALS column first appeared, many readers still had no clear sense of what was meant by a guarantee. For instance, in the December 1979 issue, a reader named Ding Yuzhu wrote to the column to ask whether he, as the guarantor, needed to pay the debt to the commune

[27] In this context, guarantee refers to a situation whereby a third party (i.e., the guarantor) guarantees to pay the debtor's debt to the creditor in cases in which the debtor cannot pay her own debt.

when his out-of-town friend Zhao (i.e., the debtor) could not fulfill the obligation. The column lawyer offered the following reply:

> The debtor Zhao did not pay his debt when it was due, so you as the guarantor should fulfill the legal obligation according to the agreement. That is to say, this debt, which Zhao did not pay by the due date, should be paid by you as his substitute. Given the situation described in the letter, we consider that the commune's request for you to pay this debt is fair and reasonable, and it is also in accordance with the spirit of our laws. After you have paid the debt for Zhao, you certainly have the right to request that he pay you back for the debt you have paid on his behalf. Therefore, you should make the payment to the commune promptly and ask Zhao to repay you. This is the correct attitude. (#19790512)

In 1979, there was no formal civil code in China except for the Marriage Law, and all commercial transactions were governed by informal rules and customs. Accordingly, in her reply, the column lawyer emphasized that the commune's payment request was "fair and reasonable" and in accordance with "the spirit of our laws." Then she urged the guarantor to make the payment with "the right attitude," but she did not mention any legal sanction if he failed to do so. This suggests the powerlessness of law in a society where the enforcement of contracts still relies on extralegal authorities (i.e., the commune). Also note that the phrase "we consider" was used both in this reply and in the 1980 case on de facto marriage reported above (#19800107). Column lawyers very commonly used this phrase in the early years when formal statutes were nonexistent.

In the mid-1980s, an important new civil law statute was put into practice: the 1986 General Principles of Civil Law. This was the first major general statute on civil law since the PRC had been established, and it fundamentally changed the way civil disputes were resolved by providing lawyers and judges with a relatively clear system of rules. From 1986 to 2003, this statute was cited 236 times by the column lawyers in their legal advice, one of the highest rates among all statutes (Table 8.2). In addition, during this period, rapid social change largely had destroyed the socialist commune system, and questions regarding guarantees in the column letters changed from simple confirmation of the payment obligation to more complicated issues. A good case in point is the guarantor's obligation when the creditor and the debtor alter their loan contract. In explaining this issue, the column lawyers used diverse strategies and language over time. For example, in a May 1988 case titled "If Both Parties Agree to Postpone Payment of the Loan, Does the Original Guarantor for the Contract Still Have Any Obligations?" the column lawyer replied in the following way:

> The guarantee of a debt is a certain legal form or means made by the two parties of the debt according to the legal prescription or agreement to guarantee the fulfillment of the debt. It has the functions of supervising the debtor's fulfillment of the debt and protecting the creditor's civil rights. The General Principle of Civil Law in our country prescribes four types of debt guarantees, including guarantor, mortgage, down payment, and lien. The guarantor can be a natural person or a juridical person, who guarantees to the creditor that the debtor will fulfill the obligation. When the debtor does not fulfill the obligation, the guarantor assumes all or part of the obligation according to the originally agreed upon scope of the guarantee. If the guarantee contract does not explicitly prescribe the scope of the guarantee, it should be considered to be a guarantee for the entire obligation. The guarantor only assumes liability for the content of the guarantee that he agreed to and signed (or sealed) in the guarantee contract. During the fulfillment of the contract, if the two parties (debtor and creditor) reach a written agreement to postpone payment without informing and receiving consent from the guarantor, then it should be considered a new legal relationship and the original guarantee contract should be dissolved. The guarantor no longer assumes the liability for this new payment agreement. (#19880507)

The level of abstraction in this reply is astounding. Although only one statute is cited, the column lawyer uses purely professional or even technical terms and language to explain the guarantor's obligations. From a legal point of view, without a specific statute on guarantee at the time, the lawyer makes a very sound interpretation of the meaning of a guarantee in civil law according to legal doctrine. Nonetheless, for common people, this reply would be extremely difficult to understand. The implication of this case is twofold: On the one hand, it shows the rapid rationalization of the formal law and lawyers' professional knowledge; on the other hand, it also suggests the obvious discontinuities that this process generated between law and society. Caught in such a discontinuity, the column lawyer chose to stick to the abstract formal law and to ignore the social demand of ordinary citizens to understand the law and to seek a clear and simple answer to their questions. For the column readers, however, here the law became an external authority that they stood by but could never get inside.[28]

[28] See Ewick and Silbey, *The Common Place of Law*.

Six years later, a very similar case appeared in the DALS column (#19940204). The only difference is that this time, the loan was between a company and a construction bank, and the guarantor was a commercial agency. The bank and the company made a new payment agreement after the debt was due, but the company still could not pay the debt on time, so the construction bank sued both the company and the commercial agency. A reader named Wu Dezhen from the agency wrote to the DALS column for advice, and the column lawyer replied:

> According to the descriptions in the letter, the loan contract between the company and the construction bank is valid. Regarding whether your commercial agency still needs to assume liability after the company and the construction bank reached a new agreement, it depends on the situation. Item 2 of Article 16 of the Supreme People's Court's Several Opinions on the People's Courts' Trial of Debt and Loan Cases on August 13, 1991 prescribes: "When the loan period is due and the debtor cannot make the payment, if the creditor and debtor reach an agreement on a new payment period or interest without the consent of the guarantor, then the guarantor no longer assumes liability." According to the above judicial interpretation, the key to whether or not your commercial agency still assumes liability is to determine whether the new payment agreement between the company and the construction bank was agreed to by your commercial agency. If so, then your commercial agency should assume liability for the new payment agreement; if not, then your commercial agency would no longer assume liability. (#19940204)

Compared with the reply in the previous case, this was much easier for the readers to understand. This is partly because the promulgation of the SPC's judicial opinions on debt and loan cases in 1991 provided a simpler and more concrete solution than the General Principles of Civil Law. In addition, the column lawyer tried to connect the case facts with the law rather than merely to elaborate on legal doctrine. Note that the moral discourse and emphasis on fairness or the "spirit of the laws" in the 1979 case were completely absent in both the 1988 and 1994 cases – lawyers increasingly tended to use formal law and legal discourse when they had the option.

The formalization of law on guarantee did not stop with the 1991 SPC Opinions. In 1995 the Guarantee Law was promulgated and in 2000 the SPC issued a comprehensive interpretation. These two statutes soon became the main basis for lawyers' work on guarantee issues. In

October 2003, a similar case appeared again in the DALS column, and the column lawyer replied in the following way:

> Article 24 of the Guarantee Law of our country prescribes: "If the creditor and the debtor agree to change the contract, they should acquire the consent of the guarantor; without the guarantor's written consent, the guarantor no longer assumes liability. If there is an alternative agreement in the guarantee contract, then follow the agreement." Item 1 of Article 30 of the Supreme People's Court's Interpretation of Several Issues in Applying the Guarantee Law prescribes: "During the guarantee period, if the creditor and the debtor agree to change the quantity, price, currency, or interest of the main contract without the consent of the guarantor, and if this reduces the debt of the debtor, then the guarantor still should assume liability for the changed contract; if this increases the debt of the debtor, then the guarantor does not assume liability for the increased part." According to these regulations and the situation described in the letter, although Zhao and the bank increased the amount of the loan without the consent of your husband, your husband still should assume liability for the 100,000 yuan agreed on in the original contract; as far as the increased loan of 60,000 yuan is concerned, your husband does not assume liability. (#20032002)

Apparently, the Guarantee Law and the SPC interpretation made the issue of guarantee liability more complicated than the 1991 SPC Opinions had. However, in comparison with the previous case, in which the column lawyer used the 1991 SPC Opinions to analyze the specific conditions of the case, in this case the lawyer simply listed the two statutes and then provided a conclusion without any illustration or inference. This style of legal advice is reminiscent of the "vending machine" model in Max Weber's classic account of a modern legal system.

In short, during the twenty-five years, the column lawyers' explanations of guarantees in debt and loan cases changed from a plain but moralistic exposition to an abstract and doctrinal presentation and finally to a "vending machine" explanation. They no longer emphasized the "spirit of the law" or the "right attitude," but focused on the direct application of the legal codes, which sometimes was difficult for the readers to understand. This type of case offers a vivid illustration of the formal rationalization of ordinary legal work in Chinese society.

Labor Disputes

In addition to family life and economic life, another important aspect of ordinary Chinese people's lives is the workplace. Labor disputes – Chinese people's problems in their work-units – changed over time. Altogether, there were 109 labor cases in the DALS column, accounting for 5.25 percent of all 2,077 cases. The percentages of labor disputes remained stable from 1984 to 2003, at about 5 to 7 percent, yet the content of the cases changed dramatically, as is revealed in the following.

The meaning of labor disputes varied notably across the twenty-five years. In the early 1980s, most labor disputes were associated with criminal issues. The most frequently appearing issue was whether released former criminals were allowed to resume their former jobs or assume new positions in the work-units. In the February 1980 issue, for example, a former state official named Liu Bingshan who had spent four years in prison for obstructing a military marriage wrote to the DALS column to ask whether he could resume work in his original work-unit. (#19800203) The following is the column lawyer's reply:

> According to the spirit of the State Council's Regulation on Rewards and Punishment of Personnel in State Administrative Agencies, we consider that, if personnel in the state administrative agencies were sentenced by the people's court for imprisonment or disfranchised, they should naturally be eliminated from their positions. Thus whether or not it was a disciplinary procedure does not matter. Employees of state enterprises or administrative work-units can also be handled according to this principle. As to whether they may again be employed as state employees after being released from prison, we consider that, under the present condition in which employment problems have not been completely resolved, they may not be re-employed as state employees. Of course, when certain conditions are satisfied, for example, the original crime was minor, performance during reeducation was good, and certain work-units (including the original work-unit) need the person very much, he can be so employed (including employment in the original work-unit). However, if he is employed as an official, then it must be approved by the personnel department; if he is employed as a worker, then it must be approved by the labor department. Before approval, any quarrels with the leaders are not permitted. (#19800203)

Similar to the other two case types in the early 1980s, in this case the column lawyer emphasized the "spirit" of the law and frequently used the term "we consider" when she had no formal statute to rely upon. Moral discourse like "quarrels with leaders is not permitted" is also found in this reply. The interesting feature of the reply, however, is that the column lawyer in fact made up a rule to resolve labor issues within the work-unit. This "invasion" of legal advice into the largely closed system of work-units suggests that in its early years, the role of the DALS column exceeded providing professional advice on legal issues.

This extensive role of legal advice is more evident in a March 1986 case titled "Can Released Former Criminals Become Basic-Level Cadres after Returning to their Native Place?" (#19860303). Wang, a released former criminal, had returned to his village and maintained good conduct there. He was nominated as a new village cadre, but some village cadres argued that former criminals should not be permitted to become basic-level cadres. The village secretary general wrote to the DALS column for advice. The column lawyer gave the following interesting reply:

> Whether or not released former criminals can become cadres after returning to their native place, this question generally and simply cannot be answered with a yes or a no. It needs to be specifically analyzed. Criminals may commit serious crimes like murder, arson, robbery, rape, spreading poison, and bombing and other ordinary crimes. And criminals may behave differently during imprisonment: some indeed abandon their evil ways, embrace goodness, and become new persons; yet others are not truly reformed but just temporarily restrained themselves. After their release, they also behave differently. Cadres should be outstanding members among the people who have gained the people's trust, and not every citizen can become a cadre. Therefore, criminals of serious crimes are inappropriate to become cadres. Furthermore, we need to maintain a discreet attitude toward appointing basic-level cadres, even ordinary criminals who indeed have abandoned evil and have embraced goodness after being released. They should be closely observed and helped to prevent the "recrudescence of the old disease." The person described in the letter was involved in gambling but he behaved well after being released; of course we cannot say he absolutely should not become a basic-level cadre. Still a considerable period of testing is required to prove that he is indeed qualified both morally and professionally and that people trust him before he can become a cadre. Remember that we cannot equate good performance after being released with the moral and professional qualifications for selecting cadres. Nowadays some comrades easily believe in some "able persons" with criminal records and do not pay attention to their moral caliber, thus resulting in improper appointments and damage to the people's interest. We need to watch out for this situation. (#19860303)

In this reply, the tone of the column lawyer does not sound like a legal professional, but rather like a moral authority in a socialist society. No statute is cited and no legal reasoning is found, but therapeutic discourse like "abandoning evil, and embracing goodness" or the "recrudescence of the old disease" is found throughout the text. This case, together with the previous one, strongly suggests that labor disputes in the early years of the legal reform often were intertwined with criminal issues, and these disputes were resolved within the work-units or basic-level agencies with extralegal means. The role of lawyers in these cases, accordingly, became extralegal as well. This shows that the meaning of ordinary legal work was still intertwined with social work in the early 1980s.

Beginning in the late 1980s, however, the nature of labor disputes in the DALS column began to change dramatically. Labor contracts were more prevalent, and issues related to industrial injuries frequently appeared (e.g., #19890405, #19951901, #19960302, #19972403, #19992301, and #20021401). At the time, many companies and factories tended to hire out-of-town workers for construction or production work, and the labor rights of these workers often were poorly protected. A common strategy employers used in signing labor contracts was to add a "no responsibility for industrial injury" clause to avoid having to provide compensation should an accident occur. For example, in an October 1995 case, worker Shen Jianhua from Jiangsu Province was seriously injured when he was working in a cotton factory in Henan Province, but the factory denied his request for compensation because there was a "no responsibility for industrial injury" clause in his labor contract (#19951901). The Labor Law had already been promulgated in 1994, and the SPC also had issued a judicial interpretation on the "no responsibility for industrial injury" clause in labor contracts in 1988. Citing these two statutes, the column lawyer replied:

> This type of agreement violates the law of the state and it is void. As early as October 14, 1988, the Supreme People's Court pointed out in the Reply to Whether the "No Responsibility for Industrial Injury" Clause in Labor Contract Can Have Effect: providing workers labor protection is prescribed explicitly in the constitutional law of our country, and it is a right that workers enjoy. The employer should provide the employees with labor protection according to the law, noting "no responsibility for industrial injury" on the recruitment form is not in accordance with the prescriptions in the constitutional law and other regulations, and it also seriously violates socialist public morality, thus it is a void civil juridical act.... The Labor Law promulgated on July 5, 1994 further clarifies the rights and obligations of the two parties in labor relations.... These regulations suggest that receiving labor protection is the right of workers, the employing work-units must fulfill the corresponding obligations, and neither party can violate

the law and adhere to a so-called "no responsibility for industrial injury" clause. (#19951901)

The form and language of this reply is obviously more professional than that in the previous two cases, suggesting that by the mid-1990s, labor cases were no longer related to political and social work, but were part of a legal system that was autonomous from society. Another noteworthy phenomenon is the time lag in the lawyer's use of the statutes. Although the 1994 Labor Law had already been effective for more than a year when this reply was issued, in the column lawyer's reasoning, it merely complemented the 1988 SPC interpretation.

Overall, during the twenty-five years, the meaning of labor disputes in the DALS column changed from cases related to criminal issues and job opportunities to cases related to contractual issues and economic compensation. This shift is in accordance with the transition in Chinese law from a focus on criminal issues to a focus on civil and economic issues and the transition of Chinese society from status based to more commercialized. Accordingly, the role of lawyers in ordinary legal work also was transformed from a moral and political authority under the traditional socialist system to that of a legal professional in a market economy. As Ching Kwan Lee's recent study suggests, by the early 2000s, workers' grievances regarding "social contracts" under the socialist *danwei* (work-unit) system usually went through non-legal channels (e.g., public demonstration) rather than litigation.[29] The changing meaning of Chinese law is closely associated with this movement "from status to contract."[30]

CONCLUSION

In this chapter we have examined the work, life, and economic problems of ordinary Chinese citizens during the twenty-five years of Chinese legal reform. We have observed changes in lawyers' language, legal reasoning, and attitudes in defining and solving these problems. From inheritance in traditional families to marriage without legal recognition, from guarantees for loans to workers' industrial injuries, ordinary legal advice covered most aspects of Chinese social life. In the twenty-five-year history of the DALS legal-advice column, lawyers first relied on moral and therapeutic discourses and then began to use the powerful weapon of formal law and

[29] Ching Kwan Lee, *Against the Law: Labor Protests in China's Rustbelt and Sunbelt* (Berkeley: University of California Press, 2007).

[30] Henry S. Maine, *Ancient Law* (Boston: Beacon Press, 1963).

legal discourse. However, at the same time, their legal advice became more abstract, inferential, and sometimes too technical for ordinary readers to comprehend.

China's legal reform since 1979 has produced an increasingly large and self-sustaining system of formal law, a rapidly developing legal profession, and a disinterested and rigid manner of providing popular legal advice. In the early years of the reform, when there were few formal statutes on which to rely, lawyers made a great effort to fit their legal advice into the readers' social, political, and cultural contexts. As the legal system grew and matured, though, the lawyers' advice often became a cold "vending machine" detached from ordinary social life. At the same time, the popular attitude toward ordinary legal work in contemporary China changed from "with the law" to "before the law" and "against the law."[31] Although we do not intend to prove any causal relationship between the rationalization of lawyers' work and the changes in popular legal consciousness, throughout this chapter we have clearly observed a disjunction between the legal system and everyday life and the resultant struggles by lawyers that were generated by the rapid legal reform.

This difficulty in communication between lawyers and citizens has important consequences for ordinary legal work in China. Because the social functions of lawyers have become narrower in the process of legal reform, and lawyers' work often cannot fully respond to ordinary people's demands for resolving disputes and pursuing social justice, alternative legal-service providers emerged in this huge gap between the legal system and social life. These authorized and unauthorized practitioners include basic-level legal workers in urban communities and rural townships, "barefoot lawyers" in villages, and so forth.[32] Although they do not have a lawyer's license, these legal-service providers often appear to

[31] See, for example, Michelson, "The Practice of Law as an Obstacle to Justice"; Gallagher, "Mobilizing the Law in China"; Lee, *Against the Law*.

[32] William P. Alford, "Tasselled Loafers for Barefoot Lawyers: Transformation and Tension in the World of Chinese Legal Workers," *The China Quarterly*, no. 141 (1995): 22–38; Fu Yulin, *Nongcun jiceng falü fuwu yanjiu* (Research on Rural Basic-Level Legal Services) (Beijing: Zhongguo zhengfa daxue chubanshe, 2006); Wang Yaxin, "Nongcun falü fuwu wenti shizheng yanjiu (I)" (Empirical Research on the Problem of Rural Legal Services [I]), *Fazhi yu shehui fazhan* (Law and Social Development), no. 3 (2006): 3–46; Ying Xing, "'Ying fa ru xiang' yu 'jiejin zhengyi': Dui Zhongguo xiangcun 'chijiao lüshi' de ge'an yanjiu" ('Welcoming Law into the Countryside' and 'Access to Justice': A Case Study of the 'Barefoot Lawyers' in Rural China), *Zhengfa luntan* (Tribune of Political Science and Law), no. 1 (2007): 79–94.

have better communications with local residents than do lawyers, and they occupy important positions in the market for grassroots legal services. If this localized way of communication is also a type of expertise in legal practice, then how lawyers can use it to respond to ordinary legal needs in society becomes a crucial issue for the future development of the legal profession in China.

This leads us back to the earliest DALS column published in the August 1979 issue of the journal (see Appendix). It was the summer of 1979, when the Marriage Law was the only civil code in existence, the judicial system had just resumed operations, and the legal profession had not been formally revived, yet the column lawyer made an excellent reply in this first published correspondence in the column. She first cited two articles in the Marriage Law, elaborated on their meanings, went on to the "judicial practice of our country" to find an informal rule regarding the issue, and discussed its varying applicability in practical situations. In the reply she also emphasized the importance of being "a citizen with socialist consciousness," maintaining a harmonious family, abiding by the law and government policy, and "carrying forward a self-effacing manner" to resolve the dispute. More than twenty-five years later, when contemporary Chinese lawyers look at this piece of legal advice, they might be amused by its language and reasoning, but there also is something in it for them to learn. Compared to the cold legal discourse evident in the daily work of many contemporary Chinese lawyers, this 1979 opinion is much easier for the common people to understand and accept.

Although the legal culture of lawyers in contemporary China is modern and exogenous, the popular legal culture is largely traditional. This tension between modernity and tradition is a potential cause of many of the problems in China's legal reform. Nevertheless, in comparison with the transformation of a popular legal culture, it perhaps is easier to change the way lawyers work. The differentiation of the legal system from society may seem inevitable, but lawyers still face a choice in their daily work: They can use a cold and technical manner to alienate citizens from the law, or they can use a more considerate and caring manner to encourage citizens back into the scope of the law. After all, the essence of legal practice is not merely to wander around in a private law garden, but to go outside and serve the client and the public. The great irony for China's legal reform, however, is that when lawyers were without the law, the citizens were with the law, but now that lawyers finally are with the law, the citizens have lost their place.

APPENDIX: THE FIRST DALS LEGAL-ADVICE COLUMN, AUGUST 1979

Can the Bequest of the Grandfather be Inherited?

Letter

Comrade Editor:

My grandfather was an old doctor. He passed away recently and left some savings, furniture, and other life belongings. Now my uncle considers that because my parents have already died, the grandson does not have the right to inherit the bequest of the grandfather; my aunt already gave up her right to inherit this bequest, so the grandson is the only legal heir to grandfather's entire bequest. I cannot understand this and it has generated a dispute. May I ask Comrade Editor, can the grandson inherit the bequest of the grandfather?

Chen Xiaoming

Chen Xiaoming

Reply

Comrade Chen Xiaoming:

Article 12 of the Marriage Law of our country prescribes that "husband and wife have the right to mutually inherit a bequest," and Article 14 prescribes that "parents and children have the right to mutually inherit a bequest." That is to say, if one of the couple has passed away and left the bequest, the partner can inherit it; for the bequest of parents, sons and daughters (married or not), have the right to inherit; and vice versa, parents can also inherit the bequest of their children. In addition, in the judicial practice of our country, there is also the practice of representative inheritance (*daiwei jicheng*). If one partner or the children of the deceased had already passed away, then the grandchildren can receive the inheritance. According to this spirit, we consider that those who have the right to inherit your grandfather's bequest are first your grandmother, your father, your uncles, and your aunts. Now that your father has passed away, according to the custom of representative inheritance, you have the right to inherit the proportion of the property that should have been inherited by your father.

However, the issue of inheritance is complicated. Having the right of inheritance or not is the primary condition for deciding whether to inherit, but not all those who have the right of inheritance can divide it equally according to the number of heirs mechanistically and without analysis. First, juveniles and incapacitated heirs should be favored.... Second, the obligations that the heirs assumed to the deceased should be considered.... In addition, the heirs' economic conditions and practical life needs should also be considered.... In short, the issue of inheritance cannot be egalitarian. Therefore, as a citizen with a socialist consciousness, you should have a correct understanding and attitude in dealing with the issue of inheritance. The law of our country prescribes that the legal earnings, including the right of inheritance, of citizens shall be protected; but as far as heirs are concerned, the part of an earning from an inheritance is after all not earned through their own labor, so they should not destroy the kinship of relatives by fighting over a bequest. I believe that you and your uncle, on the basis of improving your thinking and conscience, will be able to coordinate and not abide by state law and government policy, but also carry forward a self-effacing manner, properly and pleasantly handle your dispute over the inheritance, and make more of a contribution to the construction of socialist modernization.

Legal Advisory Group
(*Democracy and the Legal System*, no. 1, August 1979)

PART III

Law from the Bottom Up

9

A Populist Threat to China's Courts?

Benjamin L. Liebman

Is the Chinese party-state too responsive to public opinion? In the case of the courts, this may be the case. Western literature has devoted extensive attention to the problems in the Chinese legal system, in particular in the courts, describing a system that continues to be undermined by a range of problems, from corruption to lack of competence to continued Communist Party intervention. Likewise, existing literature describes a legal system that often is unresponsive to individual demands for justice. In this chapter, I examine another possibility: that one impediment to the development of courts that are able to protect individual rights is that courts are too responsive to protests, petitions, and public opinion.

This chapter presents evidence that protesting, petitioning, or simply threatening to do either often is a successful means for litigants to pressure courts to rule in their favor or to alter decided cases. The ability of individuals to influence court decisions through petitioning is linked to other better-known problems in the Chinese legal system. Courts' sensitivity to the threat of unrest reflects the facts that party officials continue to interfere in court decisions and that individual judges and court leaders are dependent on party officials for their positions. Sensitivities to popular opinion and to individual protesters also reflect a political system that has placed tremendous emphasis on maintaining social stability. But the ability of petitioners and protesters to influence the courts also yields insights into broader trends in governance in China and to a central question facing China's legal system: whether courts can be effective protectors of individual rights in China's one-party system.

China's authoritarian populist justice may also yield insights into the relationship between populism and courts generally.[1] Virtually all Western literature on the topic confronts the question in the context of democratic systems, often asking whether judicial review is legitimate or examining whether courts are influenced by populist pressures. The literature on authoritarian political systems largely overlooks the role of the courts; no existing literature of which I am aware examines the role of protest in influencing court decision making. Yet evidence from China suggests that populist pressures on the courts may be even greater in a nondemocratic system, where there are few other outlets for expressing popular views. The evidence presented in this chapter likewise suggests that the top-down control that often is assumed to be a key characteristic of courts in authoritarian regimes does not make Chinese courts unresponsive to popular views. Instead, state concerns about stability are reflected in courts that are extremely responsive to populist pressures, perhaps to the detriment of adherence to rule of law principles. This suggests that the Chinese legal system is evolving in a way that conforms neither to the experience of more conventional authoritarian legal systems nor to that of countries that have transitioned to democracy.

China's experience also shows how concerns about public opinion and the threat of protest can affect courts even in cases that involve only a single individual and in which there appears to be little threat either of media coverage or escalation of the protest. Populist pressure in China can result from individual petitioners as well as from mass opinion. The influence of populist pressure on Chinese courts may also provide insights into potential sources of court legitimacy in a system in which formal legal rules appear to be increasingly diverging from popular views of justice and in which regime legitimacy continues to be based more on the ability to maintain social stability than on the fairness of the legal system.

This chapter proceeds in three parts. Section 1 provides a brief overview of the existing literature. Section 2, the bulk of the chapter, presents empirical evidence on the impact of petitioning and protests on China's courts. Section 3 discusses the implications of the evidence in section 2 for the development of China's legal and political system and for the ability of individuals to obtain justice in China. Section 3 also begins

[1] I explore the recent reemphasis on populism in China's courts in more detail elsewhere. Benjamin L. Liebman, "A Return to Populist Legality? Historical Legacies and Legal Reform," in *Mao's Invisible Hand*, ed. Sebastian Heilmann and Elizabeth Perry (Cambridge: Harvard University Asia Center, forthcoming 2011).

to explore the ways in which China's recent experiences may influence understandings of the relationship between populism and the courts and also the implications for literature on courts in authoritarian systems.

I. EXISTING LITERATURE AND BACKGROUND

Existing Literature

Western literature on how popular opinion affects the courts attempts to measure whether courts are swayed by public opinion[2] and discusses whether courts should take public opinion into account when making decisions.[3] Recent literature also examines how court decisions shape public opinion.[4] The questions raised by populist pressures on China's courts are distinct from those that are the focus of this Western literature. Cases in which popular opinion is influential rarely touch on core political or policy issues. Chinese courts remain weak actors in the Chinese political system – and thus, in most cases, cannot act contrary to the interests of other arms of the state even if they want to do so. When Chinese courts are compared with other arms of the state, there is no countermajoritarian difficulty, as courts are not alone in lacking democratic legitimacy. Also, measuring public opinion in China is extremely difficult: Most domestic discussion of "public opinion" in China refers to views expressed in the state-run and -monitored media. Although there is qualitative empirical evidence that public opinion (or claims to represent public opinion) as reflected in the Chinese media influences the courts,[5] proving this with quantitative data remains difficult.

[2] For a recent example surveying such literature and noting that the literature concludes that American courts are in fact swayed by public opinion, see Cass R. Sunstein, "If People Would Be Outraged by their Ruling, Should Judges Care?" *Stanford Law Review* 60, no. 1 (2007): 155–212. For another recent summary of such literature, see Nathaniel Persily, "Introduction," in *Public Opinion and Constitutional Controversy*, ed. Nathaniel Persily, Jack Citrin, and Patrick J. Egan (New York: Oxford University Press, 2008), p. 8.

[3] For example, see Sunstein, "If People Would Be Outraged by their Ruling, Should Judges Care?" 159, discussing both epistemic and consequentialist reasons why courts may decide to follow public opinion: There may be wisdom in mass opinion, and, in any event, it may be in the courts' interests of self-preservation to take public opinion into account.

[4] See, generally, Persily, Citrin, and Egan, eds., *Public Opinion and Constitutional Controversy*.

[5] Benjamin L. Liebman, "Watchdog or Demagogue? The Media in the Chinese Legal System," *Columbia Law Review* 105, no. 1 (2005): 1–157.

In addition, many cases in which courts in China adjust their outcomes in response to protest are not high-profile cases; they are routine cases involving a small number of parties. There are cases in which larger groups are involved, and in some cases courts appear motivated by concerns that protests may spread to a wider group. Courts are also sensitive to media reports. Nevertheless, in many cases protestors are individuals or a small number of individuals whose cases have little hope of attracting media attention. Likewise, cases in which party-state officials pressure the courts to change decisions often are not cases in which the officials have different views of the substantive law or facts; officials often intervene simply to appease petitioners.

The roots of the importance of popular views for regime legitimacy in China, including for the legal system, stretch back to Mao's mass-line ideology. Extensive Western literature has examined the mass line. The literature has also examined the legal system under Mao and state mobilization of popular opinion to use the legal system to target enemies of the state, particularly during the Cultural Revolution.[6] Furthermore, there is a growing body of scholarship on public opinion in contemporary China. Most such literature focuses either on how the media reflect and create public opinion or on how the state manages popular participation in an authoritarian system. There is a lack of literature on how public opinion shapes policy formulation. There is also extensive Western literature on protest and the rising volume of social unrest in China.[7] Most of this literature focuses on collective grievances and on state responses to protest.[8] There has been little focus on individual grievances or on how state institutions view petitioning and protests. Likewise, although recent literature attempts to measure popular confidence in the legal system,[9]

[6] Stanley B. Lubman, *Bird in a Cage: Legal Reform in China after Mao* (Stanford: Stanford University Press, 1999); Albert H. Y. Chen, *An Introduction to the Legal System of the People's Republic of China*, 3rd ed. (Hong Kong: LexisNexis Butterworths, 2004).

[7] Leading examples include Thomas P. Bernstein and Xiaobo Lü, *Taxation Without Representation in Contemporary Rural China* (New York: Cambridge University Press, 2003); Kevin J. O'Brien and Lianjiang Li, *Rightful Resistance in Rural China* (New York: Cambridge University Press, 2006).

[8] Yongshun Cai, "Local Governments and the Suppression of Popular Resistance in China," *The China Quarterly*, no. 193 (2008): 24–42; Peter L. Lorentzen, "Regularized Rioting: Strategic Toleration of Popular Protest in China," *Social Science Research Network*, June 2, 2008, http://ssrn.com/abstract=995330 (accessed September 27, 2008).

[9] Michelson and Read, Chapter 6; Yanqi Tong and Pierre Landry, "Disputing the Authoritarian State in China,"paper presented at the annual meeting of the American Political Science Association, Washington, DC, September 3, 2005, http://www.allacademic.com/meta/p40460_index.html (accessed August 26, 2008).

there are few examinations of how popular opinion influences decisions by China's courts.[10] The literature on authoritarian systems, including China, generally assumes that authoritarian regimes, although sensitive to signs of popular resistance,[11] are by nature are at odds with a serious role for public opinion. Some recent work on the Chinese system, however, has begun to take a more nuanced approach, exploring why and how the state might wish to facilitate challenges to authority.[12]

There is also important work on China's letters and visits system.[13] Most of this work describes the letters and visits system as an alternative to the formal legal system, albeit one with its own legal basis in Chinese law and one that overlaps with the courts. Some of this literature focuses on how the system works; other works examine petitioners and their complaints. By contrast, my focus is on how one set of institutions, the courts, responds to such complaints.[14]

The existing literature, whether academic, advocacy based, or in the popular media, generally paints a picture of aggrieved individuals seeking redress against an unresponsive state. Yet judges see things differently. The evidence I present suggests that courts are being forced to change decisions by petitioners whose claims lack merit. This reflects my methodology: The chapter is based largely on interviews with dozens of judges in seven provinces and provincial-level cities and on a review of materials from the courts and from judges, including articles about court efforts to manage petitions from the official press.[15] Interviews with petitioners

[10] The exception to this is writing, including my own, on how the media influence the courts.

[11] Jack A. Goldstone and Charles Tilly, "Threat (and Opportunity): Popular Action and State Response in the Dynamics of Contentious Action." In *Silence and Voice in the Study of Contentious Politics*, ed. Ronald R. Aminzade et al. (New York: Cambridge University Press, 2001), pp. 179–194.

[12] For examples, see Yongshun Cai, "Managed Participation in China," *Political Science Quarterly* 119, no. 3 (2004): 425–451; Tianjian Shi, *Political Participation in Beijing* (Cambridge: Harvard University Press, 1997); Jie Chen, *Popular Political Support in Urban China* (Washington, D.C.: Woodrow Wilson Center Press, 2004).

[13] Carl Minzner, "*Xinfang*: An Alternative to the Formal Chinese Legal Institutions," *Stanford Journal of International Law* 42, no. 1 (2006): 103–179; Laura M. Luehrmann, "Facing Citizen Complaints in China, 1951–1996," *Asian Survey* 43, no. 5 (2003): 845–866; Cai, "Managed Participation in China."

[14] Ethan Michelson has written of the need for greater understanding not only of "who gets in the door" but also of "what happens inside – in short, of how popular complaints are actually processed." Ethan Michelson, "Climbing the Dispute Pagoda: Grievances and Appeals to the Official Justice System in Rural China," *American Sociological Review* 72, no. 3 (2007): 459–485, 482.

[15] The seven provinces and cities were Beijing, Shanghai, Jilin, Hubei, Shaanxi, Guangdong, and Jiangxi. In all cases I relied on contacts in China to introduce me to judges.

inevitably would result in a different picture.[16] My goal is not to evaluate the merits of claims by the judges or petitioners. I do not dispute that many petitioners, including those challenging court decisions, have suffered wrongs or have been treated unfairly.[17] Instead, my aim is to examine how courts respond to such complaints and the implications of such responses for the development of China's legal system.

Letters, Visits, and China's Courts

In this chapter, I refer to petitioning, protesting, and the letters and visits system interchangeably. China's letters and visits system, or *xinfang*, refers to offices that exist at most levels of the party-state and at most central party and government departments to handle both written and in-person complaints. The letters and visits system serves as an outlet for popular grievances and as a mechanism for the party-state to obtain

This almost certainly biased the responses I obtained: judges with whom I spoke are likely to be better educated, and perhaps more reform minded, than other judges. They thus may be more likely than other judges to view the letters and visits system as improperly subverting what they view as the appropriate roles of judges. It is possible that the judges with whom I spoke overstated the degree of influence of petitioners on their work (because of a desire to meet the expectations of this foreign academic). But in most cases, our discussions of petitioning were only one part of broader discussions on current issues in the courts, and in a number of cases, the judges raised the issue without being prompted.

16 Some scholars in China have begun to engage in empirical studies of the nature and effectiveness of petitions regarding legal disputes, and analysis of petitioners' complaints is a promising avenue for future research – albeit one that requires cooperation from the courts. Examining the substance of the complaints and how they are handled would give insight into a central unanswered question in this chapter: What makes certain complaints or threats to protest credible? Such research may also yield insights into issues such as possible regional differences in the substance and effectiveness of petitioning, insights that are not possible with the limited data I rely on in this chapter.

17 In 2003, Zhou Zhanshun, the director of the State Letters and Visits Bureau, commented that 80 percent of all petitions, especially group petitions, were reasonable. Wang Yongqian 王永前,"Guojia xinfangju juzhang Zhou Zhanshun: Diaocha xianshi 80% shangfang youdaoli" 国家信访局局长周占顺：调查显示80%上访有道理 (Zhou Zhanshun, the Director of State Letters and Visits Bureau: Survey reveals that 80% of petitions are reasonable), *Ban yue tan*, November 20, 2003, http://www.southcn.com/news/china/zgkx/200311200686.htm (accessed August 25, 2008). A survey of 560 petitioners who came to Beijing to petition to central authorities found that 63.9 percent of them had been detained and 18.8 percent had been sanctioned criminally or through reeducation through labor system by authorities at the local level. Yu Jianrong 于建嵘, "Dui 560 ming jinjing shangfangzhe de diaocha" 对560名进京上访者的调查 (A survey of 560 petitioners to Beijing), *Falü yu shenghuo*, no. 10 (2007): 14–15.

information.[18] Although the total number of complaints raised is not made public, the system handles an enormous volume of grievances each year – far greater than the number of cases brought to court. Government letters and visits bureaus may refer complaints to other government departments, and in some cases may issue suggestions regarding how a matter should be handled, but they have no formal power to resolve disputes.[19]

Complaints regarding the courts can be filed either directly with court letters and visits offices or with letters and visits offices of other party-state departments, often those belonging to local governments, local Communist Party committees, or local people's congresses. Most of the cases discussed here are instances in which petitioners have raised their grievances with the courts directly. But judges also note pressures resulting from petitions filed with other party-state institutions.[20]

Statistics regarding letters and visits are not comprehensive. Official reports do, however, provide some sense of the volume of petitions. Official court statistics show courts handling a large volume of petitions annually, although that number has declined in recent years. Courts at all levels reported receiving 4.14 million letters and visits in 2005 (slightly fewer petitions than the total number of first-instance civil cases),[21] 3.55 million in 2006, 3.03 million in 2007, 1.52 million in 2008, and 1.06 million in 2009.[22] The total number of letters and visits received by provincial

[18] The letters and visits system is not a modern invention: It reflects a continuation of a long tradition of petitioning and of appealing directly to officials for assistance in resolving grievances. For a full discussion of the letters and visits system, see Minzner, "*Xinfang*: An Alternative to the Formal Chinese Legal Institutions," 103–179, and Luehrmann, "Facing Citizen Complaints in China, 1951–1996."

[19] *Xinfang* officials do argue that they should be given expanded powers, and some provinces have discussed giving their letters and visits offices greater authority to compel action by other state actors.

[20] Complaints can also be filed with state actors outside the *xinfang* system. As Michelson notes, most complaints to state authorities are not made through the system. Ethan Michelson, "Justice from Above or Below? Popular Strategies for Resolving Grievances in Rural China," *The China Quarterly*, no. 193 (2008): 43–64, 49.

[21] Chinese courts handled a total of roughly 5.1 million first-instance cases in 2005, including 4.4 million first-instance civil cases. Zuigao Renmin Fayuan 最高人民法院, "Zuigao Renmin Fayuan 2006 nian gongzuo baogao" 最高人民法院2006年工作报告 (2006 Supreme People's Court work report), *Zuigaofa wangzhan*, March 19, 2006, http://www.gov.cn/jrzg/2006-03/19/content_230762.htm (accessed August 25, 2008).

[22] Zuigao Renmin Fayuan 2006 nian gongzuo baogao; Zuigao Renmin Fayuan 最高人民法院, "Zuigao Renmin Fayuan 2010 nian gongzuo baogao" 最高人民法院2010年工作报告 (2010 Supreme People's Court work report), *Xinhua she*, March 18, 2010, http://

and lower-level courts from 2003 to 2007 was 18.76 million, a decrease of 55.58% compared to 1998–2002.[23] During the same period, however, the Supreme People's Court (SPC) reported a significant increase in petitions filed with the SPC itself.[24] In 2009, the number of letters and visits filed with the SPC was 210,934, compared to 140,511 in 2006.[25]

The 2006–09 figures for the total number of petitions received by courts represented dramatic declines from 1999, when the number of complaints handled by the courts peaked at 10.7 million.[26] The steep decline from the 1999 peak in complaints primarily reflects changed counting methodologies that the SPC ordered beginning in 2002.[27] For example, some courts have begun to count group petitions as a single petition and repeat petitioners only once. The reported declines may also reflect decreased complaints regarding the courts. But they also

news.xinhuanet.com/politics/2010–03/18/content_13192577.htm (accessed March 20, 2010); Zhongguo Falü Nianjian Bianweihui 中国法律年鉴编委会, 2007 *Zhongguo Falü Nianjian 2007* 中国法律年鉴 (2007 law yearbook of China) (Beijing: Law Press of China, 2007), p. 147; Zhongguo Falü Nianjian Bianweihui 中国法律年鉴编委会, 2008 *Zhongguo Falü Nianjian 2008* 中国法律年鉴 (2008 law yearbook of China) (Beijing: Law Press of China, 2008), p. 177; Zhongguo Falü Nianjian Bianweihui 中国法律年鉴编委会, 2009 *Zhongguo Falü Nianjian 2009* 中国法律年鉴 (2009 law yearbook of China) (Beijing: Law Press of China, 2009), p. 164.

23 Zuigao Renmin Fayuan 最高人民法院, "Zuigao Renmin Fayuan 2008 nian gongzuo baogao" 最高人民法院2008年工作报告 (2008 Supreme People's Court work report), *Xinhua she*, March 22, 2008, http://news.xinhuanet.com/newscenter/2008–03/22/content_7837838.htm (accessed August 25, 2008).

24 Zuigao Renmin Fayuan 2008 nian gongzuo baogao.

25 Wang Shaonan 王少南, "Chuangxin shesu xinfang gongzuo fangfa, fangbian dangshiren yifa biaoda suqiu" 创新涉诉信访工作方法, 方便当事人依法表达诉求 (Create new methods to improve litigation-related petition work, make it convenient for the parties to make their claims according to law), *Zuigao renmin fayuan wang*, March 12, 2010, http://www.court.gov.cn/lhzl/bgjd/201003/t20100312_2835.html (accessed April 2, 2010); *2007 Zhongguo Falü Nianjian*, 147.

26 Li Hongbo 李宏勃, *Fazhi xiandaihua jincheng zhong de renmin xinfang* 法制现代化进程中的人民信访 (People's letters and visits in the process of modernization of the legal system) (Beijing: Tsinghua University Press, 2007). By contrast, in 1999, China's courts handled a total of 5.7 million first-instance cases.

27 Prior to 2002, statistics on letters and visits to the courts included not only complaints regarding the courts but also the total number of all cases filed and accepted for hearing and the total number of cases filed but rejected by court filing offices. Beginning in 2002, the SPC ordered courts not to include case filings in the total number of reported letters and visits. Wang Yaxin 王亚新, "'Shefa xinfang' xianxiang de jiexi" "涉法信访"现象的解析 (Analysis of law-related petitions) (unpublished paper on file with author). As Wang Yaxin points out, however, it is likely that some, if not many, local courts were slow to adjust their counting methodologies, meaning that statistics on later years may also have included some applications for case filings. The slow adoption of the new counting methodology might help to explain the decrease in reported letters and visits after 2002 and highlights the unreliability of official statistics on petitioning. Ibid.

reflect greater emphasis in the courts on preventing letters and visits and SPC instructions to lower courts to work to reduce the total number of complaints.[28] Despite the drop in the official statistics, none of the dozens of judges interviewed for this essay mentioned a drop in pressure resulting from complaints, although many reported pressure to reduce the number of reported petitions. Most argued that pressure from letters and visits has increased in recent years. Public statements by court officials likewise suggest continued and increased pressure on the courts from petitioners. For example, in his 2009 report to the Standing Committee of the Yunnan Province People's Congress, the president of the provincial high court described the pressure on courts to avoid petitions as "huge" because of the potential for petitions to result in social instability – despite a steady decrease in litigation-related petitions since 2006.[29] Moreover, even after the decrease, the volume of petitions remains large, in particular when compared to the total number of administrative cases.[30] As the total volume of litigation in China's courts increases, the potential for petitions is likely to continue to increase.

The total number of letters and visits of all types filed with party-state letters and visits offices is even larger: Reports stated that letters and visits offices received a total of 12.65 million complaints in 2005.[31] The number of petitions declined by 15.5 percent in 2006, leaving the

[28] For example, see Zuigao Renmin Fayuan 最高人民法院, "Guanyu chongfen fahui shenpan zhineng qieshi weihu qiye he shehui wending de tongzhi" 关于充分发挥审判职能切实维护企业和社会稳定的通知 (Notice concerning fully developing adjudication ability in order to accurately maintain enterprise and social stability), *Zuigao Renmin Fayuan Gongbao*, no. 4 (2002): 112–113.

[29] Xu Qianfei 许前飞, "Yunnansheng gaoji renmin fayuan guanyu shefa shesu xinfangjian zhuanxiang gongzuo qingkuang de baogao" 云南省高级人民法院关于涉法涉诉信访件专项工作情况的报告 (Report on the special work situation of litigation- and law-related petitions by the Yunnan Province HPC), *Yunnan renda wang*, September 23, 2009, http://www.srd.yn.gov.cn/ynrdcwh/1013079018716528640/20100104/208024.html (accessed April 20, 2010).

[30] Chinese courts handled 95,000 first-instance administrative cases in 2006. The comparison is somewhat misleading, however, as most letters and visits regarding the courts do not involve direct claims against the state. Nevertheless, officials at the National Letters and Visits Office rely on the comparison between administrative cases and letters and visits to show the importance of their work. Li Lin, Mo Jihong, Lü Yanbing, Nie Xiushi, Li Xia, and Qi Jianjian 李林, 莫纪红, 吕艳滨, 聂秀时, 李霞, & 祁建建, "Tongguo fading qudao jiejue jiufen jizhi de fazhan zhuangkuang" 通过法定渠道解决纠纷机制的发展状况 (The development of the mechanism for resolving disputes through legally-stipulated routes), *Zhongguo wang*, October 23, 2007, http://www.china.com.cn/law/zhuanti/fzbg/2007-10/23/content_9110515.htm (accessed August 25, 2008).

[31] Ibid.

total greater than 10 million.[32] There do not appear to be comprehensive national data on the volume of letters and visits regarding the courts filed with other party-state institutions. Yet reports suggest that a large volume of such complaints relate to the legal system. Thus, for example, a 2004 report on the official Chinacourt.org Web site states that 40 percent of all petitions to government *xinfang* offices stem from complaints about courts, procuratorates, or the police.[33] Other reports state that in some provinces and cities, 40 to 70 percent of petitions relate to law and litigation.[34]

Regardless of the statistics, it is clear that courts spend a significant volume of their time and effort handling letters and visits. Judges report that letters and visits result in enormous pressures on the courts [35] and describe petitions as a "major problem" for the courts.[36] Interviews with judges provide anecdotal evidence on the volume of complaints in local

[32] Wei Wu and Li Yajie 魏武, & 李亚杰, "Quanguo xinfang zongliang 2006 nian zaici xiajiang, xinfang xingshi mingxian haozhuan" 全国信访总量 2006 年再次下降, 信访形势明显好转 (The total number of letters and visits nationwide has decreased again in 2006, clearly resulting in a better situation for petition work), *Xinhua she*, March 29, 2007, http://xnczq.xining.gov.cn/html/1386/30790.html (accessed August 25, 2008). The exact number is not disclosed in the report. The reported number of letters and visits continued to decrease in the subsequent two years. Zhongyang zongzhi ban 中央综治办, "Quntixing shijian ji xinfang zongliang xiajiang mubiao shixian" 群体性事件及信访总量下降目标实现 (The goal of decreasing the number of group incidents and letters and visits is realized), *Renmin wang*, February 6, 2009, http://politics.people.com.cn/GB/1026/8763391.html (accessed March 20, 2010).

[33] Ye Wenbing 叶文炳, "Shixi fayuan dangqian xinfang cunzai wenti ji duice" 试析法院当前信访存在问题及对策 (Analysis of the problems with and responses to letters and visits to courts at present), *Zhongguo fayuan wang*, January 7, 2004, http://www.chinacourt.org/public/detail.php?id=98316 (accessed August 26, 2008).

[34] Huang Shixiao 黄士孝, "Banli quanguo renda jiaoban xinfang de shijian yu sikao" 办理全国人大交办信访的实践与思考 (Practice and thoughts on the handling of letters and visits by the National People's Congress), *Renmin daibiao bao*, December 29, 2005, http://www.hljrd.gov.cn/llqy/200604290014.htm (accessed August 25, 2008); Liu Senjia 刘森甲, "Renzhen chuli shesu xinfang, qieshi weihu wending daju" 认真处理涉诉信访, 切实维护大局稳定 (Conscientiously manage litigation-related petitions seriously, so as to maintain social stability), *Qiyejia tiandi*, no. 1 (2009): 89–90; Li Mingxiang, 李明向, "Qianxi shesu xinfang anjian de yuanyin, tedian ji zhili cuoshi" 浅析涉诉信访案件的特点, 原因及治理措施 (A preliminary analysis of the characteristics and causes of and measures for managing litigation-related petitions), *Journal of Huanghe Science and Techonolgy University*, no. 1 (2009): 88–90.

[35] Interview 2007–13.

[36] Interview 2007–12. Quantifying the amount of time judges spend is difficult, and judges in China often have a range of responsibilities in addition to hearing and deciding cases. But judges note that they are affected not only by the quantity of time spent, but also by the significant pressure that results from petitioning.

courts. Judges at one intermediate court in a major city in central China said that they handled more than one hundred cases with petitions or protests in 2006.[37] Most complaints related to cases being handled by the court itself, but some were complaints regarding lower court cases.[38] One judge in a case-filing division in a basic-level county court reported that the court has sixty to seventy cases that result in petitions or protests out of about two thousand total cases per year.[39] Intermediate courts receive the greatest volume of petitions and protests, because most cases become final after review in intermediate courts and because they receive complaints relating both to their own decisions and to those of lower courts.[40]

Numerous reports in the media have detailed court statements that the volume of letters and visits is affecting their work. In his 2004 Work Report, for example, then–SPC President Xiao Yang noted that the lack of restrictions on petitions means that petitions from litigants "have become a very burdensome task for the Supreme People's Court."[41] The SPC itself has sent mixed messages to lower courts, calling on them to reduce the number of complaints but also to make it easier for those with grievances to file petitions.[42] Reports from and about the courts also make clear that resolving grievances raised through petitions and protests is a crucial element of judges' work.[43] In interviews, judges at all levels – and in regions ranging from rural county courts to courts in Shanghai – confirm that cases that involve either actual petitions or protests or the threat thereof occupy a disproportionate amount of their time and that they are under pressure to resolve cases so as to prevent petitions and protests.[44]

37 Interview 2007–26.

38 Interview 2007–26.

39 Interview 2006–51.

40 Interview 2007–26; Interview 2006–32.

41 Zuigao Renmin Fayuan 最高人民法院, "Zuigao Renmin Fayuan 2004 nian gongzuo baogao" 最高人民法院2004年工作报告 (2004 Supreme People's Court work report), *Zuigao Renmin Fayuan Gongbao*, no. 4 (2004): 5–11.

42 For example, the SPC has called for courts to accept filings and petitions via the Internet. Zuigao Renmin Fayuan 2006 nian gongzuo baogao. Although facilitating the filing of complaints by aggrieved individuals may appear at odds with efforts to reduce the total number of complaints, making it easier to file complaints may also reduce the likelihood that petitioners will resort to more confrontational methods, including protests.

43 Zuigao Renmin Fayuan "Guanyu chongfen fahui shenpan zhineng qieshi weihu qiye he shehui wending de tongzhi."

44 Interview 2006–57. Commentators describe petitions as a cause of psychological pressure on judges. Tao Canhua and Chen Hui 陶灿华 & 陈慧, "Jiceng faguan xinli yalida de yuanyin fenxi yu jianqin jianyi" 基层法官心理压力大的原因分析与减轻建议 (Analysis of the causes of large psychological pressure on local judges and suggestions for reducing such pressure), *Renmin fayuan wang*, March 9, 2010, http://ahxfy.chinacourt.org/public/detail.php?id=352 (accessed March 20, 2010).

Some commentators have noted that the work burden on courts has increased as petitioning has attracted increased public attention in recent years.[45] In some cases, judges have cited pressure from petitions as a reason for quitting their jobs.[46] Courts and judges are also evaluated based on their success in reducing and resolving petitions, a topic to which I return below in Section 2.

II. THE IMPACT OF PETITIONING ON CHINA'S COURTS

Sources of Grievances

What types of cases are most likely to result in petitions and protests? Asked to identify such cases, judges distinguish cases based on substantive classification – the nature of the underlying dispute – or on whether the grievances have merit. Judges identify groups of cases that are likely to generate petitions and protests; they also argue that many petitions are from litigants who lack legal knowledge, have no relationship to court disputes or reflect cases in which litigants may have valid grievances but lack legal recourse for such complaints.

Certain types of cases are likely to result in letters and visits. First, judges note that criminal cases in general and death sentences in particular frequently result in complaints from both the families of defendants and from victims and their families. Complaints from family members of the condemned are perhaps to be expected. But a court official noted the importance of handling complaints by victims and their families as well. Victims frequently protest when they fail to receive civil compensation

[45] Xu Wei 徐薇, "Jiaqiang shesu xinfang gongzuo de sikao" 加强涉诉信访工作的思考 (Thoughts on strengthening work on litigation-related petitions), *Henan ping'an wang*, January 19, 2010, http://www.hapa.gov.cn/Article/pajszt/pacj/pacjzw/201001/130841.html (accessed April 30, 2010).

[46] "Chengdushi Jinniuqu Renmin Fayuan jianjie" 成都市金牛区人民法院简介 (A brief introduction to the Jinniu District people's court of Chengdu municipality), *Jinniuqu fayuan wang*, November 24, 2006, http://www.jnqfy.cn/remark.asp?bh=16 (accessed April 20, 2010); Cao Xiaole, Dong Xin, Du Wen, and Cai Xiaoli 曹晓乐, 董馨, 杜雯, & 蔡小莉, "Jinniu Fayuan 17 faguan tiqian tuixiu, pingjun 50 lai sui" 金牛法院17法官提前退休, 平均50来岁 (Seventeen judges in the Jinniu Court retire early, the average age was around 50 years old), *Xinmin wang*, April 28, 2010, http://news.xinmin.cn/rollnews/2010/04/28/4639549.html (accessed May 16, 2010); Fu Xiangjun 符向军, "Faguan weihe yaoqiu tiqian tuixiu?" 法官为何要求提前退休? (Why did the judges apply for early retirement?), *Jiangsu fayuan wang*, May 4, 2010, http://www.jsfy.gov.cn/rdsp/2010/05/04094138570.html (accessed May 16, 2010).

awarded to them at trial – generally because the defendant lacks the means to pay such judgments.[47] Family members also sometimes petition in cases in which a death sentence is not imposed. Reports note the importance of courts acting proactively so as to prevent complaints from escalating and disrupting social stability.[48]

Statements from the SPC also reflect concerns regarding the risk of petitions and protests relating to capital cases. In response to an expected rise in petitions to the SPC resulting from its decision in 2006 to assume responsibility for final review of death sentences, in 2006 the court announced a new system for handling petitions relating to death sentences.[49] Judges also report that courts or local governments may pay compensation to crime victims when judgments cannot be enforced – in some cases, as much as 300,000 to 400,000 yuan – to reduce the risk of protest.[50]

A second group of cases that frequently result in petitions is claims for which court judgments have not been enforced.[51] Judges argue that courts often are not to blame for their inability to enforce decisions; enforcing decisions requires the cooperation of other government departments. One judge in Xi'an recounted how a successful plaintiff in a civil case resulting from an auto accident repeatedly protested outside the court. The defendant had no assets, and thus the court had no means of enforcing the decision. In the end, the court paid a portion of the judgment to the protestor from its own funds to convince her to stop protesting – although the protestor returned a few months later complaining that she had spent all of the money.

A third category is cases in which plaintiffs lose because of their inability to produce evidence to support their claims. In many cases, litigants who have suffered harm lack the ability to obtain crucial evidence. Thus, for example, one media report regarding environmental pollution in Nanjing noted that one district in Nanjing received 7,400 complaints relating to environmental pollution, not one of which was resolved through the

47 Interview 2007–25; Interview 2007–26.

48 Zhu Yongbin 朱永斌, "Sixing'an jinjing shangfang huozengduo, zuigaofa jiang jian youxiao xinfang jizhi" 死刑案进京上访或增多, 最高法院将建有效信访机制 (There may be an increasing number of letters and visits to Beijing concerning death penalty cases, the Supreme Court will establish an effective system), *Zhongxin wang*, December 29, 2006, http://news.eastday.com/c/20061229/userobject1ai2538274.html (accessed August 26, 2008).

49 Ibid.

50 Interview 2007–25.

51 Interview 2007–18; Interview 2007–20; Interview 2007–23.

courts because of the difficulties plaintiffs faced in obtaining evidence.[52] Judges argue that many litigants lack understanding of their burden of proof and then are unhappy when their claims are dismissed because of lack of evidence.

A fourth, broad category of cases involves claims that are only partially under the courts' jurisdiction. Judges complain that many cases relate to sensitive topics such as land disputes, housing relocation, enterprise reform, and bankruptcy claims. Judges argue that these cases are simply "too complex" for courts to resolve on their own or even to accept.[53] These disputes reflect "problems in society," and as such are not issues that courts can resolve on their own.[54] Yet courts frequently become a locus of protest for aggrieved individuals in such disputes. Such cases are particularly dangerous for the courts, as they are most likely to result in group litigation and protests; court officials thus note the importance of coordinating responses with local party committees.[55]

A fifth category of petitioners is those with grievances who lack a legal basis for their claims. Many cases resulting in letters and visits involve individuals who are facing real financial hardships and who lack access to any form of social security.[56] As one judge explained, "[M]any of these cases are not because of [the courts]; the person sues, but the real issue is with their life."[57] A related group of cases involves petitioners with "historical grievances" – often claims for compensation from the state that predate the 1995 passage of the State Compensation Law or even the Cultural Revolution.[58] Judges say that such petitions are difficult to resolve through law.

Judges contend that many petitioners' claims are utterly without merit and blame such petitions on ordinary people's lack of understanding of law. They also argue that some petitioners are using letters and visits to resolve issues that cannot be resolved through law.[59] Judges say that many petitioners argue that they should be compensated because they are the

52 Bao Yonghui and Lü Guoqing 包永辉 & 吕国庆, "Jiangsu Hebei deng sheng bufen qunzhong yueji xinfang shijian diaocha" 江苏河北等省部分群众越级信访事件调查 (Investigation into petitions bypassing the ordinary level in Jiangsu and Hebei Provinces), *Liaowang xinwen zhoukan*, October 30, 2004, http://news.xinhuanet.com/newscenter/2004–10/30/content_2156474.htm (accessed August 27, 2008).

53 Interview 2006–33.

54 Interview 2007–25; Interview 2006–60; Ye Wenbing, "Shixi fayuan dangqian xinfang cunzai wenti ji duice."

55 Ibid.

56 Interview 2007–14.

57 Interview 2007–25.

58 Interview 2006–51.

59 Interview 2007–18; Interview 2007–19; Interview 2006–32.

weak party – without having a legal basis for their claims.[60] Petitioners simply use letters and visits to the courts to try to obtain compensation – and are often successful in doing so, depending on how local party-state leaders view the matter.[61] Judges note that they are caught in a bind: They are under pressure to emphasize cases that result in petitions, even when such claims lack legal merit. At the same time, they know that if they do provide assistance, they may encourage yet more petitions and protests.[62] Academics likewise argue that many petitioners lack both understanding of the law and trust in the courts.[63] Many problems result from petitioners having excessively high hopes of what the law and the courts can provide.[64]

"Extreme" or "repeat" petitioners are particularly troublesome for courts. Some such petitioners maintain their protests for more than a decade.[65] Repeat petitioners may cause severe disruption to the courts' handling of other business and may pose a threat to the judges' safety.[66] Petitioners who threaten suicide are also particularly worrisome for

[60] Interview 2006–35.

[61] Interview 2006–51.

[62] Interview 2006–32.

[63] Tian Menghua 田孟华, "Lun nongcun jiceng renmin shesu fayuan shangfang de chengyin yu duice" 论农村基层人民法院涉诉上访的成因与对策 (On the causes of and solutions to litigation-related petitions in rural basic-level people's courts), *Chongqing sanxia xueyuan xuebao* 22, no. 2 (2006): 91–93. The author notes, however, that the courts themselves are at least partially responsible for solving this problem, as they need to do a better job of raising the litigants' legal awareness and understanding of the law.

[64] Liang Yanping, Mao Ruijiang, and Rong Jianli 梁艳萍, 毛瑞江, & 荣建礼, "Guanyu fayuan goujian chuli shefa shangfang wenti changxiao jizhi de sikao" 关于法院构建处理涉法上访问题长效机制的思考 (Thoughts on the question concerning the establishment of a long-term mechanism for courts to resolve law-related letters and visits), *Heihe xuekan*, no. 6 (2004): 80–82.

[65] Interview 2006–51.

[66] Jun Yang 君洋, "Fayuan yu shangsuzhe de jiuchan" 法院与上访者的纠缠 (The entanglement of courts with petitioners), *Falü yu shenghuo*, no. 4 (2004): 30–32. Judges' concerns about their physical safety have some basis. In some cases petitioners have turned violent, attacking judges after their petitions were refused by the court. Newspaper reports suggest a rising number of incidents of violence against court personnel by disgruntled litigants. For examples, see Qing Xinhai 青兴海, "Sichuan sheng Guangyuan shi zhongyuan fasheng zishaxing baozha, zaocheng yisi yishang" 四川省广元市中院发生自杀性爆炸，造成1死1伤 (Suicide explosion at Guangyuan intermediate court in Sichuan Province leads to one death and one injury), *Haikou wanbao*, April 6, 2006, http://news.sohu.com/20060406/n242674710.shtml (accessed August 26, 2008); Ke Honghai 柯鸿海, "Hunan Yongxin xian fayuan fasheng baozha, yuanzhang bei zhashang, faguan bei zhasi" 湖南永兴县法院发生爆炸，院长被炸伤庭长被炸死 (Explosion at Yongxin County District Court in Hunan injures president of the court and kills one judge), *Xinjing bao*, March 4, 2005, http://news.sina.com.cn/c/2005-03-04/04395981518.shtml (accessed September 27, 2008).

judges, who are likely to be held responsible for petitioner suicides.[67] One lawyer in a medium-sized city described a case in which a court changed its decision and awarded compensation to a petitioner who had threatened to commit suicide if the court did not rule in his favor. The lawyer argued that the courts were "giving up law in order to obtain a stable society."[68] Likewise petitioners who take their complaints to Beijing are of particular concern to judges.[69] Judges will generally come under pressure from higher courts, people's congresses, and party committees to resolve complaints that petitioners take to Beijing. Court officials participate in local government efforts to prevent petitioners from going to Beijing or to persuade petitioners who go to Beijing to return home.[70] Some courts send judges to Beijing, in particular during the annual meeting of the National People's Congress (NPC), to be on standby in case petitioners from their city travel to Beijing to raise complaints about cases.[71] Judges will meet with the petitioners in Beijing and may accede to some of the petitioners' demands.[72] In extreme cases, they may detain petitioners to force them to return home.[73]

Judges and commentators acknowledge, however, that many petitioners' claims have merit and reflect problems in the courts.[74] One judge noted that many complaints concern procedural mistakes that give rise to doubts by litigants, such as delays in scheduling court hearings.[75] Some complaints concern judges' negative attitudes toward the parties.[76]

67 Liu Guoyu 刘国禹, "Tan shesu xinfang yu fayuan fazhan de guanxi" 谈涉诉信访与法院发展的关系 (Discussion on the relationship between petitions involving litigation and development of the courts), *Zhongguo fayuan wang boke*, August 15, 2007, http://blog.chinacourt.org/wp-profile1.php?p=74070&author=11434 (accessed August 27, 2008).

68 Interview 2006–37.

69 Interview 2007–26.

70 Wang Shu 王姝, "Beijing fayuan dui zhongda shesu xinfang anjian shixing lingdao baoan zhidu" 北京法院对重大涉诉信访案将实行领导包案制度 (Beijing courts will implement a responsibility system for leaders for major petitions involving litigation), *Zhongguo xinwen wang*, July 28, 2005, http://news.qq.com/a/20050728/000926.htm (accessed September 27, 2008). In Anhui, court regulations make explicit that lower courts shall be responsible for working to urge petitioners to return home. "Anhui sheng gaoji renmin fayuan xinfang gongzuo zerenzhi" 安徽省高级人民法院信访工作责任制 (The responsibility system for petition work at the Anhui HPC), Art. 12, *Anhui sheng gaoji renmin fayuan wangzhan*, April 23, 2004, http://www.ahcourt.gov.cn/ahgy/flfg/node16/userobject1ai832.html (accessed September 27, 2008).

71 Interview 2007–26; Interview 2007–25.

72 Interview 2007–25.

73 Interview 2007–25.

74 For example, see Ye Wenbing, "Shixi fayuan dangqian xinfang cunzai wenti ji duice."

75 Ibid.

76 For example, of the 2656 petitions to basic-level and intermediate courts in Shangqiu Municipality in Henan Province in 2008, 6.9 percent (183 cases) complained about judges' "bad attitudes" or impolite language. Song Haiping 宋海泙, "Guanyu yufang

Enforcement problems, such as delays in enforcement and wrongful enforcement against the property of a third party, also are sources of petitions.[77] Similarly, in some cases litigants may have a valid complaint about the substance of the case.[78] One judge responsible for letters and visits in a first-instance county court noted that many petitioners have legitimate grievances regarding problems in the courts. The judge argued that most ordinary people will not protest unless they have a significant reason for doing so.[79] Likewise, commentators argue that some petitions reflect the low quality of work in Chinese courts as well as judges' failure to recognize the potential social impact of their cases.[80]

Judges are not only the targets of petitions: Some judges use the letters and visits system to address their own grievances. One report noted how a judge petitioned for seven years to prove that he had been incorrectly sanctioned by his court for failing to follow a decision of the court adjudication committee. The dispute arose after the judge refused the court president's instruction that he delay issuing a decision against the local government construction bureau.[81] In another case, a judge from Chongqing petitioned to the national letters and visits bureau of the State Council after a prominent defendant in a case he had handled refused to obey a court order to pay 3.5 million yuan in back pay to more than two hundred migrant workers.[82] The letters and visits bureau issued a written instruction that the money should be paid; the defendant, China

he jianshao shefa shesu xinfang de jidian sikao" 关于预防和减少涉法涉诉信访的几点思考 (Some thoughts on how to prevent and reduce litigation- and law-related petitions). *Shangqiu ping'an wang*, March 18, 2009, http://www.sqpaw.gov.cn/Article/ShowArticle.asp?ArticleID=194 (accessed April 2, 2010).

77 Cao Zhengzhi and Tang Chongde 曹征知 & 唐崇德, "Jiceng renmin fayuan shesu xinfang nanti pojie duice" 基层人民法院涉诉信访难题破解对策 (Countermeasures for dealing with litigation-related petitions in basic-level courts), *Zhongguo lunwen lianmeng*, June 7, 2009, http://www.studa.net/sifazhidu/090603/11135553.html (accessed March 20, 2010).

78 Interview 2006–51.

79 Interview 2006–51.

80 Liang Yanping and Mao Ruijiang, "Guanyu fayuan goujian chuli shefa shangfang wenti changxiao jizhi de sikao."

81 Huang Guangming 黄广明, "Yiming faguan 'kangshang' de daijia" 一名法官"抗上"的代价 (The price for a judge who "fought against his superiors"), *Nanfang zhoumo*, March 23, 2001, http://news.huash.com/2006-11/22/content_5906458.htm (accessed August 27, 2008). As a result, the judge had his pay docked and promotion blocked. Although the judge eventually won positive media coverage of his grievance, it is unclear whether he succeeded in having the decision rescinded or was compensated.

82 Jiang Yingshuang 姜英爽, "Faguan shangshu zongli dai mingong taoxin" 上书总理代民工讨薪 (Judge petitions to the Premier on behalf of peasants seeking salary), *Nanfang dushi bao*, December 25, 2004, http://news.sina.com.cn/o/2004-12-25/09264624506s.shtml (accessed August 27, 2008).

National Railway Corporation, then promptly paid the judgment. Similarly, three judges from Hunan Province petitioned to the provincial people's congress in neighboring Guangdong to request help in executing a judgment; local officials in Guangdong had refused to obey the court order and had threatened to detain the judges when they sought to enforce their judgment.[83]

Impact on the Courts

What impact do letters and visits have on court decision making? The question is difficult to answer empirically. Some of the most important consequences may be hidden: information about petitioners and final court decisions often is not publicly available. Many, if not most, letters and visits to the courts likely have little impact. Nevertheless, evidence also supports the conclusion that petitions and protests have a significant impact on how courts handle at least some cases. Judges identify three specific consequences of cases that result in petitions. Courts may change their decisions, may agree to rehear a case that has resulted in a petition, or may seek to quiet petitioners by paying compensation. Courts may also, however, respond to extreme petitioning by arranging for petitioners to be detained.

Numerous accounts in the Chinese media have detailed how petitioners have used the letters and visits system to force courts to change or reverse unjust decisions. Thus, for example, a 2006 report detailed how a petitioner won compensation from a local court after years of petitioning. The court had ordered the plaintiff's assets seized in an economic dispute. After eight years of complaints to local party and government officials, the local intermediate court ordered the original court to compensate the petitioner for his losses.[84] Likewise, a report praising the Yingkou Intermediate Court in Liaoning Province for its success in handling letters and

[83] Zhao Wenming 赵文明, "Zhixing gongwu zao ganshe, Hunan faguan weihe lunwei 'shangfanghu'" 执行公务遭干涉，湖南法官为何沦为"上访户" (Interfered with while carrying out enforcement duties, why Hunan judges are reduced to being "petitioners"), *Xinhua wang*, February 5, 2007, http://news.china.com/zh_cn/news100/11038989/20070205/13922343.html (accessed August 27, 2008). In another example, ten judges from Fuping County in Hebei Province petitioned for ten years to claim unpaid salaries. "Hebei fupingxian faguan jinjing taoxin" 河北阜平县法官进京讨薪 (Judges in Fuping County in Hebei Province come to Beijing to claim their salaries), *Xinjing bao*, February 19, 2008, http://www.chinanews.com.cn/sh/news/2008/02-19/1166261.shtml (accessed April 2, 2010).

[84] "Shanxi shouli shimin zhuanggao difang fayuan shengsu" 山西首例市民状告地方法院案胜诉 (The first case by a citizen against a court in Shanxi is successful), *Shanxi wanbao*,

visits noted that the court president had visited an elderly petitioner who had petitioned sixty-seven times regarding his son's death. The court president "decided on the spot" that the petitioner was telling the truth and that the case should be retried.[85] Court officials were quoted as stating that no matter what, they would change decisions that were wrong.

Petitioners' ability to persuade or pressure courts to change decisions is in some cases tied to their ability to attract the attention of senior party officials, people's congress representatives, or the media. Judges complain that petitioners frequently bring complaints directly to the local party or government to pressure the courts.[86] Judges report that the fact that a complaint is made is often sufficient to cause party officials to interfere in the courts.[87] For instance, media reports recounted how a petitioner who won a case concerning a loan agreement in Jiangsu was unable to enforce the award for more than six years, allegedly because of corruption involving a judge. After the petitioner's case was covered by the official Xinhua News Agency, thus attracting the attention of the national leaders, the case was quickly resolved. One report on the case noted that it highlighted a problem with the petitioning system: If a petitioner fails to obtain the attention of a senior official, it is likely that the grievance will not be addressed.[88] Petitions to people's congresses about the courts can be particularly influential: A report about another case detailed how a petition to a people's congress and subsequent inquiry about the case from the congress to the court that had decided the case caused the court to review and change its outcome.[89] Although media

November 29, 2006, http://www.law-lib.com/fzdt/newshtml/gzaj/20061129090814.htm (accessed August 27, 2008).

[85] Wang Zhi, "'Ling shangfang,' yige shangfang dahu de xinwen diaocha" "零上访"一个上访大户的新闻调查 ("Zero letters and visits": A news investigation into a court overwhelmed by petitions), *Minzhu yu fazhi*, April 25, 2006, http://old.chinalaw.org.cn/media/shownews.asp?id=584 (accessed August 27, 2008).

[86] Interview 2007–25.

[87] Interview 2006–52.

[88] Bao Yonghui and Lü Guoqing, "Jiangsu Hebei deng sheng bufen qunzhong yueji shangfang diaocha." For a discussion of a case in which a local court issued a decision favorable to a petitioner after the petitioner sought assistance from the local party discipline office, see Li Hongbo, *Fazhi xiandaihua jincheng zhong de renmin xinfang*.

[89] Zhai Hao 翟昊, "Yu xinfang yu jiandu zhi zhong" 寓信访于监督之中 (Incorporating letters and visits system into supervision), *Renmin wang*, February 17, 2006, http://npc.people.com.cn/GB/25015/4116961.html (accessed August 27, 2008).

In a separate case, in Guang'an, in Sichuan, the municipal people's congress determined that a petition from a litigant raised a valid complaint regarding a local court. The standing committee of the municipal people's congress determined that the court had been in error and issued a letter asking the court to review the case and correct its mistake. The court followed the opinion of the municipal people's congress and accounts generally recount how party leaders intervene to force courts to correct unjust decisions, judges complain of being told by party leaders to "manage" or resolve a case without regard to its underlying merits.[90]

Yet the ability of petitioners to influence judges is not limited to cases that attract the attention of party officials or the media. In interviews, judges commented that it is common to change decisions as a result of petitions, both in cases in which the complaints raise valid claims and in cases in which the original decision was correct.[91] As an example, a judge described a tort case in which liability was apportioned 80 percent to one party and 20 percent to the other party. After the party judged to be 80 percent at fault petitioned, the court adjusted the liability determination modestly so as to reduce the petitioner's share of liability.[92]

Changes generally come through rehearing procedures.[93] Sometimes, however, pressure from petitioners results in cases being changed on appeal. Not all changes to decisions are the result of petitions; judges note that changing decisions on appeal or in rehearing procedures is common.[94] Nevertheless, judges also note that letters and visits can have

revised the holding. The vice director of Guang'an People's Congress Standing Committee said that "the court should be praised for the quick response to the congress." Xiao Mingfeng and Lin Hui 肖明 & 锋林辉, "Guang'an zhongyuan yifa gaipan liangqi ge'an" 广安中院依法改判两起个案 (Guang'an Intermediate Court changes the decision according to law in two individual cases), *Sichuan fazhi bao*, February 23, 2005, http://news.sohu.com/20050223/n224405746.shtml (accessed August 27, 2008).

90 Interview 2006–52. Likewise, drastic actions, or threats thereof, by petitioners can be a particularly effective means for applying pressure because they are likely to attract attention from officials outside the courts. One report noted a case in which a petitioner committed suicide after his complaints were not addressed. In response, the Shanxi HPC revoked the lower-court judgment and ordered a 70,000-yuan payment to the deceased's family. Li Hongbo, *Fazhi xiandaihua jincheng zhong de renmin xinfang*.

91 Interview 2007–13.

92 Interview 2006–33.

93 Under Chinese law, parties to a case may request that the courts rehear a case within two years of the court decision becoming final and effective; courts have the discretion whether or not to do so. Courts may also decide, on their own initiative, to rehear a case at any time. The courts also must rehear a case when asked to do so by procuratorates; procuratorate requests are not time bound.

94 In one Shenzhen court, a judge in the case-supervision division, which is responsible for rehearings, estimated that as many as forty cases per year are changed through rehearing procedures. Interview 2007–12. Similarly, a judge in a municipal intermediate court noted that 40 to 50 percent of all appellate civil cases are changed in some way, sometimes because of pressure from petitioners. Interview 2007–13. Nationally, statistics show that about one-third of the cases subject to rehearing are changed: In 2006, courts concluded 48,286 rehearing cases, of which 15,568 involved changes to the original decision. Zuigao Renmin Fayuan 最高人民法院, "Zuigao Renmin Fayuan 2007 nian gongzuo baogao" 最高人民法院 2007 年工作报告 (2007 Supreme People's Court work report), *Xinhua she*, March 21, 2007, http://news.xinhuanet.com/legal/2007–03/21/

a major impact: As one judge said, in cases giving rise to petitions and protests, the pressure on courts is "huge."[95] In some cases, however, changing decisions may result in the other party to the case starting to petition.[96]

Some judges acknowledge ignoring the law on the books or reaching strained interpretations of the law to assuage petitioners.[97] Judges explicitly acknowledge the need to balance their duty to apply the law fairly with their obligations to reduce protests and petitions. As one judge explained, "We not only have to resolve cases on the law; we also need to act according to our national conditions. We have social responsibility."[98] Such social responsibility entails working to reduce letters and visits, and thus the potential for social unrest, both through explaining court decisions to litigants and adjusting decisions so as to minimize complaints. For example, SPC President Wang Shengjun stated in early 2010 that to guarantee the success of the 2010 World Expo in Shanghai, courts should focus on deciding cases and resolving problems so as to terminate petitions and prevent and resolve contradictions before and during the Expo.[99]

Other judges say that they will not violate the law in changing decisions, but that they may send a report on the case to the local party political-legal committee outlining a range of outcomes that would be permissible under existing laws, thus effectively asking the political-legal committee to choose among legally permissible outcomes.[100] Yet judges also note that they can frequently alter cases without issuing decisions that violate the law. As one judge explained, judges have tremendous discretion under Chinese law, so even if they are influenced by petitioners, they

content_5877470.htm (accessed August 25, 2008). Courts reported changing decisions in 11,669 of the 32,000 cases reheard nationwide in 2009. Zuigao Renmin Fayuan 2010 nian gongzuo baogao.

95 Interview 2007–19; see also Interview 2006–32 (stating that letters and visits or the threat thereof will result in pressure on the courts); Interview 2006–34 (describing pressure from letters and visits as "natural").

96 Yu Xisheng, 于喜胜, "Lun shesu xinfang zhidu de gaige he wanshan" 论涉诉信访制度的改革和完善 (On the reform and improvement of the litigation-related petition system), *Zhongguo fayuan wang*, April 23, 2008, http://www.chinacourt.org/html/article/200804/23/297913.shtml (accessed March 26, 2010).

97 Interview 2006–76.

98 Interview 2007–19.

99 Gao Yuan 高远, "Zuigaoyuan yuanzhang Wang Shengjun: wei shibohui tigong gongzheng gaoxiao de sifa baozhang" 最高院院长王胜俊：为世博会提供公正高效的司法保障 (Wang Shengjun, President of the SPC: providing fair and efficient judicial guarantees for the World Expo), *Xinmin wang*, April 16, 2010, http://sh.xinmin.cn/minsheng/2010/04/16/4473642.html (accessed April 30, 2010).

100 Interview 2006–57.

still may be able to issue judgments that accord with legal standards.[101] Other judges argue that they are unlikely to change the outcome of cases involving petitioners, but that they will handle such cases with more care than they would routine cases.[102]

Judges say that the attitude of local party leaders will have a significant impact on how courts view and handle petitions. Local officials may differ significantly in their reactions to petitions and protests concerning the courts, with some blaming the courts for any complaints they receive about the courts and others being more willing to accept that the petitions may be without merit. Judges in one city painted a picture of local authorities being largely cooperative, often helping the court resolve cases involving petitioners. For example, in suits against employers, the local government may pressure the employer to work with the court to resolve a dispute.[103] Nevertheless, judges say that cases in which petitioners raise complaints directly to party officials often are problematic.

Judges also note that even in cases in which they do not change outcomes, they may work with the parties to try to assuage the petitioners – with the same practical result as if they had changed the decision. Thus, judges frequently will seek to mediate cases involving petitioners, with a view to pressuring the other side to agree to pay an additional amount to settle the case. Mediation to resolve petitions is particularly common when a defendant fails to pay a judgment.[104] For example, another report detailed petitioning by a plaintiff who had been severely injured in a traffic accident. The defendant had paid only 130,000 yuan of a 270,000-yuan judgment. After petitioning by the plaintiff, the court intervened and mediated between the parties. In the end, the defendant paid the full balance of the judgment.[105]

A second method for mollifying petitioners is for the courts to agree to rehear cases, even when they have no intention of changing the outcome. Even judges who say that it is rare to alter outcomes because of pressure from petitioners acknowledge that they may reopen cases and permit petitioners another opportunity to argue their cases.[106] Doing so, report

[101] Interview 2006–14.

[102] Interview 2006–154.

[103] Interview 2007–26.

[104] Interview 2007–18.

[105] Liang Shanchuan 梁山川, "Wangsheng fayuan zhuanbian xinfang gongzuo fangshi jian chengxiao" 万盛法院转变信访工作方式见成效 (Wansheng district court's new method of letters and visits work shows results), *Chongqing diwu zhongji renmin fayuan wangzhan*, January 3, 2008, http://www.cq5zfy.gov.cn/news/view/id/9461 (accessed September 22, 2008).

[106] Interview 2007–26.

the judges, helps to convince petitioners that their grievances are being taken seriously.[107] Agreeing to rehear cases also allows the courts to mediate disputes, perhaps applying pressure on the other party to meet some of the petitioners' demands.[108] One judge responsible for letters and visits commented that 20 to 30 percent of petitions are resolved simply by agreeing to reopen the case.[109]

Judges note a rise in the total number of cases that are reheard and say that this is due to increased pressure from petitioners.[110] Judges also argue that procuratorates are increasingly filing *kangsu*, or objection to suit petitions, which compel the courts to rehear cases, to assuage petitioners.[111] Although judges say they often agree to rehear cases simply to appease the petitioners, they also acknowledge that some cases involve issues in which the petitioners have a genuine disagreement with the court on legal issues. In such cases, holding a rehearing may help to resolve the disagreement.[112]

A third response to pressure from petitioners is to pay, or arrange payment to, those with complaints. This practice is not unique to the courts: Cai, O'Brien, and Li others have noted the common practice of local governments making payments to protestors to prevent escalation.[113] Judges say that courts sometimes will pay petitioners directly to persuade them to stop protesting.[114] Often, however, such payments are relatively

[107] Interview 2006–32.

[108] Interview 2007–27; Interview 2006–32; Interview 2007–25.

[109] Interview 2007–25.

[110] Interview 2006–32. For example, a judge in the supervision division of an intermediate court in central China said that many rehearing cases result from petitions – and that approximately 30 percent of reheard cases result in changed decisions. Interview 2006 34.

[111] Interview 2006–37.

[112] Interview 2006–51.

[113] Cai, "Local Governments and the Suppression of Popular Resistance in China," 27, 37–48; O'Brien and Li, *Rightful Resistance in Rural China*.

[114] Interview 2006–32. For a report on court payments to petitioners facing economic difficulties, see "Jindong fayuan xinfang gongzuo cheng 'yijiangyijianyiwu' lianghao taishi" 金东法院信访工作呈"一降一减一无"良好态势 (Jindong letters and visits work becomes "one drop, one reduction, one elimination"), *Jinhua shi zhongji renmin fayuan wangzhan*, July 19, 2007, http://www.jhcourt.cn/news/news_detail.asp?id=1242 (accessed August 27, 2008). For a report on court payments to persuade petitioners to stop petitioning, see Zhang Jian 张健, "Sifa quanwei de queshi yu chongsu – jiceng fayuan shesu xinfang wei shijiao" 司法权威的缺失与重塑 – 基层法院涉诉信访为视角 (The absence and reconstruction of judicial authority – From the perspective of litigation-related petitions at basic-level courts), *Gongzheng sifa yu goujian hexie shehui* 公正司法与构建和谐社会, ed. Wan E'xiang 万鄂湘 (Beijing: Renmin Fayuan Chubanshe, 2006), pp. 256–264.

small.[115] Some courts have dedicated funds available for paying petitioners – although judges point out that such funds are modest compared to similar funds maintained by local governments.[116] Judges sometimes will also personally make payments to petitioners.[117]

More often, however, the courts will consult with other party-state authorities in an attempt to arrange for the petitioners to be compensated.[118] For example, courts will consult with the local department of civil affairs in an attempt to obtain some form of social compensation or support for individuals who have raised grievances.[119] In some cases, such payments are contingent on obtaining a signed agreement from the petitioner that he will cease petitioning.[120] This method appears largely effective, although the validity of the agreement could be challenged in theory.[121] In one county, officials reported that 83 percent of repeat petitioners signed agreements with the court in which they agreed to cease petitioning and that 88.6 percent of those who signed agreements did in fact cease petitioning.[122] Judges note that persuading other authorities to pay petitioners not only saves the courts from having to pay themselves, but it also means that judges can avoid having cases classified as incorrect.[123] It is also a logical step given that courts generally must rely on local authorities to enforce decisions; the courts' own enforcement powers are weak. In other cases, however, judges report being ordered

[115] Interview 2006–33.

[116] Interview 2006–57.

[117] Similarly, courts sometimes require judges to reimburse the court for payment to petitioners. For example, in 2005, the Jiangsu Province HPC issued a rule requiring judges whose incorrect decisions result in state compensation to petitioners to reimburse the court. Wang Yijun 王亦君, "Jiangsu gaoyuan chutai xingui: panle hutu an, faguan yao peiqian" 江苏高院出台新规：判了糊涂案，法官要赔钱 (The High Court of Jiangsu Province issues a new rule: judges who issue a muddled opinion shall pay compensation), *Xinhua wang*, August 6, 2005, http://news.xinhuanet.com/newscenter/2005–08/06/content_3316425.htm (accessed April 24, 2010).

[118] Interview 2007–18; Interview 2006–33; Interview 2007–23.

[119] Interview 2007–18.

[120] Interview 2006–51.

[121] Wang Huahai and Jiang Wujun 王华海 & 蒋武君, "Xifang xieyi de jiongjing yu chulu" 息访协议的窘境与出路 (The predicament of agreements to cease petitions and a solution), *Fazhi yanjiu*, no. 11 (2008): 63–67.

[122] Wang Huahai and Jiang Wujun, "Xifang xieyi de jiongjing yu chulu." In some cases, local governments have sued petitioners to demand repayment and have brought extortion charges against petitioners who continued petitioning despite having signed an agreement in which they agreed to stop petitioning. Jin Mingda 金明大, "Liuxun fangmin bei yi shexian qiaozha lesuo zui daibu" 六旬访民被以涉嫌敲诈勒索罪逮捕 (A sixty-year-old petitioner was arrested on suspicion of the crime of extortion), *Dongfang wang*, November 10, 2009, http://news.sina.com.cn/s/2009–11-10/145419016501.shtml (accessed April 27, 2010).

[123] Interview 2006–3.

by local governments to pay the petitioners themselves or in addition to government payments.[124]

Judges may also seek to obtain additional compensation from the other parties to a case. This is particularly the case where the defendant is perceived as being powerful compared to the petitioner/plaintiff.[125] In one court in central China, judges responsible for letters and visits said that in some cases they may ask defendants to pay the petitioners, even when there is no legal requirement to do so, to convince the plaintiffs to cease petitioning.[126] Likewise, other judges say that they may ask the defendants to pay the petitioners, in particular when the courts are worried that the petitioners will cause significant disruptions.[127]

One way the courts compensate petitioners is through "assistance funds." The creation of these funds reflects general concerns about the widening gap between the rich and poor in China; they are not exclusively used for petitioners. Data on how such funds are used are difficult to obtain, but judges note that a significant factor behind the creation of such funds is concern with reducing the number of letters and visits. Funds have been created to provide relief to individuals who are unable to have their court decisions enforced, to compensate crime victims, and to pay victims of automobile accidents when the other party to the accident either cannot be located or has no insurance.[128] All three categories of cases are reported to be frequent sources of complaints by petitioners.[129] In 2008, for example, the Beijing Higher People's Court (HPC), together with the Municipal Civil Affairs Bureau and other Beijing

[124] Interview 2006–33.

[125] Interview 2006–57.

[126] Interview 2006–32.

[127] Interview 2007–23.

[128] Liu Wenhui 刘文晖, "Guojia buchang beihairen, zhidu bi qian geng zhongyao" 国家补偿被害人，制度比钱更重要 (State compensation of victims, the system is more important than money), *Jiancha ribao*, May 23, 2007, http://www.bianhu.com.cn/rdzz/tbgz/20070524/105324.htm (accessed August 25, 2008); Yang Wenhao 杨文浩, "Xingshi beihairen guojia jiuzhu zhidu ruhe yuechu zhimian" 刑事被害人国家救助制度如何"跃出纸面" (How will the state assistance system for crime victims come out), *Beijing qingnian bao*, January 9, 2007, http://www.chinacourt.org/public/detail.php?id=229998 (accessed August 25, 2008); Wang Bixue 王比学, "Sheilai fuwei xingshi shouhairen" 谁来抚慰刑事受害人 (Who is responsible for compensating victims in criminal cases?), *Renmin ribao*, August 9, 2006, http://qdfy.chinacourt.org/public/detail.php?id=1230 (accessed August 25, 2008); Interview 2007–26.

[129] Xia Haijun and Xu Mingcheng 夏海军 & 徐明成, "Jidongche disanzhe zeren baoxian zhidu tantao" 机动车第三者责任保险制度探讨 (Discussion of third-person liability insurance for car accidents), *Falü jiaoyu wang*, http://www.chinalawedu.com/news/2005%5C11%5Cli836715210121150027600.html (accessed August 27, 2008); "Shei lai zhengjiu zhege jia?" 谁来拯救这个家 (Who will save this family?), *Hainan ribao*, August 2, 2007, http://www.hi.si.gov.cn/zhengce/read.asp?id=1041 (accessed August 27, 2008).

government departments, issued rules stating that petitioners in cases that may impact social stability are eligible for assistance if they face economic difficulties but otherwise are not eligible for social security payments, they agree to stop petitioning, and their requests are reasonable.[130] In 2009, Guangdong Province promulgated rules concerning judicial assistance in enforcement cases that likewise excluded from payment those petitioners who refused to stop "unreasonable petitioning."[131]

The three types of effects discussed here are steps courts take after cases have been decided. This reflects the fact that most petitioners raise their grievances only after they obtain a decision.[132] Yet there are also less perceptible effects on how courts handle cases even before petitioners file grievances. Judges note that they are aware of the types of cases and litigants likely to generate letters and visits. They pay particular attention to cases likely to result in protests or petitions.[133] They also comment that they may refer cases likely to have a significant social impact to the court adjudication committee; doing so means that they will not themselves be responsible if the decision results in protests.[134] Whether or not such pressure results in altered outcomes is difficult to assess. Nevertheless, it

[130] Beijing Gaoji Renmin Fayuan 北京高级人民法院, "Beijing shi shishi sifa jiuzhu zhidu guanli banfa (shixing)" 北京市实施司法救助制度管理办法(试行) (Beijing Municipality implements Measures for the Management of Judicial Assistance (for trial implementation), *Beijing shi shehui jiuzhu xinxi wang*, August 15, 2008, http://bjshjz.bjmzj.gov.cn/ViewWWInfoAction.do?type=001001002007&id=1247 (accessed April 20, 2010).

[131] Guangdong Gaoji Renmin Fayuan 广东高级人民法院, "Guangdong Sheng Gaoji Renmin Fayuan guanyu zhixing anjian tekun qunti sifa jiuzhu de guiding (shixing)" 广东省高级人民法院关于执行案件特困群体司法救助的规定(试行) (Regulations of the Guangdong Province HPC concerning judicial assistance to persons facing special difficulties in enforcement cases [for trial implementation]), *Guangdong fayuan wang*, December 15, 2009, http://www.gdcourts.gov.cn/gzzdyj/t20091230_28143.html (accessed March 20, 2010). In 2009, the SPC issued a notice stating that local courts should work together with other government departments to facilitate the creation of judicial assistance funds to be used to reduce the burdens of litigants facing economic difficulties, including in cases in which judgments have not been enforced. Zuigao Renmin Fayuan 最高人民法院, "Zuigao Renmin Fayuan guuanyu jiyibu jiaqiang sifa bianmin gongzuo de ruogan yijia" 最高人民法院关于进一步加强司法便民工作的若干意见 (Some views of the Supreme People's Court concerning further strengthening the work of making the judicial system convenient for the people), *Xinhua wang*, March 10, 2009, http://news.xinhuanet.com/legal/2009–03/10/content_10981330.htm (accessed April 20, 2010).

[132] Interview 2006–15. Court officials responsible for handling petitions likewise comment that even if they receive petitions while a case is pending, they generally will wait until the case is concluded before they address the complaint. The one exception, however, is that they may intervene more quickly if a complaint is raised about a particular judge. Interview 2007–26.

[133] Interview 2007–13.

[134] Interview 2006–54.

is clear that courts are also devoting significant resources to preventing letters and visits before they arise.

Why Courts and Judges Care: Efforts to Manage Petitioning

Emphasis on letters and visits reflects both the Chinese party-state's concern with managing petitions and the importance of petitions in determining courts' standing with superior party-state institutions.[135] Petitions demand court resources; they also make courts and individual judges look bad in the eyes of their superiors. The importance of letters and visits is reflected in court attempts to prevent letters and visits and in compensation schemes that reward judges for preventing petitions and punish those who fail to do so. This section surveys general responses by courts to petitioning, providing evidence both of the effect of petitioning on the courts and of why courts care about letters and visits.

Preventing and handling letters and visits consumes significant court resources. The SPC is reported to have as many as eighty judges working on letters and visits.[136] Virtually every judge interviewed for this chapter agreed that reducing letters and visits is a goal of all courts and that letters and visits are resulting in significant pressure on courts.[137] Some courts have set targets of "zero petitions." Courts are not unique in this regard; other government departments likewise have taken steps both to address grievances and to reduce the number of letters and visits. Nevertheless, court efforts appear striking insofar as they interfere with, and influence, their handling of disputes before the courts.

Much of the emphasis on reducing petitions comes from the top. In 2002, the SPC issued a notice instructing all courts nationwide to emphasize resolving complaints raised by letters and visits. The court stated that handling petitions should be as important as handling cases through trial.[138] The SPC instructed lower courts to address letters and visits in the process of handling cases, to work to persuade and guide petitioners, and to change judgments in which they had erred.[139] In 2005, the SPC instructed lower courts to promote the provision of explanations of

[135] Courts are not the only institutions seeking to reduce litigation-related petitions. Lawyers report that, in some cases, they may be required to seek approval from local justice bureaus before taking cases that are likely to result in letters or visits. Interview 2006–45.

[136] Interview 2007–25.

[137] Interview 2007–18.

[138] Zuigao Renmin Fayuan, "Guanyu chongfen fahui shenpan zhineng qieshi weihu qiye he shehui wending de tongzhi."

[139] Ibid.

decisions to parties after decisions are made[140] and to promote the holding of public hearings to decide whether a case should be reheard.[141] In the following year, the court announced a new system for coordinating petitions relating to the courts to facilitate the better handling of suit-related petitions.[142] In 2007, the SPC called for renewed emphasis on the rehearing system in order to increase court transparency and, presumably, reduce petitioning.[143] More recently, in 2009, the SPC required all lower courts to establish a physical window to accept both case filings and petitions so as to better "serve the people."[144] SPC officials have pointed to the decrease both in the total number of letters and visits and in the number of collective petitions as signs that the courts are improving their handling of petitions.[145]

Lower courts have followed the SPC's instructions, increasing the resources they devote to handling letters and visits. In most courts,

[140] Zhang Na, Zhu Yunfeng, and Pan Jie 张娜, 朱云峰, & 潘杰, "Zuigaofa: Geji renmin fayuan jiang tuixing faguan panhou dayi zhidu" 最高法：各级人民法院将推行法官判后答疑制度 (SPC: All levels of courts will implement the system of providing explanations of decisions to the parties after decisions are made), *Renmin fayuan bao*, November 3, 2005, http://news.xinhuanet.com/legal/2005–11/03/content_3725454.htm (accessed August 25, 2008).

[141] Xiao Yang 肖扬, "Zuigao Renmin Fayuan guanyu kaizhan guifan sifa xingwei zhuanxiang zhenggai qingkuang de baogao" 最高人民法院关于开展规范司法行为专项整改情况的报告 (Report of the Supreme People's Court concerning developing norms for correcting some special judicial activities), *Zhongguo renda wang*, November 1, 2006, http://cms.npc.gov.cn:87/servlet/PagePreviewServlet?siteid=1&nodeid=1482&articleid=353846&type=1 (accessed April 26, 2010).

[142] Tian Yu, Yang Weihan, and Bu Yuntong 田雨, 杨维汉, &卜云彤, "Sifa huiying gongzheng yuqiu" 司法回应公正吁求 (Law responds to the demands of justice), *Xinhua wang*, March 13, 2007, http://news.xinhuanet.com/legal/2007–03/13/content_5842238.htm (accessed September 27, 2008).

[143] Zuigao Renmin Fayuan 最高人民法院, "Guanyu wei goujian shehuizhuyi hexie shehui tigong sifa baozhang de ruogan yijian" 关于为构建社会主义和谐社会提供司法保障的若干意见 (Opinion of the Supreme People's Court regarding some views on providing judicial protections for the construction of a harmonious society), *Zhongguo fayuan bao*, January 15, 2007, http://www.chinacourt.org/flwk/show1.php?file_id=115852 (accessed August 27, 2008).

[144] Zuigao Renmin Fayuan 2010 nian gongzuo baogao. The SPC also issued detailed rules concerning the operation of court letters and visits windows. See Zuigao Renmin Fayuan 最高人民法院, "Guanyu jinyibu jiaqiang renmin fayuan li'an xinfang chuangkou jianshe de ruogan yijian (shixing)" 关于进一步加强人民法院"立案信访窗口"建设的若干意见(试行) (Several opinions on strengthening the construction of courts' windows for case filings and petitions), *Zuigao renmin fayuan wang*, March 31, 2010, http://www.court.gov.cn/qwfb/sfwj/yj/201003/t20100331_3596.htm (accessed April 20, 2010).

[145] Li Hong 黎虹, "Renmin fayuan dui shensu anjian yao zuodao sange 'jianjian'" 人民法院对申诉案件要做到三个"件件" (Three "elements" the people's courts must satisfy to resolve petition cases), *Zhongguo fayuan wang*, March 13, 2007, http://www.chinacourt.org/public/detail.php?id=237943 (accessed August 27, 2008).

case-filing divisions are now responsible for petitions.[146] In 2009, the SPC itself also established a second case filing division, employing forty judges, to accept petitions.[147] This role has transformed the case-filing division from a relatively unimportant office into one of the most important and powerful in many courts.[148] As one (male) judge stated, in the past, the case-filing division "was for old people and women";[149] now it is staffed by some of the best-qualified judges.[150] The "huge importance" of letters and visits for local judges means that courts need judges who have experience "with both society and law" to handle petitions.[151] In addition to legal and social skills, psychological knowledge is also emphasized in case-filing divisions: The Zhejiang Province HPC requires every case-filing division in the province to employ at least one judge with training as a psychologist.[152]

In many courts, senior court officials also personally receive petitioners on specified days – and in some courts, only senior judges are permitted to receive petitions in person.[153] This reflects the emphasis that courts are putting on assuaging petitioners and also court leaders' belief that judges "need skill" in order to quiet petitioners. This generally involves explaining cases to petitioners, with a view to resolving the "contradictions" that give rise to protests.[154] Judges say that with sufficient work and attention, many cases involving petitioners and protesters can be resolved amicably.

Courts are also focusing on identifying potential petitioners before they lodge complaints. As one judge explained, "[O]ur first priority" is

146 Some courts have also established dedicated letters and visits offices separate from the case-filing division. Likewise, in some localities, the letters and visits offices of the local party committees have specialized divisions for handling litigation-related petitions. Interview 2007–25; Interview 2007–26.

147 Wang Shaonan, "Chuangxin shesu xinfang gongzuo fangfa, fangbian dangshiren yifa biaoda suqiu"; Zhang Weigang 张伟刚, "Zhuanyehua fengong: xianqi li'an shenpan de 'honggaitou'" 专业化分工:掀起立案审判改革的"红盖头" (Labor specialization: Lift the "red veil" of case filing adjudication reform), *Ping'an wang*, January 11, 2010, http://www.chinapeace.org.cn/zfdt/2010–01/11/c_13132513_2.htm (accessed on April 27, 2010).

148 Interview 2007–19; Interview 2006–51.

149 Interview 2006–52.

150 Interview 2006–51.

151 Interview 2006–51. For cases that have already been decided, the case-filing division will determine whether a case should be reheard. If a case is still in progress, judges in the filing division will speak about a petition either to the judges hearing the case or to their superiors. Interview 2007–19.

152 "Zhejiang quansheng li'anting kaizhan xinli zixunshi peixun gongzuo" 浙江全省立案庭开展心理咨询师培训工作 (All case filing divisions in Zhejiang Province begin psychological consultation training), *Kaoshida wang*, July 31, 2009, http://www.examda.com/xlzx/hangye/20090731/085758777.html (accessed April 2, 2010).

153 Interview 2007–13.

154 Interview 2007–23.

to prevent letters and visits.[155] Asked how they can prevent petitions, judges state that when a litigant comes to the court's case-filing office, "we can tell from their acts" whether they are the type of person who will petition and protest.[156] Some litigants will refuse to pay the court-filing fee or will threaten to protest. In such cases, judges from the filing division will warn the judges who will hear the case to be careful and to "emphasize the case," with a view to avoiding petitions and protests.[157] In cases in which litigants express their views strongly or express a great deal of emotion, the courts will try to mediate to avoid complaints after the case.[158]

The courts' goal in handling complaints is clear: to assuage the petitioners. "We try to calm them; we are concerned that [if we fail to do so], they will go to a higher court or to the local party committee."[159] Judges place particular emphasis on petitions regarding the courts that are filed with other party-state entities or with superior courts.[160] As a chief judge of a local court explained, in such cases the higher court or authorities will ask the court handling the case about the matter; the court will prepare a written response.[161] The case-filing division will also examine the case to see if there have been any mistakes in the court's handling of the case.[162] Numerous reports have likewise emphasized the need for courts to work with local people's congresses, government, and party officials to resolve letters and visits relating to cases.[163]

Judges complain that petitioners act strategically when they raise their grievances with other party-state officials. According to one judge, litigants know that the party is the boss, and they will go to party letters and visits bureaus to raise their grievances.[164] Litigants are also aware that doing so will result in pressure on the courts to resolve the matter. Courts

155 Interview 2007–26.
156 Interview 2007–25.
157 Interview 2007–25.
158 Interview 2007–26.
159 Interview 2007–19.
160 Interview 2007–18.
161 Interview 2007–18. Either the case-filing division or the judges responsible for the case will prepare the written response. Interview 2007–13; Interview 2007–17; Interview 2006–51; Interview 2006–57. Judges sometimes must also prepare reports for their own courts' filing divisions in response to complaints, but doing so is more common when enquiries come from superior courts or other party-state offices. Interview 2007–13.
162 Interview 2006–51.
163 For example, see Li Hong, "Renmin fayuan dui shensu anjian yao zuodao sange 'jian-jian.'"
164 Interview 2006–51.

have taken a range of novel approaches to addressing petitions – some of which appear designed to pressure judges to act proactively to prevent petitions. In Hebei Province, for example, court regulations provide that petitions are to be addressed by higher courts – meaning the court directly above the court where the case is pending.[165] A vice president of the Hebei HPC explained that the new procedures were designed to overcome the perceived reluctance of judges to change their decisions in cases they had personally decided.[166] Other courts, however, have taken different approaches. In Hubei, petitioners are explicitly permitted to meet with the presiding judge who handled their case – presumably both to pressure judges to act to prevent petitions and also to mollify petitioners.[167] In Nanhe County in Hebei Province, all judges' mobile phone numbers are disclosed to the public, and judges are required to keep their phones on twenty-four hours a day, seven days a week, to receive complaints from petitioners.[168] In a local court in Xinjiang, petitioners are allowed to select a judge to decide the case after reading judges' resumes.[169] Other courts hold dedicated days devoted to handling complaints or have announced that they have raised their work quality so as to eliminate complaints

[165] "Jianshao xinfang fasheng Hebei fayuan shensu anjian shangti yiji guanxia" 减少信访发生，河北法院申诉案件上提_级管辖 (Hebei courts raise the jurisdiction level for rehearing cases), *Xinhua wang*, January 10, 2006, http://www.ce.cn/xwzx/gnsz/gdxw/200601/10/t20060110_5781631.shtml (accessed August 27, 2008).

[166] Ibid.

[167] Yu Kai 余凯, "Shenggaoyuan gaige xinfang zhidu, pan'an faguan yu shangfang qunzhong "mianduimian" 省高院改革信访制度判案法官与上访群众"面对面" (The provincial high court reforms the letters and visits system, the masses can petition "face to face" to the judge who presided over the case), *Hubei ribao*, April 16, 2004, http://www.cnhubei.com/200404/ca443760.htm (accessed August 25, 2008).

[168] Ding Lixin and Wang Tiefeng 丁力辛 & 王铁峰, "Nanhe fayuan: qinmin jucuo wennuan baixinxin" 南和法院：亲民举措温暖百姓心 (Nanhe court: measures convenient to the public warmed their hearts), *Hebei fazhi bao*, March 3, 2010, http://www.yzlegal.com/shownews.asp?news_id=7257 (accessed March 20, 2010). Some scholars have criticized such measures both for making judges public figures and for facilitating corruption. "Chongqing fayuan zhili sifa fubai xilie fanfu dadongzuo yin guanzhu" 重庆法院治理司法腐败系列反腐大动作引关注 (A series of major anticorruption activities by the Chongqing courts to manage judicial corruption attract attention), *Chongqing fayuan wang*, October, 27, 2009, http://cqfy.chinacourt.org/public/detail.php?id=52240 (accessed April 27, 2010).

[169] Yang Yingchun 杨英春, "Wushi tianshanqu fayuan shouchuang xinfang dangshiren tiao faguan zhidu" 乌市天山区法院首创信访当事人挑法官制度 (The court of Tianshan District in Urumchi Muncipality is first to create the system of parties in petition cases selecting judges), *Xinjiang ribao*, December 15, 2008, http://bt.cinhuanet.com/2008–12/15/content_15187982.htm (accessed April 2, 2010).

altogether.[170] Numerous reports detail the courts' success in resolving complaints to the satisfaction of petitioners.[171]

Reports have also noted that judges not only receive petitions; they are also responsible for proactively visiting petitioners to try to prevent grievances from escalating.[172] One report from the Jiangsu Province HPC Web site notes that courts have too often been solely reactive in handling petitions. The report called on judges to be proactive and to resolve petitions before they escalate.[173] From January 11 to 20, 2010, the Henan Province HPC held a campaign in which "10,000 judges in Henan visited 10,000 petitioners." The judges focused on petitions referred to the courts from other authorities, cases in which petitioners had gone to Beijing or the provincial capital to petition, and cases involving important local enterprises.[174] SPC officials have also noted the importance of "prevention work" in reducing the number of petitions, as well as

170 "Zhuozhou changtong xinfang qudao, jiashi jiejue wenti" 涿州畅通信访渠道, 扎实解决问题 (Zhuozhou opens letters and visits route to provide solid solutions to problems), *Zhongguo jijian jiancha bao*, December 16, 2004, http://www.jjjc.hh.cn/wddt/wddt/2004/2004–12/2004–12-16/1103175081_19/ (accessed August 27, 2008).

171 For a report that a court claimed to have resolved all cases resulting in letters and visits to petitioners' satisfaction, see Liu Xiaobo and Tang Fengwei 刘晓波 & 唐风伟, "Bian shangfang wei xiafang, Heilongjiang pojie zhixing xinfang gongzuo nanti" 变上访为下访, 黑龙江破解执行信访工作难题 (From petition to reaching-out, Heilongjiang resolved the difficulties in petitions regarding enforcement of court awards), *Renmin fayuan bao*, April 7, 2007, http://www.chinacourt.org/public/detail.php?id=241437 (accessed August 25, 2008). Another court noted its success in preventing letters and visits by concentrating on cases with potential large social impact. "Jindong fayuan xinfang gongzuo." The Yingkou Intermediate People's Court in Liaoning Province announced that it succeeded in eliminating all letters and visits concerning cases. The court previously had had one of the highest rates of complaints of any court in the province, with the total number of petitions in one year nearing one thousand. Media reports praised court officials for visiting petitioners at home to address their complaints and to persuade them to stop petitioning. Also, the court announced that as part of its efforts to address letters and visits, it was honoring nineteen judges who had not issued an incorrect decision in the previous ten years and twenty-three who had been error free for five years. Media reports also noted that the court had been singled out for praise by central party leaders. Wang Zhi, "'Ling shangfang,' yige shangfang dahu de xinwen diaocha."

172 Li Hong, "Renmin fayuan dui shensu anjian yao zuodao sange 'jianjian.'"

173 Jiao Changbao and Xu Shihong 焦长宝 & 徐施宏, "Qidong fayuan loushi 'liujiehe,' guojian hexie xinfang xin chixu" 启东法院落实"六结合" 构建和谐信访新秩序 (Qidong courts use six measures to create new harmonious letters and visits order), *Jiangsu fayuan wang*, March 12, 2007, http://www.jsfy.gov.cn/cps/site/jsfy/index_content_a20070312222380.htm (accessed September 27, 2008).

174 "Henan yaoqiu geji faguan shidang buchang changqi shangfangzhe" 河南要求各级法官适当补偿长期上访者 (Henan requires judges at all levels to compensate long-term petitioners), *Renmin wang*, January 12, 2010, http://news.cn.yahoo.com/10–01-/1028/2juos.html (accessed April 2, 2010).

of advising litigants of the risk of litigation and of educating litigants about procedures.[175] In 2008, the SPC reported sending out fourteen groups of judges to lower courts to investigate and deal with 36,727 petitions.[176]

Courts have also taken a range of steps that appear designed to win over popular trust in the courts – and thus reduce petitioning. Such steps have included holding cases in the open air in villages (even in the rain),[177] providing accommodation to indigent litigants,[178] and accompanying petitioners to petition to higher authorities when petitioners disagree with a court judgment.[179]

Courts actively reach out to cooperate with other organizations to prevent petitions. For example, to address enforcement problems, a court in Shanghai collaborates with street-level officials to monitor people subject to enforcement actions.[180] In Henan, one first-instance court invited government leaders, people's congress representatives, legal scholars, and representatives of social organizations to attend hearings concerning major or repeat applications for rehearing. The courts invited the observers to express their opinions about the cases and help with mediation.[181]

The most significant indicator of the importance courts are placing on resolving and reducing petitions is the pressure individual judges face to

[175] Li Hong, "Renmin fayuan dui shensu anjian yao zuodao sange 'jianjian.'"

[176] Zuigao Renmin Fayuan 最高人民法院, "Zuigao Renmin Fayuan 2009 nian gongzuo baogao" 最高人民法院2009年工作报告 (2009 Supreme People's Court work report), *Xinhua she*, March 17, 2009, http://news.xinhuanet.com/newscenter/2009–03/17/content_11024682_1.htm (accessed August 25, 2009).

[177] Song Haiping, "Guanyu yufang he jianshao shefa shesu xinfang de jidian sikao."

[178] Han Jingwei and Guo Zhenzhen 韩景玮 & 郭珍珍, "Henan Gaoyuan fatongzhi wei tekun dangshiren jiejue shisu" 河南高院发通知为特困上访者解决食宿 (Henan High Court issues a notice to provide accommodation and food to petitioners facing special difficulties), *Dahe wang*, December 17, 2009, http://news.cn.yahoo.com/09–12-/346/2js7l.html (accessed April 2, 2010).

[179] Shan Shibing 单士兵, "Faguan pei shangfang shi falü xinyang de queshi" 法官陪上访是法律信仰的缺失 (Judges accompanying petitioners indicates the lack of faith in law), *Bandao wang*, April 5, 2008, http://news.bandao.cn/news_html/200804/20080409/news_20080409_602574.shtml (accessed April 3, 2010).

[180] "Chuangxin gongzuo jizhi, jianshao shesu xinfang" 创新工作机制, 减少涉诉上访 (Create new working systems to reduce litigation-related petitions), *Nanchong renmin zhengfu wang*, June 17,2009, http://www.ncxf.gov.cn/a/detail/2009–06-17/79.html (accessed March 20, 2010).

[181] Yue Qifeng 岳奇峰, "Xinhua Qu Fayuan shixing shensu tingzheng xiaoguo hao" 新华区法院实行申诉听证效果好 (The Xinhua district court implements hearings for petitions with good effects), *Zhongguo fayuan wang*, March 30, 2010, http://www.chinacourt.org/html/article/201003/30/401644.shtml (accessed April 20, 2010).

eliminate letters and visits.[182] Judges' promotions and salaries are tied to their ability to resolve cases without generating petitions.[183] Reports note that judges are evaluated based on, and thus have their compensation tied to, whether their cases result in petitions.[184] Judges whose cases generate group petitioning are singled out for negative appraisals,[185] whereas judges who handle petitions well or prevent them altogether are praised.[186] Judges note that the fact that a case results in a petition will reflect badly on the judge, regardless of whether the original case was decided correctly.[187] In Beijing, for example, a judge will be sanctioned if he or she has three cases that result in letters or visits – without regard to whether the complaints have merit.[188]

In Anhui, a notice of the provincial high court makes explicit that judges will be sanctioned for mishandling letters and visits. One indicator of a case being mishandled is when petitioners raise their complaints to a higher-level government department. The Anhui regulations emphasize that the person or entity that first receives a letter and visit is responsible for resolving it, and that letters and visits should be resolved at the "basic level" to prevent escalation.[189] The regulations also state that

182 Stability concerns permeate all aspects of governance in China; officials outside the courts are likewise concerned about potential harm to their images due to instability. Cai, "Local Governments and the Suppression of Popular Resistance in China," 35; see also Anna Brettell, "Channeling Dissent, The Institutionalization of Environmental Complaint Resolution," *China's Embedded Activism: Opportunities and Constraints of a Social Movement*, ed. Peter Ho and Richard Edmonds (New York: Routledge, 2008), pp. 126–127, noting pressures on low-ranking environmental officials to reduce the volume of complaints.

183 Li Hong, "Renmin fayuan dui shensu anjian yao zuodao sange 'jianjian;'" Interview 2007–27.

184 Wang Shu, "'Ling shangfang,' yige shangfang dahu de xinwen diaocha"; Chen Haifa and Ji Tianfu 陈海发 & 冀天福, "Henan fayuan jianli xinfang pinggu jizhi fanghuan weiran" 河南法院建立信访评估机制防患未然 (Henan courts establish a petition evaluation system to prevent escalation), *Renmin fayuan bao*, January 16, 2008, http://law-star.com/cacnew/200801/105011155.htm (accessed August 25, 2008).

185 Li Mingjie 李明杰, "Changjizhou zhongyuan zhaokai fayuan shesu xinfang gongzuo huiyi" 昌吉州中院召开法院涉诉信访工作会议 (Changji Intermediate Court convened a conference concerning petitions relating to litigation), *Changjizhou fayuan*, July 2, 2007, http://www.xj.xinhuanet.com/pingan/2007–07/02/content_10459356.htm (accessed August 27, 2008).

186 "Faguan shuo fa: Disanzhe zerenxian buneng suiyi tuibao" 法官说法：第三者责任险不能随意退保 (Judges explain the law: insurance for third person liability cannot be arbitrarily cancelled), *Zhongguo Xuzhou wang*, June 27, 2006, http://www.cnxz.com.cn/newscenter/xznews/sjbt/2006/2006062754862.htm (accessed August 27, 2008).

187 Interview 2007–26.

188 Interview 2007–31.

189 "Anhui sheng Gaoji Renmin Fayuan xinfang gongzuo zerenzhi."

court presidents are ultimately responsible for handling letters and visits in their courts.[190] The policy governing the courts is not unique; many government departments in Anhui have similar policies, suggesting that the courts are not taking such steps on their own. But the policies are notable for two reasons. First, they emphasize the handling of letters and visits without reference to whether such petitions have merit. Second, they make clear that courts are to follow the instructions of other government departments – the explicit reference is to *lingdao jiguan*, or leadership entities – regarding the handling of serious cases involving petitioners.[191]

Courts are also renewing emphasis on mediation, in significant part because mediated cases are less likely than adjudicated cases to result in letters and visits.[192] In 2009, the SPC encouraged all courts to reemphasize the Ma Xiwu adjudication method, which focuses on mediation.[193] The total percentage of mediated cases has increased significantly in recent years, from 55 percent of all first-instance civil cases in 2006 to 62 percent in 2009.[194] The Henan Province HPC identified 2009 as its "Mediation Year" and reported that courts in the province mediated 70 percent of civil cases in 2009.[195] Similarly, the number of disputes revolved by people's mediation committees increased in 2005, the first such increase in more than a decade.[196] The number continued to increase from 2006

190 Ibid., Art. 8.

191 Ibid.

192 "Jianshao xinfang fasheng Hebei fayuan shensu anjian shangti yiji guanxia." Reports from Hebei draw an explicit link between an increase in mediation and a decrease in the number of complaints filed regarding the courts. For example, a Hebei HPC report stated that the combination of mediation with the letters and visits system had resulted in a reduction in complaints – as had other reforms, including putting more weight on the obligation of judges to explain their decisions. Zhou Yuan, Han Yuanheng, and Li Ji 周远, 韩元恒, & 李霁, "Sheng fayuan 'sige chuangxin' jie shesu xinfang nanti" 省法院"四个创新"解涉诉信访难题 (The "four new innovations" of the provincial high court to resolve the problems from letters and visits), *Hebei ribao*, February 21, 2008, http://news.sohu.com/20080221/n255276884.shtml (accessed August 25, 2008).

193 Zuigao Renmin Fayuan 2010 nian gongzuo baogao; Liebman, "A Return to Populist Legality?"

194 *2007 Zhongguo Falü Nianjian*, 1066; Zuigao Renmin Fayuan 2010 nian gongzuo baogao.

195 Chen Haifa, Ji Tianfu and Guo Lingling 陈海发, 冀天福, & 郭玲玲, "Henan gaoyuan zhaokai quansheng fayuan tiaojienian huodong zongjie biaozhang dianshi dianhua huiyi" 河南高院召开全省法院调解年活动总结表彰电视电话会议 (Henan High Court held telephone and video conference for the entire province to summarize and commend mediation year activities), *Zhongguo fayuan wang*, December 30, 2009, http://www.chinacourt.org/html/article/200912/30/388726.shtml (accessed April 20, 2010).

196 Benjamin L. Liebman, "China's Courts: Restricted Reform," *The China Quarterly*, no. 191 (September 2007): 620–638.

to 2008.[197] Concerns about petitioners are not the sole factor behind the increase in mediated cases; mediation also fits with the central party-state's emphasis on constructing a "harmonious society." Yet judges note that mediation is the most common mechanism for resolving complaints raised through letters and visits.[198] As one judge explained, the goal is to resolve all civil cases through mediation, with many disputes being subject to mediation at three levels within the court: by the judges hearing the case, by the head of the division responsible for the case, and, if necessary, by the court president.[199] Nevertheless, judges say that many cases remain difficult to resolve.[200] Similarly, recent changes to rehearing procedures appear designed in part to reduce petitioning. The changes, adopted in revisions to the Civil Procedure Law, require that rehearing petitions in civil cases be filed with courts one level above those that issued the original decision. Commentators have observed that one consequence will be to make rehearing procedures more effective and thus reduce petitioning.[201]

SPC officials portray handling petitions as a key aspect of the courts' work. Judges, however, complain that the letters and visits system is forcing them to play roles that are inappropriate for judges. "We have to solve lots of problems not related to cases," said one judge.[202] Another noted that many petitioners, and the entire letters and visits system, are not respectful of judges.[203] Petitioners use extreme or improper methods, including abusing and swearing at judges, to obtain results.[204] Others have made similar criticisms of the system. One writer in an official SPC publication argued that it is improper for judges to meet parties to a pending case without the other party being present and that allowing judges to meet with petitioners on their own invites corruption and poses

[197] *2009 Zhongguo Falü Nianjian*, 248.

[198] Interview 2007–26; Interview 2006–54; Interview 2007–18. Commentators likewise have called for an increase in mediation as a means of reducing the total number of cases and thus the total number of litigation-related *xinfang*. Guo Yangcheng 郭羊成, "Cong yuantoushang jiejue shefa shesu shangfang wenti shizai bixing" 从源头上解决涉法涉诉上访问题势在必行 (The urgency in resolving law and litigation-related petitions from their roots), *Zhongguo renda*, no. 3 (2006): 50–52; Tian Menghua, "Lun nongcun jiceng renmin fayuan shangfang de chengyin yu duice."

[199] Interview 2007–25.

[200] Interview 2007–26.

[201] Lü Botao吕伯涛, "Gaige zaishen zhidu jiejue shensu nan wenti" 改革再审制度解决申诉难问题 (Reform the retrial system to solve difficulties in retrial applications), *Qiushi zazhi*, no. 19 (2007): 38–39.

[202] Interview 2007–27.

[203] Interview 2007–25.

[204] Interview 2007–25.

risks to judges.[205] One judge blogged that the importance of petitioning reflects continued emphasis on power, not law, in the Chinese system: Judges have to prostrate themselves before local leaders to have their decisions enforced. The blogger also argued that judges are violating other parties' legal rights in order to obtain stability and noted that judges are refusing to accept cases so as to avoid pressure from petitioners.[206] The only way to address this trend is to "change the ideology of government officials."[207]

Yet the problems in the courts are real, and petitioners often have legitimate concerns. Commentators have argued that reducing petitioning requires improving the courts: Doing so is the most important step in reducing the volume of petitions.[208] Others have argued that the number of complaints regarding the courts reflects the need for greater oversight, and stricter punishment, of judges.[209]

As noted previously, official statistics report a drop in letters and visits in the courts in recent years. Such statistics may suggest that the SPC's emphasis on courts avoiding mistakes has been successful.[210] The decrease in petitions may also reflect greater efforts by judges to explain their decisions, to identify cases that might lead to petitioning, and to assist litigants to obtain satisfactory resolution of their grievances.[211] Yet some judges argue that at least a portion of the decrease reflects not fewer complaints but rather greater oversight and management of petitions by the courts.[212] In some courts, for example, petitions regarding still-pending cases are no longer classified as letters and visits – thus lowering the total number of reported cases.[213]

The emphasis on addressing petitioners' complaints reflects the party-state's emphasis on stability. Courts want to prevent escalation at all

205 Xu Xuefeng 许雪峰, "Zhiyi fayuan changmen najian" 质疑法院敞门纳谏 (Doubting whether courts have left the door open for criticism), *Renmin sifa*, no. 11 (November 2001): 41.

206 Liu Guoyu, "Tan shesu xinfang yu fayuan fazhan de guanxi."

207 Zhao Wenming, "Hunan faguan weihe lunwei shangfanghu."

208 Guo Yangcheng, "Cong yuantoushang jiejue shefa shesu shangfang wenti shizai bixing."

209 Liang Yanping and Mao Ruijiang, "Guanyu fayuan goujian chuli shefa shangfang wenti changxiao jizhi de sikao."

210 Although judges complain that petitioners frequently petition even if courts have not made any errors, reducing mistakes (in particular, technical errors) does appear to reduce the frequency of petitions. One theme in judges' discussion of petitioners is that litigants will often seize on small errors as proof that the courts must have been biased. In a system in which litigants often have little faith in the fairness of the process, any errors are likely to be viewed as evidence of greater problems.

211 Interview 2006–54.

212 Interview 2006–32.

213 Interview 2006–32.

costs, because grievances reported to the higher courts or to the party-state officials will reflect badly on the courts. As one judge explained, "[T]he policy is stability"; thus, courts do whatever is necessary to maintain stability.[214] Courts, like other party-state institutions, are committed to this policy, even if short-term concerns about stability risk undermining the courts' authority in the long term.

III. A POPULIST THREAT?

Explaining the prevalence of petitioning is straightforward: It works.[215] Petitioners "know how to use their power" to influence the courts.[216] In some cases, lawyers are now encouraging their clients to petition in order to influence court decisions.[217] As one judge argued, as long as petitioners persist with their protests, they will obtain some benefit.[218]

Explaining why the party-state encourages petitioning is more complex. One of the most striking aspects of official attitudes toward petitioning is that they seem to be in tension with other trends in the Chinese political system. As Carl Minzner and others have noted, state responsiveness to petitioning and protest encourages more petitioning and thus potential unrest.[219] The party-state makes concessions to petitioners and protesters to prevent escalation and unrest – even though the officials know that doing so may encourage others to raise their grievances in a similar fashion. This contrasts with efforts to steer more disputes into the courts, to arbitration, or to mediation, where the intent is to prevent escalation and to keep the disputes off the streets. Although the petitioning system is designed to diffuse grievances and to keep complainants from using wholly extralegal mechanisms, the system creates incentives for those with complaints to persist with and escalate their demands.

There are, as prior commentators have noted,[220] important benefits for the state in the continuation of the letters and visits system. The petitioning system provides the party-state leadership (including both officials in higher courts and officials outside the court system) with valuable information. Such alternative sources of information may be of particular

214 Interview 2006–51.

215 Interview 2007–26.

216 Interview 2006–33.

217 Interview 2006–33.

218 Interview 2006–54.

219 Minzner, "*Xinfang*: An Alternative to the Formal Chinese Legal Institutions," 178; Cai, "Managed Participation in China," 446.

220 Minzner, "*Xinfang*: An Alternative to the Formal Chinese Legal Institutions," 109; Cai, "Managed Participation in China," 435–438; Luehrmann, "Facing Citizen Complaints in China, 1951–1996," 848.

importance in an authoritarian system lacking non-state sources of information or checks on official misconduct. Petitioning, even as it threatens unrest, is consistent with China's embrace of institutional competition and the reliance on multiple party-state entities to serve as checks on malfeasance.[221] Receiving and responding to petitions may also convince individuals that their grievances are taken seriously (even if most complaints are not effective). But encouraging petitions is at least partially in tension with state efforts to use the formal legal system as a means of addressing individual grievances.[222] Encouraging petitioning also appears to be at odds with the trend toward increased institutionalization of the party-state.

The influence of petitioning on the courts reflects the perseverance of problems that undermine court authority, including the continued legitimacy of official intervention, lack of finality, and the courts' close ties to local authorities. Such influence also reflects the courts' continued weak position in the political system: Populist pressures reflect the courts' lack of authority over other arms of the party-state. It is important to note that there is nothing impermissible about the courts being influenced by petitioning. Judges who take account of petitioners' views and change or adjust court decisions are acting in line with the design of the political-legal system. In addition, many observers argue that problems in the courts mean that supervision through letters and visits is essential.[223] Yet many judges interviewed for this chapter argue that the influence of petitioning is not merely a continuation of existing problems in the courts, and they express frustration with the pressures they face. Judges argue that their positions, and those of the courts, are actually declining in the face of populist pressures from both petitioning and the media. Judges are not neutral observers of external pressures or of their own competence. Such comments may reflect more about the judges' changed conceptions

[221] I discuss the emergence of institutional competition in more detail elsewhere. See Benjamin L. Liebman, "Toward Competitive Supervision? The Media and the Courts," *The China Quarterly* (forthcoming 2011); Liebman, "Watchdog or Demagogue? The Media in the Chinese Legal System."

[222] Some scholars, however, have found that state concerns regarding social stability have led to disputes being channeled away from the courts, in part because experience with the legal system frequently breeds disillusionment. Christopher Heurlin and Susan Whiting, "Villagers Against the State: The Politics of Land Seizures in Rural China,"paper presented at the annual meeting of the American Political Science Association, Chicago, August 30, 2007, http://www.allacademic.com/meta/p209847_index.html (accessed August 27, 2008), pp. 30–32.

[223] This view is noted, for example, in Cai, "Managed Participation in China," 450.

of their own roles than about the courts' power: Judges increasingly are measuring their roles with reference to the roles judges play in other countries. Nevertheless, it is noteworthy that some judges contend that their authority is actually decreasing.[224]

It would be a mistake, however, to understand the influence of petitioning as merely reflecting weak courts. The rise of courts as a locus of protest also reflects the fact that courts have become key fora in which a wide range of disputes, from traffic accidents to disputes about housing relocations to controversial criminal matters, are raised. One reason for the large number of court-related petitions is that the courts are confronting a widening range of contested issues. The growing relevance of the courts is also manifest in the frequency with which petitioners appear to bring nonjusticiable claims to court. The fact that petitioners seek to pressure the courts, either directly or by appeals to superior party officials, suggests that the courts have a significant degree of autonomy and authority. This does not mean that the courts are becoming more independent of the party-state, only that there is a wide range of cases in which the courts have significant discretion. This discretion makes the courts particularly sensitive to petitioners and also facilitates the courts' changing of decisions when they do come under pressure. This point is similar to Tong and Landry's finding that an escalation of grievances is more likely "when policy flexibility is high."[225] It is also likely that some courts use petitioning strategically to obtain outcomes they prefer and to resist some types of interference. Thus, for example, in cases in which courts come under pressure from powerful interests, the existence of petitioning may provide the courts with an argument to resist such pressures.

Is there a populist threat to China's courts? The answer depends on one's view of the appropriate role for the courts and on whether one believes that petitioning subverts or enhances the courts' ability to apply the law fairly. Existing literature, including some of my own writing,[226] argues that courts have begun to carve out significant zones of autonomy even as they remain subject to party-state oversight. The influence of

[224] Interview 2006–58. A survey of 113 judges in Beijing's Yanqing County in 2007 found that 90 percent of them felt public opinion was biased against them. Dong Xiaojun 董晓军, "Jiucheng faguan chixu youlü" 九成法官持续忧虑 (Ninety percent of judges are continuously anxious), *Nanfang zhoumo wang*, April 7, 2010, http://www.infzm.com/content/43604 (accessed April 30, 2010).

[225] Tong and Landry, "Disputing the Authoritarian State in China."

[226] Liebman, "China's Courts: Restricted Reform."

petitioning shows that this autonomy is fragile. At the very least, courts are facing a new source of pressures, one that has arisen as the courts have taken modest steps toward increasing their own authority. The populism discussed in this chapter is only one aspect of a broader phenomenon: Courts also are extremely sensitive to popular opinion voiced through the media.[227] Likewise, judges' concerns about stability and responsiveness to petitioners reflects party-state emphasis on stability. In being responsive to petitioning, courts are acting in line with party policy. If one views the development of courts that are insulated from such external pressures and that are able to apply the law consistently as a desirable outcome, then the rise of populism is likely to be of concern. If, however, one understands courts as being primarily tools of the party, and often biased or unfair, populist pressures may be of less concern. In either case, however, it is clear that courts care about how their decisions are viewed – by party officials, by the media, and by individuals.

Perhaps the most striking aspect of the influence of court-related petitioning is that courts are concerned with individual petitioners. Most literature on protest in China focuses on how the state responds to group grievances.[228] The evidence presented in this chapter shows that the state is also concerned with individual complaints. The ability of individual petitioners to influence courts may suggest that the term "populist pressure" is inappropriate to describe this phenomenon. More research is needed to determine how widespread the phenomenon of courts being swayed by individual protestors is, and also whether there are significant regional differences in the ability of petitioning and protesting to influence courts. Nevertheless, the evidence presented in this chapter suggests that litigants, often acting alone, have learned that petitioning, or merely threatening to protest, is an effective means of swaying courts. Any act of petitioning may carry an implicit threat of escalation, but courts appear swayed even when the chances of unrest are remote. Officials face incentives to reduce the number of petitions or complaints. As a result, even an individual petitioner can become a focus of official concern. The

227 Media expressions of public opinion may represent the views of a small number of people – suggesting that "public opinion" in China refers to something very different from that discussed in Western literature on populism and the courts. Popular opinion in China, whether representing a small number of people or genuine mass opinion, is influential because of its ability to influence administrative actors.

228 For example, see Cai, "Local Governments and the Suppression of Popular Resistance in China"; O'Brien and Li, *Rightful Resistance in Rural China*; Xi Chen, "Collective Petitioning and Institutional Conversion," *Popular Contention in Contemporary China*, ed. Kevin O'Brien (Cambridge: Harvard University Press, 2008).

state responds not only to collective action; it also is swayed by individual protest. By resorting to the letters and visits system, an individual is sometimes able to obtain an outcome that would not be possible by relying on formal legal processes.

Courts everywhere are subject to various degrees of populist pressures; it would be a mistake to measure Chinese courts against an idealized standard of the role of courts in more developed legal systems. Nevertheless, the prevalence of populist pressures in China is striking and reflects a system in which political ideology and concerns about stability continue to take precedence over legal doctrine. In the short run, petitioners may win redress for their grievances. In the long run, however, a systemic preference for stability over substantive or procedural justice would appear to carry costs, both for individuals and for the state. A system of populist justice is unlikely to be consistent or fair across a range of cases. The evidence presented in this chapter suggests that we should be wary of assuming that courts in China are undergoing a fundamental transition in their roles. Courts are evolving, but not necessarily toward a Western-style system. The influence of petitioning shows that courts remain subject to extensive external pressures, continue to play a range of roles in addition to deciding cases, and do not appear to be distinguishing themselves from other state institutions in the minds of those who use the courts.

At present, the formal legal system appears less interested in outcomes that are fair or consistent than in outcomes that avoid instability. As one judge explained, law is less important than either economic development or social stability.[229] Consistent application of legal rules is not viewed as a mechanism for ensuring social stability. Social stability is obtained by buying off those who complain and by greater use of official discretion, not by replacing discretion with law. This is not a new phenomenon, and it reflects long-standing incentives for both judges and party-officials. It may also reflect continued distrust of the law and of even moderately autonomous legal institutions by party elite and the fact that senior judges are explicitly political actors. Yet tensions are becoming more apparent as legal procedures become more formal, as judges begin to develop professional identities as judges, and as courts come to apply a widening range of substantive law. The obsession with stability also highlights a key difference between populist pressures in China and in the United States (and perhaps other democratic systems): In the United States, the legitimacy of populist influence is grounded at least in part

[229] Interview 2006–52.

on what scholars refer to as the unwritten, or customary, constitution – the set of internalized constitutional norms that are safeguarded by the democratic process. Populism in China is rooted in mass-line ideology. But it also reflects continuing and perhaps growing tensions between popular conceptions of morality and increasingly important legal standards. Appeals to populism in China often appear to have little to do with the law at all, reflecting the fact that, as noted most famously by Peking University Law School dean Zhu Suli, redressing grievances and following the law may result in different outcomes.

The importance of petitioning also reflects the significance of popular opinion in the Chinese political system more broadly. Although political scientists have recognized the complex role of public opinion in contemporary China, legal scholars have paid much less attention to the topic. Populist justice in China means not only that courts are swayed by the media or by outpourings of popular opinion on the Internet. It also means that a single individual, standing with a sign stating "grievance" outside a local court, has the ability to sway a court's decision. The concern here appears not to be only with unrest; there is also discomfort about the individual's claim of injustice and apprehension that failure to respond will undermine the legitimacy of both the courts and of party rule. There are historical precedents for such developments that help to explain the perseverance of the letters and visits system. Nevertheless, this finding also contrasts somewhat with findings that costless (or nondisruptive) complaints generally fail to yield a response from the state[230] – although it may be the case that the courts view all petitions as disruptive because of the possibility that they will escalate or be raised with higher-ranking officials.

The challenges for the courts may be becoming more pronounced given their avowed commitment to embracing rule of law principles in a system that continues to derive its legitimacy from achieving outcomes that are substantively, rather than procedurally, just.[231] The influence of

[230] For example, Chen notes that petitioners are generally "powerless" in the absence of a threat of escalation. Chen, "Collective Petitioning and Institutional Conversion." Likewise, see Xi Chen, "Art of Troublemaking: Chinese Petitioners' Tactics and Their Efficacy," paper presented at the annual meeting of the American Political Science Association, Hilton Chicago and the Palmer House Hilton, Chicago, September 2, 2004, http://www.allacademic.com/meta/p59702_index.html (accessed September 16, 2008), pp. 6–7; Cai, "Managed Participation in China," 441–442.

[231] As Chapter 6 in this volume notes, this observation regarding China contrasts significantly with Tom Tyler's work on the United States, where the legitimacy of the system derives from the legitimacy of procedures and thus the system. Tom R. Tyler and Yuen

petitioning suggests that litigants – in particular, those with experience in the system – continue to lack confidence in the law or the legal system.[232] Instead, courts and petitioning are used as strategic vehicles for achieving their goals. Further research on petitioners' grievances is needed, but one important cause of complaints regarding the legal system is a lack of popular confidence in the legitimacy of legal procedures. The focus of litigants and petitioners thus becomes the outcomes, not whether the litigants have been treated fairly.[233] Indeed, in contrast to findings regarding the U.S. system,[234] there is little evidence that litigants in China believe that they benefit by belonging to a society that respects legal procedures. If so, this lack of trust in the fairness of the system suggests limits to how far the process of institutionalization and legalization can go toward addressing China's increasing volume of complaints and unrest.[235]

The influence of petitioning on the courts also provides insights into one additional theme of this volume: the development of a legal culture in China. As I have noted elsewhere,[236] the Chinese party-state has devoted enormous resources to legal education and awareness in recent years. These efforts have created rising expectations regarding the law and legal institutions that may exceed the current capacity of such institutions. The determination of petitioners to pursue their grievances may reflect greater awareness of rights among litigants. But it also suggests that a system that is increasingly focused on rights will not necessarily lead to a system in which judges and courts are the central players or make the final

J. Huo, *Trust in the Law: Encouraging Public Cooperation with the Police and Courts* (New York: Russell Sage Foundation, 2002).

[232] This is a point supported by Mary Gallagher's work. See Mary E. Gallagher, "Mobilizing the Law in China: 'Informed Disenchantment' and the Development of Legal Consciousness," *Law & Society Review* 40 (2006): 783–816, as well as Chapter 6 in this volume. By contrast, Sally Merry's work on attitudes among working-class Americans noted that working-class plaintiffs "rarely doubt the legitimacy of the law itself or the value of a legally ordered society." Sally Engle Merry, *Getting Justice and Getting Even: Legal Consciousness among Working-class Americans* (Chicago: University of Chicago Press, 1990), p. 11.

[233] Judges in China state that they are sometimes able to diffuse complaints by meeting with petitioners and persuading petitioners that their complaints have been taken seriously. In doing so, however, they appear to be stepping outside their formal roles as judges who adjudicate disputes and into more traditional roles as government officials.

[234] Tyler and Huo, *Trust in the Law: Encouraging Public Cooperation with Police and Courts*, pp. 171–172..

[235] Michelson and Read's contribution to this volume in Chapter 6 makes an important, analogous point: Procedural reforms may be of limited effect in a system focused on substantive justice.

[236] Benjamin L. Liebman, "China's Courts: Restricted Reform," 625–626. Michelson and Read make a similar point in Chapter 6 of this volume.

determinations. Likewise, the impact of petitioning suggests that greater awareness of rights is not translating into greater confidence in formal legal institutions – and may be translating into greater disenchantment.

Finally, it is worth considering what implications developments in China may have for theories of populism and the courts more generally and about how courts construct legitimacy. Extreme concerns with popular opinion, or with individualized claims of injustice, generally are not characteristics we associate with authoritarian regimes. How China balances tensions between populism and the law may go a long way toward determining both the role that the courts play in the Chinese legal system and how the Chinese party-state is able to manage populist pressures. Courts today view popular opinion and individual protest as threats to their authority, much as they see party interference as a threat. It remains to be seen whether the courts will also be able to seek legitimacy through reliance on popular opinion.[237] Their ability to do so will depend on the party-state's willingness to loosen control of public opinion and on the party-state becoming more secure with the idea that refusing to yield to petitioners or to public opinion regarding the legal system may also be a mechanism for ensuring stability and regime legitimacy.

[237] Courts have, to a degree, begun attempting to do so under the leadership of SPC President Wang Shengjun, albeit not in a way that encourages respect for the finality of legal decisions. Liebman, "A Return to Populist Legality."

10

Dispute Resolution and China's Grassroots Legal Services

Fu Yulin

As has often been pointed out, "China's major problem is still the rural problem, and one of the most important tasks of the modernization of Chinese society is the modernization of rural society; anyone who is really concerned about the happiness and sorrow of the Chinese people is certainly concerned about the life of those people at the bottom of the society."[1] China's growing gaps between urban and rural areas and between rich and poor continue to challenge China's legal reforms. Whether China becomes a rule of law state will depend on whether legal reforms can reach deep into the rural population.

This chapter examines "grassroots" legal services in China's rural areas. "Grassroots level" refers to cities and districts at the county level, township, town, and subdistrict offices, and the so-called "detached judicial tribunals." "Legal services" include a range of activities from legal representation in litigation to the handling of nonlitigation legal matters, mediation of disputes, assistance in notarization and testimony, legal consultancy, and assistance in the writing of legal documents. Grassroots legal-services offices provide legal services to a wide range of clients from governmental agencies, self-governed mass organizations,

[1] Zhu Suli, *Songfa xiaxiang: Zhongguo jiceng sifa zhidu yanjiu* (Bringing the Law to the Rural Areas: A Study of China's Grassroots Judicial System) (Beijing: Zhongguo zhengfa daxue chubanshe, 2002), p. 7.

This chapter is extracted from the project on "A Study on Grassroots Legal Services" funded by the George Washington University. The entire report can be found in *Nongcun jiceng falü yanjiu* (Researches on Rural Law Services at the Basic Level), ed. Fu Yulin (Beijing: Zhongguo zhengfa daxue chubanshe, 2006). For similar conclusions, see also Wang Yaxin, *Empirical Researches on Grassroots Legal Services*. In Law and Social Development (*Falu Yu Shehui Fazhan*) 2006.3, and also in Tsinghua Law Journal (*Tsinghua Faxue*) 2008.5, and 2009.1. Professor Wang's articles were based on investigations done in 2005 from the perspective of legal services in litigation filed in the "expedited courts" (*paichu fatin*).

government-sponsored institutions and enterprises, social entities, and individual businessmen, partnerships, and citizens within the jurisdiction.

In analyzing grassroots legal services, we find a complex relationship between these offices and other state administrative organs (local justice offices – the *sifabu*), state judicial organs (grassroots people's courts), self-governing mass organizations (people's mediation commissions), and other legal-services institutions (legal aid and law firms). We find functional overlaps, subordination, and administrative or competitive relationships in the development and evolution of these offices. When seeking to resolve disputes, Chinese rural citizens will seek out "legal," administrative, governmental, as well as self-exercised social remedies in a blended and interesting mix.[2]

Grassroots legal-services offices came into being primarily to address emerging social needs. Grassroots legal services developed from needs rather than from holistic government planning. As a result, their growth has been haphazard and their existence constantly threatened. In recent years, with the rapid development of law firms in urban areas, grassroots legal-services offices have been seriously criticized for their low-price competition and low-quality services. Changes in top leadership of judicial and administrative departments have also led to a sudden decline in legal-services offices and to proposals to replace grassroots legal-services with government-funded offices, such as legal aid and "self-governing mass organizations" – namely, the people's mediation commissions.

Although we collected data from four cities, in this chapter we discuss two representative sites: Site A in central Hubei Province and Site C (north) in western Shanxi Province. These sites were selected because

[2] For instance, according to the classifications of mediation in 1985, when the first grassroots legal-services offices were established, "civil mediations are classified into mediations by people's mediation commissions (people's mediations); mediations by grassroots mass legal-services offices (stations); mediations by colleagues, relatives, and neighbors; and mediations by people present, among others. Official mediations are grouped into mediations by courts; administrative mediations by authorities (mainly mediations by judicial assistants and by people's mediation sections or grassroots work subdivisions and sections of the county and district judicial bureaus); administrative mediations by units in charge (mainly mediations by the administrative institutions of enterprises, government-sponsored institutions, organs, and entities, including mediations by public security stations); mediations by arbitration committees and mediations by law firms (prelitigation or extralitigation mediations)." Today, the functions and personnel of legal-services offices are still close to or even the same as those of the justice offices, public security stations, and people's mediation commissions. See Ministry of Justice, ed., *Zhongguo sifa xingzheng de lilun yu shijian* (Judicial and Administrative Theory and Practice) (Beijing: Zhongguo zhengfa daxue chubanshe, 1989), p. 722.

they epitomized grassroots legal-services offices in developing and poverty areas. Through interviews and surveys, we obtained the history of these legal-services offices and their relationship within the judicial system. The scope of our investigation included not only legal-services offices (*falü fuwu suo*), but also administrative authorities (*sifa bu*) (county or city judicial bureaus), the main locations where the services are provided (grassroots courts), their competitors and substitutes (namely, law firms and the people's mediation commissions), possible future substitutes such as legal-aid centers (*falü yuanzhu zhongxin*), and service recipients or customers.

Legal-services offices provides representatives for a party, but we should not ignore the following reality about legal services in China: 1) government interference in every aspect of social life is an administrative mode with particular Chinese characteristics. In China, there are no autonomous organizations or nongovernmental organizations in the strict sense; 2) the overlap of judicial bureaus (grassroots juridical and administrative authorities of the government) and legal-services offices indicates that legal-services offices have not yet evolved from governmental institutions into autonomous social agencies; and 3) the neutrality of the courts and classification of lawyers' functions only evolved within the last decade and have not yet reached the grassroots in China.

As of July 2010, grassroots legal services remain marginalized as central policy turns to ensuring a "harmonious society." The main function of the local justice offices has transferred to mediation and renamed the "Center of Mediation And Resolution of Social Disputes" (She Hui Mao Dun Jiu Fen Tiao Jie Zhong Xin) as courts turn their attention on mediation instead of adjudication. Although the Law on Lawyers was revised in 2007 and the draft on the Law on People's Mediation (*Renmin Tiaojie Fa*) is under consideration by the NPC as of June 2010, there is no comparable new regulation on grassroots legal service issued from the Justice Department. To date, the prospect of rural legal services in China remains dim.

THE RISE AND DECLINE OF GRASSROOTS LEGAL-SERVICES OFFICES

Grassroots legal-services offices first emerged in Guangdong, Fujian, and Liaoning Provinces in the late 1980s, primarily serving rural residents in manufacturing or business disputes. They provided simple legal services, such as writing legal documents and providing legal consultancy.

In 1984, grassroots legal-services offices expanded rapidly throughout the country and quickly entered the sub-districts, factories, and mines in large- and medium-sized cities. By the end of 1989, there were 29,979 township and town legal-services offices and 90,333 township and town (subdistrict) legal-service workers in China. The township and town legal-services offices were reported to have resolved a total of 1,377,624 disputes, assisted in 1,727,265 notarizations, represented in 117,013 civil litigations, and handled 235,037 nonlitigation matters. They acted as legal consultants for 104,073 grassroots governments and enterprises, wrote 594,356 legal documents for others, provided legal consultancy for 3,986,602 persons, and retrieved economic losses of 2.12688 billion RMB.[3] The Central Committee of the Communist Party of China and the State Council recognized grassroots legal-services offices as official "political and legal grassroots organizations."[4]

After 1990, township legal-services offices were reviewed, with a focus on raising their standards, quality, and efficiency. The Ministry of Justice (MoJ) promulgated the Interim Provisions on Township and Town Legal-Services Offices and the Detailed Implementing Rules for Township and Town Legal Services, affirming that the business scope of grassroots legal-services offices is to be as extensive as that of law firms. Although the MoJ in theory issued qualification certificates for township and town legal-service workers or licenses for legal-service providers, in reality, the examination and approval authority rested with the county-level judicial bureaus.[5] By 1992, the number of township and town legal-services offices had increased by 1,087 despite the revocation and merging of unqualified offices, and the number of legal-service workers increased by 1,046. Township and town legal-service workers with junior-college and higher degrees accounted for 13.8 percent of the total, those who

[3] However, based on research conducted by this author, the authenticity of the data submitted by the grassroots authorities is questionable. One local judicial bureau told us candidly that these data have been inflated, and the figure provided to us by the bureau in private is merely half of the figure in official reports and even less in certain aspects.

[4] *Jiaqiang shehui zhi'an zonghe zhili de jueding* (Decision on Reinforcing Comprehensive Administration of Law and Order in the Society), issued by the Central Committee of the Communist Party of China and the State Council.

[5] The items of charges of grassroots legal-services offices were included in the approved category in *Guanyu yinfa guowuyuan youguan bumen lianhexia fade "Zhongjie fuwu shoufei guanli banfa" de tongzhi* (Circular concerning the Printing and Distribution of the Second Catalog for the Administration of Administrative Charges of the Relevant Departments under the State Council issued by the State Bureau of Commodities), December 22, 1999.

had attended senior high schools (technical secondary schools) accounted for 62.3 percent of the total, and 1,205 were qualified lawyers. Official documents again affirmed that grassroots legal-services offices play an important role in assisting grassroots governments in promoting administration according to the law, resolving grassroots conflicts, popularizing legal knowledge, and settling controversial legal issues. In the early 1990s, legal-services offices were an important force supplementing grassroots and basic political and legal work.[6]

From September to October 1999, the MoJ sent four survey teams to ten provinces and municipalities, including Beijing, Tianjin, Shanghai, Shandong, Jiangsu, Henan, Shaanxi, Gansu, Guangdong, and Hubei. Their research found confusion in the overlapping names and functions of these offices (such as legal-services offices, legal-services centers, legal firms, legal-services stations, legal-consultation centers, legal-services companies, and legal-consultancy companies) and an unequal geographic distribution of the legal-services offices. There were relatively more legal-services offices located in the urban areas, fewer in the countryside, and even fewer in the remote areas. There were no national standards for charging legal-service fees, resulting in varied fees charged in accordance with some interim measures issued by the province or city. Finally, approval for the legal-services offices was not uniform, with some being approved by provincial and municipal judicial departments or bureaus, others by district and county judicial bureaus, and still others by nonjudicial administrative departments such as the provincial planning committees, provincial legislative affairs offices, provincial high courts, provincial procuratorates, and provincial administrations for industry and commerce,

The MoJ also found the professional qualifications of legal-service workers to be low. Any person with some legal knowledge who had graduated from senior high school could engage in grassroots legal work. There were no uniform national, professional qualification examinations, nor were there any regulations on professional ethics and discipline. Indeed, legal-service workers were mainly retirees from administrative or judicial organs, who favored their relatives and associates when dealing with cases. Noting these problems, senior government officials suggested that legal-services offices be reformed according to market standards and participate in market competition.

[6] *Sifabu 2001 nian 6 yue 16 ri banbu de sifa tong (2001) 069 hao wenjian* (SFT [2001] No. 069 Circular issued by the Ministry of Justice, June 16, 2001).

This focus to market discipline for legal services contrasts sharply with speeches by some senior leaders who emphasized the "public service and "nonprofit" nature of legal services.[7]

As a first step, grassroots offices under the MoJ were moved from the "grassroots work" department to the lawyers and notarization department, so that legal service workers and lawyers are now under the same management system. There were greater changes in the grassroots legal-services offices in 2000. In August, "GBF (2000) no. 51" and "QBH (2000) no. 9" documents stipulated that legal-services offices "shall no longer be administratively affiliated institutions or government-sponsored institutions and shall implement a self-disciplined operational mechanism for independent operations, independent income and expenditure, independent management, and independent development in order to become partnership business organizations in conformity with the rules of the legal agency services industry."[8] In other words, grassroots legal-services offices were to be subject to market discipline.

Thereafter, the number of the grassroots legal-services offices throughout the country declined dramatically. By the end of 2000, there were a total of 34,219 grassroots legal-services offices in China, 1,164 fewer than at the end of 1999.[9] In 2002, the number of legal-services offices

[7] For example, *Guanyu jiaqianq dazhong chengshi shequ falü fuwu gongzuo de yijian* (Opinions concerning the Enhancement of the Community Legal Services Work in Large- and Medium-Sized Cities), promulgated by the Ministry of Justice in 2002; and the speech by Minister of Justice Zhang Fusen at a symposium attended by the directors of the Chinese judicial departments (bureaus) in 2003 requiring that grassroots legal services be rooted in communities, close to the people, and provide convenient services at low prices, and that the functions of grassroots legal services work in large- and medium-sized cities be "to provide public welfare and non-profit legal services relying on the neighborhood sub-districts and communities and oriented toward grassroots communities and the public" in order to meet the legal needs of the low-income and disadvantaged groups in the urban areas.

[8] In March 2000, the Ministry of Justice promulgated the *"Jiceng falü fuwusuo guanli banfa" he "Jiceng falü fuwu gongzuozhe guanli banfa"* (Administrative Measures for Grassroots Legal-services Offices and Administrative Measures for Grassroots Legal Service Workers), stipulating that "grassroots legal-services offices shall be managed and operated in accordance with the system of institutional legal persons" and realizing the "combination of administrations and institutions" with township and town governmental justice offices.

[9] For details, see *Zhongguo sifa xingzheng nianjian (1995–2002)* (Judicial and Administrative Yearbook of China, 1995–2002), ed. Ministry of Justice (Beijing: Falü chubanshe, 1995–2003). However, probably because of the effect of inertia, the total number of grassroots legal-service workers in 2000 was 121,904, 2,182 more than at the end of 1999; the business volume also increased, among which the representations for civil, economic, and administrative litigation increased by 6.3 percent from the previous year, the

decreased by 1,758 during 2001, and the number of legal-service workers decreased by 9,444.[10]

To understand the role and impact of these grassroots legal-services offices, we need to examine their relationship with other legal-service providers such as the local justice bureaus (*sifa suo*), mediation committees, and law firms. Quite often, the grassroots legal-services offices have overlapping functions with local justice bureaus/offices, mediation committees, and law firms.

"One Group of Personnel with Three Names"

Grassroots justice offices emerged in the mid-1990s as a division of the MoJ, almost ten years after the emergence of legal-services offices.[11] Yet, legal-services offices are required to carry out their work under the

people working as legal consultants for grassroots people's governments, village (neighborhood) committees, enterprises, and government-sponsored institutions increased 5.9 percent over the previous year, and the business volumes of other areas also increased. However, in 2001, the total number of grassroots legal-services offices in the country decreased drastically to 28,647 (a decrease of 5,572 from the previous year), and the total number of grassroots legal-service workers decreased by 13,919 over the previous year; except for a slight increase in litigation representations, the business volume of all other service areas declined significantly.

10 At that time, legal-services offices that were responsible for their own losses and profits throughout the country accounted for 63 percent of all established offices, of which 30 percent had been separated from the justice offices and nearly 40 percent had become independent institutional legal persons. See *Zhongguo sifa xingzheng nianjian, 2002* and the speech by Vice Minister Duan Zhengkun at the national forum of directors of judicial departments and bureaus, July 23, 2003.

11 *Sifa yu 1981 nian 11 yue banbu de "Sifa zhuliyuan gongzuo zanxing guiding* (The Interim Provisions for the Work of Judicial Assistants issued by the Ministry of Justice in November 1981) provided that full-time judicial assistants at people's communes (towns) and subdistrict offices, as judicial and administrative personnel of grassroots people's regimes, should work under the guidance of people's communes (towns), subdistrict offices, and county (district) judicial bureaus (offices), and with the guidance of grassroots courts. In the *Sifabu 1996 nian 6 yue banbu "Guanyu jiaqiang sifasuo jianshe de yijian"* (Opinions regarding Enhancement of the Construction of Justice Offices, issued by the Ministry of Justice in June 1996) grassroots justice offices have eight major functions, including the guidance and management of grassroots legal services and the resolution of civil disputes on behalf of the township and town people's governments (subdistrict offices). Other functions include assisting grassroots governments in carrying out administration according to the law, administrative law enforcement, examination, and supervision; providing guidance and administration for the people's mediation work and participating in the mediation of certain important and difficult civil disputes; organizing and carrying out legal popularization and education work; organizing the interim arrangements and assistance and educational work for persons who have been released after completion of their sentences or who have been released

leadership of the township and town people's justice offices.[12] Administratively, the justice offices are state grassroots judicial and administrative organs, whereas legal-services offices are social organizations administered and guided by the justice offices.

Grassroots justice offices are funded out of the national budget, and their personnel structures are approved and determined by the government. By contrast, grassroots legal-services offices are self-funded and responsible for their own profits or losses without any definite personnel structures. And so, although the grassroots legal-services offices may charge for their services, the grassroots justice offices may not charge for the provision of legal assistance. However, based on our surveys, we found that the relationship between the two offices is in reality "one group of personnel, with two names." We learned that a director of a legal-services office was also the judicial assistant or, later, the director of the local justice office. In many townships, these two offices have the same director and share one group of personnel. In 1990, nearly 80 percent of the legal-services offices offered services under the system of "two types of openness and one type of supervision."[13]

By contrast, the people's mediation commissions are mass organizations for the mediation of disputes, administratively located under the village and neighborhood committees but supervised by the local people's governments and the grassroots people's courts.[14] Members of the people's mediation commissions are elected by the public. People's mediation commissions do not charge for mediation of disputes, except if their mediation is successful. Their funds for carrying out their work and the subsidies for the people's mediators are covered by the village or neighborhood committee. The effectiveness of a people's mediation agreement is equivalent to that of a civil contract, but an agreement reached with the support of a grassroots legal-services office is not binding. If a party refuses to accept the agreement, the legal-service worker must file a lawsuit on behalf of the other party in the people's court.

from labor reeducation camps; taking part in comprehensive social security administration; and completing all other work assigned by the superior judicial authorities and township and town people's governments (subdistrict offices).

[12] *Sifabu banbu de "Xiangzhen falü fuwu shishi xize"* (Detailed Implementing Rules for Township and Town Legal Services, issued by the Ministry of Justice), September 1991.

[13] *Falü nianjian 1993* (Law Yearbook of China 1993) (Beijing: Falü chubanshe, 1993), p. 142.

[14] See *Guowuyuan 1989 nian 17 ri banbu de "Renmin tiaojie weiyuanhui zuzhi tiaoli"* (The Regulation on the Organization of People's Mediation Commissions), issued by the State Council, June 17, 1989.

Statutory responsibility provides that a director of a local justice office can also carry out mediation work. Thus, the justice office is aptly nicknamed "one group of personnel with three names" – that is, the director of a justice office also works as the director of both the legal-services office and the mediation commission.

Grassroots Legal-Services Offices and Law Firms

More than ten years ago, law firms spun off from administrative organs and became market oriented. In many grassroots villages, local law firms are still state-operated law firms. Similarly, grassroots legal-services offices in townships and subdistricts gradually spun off from their administrative authorities, that is, the justice offices. Since 2000, grassroots legal-services offices are not very different from the current private law firms. The rights and obligations of the grassroots legal-services offices are the same as the rights and obligations of professional lawyers as provided in the Law on Lawyers.[15] They have an obligation to "safeguard the dignity of the law and the justice of the society," to fulfill their duty in safeguarding the legal rights and benefits of the parties involved, and to perform legal assistance according to the law.

However, grassroots legal-services offices are clearly different from law firms in terms of their geographical and business scope, professional qualifications, and fee structure. While grassroots legal-services offices serve mainly various grassroots units and individuals in rural areas or urban neighborhoods in their localities, law firms are not subject to this limit. Grassroots legal-services offices cannot engage in criminal cases, whereas law firms can engage in all types of litigation, including criminal cases.

Employees in grassroots legal-services offices are required to obtain a qualification certificate for special legal services. By contrast, lawyers in law firms are required to pass a national lawyers exam organized by the MoJ, the Supreme People's Court, and the Supreme Procuratorate. Finally, law firms are free to charge very high rates,[16] but legal-service

[15] This includes the right to review relevant materials in the people's courts while conducting litigation representation activities in civil, economic, or administrative cases; to conduct investigations as required by the cases, undertaken with certification issued by the grassroots legal-services offices and the license for legal services; and to inquire about and request relevant materials from relevant units and individuals.

[16] For details, see *Sifabu, caizhengbu yu 1990 nian 9 yue 1 ri banbu de "Xiangzhen falü fuwusuo caiwu guanli banfa* (Measures on the Financial Management of Township and Town Legal-services Offices, promulgated by the Ministry of Justice and the

workers must abide by the provisions of the provincial bureau on pricing, which mandate very low rates. In many cases, the only charge is the cost, or no charge at all according to the legal-assistance standards. Legal-service workers and legal-services offices are only required to pay very low annual examination fees and have no obligation to pay taxes, whereas lawyers and law firms must pay individual income taxes and management fees.

FACTUAL INVESTIGATIONS IN TWO PROVINCES

Grassroots Legal-Services Offices in Site A of Hubei Province

Site A is a declining county-level city located in central Hubei where economic development has been slow. The total population is about 730,000, with rural population accounting for 78.6 percent. One of its noteworthy characteristics is that many people work outside the city, accounting for more than 45 percent of the local population.[17]

According to Site A's judicial bureau, the site's legal-services system consists of lawyers, legal-service workers, notary offices, mediation commissions, and legal-assistance centers. The ratio of lawyers and legal-service workers to the local population is 1 to 7,684. However, there exist "unlicensed lawyers" and other folk legal-services who either have some working experience in government or judicial departments, know about or studied law in unofficial ways, or are simply persuasive and have a certain influence in the area. Their entry into the legal-services market is based on the provisions of "citizen representation" in China's procedural law, which allows citizens to entrust the "relative" of a concerned party to represent them in litigation or non-litigation matters, but such representatives shall receive no payment. In actual practice, whether the representative is actually a "relative" of the litigant normally is not strictly reviewed.

Ministry of Finance, September 1, 1990); *Guanyu guanche "Xiangzhen falü fuwusuo caiwu guanli banfa" youguan wenti de pifu* (Reply concerning Several Issues regarding Implementation of the Measures on the Financial Management of Township and Town Legal-services Offices), issued by the Ministry of Justice, February 11, 1991; and *Guojia jiwei sifabu 1997 nian 3 yue 3 ri banbu de "Xiangzhen falü fuwusuo shoufei guanli banfa"* (Administrative Measures on the Charges of Township and Town Legal-services Offices, promulgated by the State Planning Commission and the Ministry of Justice, March 3, 1997).

[17] It has been reported that most of the people remaining in Site A are elderly and children to the extent that when there is a death in a village, there are not enough people to lift the body.

Other government workers also share the legal market. Because local government workers are only paid "four parts" of a salary, or about 60 to 70 percent, the rest must come from fees charged for the provision of legal services. As a result, the legal-services market has become one of the more important resources shared by all official and unofficial legal sectors, including the courts, public security stations, law firms, legal-services offices, and legal-assistance centers. Hoping to get more fees, judges, lawyers, and legal-service workers commonly express concern that there are too few cases.

There is a total of twelve grassroots legal-services offices and eleven township and town legal-services offices in Site A, Eleven of these offices are so-called "one group of personnel with two names," that is, justice offices also serving as legal services offices. Moreover, because of the increase in grassroots social conflicts in recent years, the city has set up social conflict mediation centers at the township and town levels, such that the corresponding justice offices actually are "one group of personnel with three names" (mediation, justice bureau, and legal services). Indeed, among the forty-six grassroots legal-service workers in the city, fifteen people are under the government finance system, serving as judicial assistants who also work as directors of the justice offices, legal-services offices, and social conflict centers.

Several offices have one to two judicial assistants in addition to the director. Although legal assistants in some areas are local cadres, increasingly they are appointed by the municipal justice bureau. Their salaries are covered by the government budget, with the monthly salary of a director being 800 to 1,000 RMB. Other than this, the justice office does not receive any other administrative funds from the government.

Additional recruited legal-service workers are not covered by the government budget. They normally obtain the qualification certificates for legal-service workers by taking the legal-services qualification examination organized by the MoJ at the local level. The application requirements and the difficulty of the questions are much lower than the lawyers' qualification examination and the judicial examination. Many legal-service workers work on a part-time basis, supplementing their incomes from farm work and other temporary work. These legal-service workers establish their employment relationship with legal-services offices by signing a contract and implementing a case-handling and commission system. Legal-services offices and legal-service workers share the fees collected from their clients. If the legal-service workers are unable to complete their tasks, they will be suspended or terminated.

The relationship between the legal-services offices and the justice offices may be roughly summarized as mutually beneficial. Theoretically, government justice offices administer, supervise, and guide the non-governmental legal-services offices. However, the actual situation is far more complicated. Their relationship includes overlapping functions. The justice office normally includes only the director, with most of the administrative work undertaken by the legal-service workers at the legal-services offices (the justice office seldom assigns the work to other local public organizations). Such work includes the popularization of legal knowledge and legal education, comprehensive management of social security, and some temporary work, such as flood prevention work assigned by party committees of the township and town offices. Legal-services offices spend at least half of their time doing such work.

The two offices also share financial interests. The legal-services offices are responsible for their own profits or losses, but they report their expenditures to the finance division of the justice bureau. Moreover, in addition to the 150 RMB in administrative fees each person must pay to the justice bureau, their income must cover the daily expenses of the justice offices, such as the expenses incurred for popularization of legal knowledge, and make up the remaining one-quarter of the salary of the justice officers. Indeed, legal-service workers individually bear all the expenses incurred from the administrative and public welfare matters assigned to them by the justice offices.

Justice/legal-services offices appoint and organize the training of the mediators in the people's mediation commission. They guide the work of the mediation commission and send legal-service workers to participate in mediations when the people's mediation commission encounter any difficulties in resolving disputes. Although mediation commissions cannot charge for the mediation, legal-services offices may. Furthermore, the mediation commission proceedings have evidentiary effect, whereas the legal-service mediations do not.

The relationship between legal-services offices and other legal-assistance centers in Site A is relatively harmonious. The boundary between them is relatively clear in terms of their work scope and mode. The major responsibilities of the legal-assistance centers are to accept and review the materials of the legal-assistance cases and then to assign private lawyers in accordance with the situation. The legal-assistance centers also have their own lawyers, but they do not compete with the legal-service workers for business.

Although grassroots legal-services offices and private law firms in Site A in theory may be competitors in the legal-services market, our surveys indicated that the intensity of such competition is somewhat unreal or exaggerated. There are far fewer cases handled by law firms than there are by the legal-services offices, but the disputes handled by the law firms are several times larger than those handled by the legal-services offices. All law firms in the city are located within the urban area, with none situated in a township or town. The legal-services offices, by contrast, are basically affiliated with township and town justice offices and are generally located in the government buildings of the townships and towns. Only two legal-services offices are affiliated with the subdistrict offices and located in the urban area.

From the perspective of market division, law firms mainly serve clients in the urban areas whereas legal-services offices mainly serve clients in the vast rural areas – that is, rural residents – in cases involving slight injuries, field irrigation, neighborhood disputes, marriage and family disputes, homestead disputes, and contractual disputes. However, 40 to 50 percent of clients in the urban areas are also farmers seeking resolution of tort disputes, neighborhood disputes, and divorce cases, and 30 percent of the clients are organizations. According to one local high-income lawyer, lawyers and legal-service workers have their own respective territories. Most of the cases accepted by the legal-service workers are family affairs and petty property disputes that private lawyers are reluctant to accept. Sometimes lawyers refer these cases to legal-service workers when they are approached by clients. In China, most lawyers and legal-service workers rely on introductions and communications from acquaintances. Although we heard that legal-service workers sometimes take cases away from lawyers by offering lower fees, such cases are quite rare.

Social Assessment of Grassroots Legal-Services Offices and Legal-Service Workers

According to interviews with more than ten judges in a grassroots court, about 70 percent of the cases heard by the civil division of the court have some kind of representation, 10 percent of whom are relatives (citizen) representation and the remaining 60 percent lawyers or legal-service workers. These judges do not discriminate between these cases. When asked whether there is any difference between lawyers and legal-service workers, several judges responded that the lawyers are more qualified and easier to communicate with. Generally, the professional ability and ethics of legal-service workers are considered lower than lawyers because of their limited legal knowledge, but higher than that of the representatives who are relatives of the litigants.

After recent reforms requiring pretrial exchange of evidence, legal-service workers and lawyers now produce evidence at the scheduled time according to the notification of the court, but ordinary people generally say, "Can't I give it to you at trial?" The survey team tried to assess how the type of case affected the scope and quality of services provided by lawyers and legal-service workers. Surprisingly, we did not find any influence.

In contrast to judges, local residents see no difference between legal-service workers and lawyers. From their point of view, they both make a living by practicing law. Because there are few lawyers in the townships and towns, it is the grassroots legal-services office that has contacts with the people in the townships and towns. As a result, it normally has very good cases.[18]

We randomly selected two litigants in the court (it happened that their representatives were not present). Both of them had found legal-service workers through acquaintances (they called them "lawyers," even though they recognized that they were different from lawyers in the urban areas). When we asked one litigant why he had not looked for a lawyer and whether he was satisfied with the services provided by the legal-service workers, he seemed irritated and said, "Of course, I looked for him because I trust him!"

When asked about their cases, legal-service workers we interviewed said that although legal service workers are only allowed to represent parties in their locality, they actually often handle cases in other regions. Legal-service workers raised two concerns regarding the proposals for further regional restrictions. Because most of their clients are introduced by acquaintances or because of the legal worker's "reputation," mandatory geographic restrictions will result in clients losing opportunities to find representatives they trust. Furthermore, because Site A has many residents working outside the city (most of them as migrant workers), the role of the Site A legal-services office in providing legal services to migrant workers outside the city is irreplaceable.

[18] Discussion with judges at the People's Court of Site A, October 27, 2003.

Legal-service workers generally know their clients. They might be neighbors of their clients or, at the least, acquaintances, or they have been introduced by acquaintances. Their relationship is much closer than that between lawyers and their clients. This provides a sense of security to their clients, especially to rural villagers who may not be well educated and have little legal knowledge. Such a close relationship also places greater pressures on the legal-service workers. After all, legal-service workers live near their clients and have to see their clients even after a case is completed. An elderly legal-service worker mentioned that "each year we accept more than 100 cases of migrant workers' work-related injuries, with each of us having thirty to forty cases."

The Relationship between Grassroots Legal-Services Offices, Public Security, and the People's Courts

As noted above, only three-fifths of the statutory salaries for officials of "justice" organs are actually paid by the government. Obtaining cases is one main way for personnel in public security offices and the courts to make up the remainder of their statutory salaries. In fact, this has turned them into players in the legal-services market. Rural citizens are often unclear about the differences between public security, the courts, and legal-services offices. Thus, when they seek legal advice, they search mainly for the entity that has a "final say," one that charges less, or one with which they are more familiar.[19]

Surprisingly, the public security office has played an important role in the township and town legal-services system. The public security office is not simply responsible for preventing disputes; it also assumes the function of dispute resolution, and it charges for this service. According to legal-service workers we interviewed, many residents want to file lawsuits, but few actually do so; instead, they go to the public security offices. This

[19] In the minds of ordinary people, the "final say" is most important for obtaining cases. It has been reported that several leaders of local gangs are quite authoritative, and people like to go to them when they are involved in disputes. These leaders then find both parties, mediate the dispute, and propose a relatively fair and reasonable plan. If one party does not accept the plan or fails to carry out the plan after accepting it, the party is not respecting the mediator and may be punished. Therefore, these leaders are highly efficient in dispute resolution. Another element that affects cases is the price. Some poor people who want to divorce but cannot afford the litigation and representation fees may simply set up barriers in their homes to "separate" from one another and to form new families.

is because they question the objectivity of judges, the high filing fees in the courts, and the difficulties in enforcing judgments.

Rural citizens feel that going to the public security office may be more effective because the public security office has the "final say." Public security office treats every dispute like a crime, and so every issue can be resolved at the public security office. The public security office will collect several hundred RMB in mediation fees if the dispute caused bodily injury or property damage, and these fees will make up the remaining one-fourth of the public security officers' salaries. But when the public security office is unable to resolve a dispute, legal-service workers will be brought in to mediate. Legal-service workers are proud of their profession. As they noted, "The public security office has handcuffs, the court has summons, but we have our teeth [meaning they rely on their mouths]."[20] In sum, public security offices obtain cases by relying on the strength of their "law enforcement."

Furthermore, there is a mutual dependency between these two offices. Legal-service workers obtain a portion of their cases from the public security office (which does not share with lawyers located in the urban areas). Whereas these two offices maintain a good cooperative relationship, the people's courts have a more controversial role in the legal-services market. We frequently read reports criticizing courts for voluntarily providing legal services. In our research, we found two striking phenomena.

First, like the public security offices, these courts provide legal services to supplement their salaries. The judges' salaries consist of six parts, with four parts covered by the government budget and the remaining two parts to be earned on their own. Previously, the government even required that the courts contribute a certain amount of the litigation fees to the local finance authority annually. As a result, judges are motivated to cultivate good personal relationships with the litigants' lawyers and legal-service workers, relying on them to bring more cases to the court.

Some judges hear cases after they have been put on the docket by the court. The criterion for review and accepting cases is sometimes driven by economic interests.[21] When judges go outside to obtain cases, they are not very different from ordinary legal-service workers and have to consider their relationships with the parties, much like their competitors

[20] The recording is taken from a symposium held in the judicial bureau of Site A, October 25, 2003.

[21] One driver caused an accident, injuring another person. The traffic public security fined the driver 2,000 RMB. The driver unexpectedly filed a lawsuit against the victim and asked him to pay him the 2,000 RMB. The case was accepted by the court.

in the legal-services market. The distinction, however, is that judges are backed by the government's coercive force and rely on their special status to participate in the competition for the legal-services market. Although courts are bound by rules and procedures to hear cases, inevitably judges may favor the party who brought in the case, at least to the extent allowed by the law.

The parties, grassroots courts, and legal-service workers are also influenced by the most recent civil judicial reform. Recent trial reforms have placed ever-greater burdens of proof and the implementation of pretrial evidence exchange on litigants. This change, in turn, has increased the need for assistance from lawyers and legal-service workers. Although judges no longer have to conduct out of court investigation to obtain information about the cases, they still summon parties and lawyers to the court and meet them individually. This means that litigants now have to pay twice the cost in litigation than previously (to the court and now to the legal-service workers), but this does not mean that the judges are more neutral, nor does it ensure a better outcome.[22]

In Site A, lawyers who nominally represent clients and judges who should be neutral to the concerned parties may even reach secret agreements to share business. At a minimum, they have to balance their long-term interests in maintaining their personal reputations and overall justice. Parties and their lawyers who can continue to provide cases may obtain more favors from the judges and, consequently, have a better reputation and may provide even more cases. Therefore, the most powerful group in the grassroots society normally has advantages in the legal-services market.

Grassroots Legal Services in County C in Shanxi Province

County C is located in the northwest part of central China. Its total area is 437.9 square kilometers. It consists of seven townships and towns and fifteen administrative villages, with a rural population of 171,000 accounting for 75 percent of the total population.[23] According to government work reports, County C has "extraordinary vitality." However, the survey team found County C to be a "sleepy village," that is, poor,

[22] See Fu Yulin, "Susong feiyong de xingzhi yu susong chengben de chengdan" (The Nature of Litigation Fees and the Burden of Litigation Costs), *Beida falü pinglun* (Peking University Law Review) 4, no. 1 (2001).

[23] From the annals of County C.

unsophisticated, and dispirited.[24] The more frequent disputes are traditional marriage and family disputes, such as alimony disputes. There are few economic disputes.

The four legal-services offices in County C, called "legal services centers," all are located in townships and towns justice office as before, but the office now bears two separate names. There are no legal-services offices located at the county level. In the government report, the legal-services system of County C is in strict accordance with the policies of the central government. Since 2001, grassroots legal services offices have been completely separated from the justice offices and marketized in accordance with central government dictates. The 2001 reform had an obvious impact on the scale of the legal-services offices and their market share in the legal-services market. The number of legal-service workers has decreased dramatically from thirty to twelve, and local legal services are now provided by private lawyers in the neighboring counties.

The relationship between legal-services offices and other legal actors in this county is distinctly different from that in Site A. First, legal-services offices in County C occupy a less important position. County statistical work reports focus not on legal-services offices but on the building of legal assistance centers, notary offices, and law firms. When asked about the role and influence of public security offices and the courts in the local legal services market, the interviewed lawyers, judges, and legal-service workers all said that the division of the functions of the various departments in County C is very clear. Courts in County C basically maintain a passive and neutral position; local public security stations do not receive payment for handling or mediating civil disputes. With the introduction of the party responsibility system (parties bearing the burden of proof) in litigation, it is very difficult to initiate judicial proceedings for disputes without legal assistance. Between 70 and 80 percent of the civil cases in the local grassroots courts involve lawyers.

The influence of the County C legal-services offices in the local justice departments is far less than that in Site A. Interviewed judges and procurators in County C (even the leaders of the justice bureau) could

[24] We do not intend to question the authenticity of the data in the report because we have neither the ability nor the basis to do so. We only want to show that there are often great differences between abstract data and specific facts; therefore, on-the-spot investigations are even more necessary.

not understand why we would even want to study the legal-service workers, as they could barely acknowledge the existence of this group. They said the professional ability of legal-service workers is weak and cannot compete with that of lawyers. When commenting on market competitiveness, an elderly legal-service worker noted, "Nowadays people need to consider five factors before filing a lawsuit: laws, reasons, money, interpersonal relationships, and power. All five are deeply involved in the entire proceedings."

Because demand is limited, only the strongest competitors in the market can survive. Business for the sole local law firm is not good and faces competition not only from legal-services offices in County C, but also from lawyers in neighboring areas where the economy is stronger. The law firm in County C is a state-owned firm on a lane not far from the county court and procuratorate office. The average annual income of the eight professional lawyers in the firm is several thousand RMB. Only one lawyer in the law firm has passed the judicial examination. This female lawyer is also famous for being the only person in the legal system, including the court and procuracy, of the entire county who passed the judicial examination.

These lawyers also try to expand their sources of cases indirectly by providing free legal services. When we asked whether there is any hostility between legal-service workers and lawyers because of competition, these lawyers expressed doubts. They said that they all face an imperfect judicial environment. One of the reasons for the scarcity of cases is that people in the rural areas are too poor to file lawsuits and are reconciled with the situation. Another stated reason is mistrust of the courts and judges. Because courts are unable to resolve many issues, people do not file lawsuits or seek out lawyers. Some cases are settled by the people's mediation commissions. There are also very few migrant workers or people working outside the area. Disputes are rare, and the local public security stations and courts do not have much to do. Consequently, there is no market for lawyers or legal-service workers.

The most popular means of dispute resolution in County C is people's mediation. There are 155 mediation commissions throughout the county, among which 38 are similar to those in Xinanjie Village. For thirteen consecutive years, the people's mediation commission in Xinanjie Village of County C has been awarded the title of an advanced unit at the provincial, district, and county levels, and since 1993, named a "Model

People's Mediation Commission" by the MoJ, The mediation commission of Xinanjie Village has been promoted throughout the county.[25]

Under arrangements by the justice bureau, we visited the model mediation commission. Xinanjie village is a large village with a relatively high population density located in southwest County C. Twenty villagers' groups are in charge of 1,650 households and more than 6,000 residents. The village committee has one vice secretary of the general party branch responsible for people's mediation work, and the director of the mediation commission is a retired soldier who also works as the public security director. This administrative area is divided into three parts, based on the current situation of the residents. Each part has a director and a deputy director.

Regular meetings of the people's mediation commission convenes on a monthly basis to study, analyze, and forecast trends in disputes. There are 33 mediation teams under the commission and a team of 218 dispute information collectors scattered among rural families, enterprises, and markets. The principal mass organizations, including the militia, the Communist Youth League, the women's organizations, and the public security organizations, are included on the mediation commission. The responsibility structure provides that the commission is responsible for all the parts, the directors and deputy directors are responsible for the teams, and the teams are responsible for the households. There are also unofficial members on the mediation commission – that is, individuals on various production teams who have good reputations and are articulate in mediations.

This mediation commission has two offices equipped with all kinds of office equipment, five motorcycles, three telephones, and five newspaper and periodical subscriptions, such as *Legal Daily* and *Democracy and the Legal System*. The monthly salary of a mediator is 180 RMB, with a job allowance and bonus of between 10 and 80 RMB. Members of the mediation teams are paid a minor monthly allowance of 10 to 30 RMB. Most surprising, the mediation commission holds complete files. Since 1976, all settled cases have been closed and filed, and all unsettled cases have been recorded. Every year, 90 percent of the accepted cases here are resolved.

[25] "Tuidong quanxian sifa xingzheng gongzuo kuaru xinshiji: Zai quanxian sifa xingzheng gongzuo huiyishang de jianghua" (Promote Judicial and Administrative Work of the Entire County in the New Century: Speech at the County Judicial and Administrative Work Conference), County C, Shanxi, 1999.

If more than five cases handled by the mediation commission are submitted to the court, the directors do not receive a bonus. Because disputes over alimony are frequent, the mediation commission has a written handbook and requires individuals with alimony and child support obligations to write their names in the handbook every month so as to oversee their payments and to prevent future disputes.

The director of the mediation commission has been a mediator for nearly twenty years, and all of the files were established gradually after he took office. Ordinary citizens trust him and are willing to turn their cases over to him. Exactly as predicted, the results of the mediation commission's work in County C are attributable to a large extent by the work of the individual mediator. Mediators in other villages are less adept than this old director who spoke like a local clan leader. Although this old director does not oppose people filing lawsuits in the court if they do not accept his mediation, we still have concerns about the systemic arrangement of a public security director who also directs the mediation committee. The risks of such an arrangement can be avoided only by the character and reputation of the person holding the directorship.

We interviewed parties from two cases in which legal-service workers served as litigation representatives. They were very grateful to these legal-service workers, whom they called "lawyers." One of the two cases was a dispute over alimony and the other was a neighborhood dispute. The difficulties in communication when we talked with these litigants made us realize that a modern justice system might not be the best option in such an area for such disputes. This also strengthened our belief that small claims lawsuits should be self-participatory and increased our expectations regarding the dispute resolution function of the mediation commission. We further pondered whether the decrease in the number of cases in the courts is the result of the success of the people's mediation or whether these two phenomena are the result of a single common reason, such as the slow economic development. If so, we wondered what kind of legal-services system will be appropriate for County C when its economy catches up with those of other areas.

SOME PRELIMINARY CONCLUSIONS

For the past thirty years, China has moved from a highly centralized planned economy to a decentralized market economy. This process is reflected in the relationship between the central government and the society, with governmental powers quietly withdrawing from grassroots society and gradually losing control over local regimes. When state power withdraws from the social control system, social conflicts lose their self-healing ability, and disputing parties must search for new ways to vent their anger when their rights are infringed upon. Multiple institutions have stepped in to serve as civil dispute resolution mechanisms, but the differentiation in the roles of these institutions is murky, often to the detriment of grass-roots citizens.

At present, legal-services offices in grassroots rural areas, especially poor areas, have maintained both an official and a social role. Although legal-services offices, as administrative institutions under the justice offices of the MoJ, theoretically are not responsible for resolving disputes (because the courts are the state institutions for dispute resolution), the reality is that ordinary Chinese citizens still regard the role of these grassroots justice offices similar to those of the courts, and cannot see the difference between legal-service workers and lawyers. Anyone who can provide them with legal services and can represent them is considered a lawyer. This is largely due to the overlapping functions and mutual dependencies of these various offices.

In fact, the future survival of grassroots justice offices will depend on the existence of legal-services offices. The return of administrative power from the central government to local governments has meant that the formerly central command governance model has been replaced by a "mutual-friction or cooperative" model with divisions along lines and segments. The central government controls through line administration by distributing documents and formulating policies; local governments control through segmented administration by distributing funds or by budget financing.

In legal affairs, the MoJ promulgates policies and assigns tasks but it does not allocate financial support. Whether justice offices, as local branches of the central judicial bureaus, will be supported by local regimes (township and county governments) will depend on the personal negotiation ability of the judicial officer and the openness of the local leadership. In developed areas like Shanghai, central government policies can be carried out quickly, albeit with frequent changes, primarily because of the financial support from the local governments. However, in areas where central policies are rarely supported by local budgets, there are far too many difficulties to implement central policies and make ends meet.

As a result, grassroots government and society have reached a tacit unconscious agreement whereby civil servants (one assistant with only "four parts of a salary") withhold a portion of the taxes contributed by taxpayers to maintain daily administrative affairs at a low cost, and must rely on fees from clients for certain services to survive. Such transactions between the justice offices and the local society can only be realized by the existence of the subdistrict legal-services offices that can charge for their services. Therefore, when compared with government lawyers, legal-services offices provide profit-making services, but when compared with private lawyers, they provide welfare services.

Since the reform of grassroots legal-services offices, some substitute legal-services institutions have emerged such as legal assistance offices and pro bono lawyers. But the legal assistance system cannot replace the grassroots legal-services system. As a judicial remedy system for special social groups, the beneficiaries of legal assistance are few, and the range of issues it addresses is limited. This is also true for pro bono lawyers, whose limited scope of their services falls primarily in the area of criminal law. In addition, although the voluntary legal-service workers may have identical or similar functions to those of legal workers, the newly recruited volunteer legal workers are generally young and inexperienced. There are also cases that could benefit from legal assistance that may not fall under the legal-assistance umbrella because of the nature of the dispute. While some of the need might be mitigated with the establishment of simpler, small-claims procedures, there will still be cases involving illiterate clients who will require some, although not necessarily full, legal assistance.

Furthermore, legal assistance offices as "free" services offered by the government will face market pressures similar to those of the legal-services offices. In the rural areas where public servants and judges are paid only three-fifths of their salaries, such free services are illusory. As we observed during our surveys, because of the pressures of central government policies and the lack of financial support by local governments, legal assistance lawyers will also compete in the market with law firms and legal-service workers for business, and they must charge fees to make up the difference in their salaries.[26]

[26] For example, the association for the handicapped appropriates tens of thousands of RMB from the funds allocated by the state to retain a law firm or a legal-services office as its legal consultant. In a dispute involving the handicapped, the legal consultant will represent the handicapped for free at the request of the association. After the establishment of the legal-assistance center, the association for the handicapped was required to allocate these funds to the legal-assistance center. In litigation involving the handicapped, the legal-assistance center will assign cases to lawyers or legal-service workers in various law firms or legal-services offices. However, because the local government is unable to afford full-time assistance lawyers in accordance with the quota required by the central government, the legal-assistance center under the judicial bureau must

Similarly, the role of the people's mediation commissions and the public security offices has grown as an autonomous social dispute resolution mechanism. Yet, as a theoretically neutral institution, the functions of the mediation commission cannot replace those of the legal-services office. When legal-service workers represent their own clients (ordinary people in the grassroots society), they always argue on behalf of their clients. This is not the case for the people's mediation commission, however. Furthermore, according to the current system, the director of the mediation commission is usually also the director of the village committee or the public security director. Because most of the current social conflicts and complaints arise from dissatisfactions about grassroots policies or grassroots government officials, the neutrality, legitimacy, and justice of the mediation commission will be compromised. In such an event, it is not difficult to imagine that the social stability gained from application of "small issues will be dealt with in the village and big issues will be dealt with in the town" is at the cost of the ordinary people at the grassroots level.[27]

We have seen that the people's mediation commissions and legal-services offices prospered because of one document and declined because of another. Considering the particular political purpose behind the policy that strengthens people's mediation (as well as court mediation), we have concerns about the regression in the protection of the parties' rights and the restoration of the traditional mediation mechanism.

Similarly, the authority of the public security offices, as governmental organs with state power, continues to be stronger than that of the courts in traditional rural society. Public security offices, as organs safeguarding public security, unavoidably become involved in some civil disputes. Although their institutional design is said to prevent the escalation of civil disputes, the "lease of power" by the public security offices only becomes possible because of gaps in the design of the grassroots legal-services system. As the boundaries among the functions of the various legal institutions become clearer, public security offices may become less involved in the resolution of civil disputes.

In sum, the size and number of the legal-services offices under government promotion and policy restrictions has declined. This is more a result of governmental policies than a market response to actual demand. The

take the lawyers of those state-owned law firms under its jurisdiction as part-time lawyers in the legal-assistance center. The pressures for survival of the part-time lawyers result in competition in the legal-services market.

[27] For relevant discussions, see Chen Xianglin's comments about the survey on County C.

grassroots legal-services offices were established and promoted during the preliminary stage of China's legal system, when there were few lawyers. Today, although lawyers are no longer scarce in large- and medium-sized cities, there is still a serious shortage of lawyers and huge demand for legal services in the vast rural areas and the regions between the countryside and the cities.

Grassroots citizens generally embrace these albeit limited number of legal-services offices. In a dense rural society of acquaintances, the advantage of grassroots legal-services offices is that they are close to those who need them. Not only are the offices convenient, but their workers are familiar, amiable, and trusted. Legal-service workers are often from the ranks of the grassroots population and are less bound by professional standards and expertise than by folk customs, market competition, and their reputation among acquaintances in the society. Compared with the one-shot transactions with strangers, the grassroots residents' desire for and the possibility of multiple transactions have strengthened the basis and credibility of the legal-service workers.

Yet, because of compulsory government policy restrictions, the number of legal-services offices has declined despite the demand. This shows that direct interference in the social life by the government through administrative actions is likely to result in unstable policies and indefinite regulations. When official support is lacking (e.g., in reality, the legal-services offices unavoidably conflict with the relevant institutional, personnel, fee, tax, and rectification reform measures), legal-services offices constantly have to adjust their means of survival.

Because lawyers are reluctant to go to rural areas, coupled with their high fees, those in the townships and towns, especially the farmers, cannot afford lawyer services. Therefore, legal-service workers can supplement the legal services provided by lawyers. From the perspective of grassroots disputants, there is almost no difference between lawyers and legal-service workers. Even some judges do not detect any obvious difference between the two. This shows that using low-cost legal-service workers to meet the demand for legal services from low-income groups and using quasi-legal professionals to handle cases that do not require high expertise may be a systemic cost-free arrangement to meet market demand. These workers could focus primarily on nonlitigation and noncriminal matters, and limit the scope of their practice to parties in local grassroots courts or represent local parties in cases filed in grassroots courts outside the region.

Ultimately, in considering what kinds of legal assistance and means of dispute resolution is appropriate for grassroots China, we should bear in mind the diversity of China's regions and the limitations of a singular model. With its huge population and many nationalities, growing gaps between the eastern and western regions, and the urban-rural divide, a diversified dispute resolution model may be necessary. The development and evolution of legal-services offices must follow an in-depth understanding of the diverse needs and demands of the various regions rather than the singular supply model of prior government policies.

11

The Constitution in the Courtroom: Constitutional Development and Civil Litigation in China

Thomas E. Kellogg

In 2004, the ethnic-minority musician and prominent local artist Xuan Ke brought suit in Lijiang City Intermediate Court in southwestern Yunnan Province, claiming that his right of reputation had been infringed by an article in the Beijing-based *Arts Criticism* magazine. The author of the article, the scholar Wu Xueyuan, argued that Xuan's music was, in fact, not a product of the local ethnic minority culture and that Xuan's misrepresentation of his music amounted to fraud.

Arts Criticism is a scholarly journal, and Wu's critique was based on academic research. Nonetheless, his language was sharp. Wu claimed that selling Naxi music was the equivalent of "selling dog meat as steak." He referred to Naxi music as "fake culture" and declared that "these falsehoods are patently absurd, and a fraud on the public." All of these phrases would later be cited by Xuan Ke as specific examples of personal attack. Wu and the magazine's editors defended against Xuan's charges by both pointing to their constitutional rights to scholarly enquiry and by attempting to demonstrate the factual veracity of the article's assertions, specifically that Naxi music was, indeed, a commercial creation of Xuan Ke.

In a verdict delivered in December 2004, the intermediate court included a reference to Chinese constitutional rights protections; it also concluded that

> (t)he criticism of Naxi classical music in this document is a scholarly question in the category of "letting one hundred schools of thought contend," and scholarly research on these questions, and publishing commentaries on

A prior version of this essay was published as *Constitutionalism with Chinese Characteristics? Constitutional development and civil litigation in China*, *International Journal of Constitutional Law*, 7 no. 2 (2009): 215–244.

> that research is a right of scholars, and should be considered appropriate behavior. This court does not pass legal judgment on scholarly questions.

Nothwithstanding this pronouncement in support of scholarly debate, the court ruled in favor of Xuan Ke, holding that the article had gone beyond the bounds of scholarly criticism and therefore was defamatory.

In essence, with the statement that courts generally should not intervene in scholarly debates, the court seemed to engage in judicial rule making. There is no requirement in Chinese statutory law that courts should refrain from judging the truthfulness of allegedly defamatory statements merely because they occur in an academic context. In fact, under Chinese law, truthfulness, or lack thereof, is usually considered a key part of a defamation case.

In creating such a rule, applicable at least to the case at hand, was the court giving concrete substance to Article 47 of the Chinese Constitution, which protects the individual right to engage in scholarly enquiry? If so, what does this decision – and dozens of others like it, in which Chinese courts seem to base their decisions, at least in part, on constitutional norms – say about the current state of legal and constitutional development in China? What does it say about the role and function of the constitutional text itself in relation to the body of Chinese law? Does the fact that Wu Xueyuan lost, and that he and his magazine were forced to pay significant damages, have any impact on our view of whether or not the court did, in fact, "interpret" or otherwise apply the constitution?

In China, the constitutional governance framework is modeled on the Soviet system. The National People's Congress (NPC), China's legislature, is the supreme organ of state power, unchecked, in theory at least, by the other branches of government. Because it operates at the apex of the state pyramid, the NPC both creates and interprets law and has – on paper – significant formal authority over the executive and judicial branches of government. For its part, the Standing Committee (SC) of the NPC is empowered to interpret and supervise the implementation of the Constitution, and it exercises much of the NPC's authority when it is not in session.

As a legal document, the Chinese Constitution generally has been viewed in the West as static, primarily hortatory, and largely irrelevant. The individual rights provisions of the Chinese Constitution are implemented, purportedly, through NPC legislation; in practice, these rights provisions – especially those that can be viewed as protecting "negative rights," including the basic rights to speech, association, and assembly –

are viewed by many as little more than empty promises, with virtually no legal effect. No independent mechanism for the redress of violations of these rights or for the review of lower-level legal documents that may violate the Constitution is contemplated by the text itself.

Thus, the Chinese Constitution has been viewed by many as essentially a political document, one that, rather than stating legally binding norms, serves as a vehicle for the enunciation of the government's current political philosophy. According to one scholar, "[S]ocialist constitutions like China's serve as barometers of the state's policies and values and reflect the current social condition."[1]

In general, scholars, both Chinese and Western, have linked the rhetorical nature of the Chinese Constitution to a lack of a meaningful – in most other countries, judicial – mechanism for the enforcement of key constitutional norms.[2] As is discussed in more detail in Section 1, the Chinese Constitution is not regarded, generally, as having direct legal application and is dependent on implementing legislation to give meaning to, and provide for the judicial application of, its provisions.

By general consensus and longtime practice, then, the courts have not counted with regard to constitutional interpretation and constitutional rights protection.[3] Most government officials have viewed China's

[1] Ann Kent, *Waiting for Rights: China's Human Rights and China's Constitutions, 1949–1989, Human Rights Quarterly* 13, no. 182 (1991): 170. In this way, as will be discussed in more detail (infra, at text accompanying note 5), the Chinese Constitution is typical of the classic Soviet-style constitutional model on which it was based. One scholar of Soviet law noted that socialist constitutions "seem to be... 'basically action programs to be translated into political practice.'" John N. Hazard, *A Soviet Model for Marxian Socialist Constitutions, Cornell Law Review* 660 (1974–1975): 985, 986.

[2] See, for example, Albert Chen, "An Introduction to the Legal System of the People's Republic of China." In Yash Ghai, *Hong Kong's New Constitutional Order: The Resumption of Chinese Sovereignty and the Basic Law* (2d ed., 1999, Hong Kong: Hong Kong University Press), p. 89. Chen notes that:

> The theoretical supremacy of the constitution may not however mean much in practice. Constitutions in communist states have traditionally been regarded as directives or guidelines for the legislature, so that the constitutional provisions are not directly enforceable in the absence of implementing legislation. This seems to be the case in China.... *Apparently courts are not allowed to rely on constitutional provisions directly in deciding a case and can only apply the ordinary legislation (if any) through which the constitution is implemented. Chinese courts do not of course enjoy the power of review of legislation with regard to its conformity to the Constitution.* (emphasis added)

[3] See Yash Ghai, supra note 2, at p. 127. "There is little point in examining in detail either the rights [protections found in the Constitution] or limitations on them, since the rights are not enforceable as such, nor is the legislation giving (or not giving) them judicially reviewable."

constitutional structure as granting the National People's Congress Standing Committee (NPCSC) exclusive authority over constitutional rights norms, which it protects through the enactment of legislation. For almost sixty years, the protection of constitutional rights, and especially any sort of judicial review of the constitutionality of national law, has been considered by many observers to be beyond the authority of the courts.

Yet this understanding of the role of the courts, and of their constitutional authority, may be undergoing a fundamental, if excruciatingly slow, shift. During the past two decades, a small but growing group of scholars, activists, lawyers, and judges have begun to challenge the NPC's putative monopoly over the Constitution, asserting that the courts both should and do have a role to play in protecting constitutional rights. For the first time in Chinese history, Chinese scholars, lawyers, and activists are attempting, through litigation, not only to assert their constitutional rights but also to change the very understanding of the structure of their government.

This chapter analyzes attempts by judges, activist lawyers, and Chinese citizens to use the courts as a mechanism for constitutional litigation, and by scholars to push for what is usually referred to as "judicialization of the constitution" (*xianfa sifahua*). It describes the small but growing body of constitutional case law, stretching back for more than two decades, that scholars have used as a key basis for their arguments in favor of a more prominent judicial role in rights enforcement. It challenges the conventional view of the Chinese Constitution as static and unchanging, arguing, instead, that attempts by actors outside, and to a lesser extent inside, the government to make the Constitution a legally operative document have changed the views of many as to the Constitution's fundamental nature. It is possible that this new understanding – which, among constitutional law scholars, at least, is extremely widespread – may lead, over time, to an evolution of the system itself.

I. THE CURRENT FRAMEWORK: KEEPING THE COURTS OUT?

Both the Chinese Constitution, and the system created by it, are products of Marxist legal theory. According to this theory, law exists not to order relationships between private individuals or between private individuals and the state but rather to maintain the dictatorship of the proletariat. After a communist government has been installed, assuming the state has successfully compelled the transition from a private economy to one that is state run, the entire distinction between public and private law begins to drop away.

Just as Soviet legal theory rejects the distinction between public and private in Western law, it emphatically rejects the notion, generally associated with Montesquieu, of the separation of powers.[4] Instead, the legislature is the highest organ of state power, and its use of its authority is not checked in any significant way by the executive or the judiciary. Because the state is the primary protector of individual rights and sees to their effectuation, and because the possibility of a dichotomy of interests between the state and the individual is denied, communist legal systems generally have not viewed constitutional rights provisions as limiting state power and therefore have not sought to set up mechanisms to guarantee individual rights against encroachment by the government.

The power of constitutional interpretation resides with the working body of the legislature, which, in the Chinese case, is the NPCSC. But, given that the two main issues that generate constitutional conflict in Western systems – the application and extent of constitutional rights protections and the separation of powers among the branches of government – are, in theory, not present in the socialist context, it is unclear how and when the constitutional interpretive authority should be used.

Since the founding of the People's Republic in 1949, China has had four separate constitutions, promulgated in 1954, 1975, 1978, and 1982. In many ways, the current 1982 Constitution is modeled on the 1954 version, which itself owes a significant intellectual debt to the 1936 Soviet Constitution.[5]

Although some recent amendments have reflected a nascent trend away from the Soviet model, virtually all the key elements of the 1982 Constitution reflect the influence of the Soviet approach to constitutionalism and the division – or, more accurately, the unification – of state power. Article 2 of the Constitution states that "all power in the

[4] *The Law of the Soviet State*, ed. Andrei Y. Vyshinsky and trans. Hugh W. Babb (New York: Macmillan, 1948), p. 312.

[5] As with all legal systems, there are significant differences between the formal system as delineated in the constitution and the system in practice. Although the NPC is the highest organ of state power, it meets too infrequently and is too large and unwieldy to exercise all of the powers granted to it under the Constitution. In practice, the NPCSC and the State Council exercise a much higher degree of authority than does the NPC itself. Although the NPC is no longer quite the docile rubber stamp it once was, it does not serve as a fully functioning legislature. The Communist Party also exercises significant influence and oversight over all major government decisions, despite the fact that it is granted no formal powers under the Constitution. For a more detailed account of China's governmental structure as it operates in practice, see Anthony Saich, *Governance and Politics of China*, 2d ed. (New York: Palgrave McMillan, 2004).

People's Republic... belongs to the people" and that "(t)he organs through which the people exercise state power are the National People's Congress and the local people's congresses."[6] Article 3 establishes that all state organs operate under the principle of democratic centralism and that "all administrative, judicial, and prosecutorial organs of the state are created by the people's congresses to which they are responsible and under whose supervision they operate."[7] Article 67 is central to the debate about constitutional rights protection; under Article 67(1), the NPCSC is empowered to "interpret the Constitution and supervise its enforcement." As of this writing, there are no known instances of the NPCSC using its constitutional authority to interpret the Constitution.[8]

One of the few concrete steps the government has taken regarding constitutional development in recent years is the passage of the Legislation Law in 2000. The Legislation Law is notable for three reasons: First, the law repeatedly references the need for laws to conform to the Constitution; second, it explicitly entertains the notion that subnational laws and regulations could, in fact, be unconstitutional and have to be either "revised" or even "nullified";[9] and third, it attempts to set up a reporting mechanism for identifying and resolving legal conflicts.[10] Finally, language in the law suggests that it could also be used to resolve constitutional conflicts;[11] however, as of this writing, that language has not yet led to a single public declaration of unconstitutionality.

[6] Constitution, Art. 2, §§ 1, 2 (P.R.C.).

[7] Id. Art. 3, §§ 1, 3 (P.R.C.). The authority of local people's congresses over local courts is reiterated in Article 128 of the Constitution; this dynamic arguably does more than any other single provision structurally to limit judicial independence in China.

[8] Some scholars have suggested that a 1957 opinion issued by the NPCSC is a nascent example of constitutional interpretation by the Standing Committee. In response to a query by a court in Tianjin, the SC declared that issuing a summons to a People's Congress delegate did not, in fact, infringe on the individual's constitutionally protected freedom of person. See *Xianfa Xue* (Constitutional Law), ed. Zhang Qianfan et al (2004, Beijing: China Law Press), pp. 118–119.

[9] *Li fa fa* (Law on Legislation), Art. 2 (adopted at the Third Session of the Ninth National People's Congress, Mar. 15, 2000) 2000 Standing Committee of the National People's Congress. The full text of the Law is available online at: http://www.china.org.cn/english/government/207419.htm.

[10] Id., Arts. 87, § 2.

[11] Id., Arts. 88, 90, 91. For more on constitutional petitioning, including a detailed account of the most famous constitutional petition, that of the *Sun Zhigang* case, see Keith J. Hand, "Using the Law for a Righteous Purpose: The Sun Zhigang Incident and Evolving Forms of Citizen Action in the People's Republic of China," *Columbia Journal of Transnational Law* 45 (2006–2007): 114. In May 2004, with much fanfare, the NPCSC established the Regulation Filing and Review Office (*fagui shencha bei'an shi;* hereinafter "Filing Office"). The office serves as the receiving agent for all legal documents that, under the Legislation Law, must be filed with the NPC, and also as the presumed

1.1. *Judicial Authority Over the Constitution*

Given the lack of action by the legislature in making use of its constitutional oversight authority, it would seem that there could be an opening for the courts to play a more active role in ensuring full adherence to constitutional norms. Yet the courts face several hurdles in their path to assume a more positive role in constitutional enforcement. In addition to the ideological and structural barriers to judicial review by the courts, the courts also must overcome settled practice, the NPC's desire to protect its own constitutional prerogatives, the courts' own lack of independence, and even formal statements by the Supreme People's Court (SPC) renouncing constitutional interpretive authority.

The best-known document released by the courts themselves disclaiming any power to apply the Constitution, directly, as a legal document pertaining to actual litigation is a 1955 SPC response[12] to a query from a lower court:

To the Xinjiang Higher People's Court:

> We have received... your Court report no. 336.... The Constitution of the People's Republic of China is the fundamental law of our nation, and it is the mother of all other laws. While delivering his report on the draft Constitution of the PRC, Chairman Liu Shaoqi noted that: "it is the most important question in the life of our nation, regulating what types of behavior are legal, or what statues must effectuate and what they must prohibit." Regarding penal matters, [the Constitution] does not regulate any issues relating to determination of guilt or punishment, and so therefore we agree with the opinion of your court, that the constitution cannot be cited in criminal decisions.[13]

In 1986, the SPC again seemed to reaffirm that the courts should not directly cite the Constitution as a source of law in judicial decisions. The 1986 Response to Query Regarding the Use of Legal Normative

recipient of any petitions filed under the Article 90 review mechanism. Though some government officials indicate that the Filing Office does engage in active review of the legality and consistency of legal documents and has even, in some cases, reached out to administrative bureaus to seek legal change, there is no indication that the Filing Office, as yet, has engaged in any constitutional review; the prospects for the Filing Office to grow into such a role seem unlikely.

[12] The Chinese term for such responses is *pifu*.

[13] The full text of the 1955 response can be found in Wang Lei, *Judicialization of the Constitution in China: Selected Cases* (2005, Beijing: Peking University Press), p. 1.

Documents by People's Courts in Judicial Decisions[14] was different from the 1955 response in that, unlike that response, it did not explicitly forbid citation to the Constitution. Instead, the document merely listed the relevant sources of law that courts should invoke in different situations. The absence of any affirmative reference to the Constitution as a source of law bolstered the established view that courts should not cite the Constitution in judicial opinions.

2. JUDICIALIZATION: BRINGING THE CONSTITUTION INTO COURT

2.1. *What Is "Judicialization of the Constitution?"*

Despite the fact that the formal system would seem to prohibit the courts from using the Constitution as a source of law in adjudicating disputes, a small but growing body of case law, much of it relating to civil litigation between two private parties, nonetheless either has cited the Constitution directly or has made apparent indirect reference to constitutional norms in deciding a case. Scholarly calls for greater use of the Constitution by the courts have both preceded and followed judicial action, such that scholars and some judges seem to be engaged in a mutually reinforcing dialogue with each other on the reinterpretation of the role of the courts in constitutional enforcement. The most commonly used term to describe the use of the Constitution by Chinese courts is "judicialization of the Constitution" (*xianfa sifahua*).

In a sense, scholars and others pushing for a greater judicial role in constitutional enforcement have benefited from the slow and steady decline of Marxist ideology as the governing value system of the People's Republic. As the rhetorical value of Marxism in Chinese society has

[14] The full text of the 1986 response can be found in id., at pp. 1–2. A partial translation reads as follows:

> To the Jiangsu Province Higher People's Court:
>
> We have received your query *(qingshi)*. Regarding the question of how People's Courts should cite legally normative documents in official court legal documents. After researching the question, we offer the following response: under the Constitution and the relevant provisions of the People's Congress and the People's Government Organization Law, state legislative power is exercised by the NPC and the Standing Committee.

The response goes on to list the various normative documents that can be cited in different adjudicative situations; the fact that the Constitution is not mentioned affirmatively as a source that may be cited is taken by many scholars to mean that it cannot be.

declined, the willingness of the government to articulate its actions, goals, and even fundamental choices in classical Marxist terms has also declined. This is true across many sectors of society. Whereas the government may make a spirited attempt to justify its market-oriented policies as part of the transition to socialism, in general it embraces pragmatic and technocratic rationales for its policy choices. The same holds true for the legal system; the government is no longer as comfortable as it once was with articulating legal and institutional choices in Marxist terms.

Given the government's unwillingness to contemplate the creation of a full-dress judicial review mechanism, scholars generally have advocated an extremely limited view of judicial authority to enforce the Constitution. In part because of deference to the NPC's own authority, scholars generally have not argued that Chinese courts possess the power to strike down either legislation or administrative regulations. Indeed, in many cases, scholars have explicitly denied that judicial enforcement of the Constitution necessitates the formal power of judicial review.[15]

Although the shifts contemplated by those pushing for judicialization are fundamental – explicitly acknowledging the ability of the courts to draw on constitutional rights provisions – they are sufficiently narrow so as to be at the very edge of political feasibility. In other words, those advocating in favor of judicialization do not question party authority or the overall structure of the one-party state. Instead, they are suggesting merely that the judiciary, still controlled by the party, should adjudicate rights-related disputes in certain contexts. In this sense, judicialization advocates are traveling well-trod ground; rather than agitating for far-reaching political reforms, an approach that would surely be viewed as crossing the line, these advocates cloak their reformist package in legal language and seek to wring both legitimacy and political cover from their comparisons with Western legal systems.

In the early years of the reform era in the late 1970s and early 1980s, before the term "judicialization of the constitution" entered the scholarly lexicon, much of the scholarly discussion concerning constitutional development centered on the creation of a new constitutional review mechanism. At the inaugural meeting of the Constitutional Law Research

[15] Wang Lei, supra note 13, p. 5: "Use of the constitution by the courts does not mean that the courts have the power to engage in judicial review, or the authority to declare laws invalid." In Wang's view, the judicialization verdicts that have been issued thus far – some of which are discussed in more detail below – illustrate the dynamic of courts making use of the Constitution without usurping the NPC's constitutional authority. Id. at 212–213.

Committee of the China Law Society, held in Guiyang, Guizhou, in October 1985, the 112 attendees debated the need for the establishment of a "constitutional supervision committee" located under the SC.[16] Others called for the creation of a "constitutional litigation system" as a way to ensure fuller implementation of the Constitution. By 1990, one leading constitutional law scholar was able to describe support among his colleagues for the creation of a constitutional review mechanism as "universal."[17] A variety of scholarly articles, a number of them exploring the benefits of Western constitutional systems for the first time, also suggested ways in which China might incorporate institutional reforms based on those models.[18]

Even as the judicialization theory has developed during the past two decades, calls for a new constitutional review mechanism have continued.[19] These calls have been echoed by senior government officials; speaking in 2003, then–Chief Justice Xiao Yang of the SPC called for the further development of the constitutional supervision system,

[16] "Zhongguo Faxuehui Xianfaxue Yanjiuhui Zai Guiyang Chengli" (The Constitutional Law Research Committee of the China Law Society Is Established in Guiyang), *Zhongguo faxue* (Legal Science in Peoples Republic of China) 1, no. 57, 57 (1986): 57.

[17] Xu Weiyi, "1990 Report on Constitutional Law Scholarship." In *Research Reports on Constitutional Development of China*, ed. Hu Jinguang and Han Dayuan (2004, Beijing: China Law Press), p. 611. This consensus has held to the present day: Leading constitutional law scholar Zhang Qianfan, writing in 2003, described the current "consensus which has gradually emerged among legal scholars ... [that] China has not just a need, but in fact an urgent imperative, to take the constitution seriously as the fundamental legal document of the nation." For Zhang, taking the Constitution seriously would include the creation of a constitutional review mechanism. Zhang Qianfan, "Renzhen Duidai Xianfa" (Taking Constitutional Law Seriously), *Peking University Law Journal* 15, no. 560 (2003): 560

[18] See, for example, Hu Jinguang, "Lun Xianfa Jiandu Zhidu" (Regarding Constitutional Supervision Systems), *Zhongguo faxue* (Legal Sci. in P.R.C.) 1 (1985): 72.

[19] According to one widely used constitutional text:

> In the social and political life of our country, some incidents have emerged in which the question of whether certain normative legal documents violate the constitution has arisen. But neither the NPC nor the Standing Committee have yet implemented their constitutional review process under the Constitution and the Legislative Law. Our country's constitutional review system still needs institutions to assist the NPC and the Standing Committee in fulfilling their constitutional review duties. These institutions can put forward conditions and principles necessary for constitutional review, and put forward more detailed regulations for the constitutional review process, the constitutional review method, constitutional review measures, and the effect of constitutional review, among other matters. In this way our constitutional review system will be much more operational.

Hu Jinguang, ed., *Xianfa xue yuanli yu anli jiaocheng* (Textbook on Constitutional Law Principles and Cases) (2006, Beijing: Peking University Press), p. 134.

saying that progress was needed "without a single moment's delay."[20] Given the lack of progress in recent years, many scholars have become pragmatists, willing to support any path – including further development of the existing structure or the creation of new mechanisms – toward meaningful constitutional enforcement.[21]

Credit for coining the phrase "judicialization of the constitution" generally is given to Hu Jinguang, professor of constitutional law at People's University. Professor Hu's 1993 article "An Exploration of the Inevitability and Feasibility of Judicialization of the Constitution" introduced the term "judicialization" into the scholarly debate, reinforcing the notion that the court system could make progress on a limited form of judicial review – or at least constitutional rights enforcement – without the creation of an independent constitutional review mechanism. Hu's article, which, at just over a page, reads more like an outline than a full-blown scholarly work, first noted the historical "trend" of judicialization. Hu pointed out that a number of European civil law countries and former Soviet bloc countries, many of which lacked a long-standing tradition of constitutionalism, had adopted constitutional review mechanisms in recent years.

To Hu, this comparative experience indicated that the judicialization of the Chinese Constitution was not only "inevitable" but also "necessary." To bolster his case, Hu highlighted some of the benefits of a constitutional review power vested in the courts, including the institutional expertise of the courts in comparing laws that seem to be in conflict and avoiding the difficulties that arise when legislators are called upon to judge the constitutionality of their own handiwork. Hu also argued that, successes notwithstanding, the first decade of experience under the 1982 Constitution indicated that there were still some shortcomings in terms of its "authoritativeness." Allowing the courts to make use of the Constitution, Hu implied, might help to address this problem.

Hu concluded with three suggested next steps: First, scholars should continue to research constitutional questions; next, courts should be allowed to pass constitutional judgment on sublegislative normative documents, such as administrative regulations; and third, under special circumstances, the SPC or other specially created body should be allowed to review legislation and resolve disputes regarding the separation of powers.

[20] *Constitutional Law*, supra note 8, at p. 97.

[21] Interview with Hu Jinguang, professor of Constitutional Law, People's University, in Beijing, China (January 2008).

Hu's article is interesting in that it seems to use the term "judicialization" almost interchangeably with Western-style judicial review, and it also calls openly for the SPC to be empowered to engage in judicial review. In what might be viewed as a strategic retrenchment, later scholars who would make use of the term "judicialization" nevertheless go to great pains to deny that judicialization was the same as judicial review, or that judicialization represented any significant threat to the authority of the People's Congress. Hu himself would eventually adopt a change in terminology. In 1997, he published a slightly longer piece, again advocating the "inevitability" and "necessity" of the use of Constitution by the judiciary. In this later piece, titled "An Exploration of the Judicial Usability of the Chinese Constitution," Hu referred to his proposed reforms as "judicial usability," a term that, in his view, emphasized the shared nature of authority over the Constitution.[22] His recommendations for the next steps, which included more scholarly research on constitutional questions and the creation of a constitutional supervision committee, were more modest than the proposals he had put forward in his 1993 article.

The most prominent scholarly articulation of the judicialization concept occurred in 2000 with the publication of *Judicialization of the Constitution* by Beijing University law scholar Wang Lei. In his book – and in a case book published in 2003 – Wang put forward one of the most influential statements of what judicialization might mean. Interestingly, in his embrace of the concept of judicialization, Wang explicitly distanced himself from scholars who push for institutional reforms. According to Wang, the advocates of the development of new institutions misunderstand the "essence" of Chinese constitutionalism. For Wang, judicialization "tells the whole story of constitutional implementation in China."[23] Although Wang avoided an explicit definition of the term judicialization, he did emphasize the Constitution's legal nature and its direct legal effect. As such, Wang argues, it is a source of law that courts can draw upon in adjudicating cases.

In many ways, Wang's theory of judicialization is highly circumscribed. As previously noted, Wang declined to link judicialization with the power of judicial review of legislation. Although lower-level courts do not have the authority to interpret the Constitution, so as to avoid the appearance of conflict with the constitutional structure, Wang argued that the SPC is, in fact, so empowered.[24] He also explicitly rejected the

[22] According to Hu, the term "judicialization" incorrectly implies full authority of the courts of the Constitution, to the exclusion of other institutional actors, including the NPC. Id.

[23] Wang Lei, supra note 13, at p. 147.

[24] Id. at pp. 145–146.

notion that judicialization would allow Chinese courts to serve as a check on abuse of authority by other state organs, in a manner similar to the separation of powers in the United States.[25] It was this more limited approach that was embodied in the small but significant body of case law that referenced the Constitution during the 1980s and 1990s, and that also would be the focus of the 2001 *Qi Yuling* case (discussed in section 3).[26]

Yet, by largely ceding the interpretive ground, Wang and other advocates in favor of judicialization may have ensured that their arguments, even if eventually accepted, may have little actual impact. It is the explication and elucidation of constitutional norms through jurisprudence that leads to the creation of meaningful constitutional rights doctrine and creates concrete and binding rights obligations on states. Without the ability to actually interpret constitutional rights provisions in a way that limits state power, it is difficult to see how the courts can make use of the Constitution in any meaningful way.

2.2. *Alternative Arguments*

Other scholars, building on Wang's work, have put forward alternative readings of the Constitution, arguing that, far from prohibiting judicial enforcement of constitutional rights protections, the 1982 Constitution in fact mandates a role for the courts.

The most significant barrier to increased judicial use of the Constitution is Article 67, which, as previously noted, vests the NPCSC with the power to "interpret" the Constitution and to "supervise its enforcement." One alternative reading of Article 67, put forward by the Sichuan University law scholar Zhou Wei, among others, proposes reading that article in a broader context: Although Article 67 makes clear that the SC has interpretive power over the Constitution, it does not grant a monopoly over constitutional interpretation to the NPCSC, nor does it forbid other state organs from making use of the Constitution as a legal document.[27]

[25] Id. at p. 144.
[26] In the Qi Yuling case, the SPC approved a plaintiff's cause of action in a tort case based on the plaintiff's claim that her constitutional right to education had been infringed. The SPC's approval seemed to suggest that the Chinese constitution is in fact enforceable in Chinese courts. For a longer account of the Qi Yuling case, see infra.
[27] Zhou Wei, *Xianfa Jiben Quanli Sifa Jiuji Yanjiu* (Research on the Judicial Protection of Basic Rights) (2002, Beijing: China People's Public Security University Press), p. 129.

Constitutional law scholar Cai Dingjian has argued that, just as the SC's power to interpret statutes under Article 67(4) of the Constitution is shared by both the courts and the procuratorate, so too can the SC's constitutional interpretive authority be viewed, properly, as split between different institutional actors, including the courts. In Professor Cai's reading, Article 67(1) does not grant *exclusive* interpretive authority but rather *final* interpretive authority: If the SC disagreed with the judiciary's reading of a particular constitutional provision, it would have the authority to nullify it.[28]

For some, the alternative reading of the Constitution can be taken one step further, not only to permit judicial enforcement of constitutional rights norms but also to compel it.[29] Scholars who support this reading of the Constitution believe that Article 67 must be read in tandem with the Constitution as a whole. Article 123, for example, names the People's Courts as the nation's sole adjudicatory body. Neither Article 123 itself nor Articles 124 to 128, which further define the powers and duties of the court system, explicitly exclude cases that have an impact on basic constitutional rights from the jurisdiction of the People's Court system. If the courts reject certain constitutional rights claims brought before them, so the argument goes, they are both neglecting their duty as the judicial organs of the state and failing to give substance to Article 5 of the Constitution, which states that China is a country ruled by law.[30]

A still more creative reading of Article 67 and the authority it grants the NPCSC to "supervise the enforcement" of the Constitution has been put forth. Article 67 is said to create a quasi-judicial review authority to be exercised in situations in which lower-level people's congresses or administrative agencies issue normative documents that contradict the Constitution;[31] this authority, rooted in Article 67, does not relate to the adjudication of individual cases in which a violation of individual rights is alleged. This latter supervisory role, it is argued, is properly left to the courts. To avoid the appearance of undercutting the NPCSC's interpretive authority, this alternative analysis attempts to draw a line between measuring the constitutionality of laws and regulations – which

28 *Constitutional Law*, supra note 8, at p. 113.

29 Zhou Wei, supra note 27, at p. 130.

30 Id. at p. 131. Zhou approvingly cites the conclusion of another scholar that, "the supremacy of the constitution and the function of the people's courts means that people's courts do not have the authority to refuse to make use of the constitution; instead, both the constitution and laws approved by the legislature should be used by the people's courts." Id. at pp. 130–131.

31 Id. at p. 134.

is ceded, perhaps too quickly, to the NPCSC – and applying constitutional rights protections to individual cases. This approach does raise a serious concern: How can constitutional provisions be applied without first being interpreted, either explicitly or implicitly? This division of labor between the NPCSC and the courts also leaves state behavior, as long as it is covered by law, beyond the reach of judicial review.

Various scholars have also argued that both the 1955 and the 1986 responses should be read narrowly; on its face, the 1955 response prohibits the direct use of the Constitution only in criminal law cases. The 1986 response does not expressly forbid the use of the Constitution in any situation; it can be read as a mere reminder to the courts that they should turn first to legislation and relevant regulations before seeking answers from the constitutional text.[32] Neither document, scholars argue, was meant to keep the courts off the constitutional terrain altogether.

Tsinghua University law scholar Wang Zhenmin has suggested that the SPC's interpretation in the 2001 *Qi Yuling* case, in which it seemed to embrace openly the use of the Constitution by courts in some situations, effectively nullified the 1955 and 1986 documents.[33] In addition, Professor Wang argued, regardless of their content, SPC interpretations cannot cancel out constitutional norms, including constitutional rights protections or the supposed constitutional authority to apply them in court.

Given these and other arguments in favor of constitutional adjudication, many scholars have concluded that it is only established *practice* that holds the courts back.[34] After actors within the system decide to end that practice, these scholars contend, there will be no institutional or structural barriers to deter them.

2.3. *Judicialization in Practice: Early Cases*

The earliest known case in which a court made reference to constitutional norms is the 1988 *Democracy and Law* case, also referred to by the title of the article in question, "The Twenty-Year Riddle of the 'Madwoman.'"[35]

[32] Zhang Qianfan, supra note 17, at 561.
[33] Wang Zhenmin, *Zhongguo Weixian Shencha Zhidu* (China's Constitutional Review System) (2004, Beijing: China University of Politics and Law Press), p. 183.
[34] Id. at p. 169.
[35] The Shanghai court's verdict can be found in Wang Lei, supra note 13, at pp. 1–3.

Published in 1985, "Riddle" told the story of Shanghai resident Shi Rong, who allegedly had had his wife committed to a psychiatric institution on false grounds. The plaintiff apparently supplied documentary evidence to the magazine that his wife was mentally ill before the story ran; in court, Shi also provided affidavits from medical professionals supporting his claims.

In its ruling, the Shanghai Intermediate People's Court held that, although "the state protects citizens' right to free expression and freedom of the press," nonetheless, the individual right to reputation is also protected by law. The court ruled, therefore, that the journalists were liable for damages. The case has been cited by many scholars as an early attempt by a lower-level court to define the boundaries of the constitutional right to free expression.

The most prominent early judicialization case occurred in the late 1980s. In 1986, Zhang Guosheng signed a contract to work for Ms. Zhang Xuezhen (no relation), the proprietor of the Workers New Village Youth Cooperative Service Center in Tianjin.[36] The labor contract that Zhang Guosheng signed included a provision stating that the employer was not responsible for any injuries suffered in the course of employment. Soon after beginning work, Zhang was seriously injured on the job. He later died in the hospital.

His father and sister, Zhang Lianqi and Zhang Guoli, incurred more than 17,000 yuan (about U.S.$4,600 at that time) in costs while obtaining treatment for their son.[37] After Zhang Guosheng's death, his family approached his employer for compensation. When negotiations between the family and the employer broke down, Zhang Lianqi and Zhang Guoli brought suit in the Tanggu District Court in Tianjin. The case presented a difficult problem: At the time of the litigation, China's contract law did not prohibit clauses such as the one that Zhang Guosheng had agreed to, absolving the employer of any responsibility in the case of injury.[38] The Tianjin court, unsure about how to handle the case, requested guidance from the SPC.

In October 1988, the SPC issued its answer. Invoking the Chinese Constitution as a constitution that "protects workers,"[39] the SPC ruled that

[36] *Constitutional Law*, supra note 8, at p. 114.

[37] The exchange rate for U.S. dollars and Chinese yuan in 1986 was roughly 1:3.7. The current exchange rate is 1:6.8.

[38] The Labor Law and the Labor Contract Law, both of which would cover such situations today, did not come into force until 1995 and 2008, respectively.

[39] Id.

the contractual provision in question was both unconstitutional and in violation of Chinese law.[40] The contract provision was therefore invalid. The Tianjin court, in accordance with the SPC's guidance, ruled in favor of Zhang Guosheng's family in December 1988, ordering the employer to pay the family RMB 18,000. The case provided what in the future would become a much-followed model, whereby the Constitution would fill gaps in existing law. It was also representative of a future pattern in that the court's ruling led to legislation that codified the court's decision.

Some scholars have included, as instances within the judicialization trend, various cases that, although they do not explicitly mention the Constitution, nonetheless raise questions related to constitutional rights norms. Consider, for example, the following: In 1992, two individuals, Ni Peilu and Wang Ying, brought suit against the China World Trade Center, claiming that the World Trade Center had infringed their right of reputation by searching their bags while the two were on the premises, presumably because of concerns that the two had stolen items. The World Trade Center defended itself by pointing to a sign it had posted indicating that bags were subject to search.

The plaintiffs had to try their luck with the right-of-reputation claim because there was no private cause of action for illegal search, although Chinese criminal law prohibits illegal restrictions on the individual's freedom of person.[41] Moreover, Article 37 of the Chinese Constitution also protects Chinese citizens' freedom of person. The court ruled in favor of the plaintiffs, though its legal reasoning was somewhat strained. The court reasoned that all acts must have a legal basis, and that, because there was no legal basis for the World Trade Center's decision to engage in a search of the two customers, its claim to putting them on notice with a sign had no legal effect.

As this case indicates, judicialization cases both present the opportunity for innovation and raise potential problems. The analysis by the court in the *Ni and Wang* case turns the conventional approach – that an action is presumed legal unless it has been prohibited by law – on its head, and it has been called into question by some legal scholars, despite

[40] The SPC declined to identify which laws and regulations the contract provision violated; scholars have been unable to identify any laws in force at that time that would prohibit such a contractual provision.

[41] Criminal Law, Art. 238 (adopted at the Second Session of the Fifth National People's Congress on July 1, 1979; revised at the Fifth Session of the Eighth National People's Congress on March 14, 1997 and promulgated by Order No. 83 of the President of the People's Republic of China on March 14, 1997). Prior to the 1997 revision of the Criminal Law, illegal search was covered by Article 144.

the fact that the court's decision was cited with some approval by the SPC, which published it in its *Gazette*.[42]

However, as some scholars have argued, this case is about a conflict between a private law contract and Article 37 of the Constitution. Instead of hiding behind faulty reasoning to reach the "correct" result, some scholars believe, the court should have based its decision on the relevant constitutional provision, which would have enabled it to present a much more strongly reasoned verdict.

Though somewhat flawed, the case does illustrate some of judicialization's key dynamics as currently conceptualized in China. First, the case involved two private actors and did not present questions either of abuse of state power or of the constitutionality of specific laws or regulations. Second, the court seemed to be acting, at least in part, according to a notion of fairness, in light of what it thought the "right" result should be, even in the absence of specific legal norms that would justify such an outcome. Third, the court's reasoning, if indeed it was implicitly importing constitutional values, was difficult to follow. Finally, because there was no opportunity for the court to expound on the constitutional principles involved, it could not enunciate a rights jurisprudence that would both define and reasonably limit the individual rights protections found under Article 37 of the Constitution.[43]

Even with such flaws, cases like these have led scholars to cite this limited use of the Constitution by courts both as evidence that the courts can be entrusted with such authority and as support for their argument that judicial citation of the Constitution is, indeed, permitted under the Chinese constitutional framework:

> If we engage in a more in-depth analysis of these cases, it is not difficult to conclude that: beginning in the mid-1990s, courts across China have accepted a number of cases that, both formally and substantively, are in fact constitutional cases. The courts have accepted these cases regarding rights in dispute, and have in fact issued decisions. Perhaps these cases may not meet the scholarly definition of constitutional litigation, and perhaps they cannot be compared to scholarly litigation in other countries, but no one can deny that these cases are in the category of basic constitutional rights cases resolved by the courts.[44]

[42] Zhou Wei, supra note 27, at p. 153.

[43] Such exposition is especially needed when, as in this case, it is unclear whether or not the right being claimed would actually apply to the facts of the case: It is unclear whether Article 37 would mean that security guards should never be allowed to search an individual; regardless, such a conclusion is not immediately apparent on the basis of the text of Article 37.

[44] Zhou Wei, supra note 27, at p. 179.

Admittedly, there is an element of circularity in this analysis: The fact that these cases have taken place, it is suggested, means that such innovations must be permissible under the current system. At the very least, the small but growing number of cases – more than thirty by one count, made in 2003 – in which the courts have made reference to constitutional norms does indicate that at least some judges want to revisit the orthodox view of the division of powers under the Constitution.

3. AN ABORTIVE BREAKTHROUGH: THE QI YULING CASE

On the heels of both judicial gestures toward constitutional decision making and the growth of the scholarly conversation regarding judicialization came the 2001 *Qi Yuling* case. The case sprang from a garden-variety civil dispute about identity theft. In 1990, Chen Xiaoqi, a classmate of Qi Yuling at the Eighth Middle School in Tengzhou, Shandong Province, stole Qi's college entrance test scores and successfully used them to get into a local business school under Qi's name. Qi did not find out about the identity theft until years later, and when she did, she sued.

Qi's identity theft claim was on solid ground: The right to one's own identity is protected by the General Principles of Civil Law, and there was little doubt that Chen's actions had violated Qi's civil rights. But Qi also sought to recover damages on the grounds that Chen had violated her constitutional right to education. The provincial court in Shandong, hearing the case on appeal, sought guidance from the SPC on the constitutional rights claim, and the SPC answered that Qi could recover damages for the infringement of her right to education. In its answer, the SPC seemed to suggest that the Chinese Constitution was directly enforceable by Chinese courts, at least in some cases.

When seen in the context of earlier judicial use of the Constitution, the SPC's answer in the *Qi Yuling* case seems to be an attempt to formalize the authority exercised both by itself and by lower-level courts in prior cases. As with the 1988 *Zhang Lianqi* contract case, the Court was not attempting to pass constitutional judgment on national law, but instead saw itself as using the Constitution to fill a legal gap. As with most of the earlier cases, the litigation concerned two private actors engaged in a civil law dispute and had little to do with the protection of individual rights against infringement by the state.

Unsurprisingly, the SPC's intervention led to an explosion of commentary. For many, the value of the case was more symbolic than legal. In issuing its response, the SPC highlighted some of the shortcomings of the current system and focused both scholarly and public attention on the need for action. In essence, the *Qi Yuling* case provided a much-needed opportunity for a wide-ranging public discussion of a range of issues, including constitutional development, the shortcomings of China's current legal structure, rights protection under the law, and even, in an indirect manner, the slow pace of political reform.[45]

The scholarly response has not been all positive, however. Some scholars have voiced doubts that the development of a constitutional review system should be the first priority for legal reform.[46] Others, citing the history of China's 1982 Constitution as a primarily socialist document, have questioned the appropriateness of the SPC's intervention under the existing framework of "parliamentary supremacy."[47] Shanghai-based scholar Tong Zhiwei has argued that supporters of judicialization are engaging in a bit of constitutional sleight of hand, attempting to usurp the NPCSC's constitutional interpretive authority:

> [Judicialization of the constitution] means advocating that the NPC and the Standing Committee's authority to engage in supervision of constitutional implementation and the NPC and the Standing Committee's authority to engage in constitutional interpretation both be turned over to the SPC. It means that [the] SPC can engage in constitutional review of NPC and Standing Committee legislation. It means that the state's highest judicial organ and the supreme organ of state power are in fact the same or occupy equal constitutional status. In a word, it means a fundamental change to our nation's system of organization of political authority.[48]

Still other scholars have focused on what constitutional review might mean in practice. Senior constitutional law scholar Ji Weidong, though supportive of the SPC's move in the *Qi Yuling* case, expressed concern that China's judiciary, rife with corruption, overworked, and often lacking technical legal proficiency, might not be able to handle constitutional

[45] Tong Zhiwei, "Xianfa sifa shiyong yanjiu zhong de jige wenti" (Various Problems in Research on Usability of the Constitution). In *Xianfa yanjiu* (Studies on Constitutionalism) 1 (2002): 271–284.

[46] Liu Songshan, "Weixian shencha re de liang sikao" (Thoughts on Cooling Down the Constitutional Review Fever), *Faxue* (Legal Studies) 1 (2004): 36.

[47] Zhai Xiaobo, "Daiyi jiguan zhishang de renmin xianzheng" (People's Constitutional Governance Under the Parliamentary Supremacy System), *Tsinghua Law Review* 1 (2007): 35, 36.

[48] Tong Zhiwei, supra at note 45, at 271–284. See also Jiang Shigong, "Xianfa sifahua de beilun" (The Erroneous Theorizing of Judicialization of the Constitution), *Zhongguo kexue* (P.R.C. Soc. Sci.) 2 (2003): 18–19.

enforcement responsibilities.[49] Other scholars, echoing Ji's concerns, have suggested that what China needs most at present is not a constitutional review mechanism but, rather, measures to increase judicial independence.[50] Only after the judiciary has been better insulated from outside pressures, these scholars argue, will it be able to make proper use of constitutional review authority.

A number of scholars limited their comments to the case itself, pointing out what they saw as flaws in the court's reasoning and highlighting the ways in which the *Qi Yuling* decision was different from "real" constitutional litigation. Even as they pointed out the case's various flaws, however, most commentators urged support for the SPC's move. In a widely cited interview published in the leading intellectual weekly *Southern Weekend*, senior legal scholar Jiang Ming'an appealed to his colleagues inside the academy to support the SPC's gradualist approach:

> I believe that the scholarly community needs to understand the motivations of the Supreme People's Court. For decades, our Constitution has been packed away and put on a high shelf. For judges adjudicating cases, the Constitution was considered a "restricted area." Perhaps this has to do with the fact that some of the rights found in the Constitution are sensitive. Given that the rights touched on in this case are not sensitive, it was relatively easy to handle. We have been waiting for decades, and finally we have arrived at this opportunity which was difficult to come by. We scholars should strongly push forward with it.[51]

In the same interview, China University of Politics and Law scholar Jiang Ping expressed the hope that the *Qi Yuling* ruling would spark further constitutional litigation. In that hope, he was right, although, as we will see below, the cases that have followed have not yet led to the institutional changes that Jiang – and others, no doubt – had anticipated.

Any optimism about official attitudes toward constitutional reform generated by Qi Yuling proved short-lived. In December 2008, less than

49 Ji Weidong, "Hexianxing shencha yu sifaquan de qianghua" (Constitutional Review and the Strengthening of Judicial Power), *Zhongguo kexue* (P.R.C. Soc. Sci.) 2 (2002): 4.

50 Author interview with Chinese academic, Beijing, January 2008. The interviewee asked not to be named.

51 "Jiang Ming'an, Jiang Ping, He Weifang, Cai Dingjian: Xianfa Sifahua Sirentan (Jiang Ming'an, Jiang Ping, He Weifang, Cai Dingjian: Roundtable Discussion on Judicialization of the Constitution)," *Nanfang Zhoumo* (Southern Weekend) (August 13, 2001).

eight years after the SPC issued its famous interpretation, it quietly withdrew it, stating that the interpretation "no longer applied" and therefore was withdrawn.[52]

To be sure, certain aspects of the SPC's interpretation would come under criticism from scholars across the political spectrum after 2001. Nonetheless, the key concept of judicial review advanced by the Interpretation continued to enjoy strong support from the academic community. In its report on the invalidation of the *Qi Yuling* interpretation, *Caijing* magazine noted:

> There was no lack of legal academics who challenged the appropriateness of direct application of constitutional provisions in that particular case. But on the question of whether the constitution could serve as a basis for court judgments, scholars without exception answered in the affirmative.[53]

Writing in the Guangzhou-based *Southern Metropolitan Daily* in the aftermath of the *Qi Yuling* revocation, Beijing University Professor Zhang Qianfan tried to minimize the impact of the court's move. "Courts not only can apply and interpret the Constitution," Zhang wrote, but "they have no power to avoid constitutional questions."[54] According to Zhang, the SPC's interpretation had given the Chinese people "a ray of hope" that the constitutional document would become a legal reality. Zhang expressed concern that the cancellation of *Qi Yuling* would "transmit to society the inaccurate information" that the Constitution is without legal effect.

One could argue that the situation as of early December 2008, though far from ideal, represented a fair compromise: The *Qi Yuling* interpretation, though effectively defunct, was still formally valid and served as something of a minor talisman for those who are pushing, both in the academy and in the courtroom, for a greater judicial role in constitutional rights protection. There was little danger of additional reformist constitutional activity by the SPC, yet state, society, and individual litigants benefited from the constitutional litigation that was carried out in *Qi*'s name.

[52] Thomas E. Kellogg, "The Death of Constitutional Litigation in China?", *China Brief*, April 2009.

[53] Ye Doudou, "Qi Yuling Case Judicial Interpretation Annulled," *Caijing*, February 2, 2009.

[54] Zhang Qianfan, "Courts Have No Power to Avoid the Constitution," *Southern Metropolitan Daily*, January 7, 2009.

Why, then, formally withdraw the *Qi Yuling* interpretation? Little is known about the politics behind the SPC's move. Although the SPC has been pruning outdated interpretations, it seems unlikely that *Qi Yuling* was fully a part of that process. Other cancelled interpretations had been superceded by new laws and regulations,[55] but progress on *Qi Yuling* had been more or less at a standstill for several years. Moreover, neither the SPC nor the NPC followed the cancellation of the *Qi* interpretation with an alternative plan for constitutional development.

Some observers believe that the decision to revoke *Qi Yuling* is tied to the new judicial reform policy, referred to as the "three supremes," implemented by SPC President Wang Shengjun.[56] Since taking office in March 2008, Wang has departed from the approach mapped out by his predecessor Xiao Yang. Instead of emphasizing the role of the courts as neutral adjudicators of disputes, he instead has called on judges to consider both the interests of the Communist Party and public opinion.[57] Legal rules are also a part of the picture, but the law is by no means above party interests.

It is easy to see how this new theoretical framework would be incompatible with the long-term goals of *Qi Yuling*. Whereas *Qi Yuling* attempted to kick-start a process of constitutional adjudication, one in which judges would engage in a dialogue with litigants and each other as to the meaning and applicability of the constitutional text, the three supremes downgrades the importance of law to the judicial process. Instead, it embraces politics, party policy, and flexibility as its key virtues, and excessive adherence to the law as a vice.

It is impossible to know what connection, if any, exists between the new populist court reform policy, the revocation of *Qi Yuling*, and the downfall of SPC Vice President Huang Songyou.[58] Huang, the man most closely associated with the 2001 Interpretation, was taken into custody – specifically, a form of detention for Communist Party members known as

[55] Ye Doudou, "Qi Yuling Case Judicial Interpretation Annulled," *Caijing*, February 2, 2009.

[56] For more on Wang's "three supremes" theory, see Wang Shengjun, "Fully Implement the Work of the 17th Party Congress, Resolutely Carry Out the Work of the People's Courts," *Seeking Truth*, August 16, 2008, http://www.qsjournal.com.cn/qs/20080816/GB/qs%5E485%5E0%5E1.htm.

[57] Jerome Cohen, "Body Blow for the Judiciary," *South China Morning Post*, October 23, 2008.

[58] Huang, an SPC judge at the time of the Qi Yuling interpretation, was promoted to SPC vice president in 2002.

shuanggui – in mid-October 2008.[59] According to media reports, Huang was brought down for "abuse of power for personal gain, serious economic irregularities, and degenerate behavior in his personal life."[60] In particular, Huang was linked to a corruption scheme involving Guangdong High Court Judge Yang Xiancai.[61] In January 2010, Huang was convicted by a court in Hebei Province of taking bribes of just under 4 million yuan and sentenced to life in prison.[62] He was also stripped of his Communist Party membership and banned for life from holding public office.

Even before its revocation, *Qi Yuling* had its critics, including a small minority who viewed the case as a failure. Those who would call *Qi Yuling* a failure miss the importance of the debate generated by the case. The SPC interpretation moved the question of constitutionalism from the fringes of Chinese academic debate to its center and spurred a wide-ranging public conversation about the merits of more robust constitutional review. Lawyers and academics were encouraged by the case to bring constitutional arguments in Chinese courts, which in many instances spurred additional waves of public conversation and debate about constitutional development in China. And public rights awareness continues to grow: A 2002 survey showed that two-thirds of respondents expected the constitution to restrain government power and protect individual rights. An equal number connected corruption in China to a lack of meaningful, constitutionally based checks and balances among the branches of government.[63] Qi Yuling played a role in the evolution of public rights consciousness in China and may yet play a renewed role in the reform of the system of constitutional litigation in China.

[59] *Shuanggui*, which translates literally as "double regulation," is a form of detention used on party officials; it is very common in corruption cases. Party officials are detained by a Party Commission on Discipline Inspection and investigated for wrongdoing; only after the party process has played out is the individual brought into the formal criminal process. For more on *shuanggui*, see Flora Sapio, "Shuanggui and Extralegal Detention in China," *China Information*, March 2008, vol. 22, no. 1.

[60] Qin Xudong and Wang Heyan, "Supreme People's Court Vice President Huang Songyou Removed From Office," *Caijing*, October 28, 2008.

[61] For more on Yang's detention and the case that forms the center of the investigation of Yang and Huang, see Wang Xiaolin and Qin Xudong, "Guangdong Province High Court Enforcement Department Former Department Chief Yang Xiancai Enters into 'Shuanggui,'" *Caijing*, July 9, 2008.

[62] Rao Zhi and Zhang Youyi, "Huang Songyou sentenced to life in prison" (Huang Songyou Yishen Beipan Wuqi Tuxing), *Caijing*, January 19, 2010.

[63] Jianfu Chen, *Chinese Law: Context and Transformation* (2008, Leiden, the Netherlands: Martinus Nijhoff Publishers), p. 143.

4. CASE STUDY: THE ZHANG XIANZHU CASE AND HEPATITIS B LITIGATION

Perhaps the most successful example of judicialization litigation in China is the series of hepatitis B discrimination cases brought during the past five years. Relying on Article 33 of the Constitution – China's equal protection clause[64] – litigants have challenged decisions by both public and private actors to exclude hepatitis B–positive individuals from the workplace. Beginning in 2002, more than forty hepatitis B cases have been brought by litigants across China, some of which have resulted in reinstatement of the plaintiffs to their jobs or schools.[65] Overall, these cases have resulted in concrete legislative changes that better protect the rights of persons with hepatitis B.

The decision to focus on hepatitis B discrimination is, first and foremost, a strategic one: Discrimination implicates constitutional rights, but – at least in the Chinese context – does not directly challenge government power in the way that other constitutional rights claims might. Discrimination is less politically sensitive, and equality claims are likelier to be understood and supported by the general public than the more abstract political rights claims. Finally, in the case of hepatitis B discrimination, the defendant's rationale for engaging in discriminatory behavior – the protection of public health – often lacks a sufficient scientific basis, making it especially vulnerable to legal challenge.

Also crucial to the constitutional component of discrimination litigation is the fact that Chinese antidiscrimination law is underdeveloped, overly vague, and generally weak on enforcement provisions.[66] China's Labor Law, for example, specifically prohibits discrimination on the basis of ethnicity, race, gender, or religious belief,[67] but it does not include any

[64] Constitution, Art. 33 (P.R.C.) reads as follows:

> Article 33. All persons holding the nationality of the People's Republic of China are citizens of the People's Republic of China. All citizens of the People's Republic of China are equal before the law. Every citizen enjoys the rights and at the same time must perform the duties prescribed by the Constitution and the law.

[65] Author interview (January 2008). The interviewee asked not to be named.

[66] For a general overview of employment discrimination law in China, see Ronald C. Brown, "China's Employment Discrimination Laws During Economic Transition," *Columbia Journal of Asian Law* 19 (2006): 361.

[67] Labor Law, Art. 12 (Adopted at the Eighth Meeting of the Standing Committee of the Eighth National People's Congress on July 5, 1994; promulgated by Order No.28 of the President of the People's Republic of China on July 5, 1994. Effective as of January 1, 1995). See also id., Art. 3 (requiring employers to treat employees equally).

specific provisions regarding health status. The numerous gaps in the law, though detrimental to individual plaintiffs' chances for a positive outcome, nonetheless allow plaintiffs' lawyers to construct their legal arguments, in part, on Article 33's equal protection grounds.

The rise of hepatitis B litigation was spurred by a handful of trailblazing lawsuits brought against employers and others alleging improper discrimination on the basis of height, place of origin, and government employment status. In perhaps the most prominent case, a Sichuan University law student brought suit against a Chengdu branch of the China Construction Bank for imposing height requirements on all new employees. In May 2001, the Wuhou District People's Court accepted the case; the bank, however, withdrew the requirement before the case could be adjudicated. The court then dismissed the case, despite protestations from the plaintiff and plaintiff's counsel, both of whom were hoping to use the case to advance the development of constitutional antidiscrimination norms.

Though, at first blush, discrimination against hepatitis B carriers would seem to lack the drama of the great struggles against racial and gender discrimination in the United States and elsewhere, the problem is nonetheless a serious one. More than 10 percent of the Chinese population – approximately 120 million people, which is roughly equal to the entire populations of France and the United Kingdom combined – are believed to be hepatitis B carriers, and the practice of testing potential employees for the disease, and excluding those who test positive, is believed to be widespread. Before the government issued new regulations that prohibited discrimination against hepatitis B carriers in public employment, many government agencies had adopted policies that prohibited the hiring of individuals with hepatitis B. Carriers of the disease also have been barred from primary schools, secondary schools, and universities.[68]

From a public health standpoint, workplace bans against people with hepatitis B would seem to make little sense. Hepatitis B cannot be transmitted through casual workplace contact; it is only transmitted by means of bodily fluids.[69] Yet discrimination persists, due in part to social attitudes and widespread misunderstanding about the actual health risks the disease poses. According to one survey of hepatitis B carriers conducted

[68] For a brief account of hepatitis B discrimination in the public education sector, see Thomas E. Kellogg, "Courageous Explorers? Education Litigation and Judicial Innovation in China," *Harvard Human Rights Journal* 20 (2007): 141, 185–187.

[69] U.S. Centers for Disease Control and Prevention, "Hepatitis B Information for the Public," http://www.cdc.gov/hepatitis/HepatitisB.htm (accessed November 11, 2008).

by experts from Beijing University Law School, 56 percent of hepatitis B carriers have experienced difficulties during the recruitment process; of those, 72.3 percent were rejected on the basis of being classified as "substandard" (*bu hege*) on their physical exam.[70] Problems continue even after the recruitment process is over and the employment relationship has begun. Of survey respondents who were hepatitis B carriers, 32 percent had been dismissed from a job at least once; of those, 70.8 percent were specifically told that the reason for dismissal was their hepatitis B status. An additional 18.8 percent believed that the actual reasons given for their dismissal were a pretext for removing them from the workplace on the basis of their hepatitis B status.

A key factor in the rise of hepatitis B discrimination litigation in China has been the active engagement of civil society groups. Without the energetic assistance of nongovernmental organizations (NGOs), it is unlikely that the small wave of lawsuits that has been launched would have gotten underway. One group in particular, Sincerity (*gandan xiangzao*), has played a crucial role in focusing public attention on the problem of hepatitis B discrimination and in attempting to generate an effective legal response that includes both litigation and legislative advocacy. Founded in September 2001, Sincerity and its successor organization, Yirenping, began as a forum for persons with hepatitis B to communicate with each other, share experiences, and exchange information about treatment. In April 2003, the group began to focus on strategies to protect the legal rights and interests of hepatitis B–positive persons and has been a key player in many of the cases that have gone to court during the past five years. Its role has included encouraging its members to take legal action, helping to put individuals who have been discriminated against in touch with lawyers willing to take their cases, and providing medical information and experts to lawyers involved in antidiscrimination litigation.

Sincerity has also actively lobbied the government. In November 2003, for example, it sent a petition signed by more than sixteen hundred individuals to the NPCSC, the Ministry of Health, and the State Council Office of Legislative Affairs requesting that the NPCSC review the constitutionality of various provincial and local laws relating to civil service recruitment that limited or prohibited recruitment of persons with

70 Ye Jingyi and Shi Yuxiao, "Discrimination on the Basis of Health and Disability: An Analysis of Chinese Employment Discrimination Law Through The Lens of Hepatitis B Discrimination Cases." In *Employment Discrimination: International Standards and National Practice* (2006), p. 319.

or carrying hepatitis B.[71] Sincerity has also directed its public action efforts toward the private sector. In August 2007, the group, which by then had become Yirenping, submitted a petition to the Beijing office of Hewlett-Packard, signed by more than five thousand persons, protesting the alleged firing of twenty-two employees with the hepatitis B virus from a key supplier based in Suzhou.[72] Many experts view these acts of public mobilization as central to sustaining government attention to the issue.

Another key factor in the rise of hepatitis B discrimination litigation was an unfortunate incident that took place in April 2003. After being rejected from government employment on the basis of his hepatitis B status, twenty-two-year-old college senior Zhou Yichao attacked two local government officials in Zhejiang Province whom he viewed as responsible for his rejection, killing one and seriously wounding the other.[73] Zhou was executed in March 2004. The impact of this case was significant. It helped focus public and government attention on the severity of the problem of hepatitis B discrimination just months before the first high-profile hepatitis B case, the *Zhang Xianzhu* case, was filed.

4.1. *The* Zhang Xianzhu *Case*

On June 30, 2003, Zhang Xianzhu, a twenty-two-year-old university graduate looking for a job, took the civil service exam offered by the Wuhu City Personnel Office in Anhui Province. Zhang passed both the written and the oral examination with flying colors, receiving the highest test grade among the thirty applicants in Wuhu City for that recruitment cycle.[74] Zhang believed that he had landed a job in economic administration for the District Committee Office in Wuhu.[75]

[71] "Wo shi yigan huanzhe, dan wo bushi yideng gongmin" (I Have Hepatitis B, but I Am Not a Second-class Citizen), *Nanfang zhoumou* (Southern Weekend), December 25, 2003.

[72] "Five Thousand Petitioners Demand Hewlett-Packard Take Action Against Hepatitis B Discrimination," *China Labor Bulletin*, September 3, 2007, http://www.china-labour.org.hk/en/node/49836.

[73] "Dismantling Discrimination," *China Daily*, March 9, 2004. For an extended account of the case, see "Daxue biyesheng heyi dongshaji?" (Why do college graduates kill?), *Nanfang zhoumou* (Southern Weekend), April 21, 2003.

[74] "Yigan qishi diyi an zhurengong de yinju shenghuo" (The Secluded Life of the Central Protagonist in the First Hepatitis B Discrimination Case), *Yancheng Evening News*, June 18, 2004 (hereinafter *Secluded Life*).

[75] Shen Wulingfeng, "Verdict Announced Today in China's First Hepatitis B Discrimination Case: Court Does Not Support Plaintiff's Request for Employment," China News Net, April 2, 2004, http://news.sohu.com/2004/04/02/32/news219713299.shtml.

It was then that Zhang's troubles began. He submitted to a physical in the second half of September 2003, at which time it was discovered that he was a carrier of hepatitis B. On the basis of his hepatitis B status, he was denied a position in the local bureaucracy. He was verbally informed of the decision on September 25, 2003. In November, after an attempt at administrative reconsideration failed, Zhang filed suit in Xinwu District People's Court in Wuhu City. Zhang's lawyer in the case was the prominent legal scholar and constitutional lawyer Zhou Wei. Zhou's involvement in the case would prove to be critically important, and the attention that his participation garnered would play a key role in generating a legal response from the central government.

Zhou Wei's involvement in the case began in a somewhat nontraditional manner and illustrates the more sophisticated ways in which activist lawyers and litigants whose cases raise important constitutional concerns are beginning to find each other. Without the online support groups set up by civil society organizations, Zhang and Zhou might never have connected. Zhang had joined an online chat support group, hosted by Sincerity, devoted to the needs and concerns of hepatitis B–positive persons, and Zhang and Zhou initially made contact through Sincerity.[76]

Zhou, a professor at Sichuan University Law School, was fresh from his success in the *Jiang Tao* case and was looking for a way to continue his constitutional litigation work, which, as he put it, was one method of "marrying theory and practice."[77] At about the time of Zhang Xianzhu's removal from the government hiring process, Zhou had begun looking at hepatitis B discrimination as a potentially fruitful area to explore. Although the Zhou Yichao tragedy had made headlines nationwide, as of mid-2003, no successful legal claim had yet been brought challenging the legality of a government agency's refusal to employ an otherwise qualified applicant on the basis of his or her hepatitis B status.

Zhou, seeing a potential opportunity to continue to push legal development through litigation, agreed to take Zhang's case:

> After being in regular contact [with Zhang Xianzhu], I decided to take the case on a pro bono basis. I had long ago concluded that medical standards like this one violated the constitution, and hoped through this case to

[76] Zhou Mu, "Hepatitis B Discrimination Case Begins: An Interview with Lawyer Zhou Wei," *Chengdu Evening News*, December 20, 2003.

[77] Zhou Wei, *Zhongguo de laodong jiuye qishi: falu yu xianshi* (Employment Discrimination in China: Legislation and Reality) (2006, Beijing: China Law Press), p. 1.

> challenge various provincial regulations of this type, and in so doing to ensure fairness for hepatitis B carriers and to avoid a repeat occurrence of the Zhou Yichao tragedy. This is a part of the population that a civilized society should respect, tolerate, and understand. Society should allow them regular participation in labor and employment, and safeguard their own basic needs. Also... this was a chance to fuse theory and practice, to use facts to demonstrate the theoretical value and social benefits of my research.[78]

Media attention to the case was intense. From the moment Zhou filed suit on behalf of Zhang to the final verdict and beyond, Zhang's lawsuit received extensive press coverage, including from China's top electronic and print outlets, such as *Southern Weekend*, *Southern Metropolitan Daily*, and *Caijing*. Both CCTV and China Central Broadcasting also ran numerous reports on the case, and the Wuhu City courtroom was packed with both hepatitis B carriers and journalists on the day the verdict was announced. The press was very much in Zhang's corner, not least as a result of Zhou Wei's engagement with journalists on his client's behalf. Even the longtime party mouthpiece *People's Daily* reported favorably on Zhang's suit, eventually declaring the verdict a "victory" for both Zhang and for China's 120 million hepatitis B carriers.[79]

Presumably suspecting that no court would rule in his client's favor solely on the basis of constitutional claims, Zhou Wei – in his statement to the court – argued, first and foremost, that the rejection of Zhang's qualification for employment was illegal. Only after vigorously arguing his case on legal grounds did Zhou turn to the constitutional arguments.

Central to the case was the local government's use of the Anhui Province National Civil Service Recruitment Physical Examination Standards. The provincial regulations listed various test results that could lead to the conclusion that an individual was ineligible for government service. But the provincial standards did not specifically stipulate that persons who received the results that Zhang had received were unfit for government service. Therefore, Zhou argued, the hospital's conclusion

[78] Id. at pp. 2–3. Just before Zhou decided to involve himself in the *Zhang Xianzhu* case, he had received a grant from the Chinese Social Sciences Foundation to continue his research on constitutional review mechanisms; he viewed the *Zhang Xianzhu* case as a key part of that research work. Id. at pp. 1–3. In a way, the government was funding research on systems, innovations, and litigation strategies that could undermine its own unchecked authority.

[79] Du Wenjuan, "Zhang Xianzhu Safeguards the Rights of 120 Million People," *Renmin ribao* (People's Daily), May 13, 2005.

that Zhang was unfit to serve was "subjective" and "arbitrary" and lacking a basis in law. It was therefore, in Zhou's view, invalid.[80]

Zhou's argument that the hospital's exclusion of Zhang violated various national laws and regulations was also compelling.[81] Article 14 of the Law on the Prevention and Control of Infectious Diseases, for example, listed various occupations from which people not certifiably free of hepatitis B may be prohibited, including various jobs related to the handing of foodstuffs and the treatment of public water supplies. Also, Article 26(2) of the Food Safety Law excluded persons with some types of hepatitis from certain jobs related to the importation of food. Zhang, of course, was applying for an office position, and, as he and Zhou argued, in the absence of a specific prohibition, the central government clearly intended that he be allowed to hold the job for which he was applying.

Zhou's primary constitutional argument was that the province's physical exam regulations violated Zhang's right to equality under Article 33 of the Constitution. Specifically, he argued that, because the exclusion of some individuals on the basis of hepatitis B status under the provincial regulations lacked "rationality, appropriateness, or necessity" and because it was not connected to any "government, public, or societal interest," those provisions violated the constitutional principle of equality.[82] This argument is key in that it attempts to render Article 33 operational by creating a "rational basis" test by which government regulations could be scrutinized.

Zhou also argued that, because the physical exam regulations lacked a sufficient legislative basis, they undercut the NPC's constitutional duty to administer the country according to law under Article 2(3) of the Constitution. Additionally, they infringed the exclusive authority to legislate on matters affecting citizens' rights and interests allocated to the NPC under Article 8(5) of the Legislative Law. Finally, Zhou asserted that the local government had infringed Zhang's right to work under Article 42 of the Constitution, and his right to personal dignity under Article 38 of the Constitution.

Perhaps with an eye to future legislative debates within the halls of government, Zhou also provided extensive arguments as to why the standard applied by the provincial regulations was, in fact, irrational. Zhou pointed out, for example, that the exclusion of individuals with

80 Court submission, Zhang Xianzhu v. Personnel Affairs Bureau of Wuhu, November 18, 2003, reprinted in Zhou Wei, supra note 77, at pp. 330–331. The provincial regulations were geared toward excluding individuals who had active hepatitis, which can be more easily transmitted to others.

81 Id. at pp. 332–333.

82 Id. at p. 338.

hepatitis B from employment lacked a sound basis in medical science, given that hepatitis B is generally not communicable in an office environment and therefore creates no risk for the employee's colleagues. Zhang also argued that the exclusion lacked a basis in "social reality"; given that roughly 10 percent of the Chinese population is infected with hepatitis B, it would be impossible to isolate more than 120 million people from the rest of the population.

Zhou also put forward a detailed argument regarding the court's jurisdiction over the case under the Administrative Litigation Law, which the court accepted as part of its ruling.

The court issued its ruling to a crowded courtroom on April 2, 2004. It declined to find that the local regulations were in conflict with either national regulations or the Constitution. Instead, it found that the provincial health test standards were created in accordance with the State Council's National Civil Servant Temporary Regulations and neither went beyond the scope of the Temporary Regulations nor violated any specific prohibition found in those regulations. The court, however, did find that the People's Liberation Army No. 86 Hospital failed to adhere fully to the provincial standards in reaching the conclusion that Zhang's health was substandard. Therefore, the court held that the local personnel bureau's adoption of that conclusion and its decision to remove Zhang from the recruitment process lacked a factual basis. However, given that the recruitment period had ended and the job had been filled by the second person on the list, the court held that it was powerless to order any remedy.[83] Zhang had won a symbolic victory, but he left the courtroom as he started, with no job and no court order compelling the local personnel bureau to give him one.[84]

Perhaps unsurprisingly, the court did not rule on the constitutional arguments put forward by Zhou, although it did note in its decision that Zhou had raised constitutional claims to equality, the right to work, and the right to privacy.[85] Overall, the court's approach was moderate; it did not review the viability of the provincial rule itself. Instead, it merely found problems with its application to Zhang. Although the court's mention of the plaintiff's constitutional rights claims can be interpreted as a tacit embrace of the idea that constitutional rights should be justiciable,

[83] Zhang Xianzhu, in Zhou Wei, supra note 77, at pp. 355–356. The court did, however, order the defendant to pay RMB 100 in court costs.

[84] The local personnel bureau appealed the decision, but the decision was upheld in a one-paragraph decision issued by the Wuhu City Intermediate People's Court on May 13, 2004. Zhou Wei, supra note 77, at pp. 384–385.

[85] Zhang Xianzhu, in Zhou Wei, supra note 77, at p. 354.

nonetheless the court's failure to grapple more explicitly and meaningfully with the constitutional arguments put forward by Zhou undercuts the claims by some scholars that the *Zhang Xianzhu* case is an important *constitutional* case.

Some scholars have argued that the *Zhang Xianzhu* case represents a missed opportunity. If the court had found the provincial regulations to be without basis in national law, then the court could have reached out to the Constitution to see if the regulations passed constitutional muster instead of merely declaring the regulations invalid.[86] Assuming it agreed with Zhou's arguments about the viability of the regulations under China's equal protection clause, the court could then have declared the regulations inoperative because of the constitutional conflict. In so doing, the court certainly would have exposed itself to potential political risk, but it would have created, as well, the possibility for a breakthrough moment in China's constitutional development. Such a decision would have been the first time that an administrative rule had been declared inapplicable on constitutional grounds.[87]

4.2. *After* Zhang: *Legislation, Litigation, and Social Awareness*

Although the court ruled in favor of Zhang, it neither prescribed a remedy nor ruled on the constitutional arguments presented by Zhou. Nonetheless, the fact that the court ruled in Zhang's favor was viewed as a victory, and the verdict in the case received nationwide attention.[88] The April

[86] Author interview (September 17, 2007).

[87] It is possible that the risk created by such a decision would have been somewhat less than the pressure created in the small number of cases – including the famous "seed case" – in which local courts declared invalid laws created by local people's congresses that conflict with national law. In the *Zhang Xianzhu* case, the normative document in question was an administrative regulation, one that, presumably, the local government and the local people's congress had little interest in protecting. Whether or not there would be any difference between the political furor generated by the seed case and the circumstances presented by the *Zhang* case is, of course, an open question, given that no court has yet openly invalidated an administrative regulation due to conflicts with constitutional norms. For more on the seed case, see Jim Yardley, "A Judge Tests China's Courts, Making History," *New York Times*, November 28, 2005.

[88] Zhang himself told a journalist after the verdict that the final outcome of the case was less important than the attention that his lawsuit brought to the issue. Speaking to a reporter from the *Yangcheng Evening News*, Zhang said: "Actually, even before the verdict was announced, I already felt that the final result of the lawsuit was unimportant. The case had already gotten the attention of NPC representatives, the media, medical doctors, and various segments of society, and the country had already begun to take this problem seriously." *Secluded Life*, supra note 74.

2004 verdict has been widely discussed in academic and professional legal circles and is regarded, generally, as one of China's first successful constitutional litigation cases. Other lawyers following in Zhou Wei's footsteps have brought more than thirty hepatitis B discrimination cases, against both private and public actors, in cities across China in the four years since the *Zhang* verdict was announced.

The case, with the public attention it garnered, had several effects: First, it helped to galvanize and strengthen a nascent social movement, which itself would play a key role in continuing to push the issue, both in the courts and in society as a whole. Second, the case brought significant media attention to the issue for the first time, thus creating public pressure for a response from the government. Finally, the case captured the attention of senior government officials, who demanded an immediate response from the bureaucracy. The relevant ministries responded with new rules to limit the ability of local governments to make personnel decisions on the basis of hepatitis B status.

Had the *Zhang Xianzhu* case begun and ended with Zhang himself, it would have been an important, if limited, victory. Zhang had his day in court; still, by framing his plight as a constitutional antidiscrimination issue, he managed to reach a nationwide audience. Moreover, Zhang's case also served as an important progenitor of a small wave of follow-up litigation, focused on both public and private actors and bent on the attempt to force employers to change their hiring practices related to hepatitis B carriers.

Between 2002 and 2007, more than forty hepatitis B discrimination cases have been filed against a range of defendants, including, as in the *Zhang* case, public sector employers, private sector employers, and public schools and universities. Taken as a whole, the litigation presents some interesting dynamics. First, the cases have sprung up nationwide, in locales as diverse as Shanghai, Beijing, Xinjiang, and rural Anhui. The defendants also represent a wide range of actors, both governmental and nongovernmental, indicating both the scope of the problem and the vibrancy of the litigation response.

More recent cases against private employers, many of them in China's booming southern provinces, indicate a change in the stakes of the game: Whereas earlier litigation was focused more on securing the right of the individual to return to work or school, the more recent cases have made significant claims for emotional damages, often as high as several hundred thousand *yuan*. Whether these significantly larger damage claims will have a positive or negative impact on litigation going forward is as yet unclear. Significant monetary awards, if indeed they are granted by the courts, could create far greater incentives for pursuing hepatitis B discrimination litigation, leading to more cases and, possibly, greater compliance by employers. On the other hand, the introduction of large sums into these cases could submerge the constitutional and social justice goals that were an integral part of the overall strategy, as first articulated by Zhou Wei and others.

Perhaps the most tangible result of the *Zhang Xianzhu* case was the relatively quick regulatory response from the government. Government officials publicly acknowledged the influence that both the *Zhang* case and the Zhou Yichao tragedy had on Beijing's decision to act:

> The 2003 Zhejiang *Zhou Yichao* case and the Anhui *Zhang Xianzhu* case caused people to pay attention to the health examination standards for civil servants and led to a multifaceted discussion. Senior leaders within the State Council attached great importance to this issue and issued specific orders, asking the personnel bureau, in coordination with other relevant bureaus, to research the question and put forward some suggestions for reform. After that, the personnel bureau and the Ministry of Health got in touch and started the work of drafting the notice and standards on physical examinations for recruitment of civil servants.[89]

Some observers have analyzed the government response to such litigation in constitutional terms:

> When courts accept hepatitis B cases, this can lead state and society, including both legislative and administrative organs, to pay significant attention to the problem and spur the legislature to take seriously the authoritative position of the Constitution, and also to take seriously the specificity and the actual protectiveness of constitutional basic rights provisions. Such cases can also spur administrative agencies to comprehensively and thoroughly discuss their own behavior, and to change quickly those discriminatory practices that violate the spirit of equality of the Constitution. To do so would realistically establish the idea of putting people first in public administration.[90]

In the wake of this case, provincial governments in Zhejiang, Sichuan, Fujian, Guangdong, and elsewhere began to revise their regulations in

89 *China Personnel News*, http://www.rensb.com/showarticle.php?articleID=343 (accessed November 11, 2008).

90 "Applause for the Court Accepting the 'Hepatitis B Discrimination Case,'" *Southern Metropolitan Daily* (Guangzhou).

light of the court's holding.[91] The first response from the central government on hepatitis B was a revision, in August 2004, of the Law on the Prevention and Control of Infectious Diseases. The government added a provision prohibiting discrimination against "individuals with infectious diseases, infectious disease carriers, or those suspected of having infectious diseases."[92]

A more direct response to the *Zhang* case was the provision of new national regulations, issued jointly by the Ministry of Health and the Ministry of Personnel, regarding medical examinations for public servants. Under the new regulations, circulated for public comment in August 2004[93] and then issued in January 2005, hepatitis B carriers are specifically declared to be eligible for employment, subject to additional testing to confirm that their hepatitis is not "active."[94] The issuance of these regulations marked the first time the national government had put forward comprehensive and unified standards for physical exams for public sector recruitment.[95]

Most recently, in August 2007, NPCSC passed the Employment Promotion Law,[96] which explicitly bans discrimination against both employees and job seekers, thereby eliminating an ambiguity in prior law by clearly covering job seekers who had yet to enter into an employment relationship with their prospective employer.

The Employment Promotion Law's focus on discrimination against individuals with infectious diseases was brought about by, in part,

91 "'The First Hepatitis B Case' Continues: Local Government Bureaus Amend Their Regulations," *China Youth Daily*, April 5, 2004.

92 Law on Prevention and Control of Infectious Diseases, Art. 16 (adopted at the 6th Meeting of the Standing Committee of the Seventh National People's Congress on February 21, 1989.
(P.R.C.). The Law was revised on August 28, 2004.

93 Chang Ailing, "Chinese Government Adopting Measures to Protect the Rights and Interests of Hepatitis B Pathogen Carriers," *Xinhua*, August 10, 2004.

94 National Standards for Medical Exams for Public Servants (promulgated jointly by the Ministry of Health and the Ministry of Personnel, January 20, 2005) (P.R.C.). Article 7 reads as follows:

> Various types of serious, chronic cases of hepatitis, such cases are not standard. For hepatitis B carriers, once they have been tested to eliminate the possibility of active hepatitis, then they are standard.

95 "Casting Aside "Hepatitis Discrimination" Reflects Respect for Popular Will," *Xin Jing Bao* (Beijing News), August 2, 2004, http://tech.163.com/04/0802/10/0SP95LOG0009153U.html. According to the *Beijing News*'s analysis, the new standards reflected government responsiveness to the will of the people, which was itself reflected in the public's response to the *Zhang Xianzhu* case. Id.

96 Employment Promotion Law (issued by the National People's Congress Standing Committee, August 30, 2007, effective January 1, 2008) (P.R.C.).

extensive commentary from the public, organized by NGOs dedicated to public health issues, all of which were calling for the inclusion of such provisions in the final version of the law.[97] Active public participation in the legal drafting process – the NPCSC received thousands of comments and suggestions from the public on the draft law during the comment period, many of them related to public health discrimination – was crucial to the inclusion of strong antidiscrimination provisions in the text of the law itself.

5. CONCLUSION: FURTHER BARRIERS AHEAD?

The wave of lawsuits generated in the aftermath of the *Zhang Xianzhu* case is, in itself, a form of progress. Whereas in 2003, constitutional law scholar Wang Lei was able to identify thirty-three "constitutional" cases since the beginning of the reform era, since 2002, more than forty hepatitis B discrimination cases have been brought in courts throughout China, many of them making constitutional rights arguments. In addition, dozens of other cases making a range of rights claims have been brought across China.[98]

The proliferation of rights-based cases in recent years may have been a factor in the government's decision to tighten controls on civil society, in particular on those lawyers and civil society groups who have taken the lead in bringing constitutional cases to court.

The most serious blow came in July 2009 with the shuttering of the Beijing-based Open Constitutional Initiative, also known by its Chinese name, Gongmeng. On July 17, Beijing City tax authorities presented Gongmeng with a bill of roughly $200,000, which included both unpaid taxes and heavy penalties for nonpayment. The government claimed that Gongmeng had failed to pay taxes on grants made to the organization by Yale University; the tax charges were seen by many as politically motivated.[99] Xu Zhiyong, the founder of Gongmeng and a leading *weiquan*, or rights-defending, lawyer in Beijing, was taken into custody soon after the tax allegations came to light. He was released on August 23, 2009, after a concerted international campaign on his behalf by both

[97] "Public Responds to Draft Employment Law," *Xinhua*, April 5, 2007.

[98] Zhou Wei and Li Cheng, *The Constitution in Court: Equality, Freedom, and Anti-Discrimination Public Interest Litigation* (unpublished manuscript, on file with author).

[99] Edward Wong, "China Shuts Down Office of Volunteer Lawyers," *New York Times*, July 18, 2009.

Western governments and international human rights NGOs.[100] Xu also lost his teaching post at the Beijing University of Post and Telecommunications in the wake of his nearly month-long detention.

Xu and his Gongmeng colleagues have attempted to continue the work of the organization even though the organization itself no longer exists. However, the loss of an institutional home and platform did take a toll on Xu and his colleagues' cutting-edge rights litigation work.

Also in July 2009, police raided the Beijing offices of Yirenping, which had been centrally involved in the Hepatitis B antidiscrimination litigation described above. Authorities confiscated copies of an antidiscrimination newsletter put out by the organization, claiming that the organization had not obtained the proper permit for such a publication and was therefore engaging in illegal activity. Although it managed to avoid closure, Yirenping's difficulties with the government continued in early 2010, at which time it was subjected to a prolonged investigation regarding its activities and tax status.[101]

Perhaps the most surprising development was the closure of the Beijing University Center for Women's Law Studies and Legal Services by Beijing University officials in March 2010.[102] Long a fixture of China's public interest law scene, the Center, founded in 1995 by leading rights lawyer and activist Guo Jianmei, received word from the university in 2009 that there were concerns about the Center's work. Negotiations with the university regarding the Center's status failed to yield a solution, and the University posted an announcement on its Web site on March 25 that the Center was being closed.

Although the Beijing University Center was less active in constitutional litigation, it was a key player in public interest litigation more generally and also served as an important training ground for more mainstream public interest lawyers, whose work very much complements the more controversial cases taken on by *weiquan* lawyers like Xu Zhiyong. Its closure was seen by many in China as a signal of the government's increasing wariness of innovative rights-based litigation of all kinds and of the difficulties in pursuing such work in an ever more precarious legal and political environment.

[100] Jane Macartney, "Campaigning lawyer Xu Zhiyong released after arrest for tax evasion," *Times of London*, August 23, 2009.

[101] Peter Ford, "Law chokes Chinese NGOs' foreign funding," *Christian Science Monitor*, May 20, 2010.

[102] Keith B. Richburg, "China's crackdown on nonprofit groups prompts new fears among activists," *The Washington Post*, May 11, 2010.

Even as various organizations experience difficulties, however, lawyers across China continue to bring cases which push new and innovative constitutional theories into Chinese courts. Yet the success, in recent years, of some of the lawsuits that have been brought are indicative of the limits of the current strategy that legal advocates have adopted. Although some lawsuits have been successful in terms of generating real and ongoing legislative change to more effectively protect the rights of individuals, neither the courts nor the government have responded in any significant way to the constitutional arguments that lawyers and activists have raised. In other words, the lawyers bringing these cases have yet to make any progress – beyond, of course, the important success of stirring public debate – in the pursuit of the transformative structural constitutional goals that are very much at the heart of their work.

In that sense, it can be said that the scholars and activists pushing the judicialization concept thus far have fallen short of their goal of "legalizing" the Constitution. Obstacles abound: The orthodox understanding of the Constitution that excludes its judicial enforcement still maintains its adherents within the highest reaches of government. More importantly, the party may be reluctant to bind itself to constitutional norms to which it is not yet ready to adhere. Yet in spite of these barriers, judicialization advocates have managed to infuse the Constitution with a symbolic value and a rhetorical force it did not have in the early years of the reform era.

It is possible that, over time, this newly generated rhetorical force will change expectations within China regarding the Constitution's fundamental nature and purpose. The constitutional arguments advanced by reformist scholars and lawyers have gained traction, to some degree, because they have resonated with at least some judges, an unknown number of government officials, and the general public. If more and more Chinese citizens begin to see constitutional rights as both relevant to their own lives and legally enforceable, then the government may face growing public pressure to respond with more far-reaching reforms.[103]

This slowly evolving transformation in public consciousness – though a far cry from the broad structural changes repeatedly proposed – may be the most significant contribution of the scholars, lawyers, and activists

[103] For an analysis of constitutional petition mechanisms that links progress on constitutional development to the party-state's search for legitimacy, see Keith J. Hand, "Citizens Engage the Constitution: The Sun Zhigang Incident and Constitutional Review Proposals in the People's Republic of China." In *Building Constitutionalism in China*, ed. Stephanie Balme and Michael Dowdle (The Sciences Po Series in International Relations and Political Economy; 2009, New York: Palgrave Macmillan), pp. 221–242.

who have been pushing for judicialization. At present, most observers do not believe that the government has constitutional development on its near-term agenda.[104] For many, constitutional development in China seems to have stalled. Given the apparent lack of political support within the government for constitutional reform, the next step for reformist scholars and lawyers may be to find ways to build on the evolving public consciousness, to deepen the public understanding of constitutional values, and to broaden the extent of public support for meaningful change.

[104] Thomas E. Kellogg and Keith Hand, "NPCSC: The Vanguard of China's Constitution?" *China Brief*, January 17, 2008, p. 4, http://www.jamestown.org/single/?no_cache=1&tx_ttnews%5Btt_news%5D=4666.

Conclusion: Chinese Justice from the Bottom Up

Margaret Y. K. Woo

The Old Latin maxim *ex oriente lux, ex occidente lex* (from the East, light; from the West, law) evinces a deep assumption about the relationship between the East and law – that is, although civilization began in the East, the West is the source of rationality and law. Indeed, much of this assumption lies in present-day "rule of law" programs as they are often transported from the West to transitional economies in the East and South. Rule of law, with its rationality and predictability, is said to be fundamental to a market economy. Its ability to check abusive arbitrary powers is believed to go hand in hand with democratic polities. Pointing to today's industrial democracies, reformers have concluded that rule of law is necessary for economic development and political liberalization.

Yet the challenges to these assumptions are numerous, ranging from whether there is such an East/West divide and, if so, whether the East is really antithetical to law; to the definition of "rule of law" itself and whether legal institutions are indeed transplantable. Furthermore, even as the rule of law has become a new rallying cry for global missionaries, reformers recognize that the rule of law is an exceedingly elusive notion. If "it is not already firmly in place, the rule of law appears mysteriously difficult to establish."[1]

In its thirty years of economic reforms, China has challenged the pairing of law, markets, and democracy. Its "socialism with Chinese characteristics" strategy maintains tight political control while allowing economic freedom in the marketplace. Similarly, the thirty years of legal reforms now permit law and legal institutions to handle civil and economic disputes, but they must steer clear of political disputes. Scholars

[1] Brian Z. Tamanaha, *On the Rule of Law: History, Politics, Theory* (Cambridge and New York: Cambridge University Press, 2004), p. 4.

critical of Chinese legal reforms correctly point to the limits on judicial independence and the top-down state control of the legal profession as obstacles to the "rule of law." In addition to ideological influences, Chinese courts are said to suffer from a host of practical problems, such as lack of trained personnel, limited funding, and a restrictive bureaucratic structure. This has led some scholars to refer to Chinese legal reforms as a "bird in the cage."[2]

Nor is the history of courts in authoritarian countries encouraging to Chinese legal reformers hoping for political liberalization. Courts in authoritarian countries are known to primarily serve state goals – whether maintaining social control, legitimating the regime, or controlling administrative agents and maintaining elite cohesion.[3] Authoritarian regimes establish courts to check low-level corruption and bureaucratic arbitrariness but, at the same time, suppress local dissent and bolster the credibility of the central regime. Arguably, authoritarian regimes and courts go hand in hand, but primarily to serve state goals.

Yet, despite the difficulties with the Chinese legal reforms, official statistics reveal that ordinary citizens are using the legal system at a growing rate. For example, in 1995, more than 2 million (2,718,533) civil lawsuits were accepted for adjudication by Chinese courts, a 14.04 percent increase from 1994. As late as 2006, the number of lawsuits filed by Chinese lawyers, though not as high as in the mid-1990s, was still increased by 54 percent from 2001. Chinese civil cases are primarily in the areas of family law, debt, and housing, with personal injury cases increasing by a whopping 60 percent from the late 1990s to 2003.[4] These cases, representing the daily and immediate contested values of a society in transition, deal with conflicts in personal interactions – between family, friends, and neighbors.

[2] *See* Stanley B. Lubman, *Bird in a Cage: Legal Reform in China after Mao* (Stanford: Stanford University Press, 1999).

[3] Tom Ginsburg and Tamir Moustafa, eds., *Rule By Law: The Politics of Courts in Authoritarian Regimes* (Cambridge: Cambridge University Press, 2008). The World Bank reports that, since 1990, it has spent $2.9 billion and has supported 330 rule of law projects. David M. Trubek, "*The 'Rule of Law' in Development Assistance: Past, Present, and Future.*" In *The New Law and Economic Development*, ed. David M. Trubek and Alvaro Santos (Cambridge: Cambridge University Press, 2006), p. 74.

[4] In 2003, the Supreme People's Court also noted that contract cases increased by 9 percent, divorce and family law cases increased by 5 percent, commercial cases increased by 39 percent, and administrative appeals increased by 65 percent, but labor cases increased by only 1.7 percent See *Zuigao renmin fayuan gongzuo baogao* (Supreme People's Court Work Report), March 11, 2003, http://www.people.com.cn/GB/shizheng/19/20030322/950241.html (accessed December 15, 2010).

This jump in the use of courts by Chinese citizens is perhaps unsurprising. Economic reforms are clearly fueling tensions and conflicts in Chinese society. Laid-off workers protest the misuse of company assets by managers in the newly privatized economy, and farmers are angered by unbearable taxes and land confiscations by callous officials. Chinese citizens are using the courts as dispute-resolution mechanisms as the influence of the *danwei* and the neighborhood committees is dwindling.[5] A recent frank report by a research group under the Central Committee of the Chinese Communist Party (CCP) describes concern about the spread of "collective protests and group incidents" arising from greater economic inequities and official corruption.[6] Party officials, worried that the masses are "tense, with conflicts on the rise," are calling for a strengthening of the legal system. Acknowledging that victims of change must be fairly compensated, Chinese officials hope that limited use of the legal system will diffuse the escalating social tensions.

Although the need for law is great, the use of law and the legal system by Chinese citizens has followed an uneasy path. In the 1990s, the Chinese state encouraged the use of the formal courts by private citizens and placed greater emphasis on promoting the neutrality of adjudicators. Hoping that courts can assist in stabilizing society and reining in local bureaucrats, the Supreme People's Court (SPC) decreed that Chinese courts should "further improve the work of trying civil cases, protect the civil rights and interests of citizens and legal persons according to the law, and promote the just, safe, civilized, and healthy development of society."[7] More recent fears of instability, however, have resulted in a return to an emphasis on mediatory and conciliation methods, greater consideration of the social and political context of cases, and greater state control of courts and the judiciary.

After taking office in March 2008, new SPC President Wang Shengjun retracted the path set forth by his predecessor Xiao Yang. He shifted the

[5] Andrew G. Walder, "The Decline of Communist Power: Elements of a Theory of Institutional Change," *Theory and Society* 23 (April 1994): 297–323; Yu Xie, Qing Lai, and Xiaogang Wu, "*Danwei* and Social Inequality in Contemporary Urban China." In *Research in the Sociology of Work*, ed. Nina Bandelj (Greenwich, Conn.: JAI Press, 2009), vol. 19, pp. 283–306.

[6] Erik Eckholm, "China's Inner Circle Reveals Big Unrest, and Lists Causes," *New York Times*, June 3, 2001, p. 8.

[7] "Supreme People's Court Work Report," delivered by Supreme People's Court President Ren Jianxin at the Fourth Session of the Eighth National People's Congress in Beijing, Xinhua news agency, 12 Mar 96 in *BBC Summary of World Broadcasts Part 3 Asia-Pacific*, 9 Apr 96, p. S1.

role of the courts as neutral adjudicators, calling on judges to consider the "three Supremes" in judicial decision making – the supremacy of party work, the supremacy of the people's interests, and the supremacy of the Constitution and the law. As China approaches its thirtieth year of legal reform, China's justice minister declared that above all, lawyers should obey the Communist Party and help foster a harmonious society. To improve discipline, the minister added, party liaisons should be sent to all law firms in China to "guide their work."[8]

Apart from top-down dictates, how the thirty years of legal reform have fared in China depends largely on how law has been received by ordinary Chinese citizens and how these citizens have utilized the legal system. Has the wavering course of legal reforms in China empowered citizens, or has it served only state goals? Is the present retrenchment short-lived or, on the flip side of the same question, have the thirty years of legal reforms penetrated Chinese legal culture?

The authors in this volume present a complex picture of law reforms in China by focusing on on-the-ground implementation of the reforms. The chapters in this volume examine the role of legal institutions and actors in adapting and diffusing norms introduced through top-down reforms and the concomitant complex indigenous grassroots responses. Equally important, the chapters illustrate the importance of empirical work and the disaggregation of data that is so necessary to clarify the picture for a country as vast and diverse as China.

Several preliminary conclusions can be drawn from these chapters, offering insights into both China's specific adaptations of rule of law and, more generally, how rule of law occurs. First, institutions do matter, but they exist in a broad interdependent matrix, the dynamics of which cannot be ignored, particularly as they play out in the local context. It is the local site that diffuses top-down norms and the local context that provides the direct incentives or disincentives to legal actors in implementing reforms. Second, historical legacy is important for legal reformers, because it reaches deep into the memories of ordinary citizens and colors their receptivity to changes within the legal system. But even as historical memories can influence the legal culture, the culture is further

[8] Human Rights Watch, "Guiding Opinions of the All China Lawyers Association on Lawyers Handling Mass Cases," http://china.hrw.org/timeline/2006/a_great_danger_for_lawyers/appendix_i_guiding_opinions_of_the_all_china_lawyers_associ (accessed December 16, 2010);); *see also* "China: Curbs on Lawyers Could Intensify Social Unrest," December 12, 2006, http://www.hrw.org/en/news/2006/12/11/china-curbs-lawyers-could-intensify-social-unrest (accessed December 16, 2010).

defined by actual experiences with the legal system, and, importantly, by an individual's status within the system. As such, expectations can outpace actual experience, and the resulting disappointment engendered can undermine any reform progress. Third, formal legal process can create greater predictability but, if ossified, can impede democratic development. When legal reforms are not structured to encourage greater participation by those trying to use the system, formal legality can be a barrier leading popular voices back into the streets and to channels outside the system.

As a whole, the chapters in this volume underscore the constant tug and pull between historical determinism and actual experiences on legal culture, the potential fragmentation of diffuse sources of law, and, finally, the growing technical alienation and the danger of high levels of unmet expectations facing Chinese citizens today. Excessive formalism can be counterproductive absent the mediating forces of democratic legal professionals, whether lawyers or judges – those professionals trained not only in law but also in representation that gives greater voice to ordinary citizens.

INSTITUTIONAL DYNAMICS, LEGAL CULTURE, AND HISTORICAL LEGACY

The history of Chinese legal reform cannot be explained by a simple unidirectional trajectory. Indeed, the thirty years of Chinese legal reform have wavered between informality and mediation to more formality and adjudication and now back again. This is confirmed by the careful analysis of state policy documents (see Chapter 1) and the historical tracing of popular legal publications (see Chapter 8). In Chapter 1, Fu and Cullen point out that, although the first ten years (1979–1989) of China's legal reforms saw the enactment of substantive legislation, the next ten years (the 1990s) saw greater attention to improvements in the legal process, and in the last ten years (the 2000s), there has been a return to a focus on informality and mediation. Although this fluctuation can be explained by top-down policies by the CCP, it can also be explained by institutional dynamics and clarified by local institutional interplay. Indeed, top-down policies have no bite absent implementation by local legal institutions.

By legal institutions, I refer to those bodies (formal and informal) charged by society to make, administer, enforce, or adjudicate its laws or policies. Many of the international law reform projects of the 1990s relied on the arguments of Douglass North and other new institutional economists to focus on the legal institutional framework as the basis for creating incentives for changes in behavior.[9] But rule of law projects have largely been state-centric, with a special emphasis on elite state actors implementing top-down change, mostly by transplanting institutions wholesale from other countries. By contrast, the authors in this volume point out that a focus on institutions must take into account the social context within which these institutions operate, their interactions with other institutions, and the idea that there are multiple competing sites for law in China today. Most importantly, the authors note the importance of localized grassroots efforts that often can serve as the basis for more enduring legal change.

Thus, as Fu and Cullen pointed out in Chapter 1, much of the second phase of Chinese legal reform is traceable to the SPC, which has proven to be a stubborn institution that has spearheaded many procedural initiatives. However, even as the SPC switched gears to refocus attention on mediation, the response has been strategic reporting by on the ground actors, such as by grassroots courts who "count cases that have been withdrawn by plaintiffs as cases mediated. In doing so, judges appear to have embraced the rhetoric of mediation and at the same time diluted its impact." Similarly, Minzner notes in Chapter 2 that, despite some far-reaching reforms implemented by the SPC, local provincial regulations on promotions and punishment of judges can serve as a disincentive for judicial independence and hamper reform at the local level. Judges in China, like judges everywhere, are as affected by their immediate career advancement as they are by broad political campaigns in completing their judicial work.

Furthermore, institutions have a way of building up momentum on their own and in interaction with one another in surprising ways. For example, in Chapter 3, Douglas Glob demonstrates that it is the bottom-level implementation of the top-down reforms that matters. It is local *fazhi ban* (FZB) (legal-affairs offices) that exercise a gatekeeping and agenda-setting influence over rule making, mediate administrative conflicts that arise between government organs, and also emphasize, implement, and enforce administrative procedure. Thus, it is these local offices that actually give meaning to the top-down initiatives and adapt such initiatives to local conditions. Such local legal offices serve the (as yet unexamined) function of bridging national laws with local norms.

It is the tensions and interactions between institutions such as the *fazhi ban* and the *sifa si or sifa ting* (justice departments) that critically affect

[9] *See* Trubek, "The 'Rule of Law' in Development Assistance: Past, Present and Future," 74.

how law is actually implemented at the local levels. Indeed, the *fazhi ban/sifa ting* rivalry appears to have the potential to propel legal development and make it more self-enforcing. The FZB's authority has expanded as its role has grown in rule making and in mediating the "legality gap" at the local level. Institutional rivalry between local FZBs and local justice departments may contribute to the development of legal institutions at the grassroots level. Because legal resources are scarce in some localities, such rivalry, despite existing budget constraints, has spurred legal activities and served the role of bringing law to the grassroots.

However, such institutional vibrancy may lead to problems as well as solutions. In China, there is always the danger of fragmentation and local protectionalism. Legal and normative pluralism can also lead to the fragmentation of the state into competing agencies and competing levels of government. There is "justice," or at least legality, in many institutions: In China, this can be the procuracy, the courts, governmental and legislative legal affairs offices, legal services and "justice offices," and the providers of mediation and arbitration. Disputants resort to different legal, normative, and coalitional enforcement mechanisms depending on their perceptions of each office's receptivity to their claims. But unless there is coherence among these different institutional sites, such diverse fora may lead to a sense of bifurcated justice.

Multiple institutions and sites may increase efficiency by funneling different disputes to different fora, but as disputants receive varying resolutions for the same dispute, the differing outcomes may compromise consistency and undermine the legitimacy of the legal system as a whole. Furthermore, such a system may provide specialized tribunals to those with sufficient political clout, thus benefiting those who are already privileged within the system and, in the process, instilling a greater sense of inequality. In sum, institutions matter, but in the specific contexts of their interactions with one another. Reformers must be cognizant of the need to understand the multifaceted effects of local as well as national institutional change.

HISTORICAL CONTEXT OR HISTORICAL DETERMINISM?

If context matters, how much does it matter? Political economists have long emphasized the centrality of path dependency in the evolution of social institutions. That is, institutional reforms are never written on a tabula rasa; rather, they operate within a complex set of historical particularities – economic, political, and social – that continue to shape the evolution of the existing institutions. These historical particularities impact the nature and scope of feasible institutional reforms. The authors in this volume give added weight to the idea that China's reformers must pay special attention to the historical context. If Pierre Landry and, to a large extent, Carl Minzner are correct, legal reforms in China will not mimic those in the West but will take on an entirely different formulation as an offshoot of China's historical past.

Landry's research argues that legal memories can occur across generations through socialization in the household or in the community where historical experiences are retained. Such memories shape the legal culture, and reforms work better in communities with favorable historical memories of the existing legal institutions. In Chapter 5, Landry's findings in his nationwide survey demonstrate that villagers' memories are long and that legal institutions with roots in the early Maoist era and Nationalist legacies are viewed with more optimism than those without such roots. During the early years of the People's Republic, state institutions were viewed with great respect, and this legacy endures to color Chinese citizens' views of legal institutions today. Landry's data further challenge the general assumption that villagers prefer informal to formal legal mechanisms and that displacing such preferences will be more difficult in the rural areas than in the urban areas. Landry finds that rural villagers with positive memories of formal legal institutions by and large express a preference for formal state dispute-resolution mechanisms.

Similarly, Minzner, viewing the Chinese judiciary as informed by the Chinese imperial civil service system, concludes that even modern legal institutions maintain traces from the imperial past. As during imperial times, the Chinese judiciary today is subject to an elaborate grid of locally set incentives and discipline. Chinese judges are promoted or demoted depending on a point system that takes into consideration job performance, number of cases processed, and number of reversals of decisions, as well as judicial misconduct. The Chinese system of discipline and promotion means that Chinese judges are under constant pressures to avoid adjudicating cases that may be reversed, as their pay and promotion largely depend on the efficient and "correct" resolution of disputes.

Although some scholars attribute this discipline and promotion system to socialist tradition, Minzner points to the traditional Chinese distrust of formal legality and the imperial system of treating magistrates as civil servants within an immense bureaucracy. Because of the close supervision of their work, Chinese judges are more risk adverse and tend to seek upper-level approval prior to rendering judgments, if they render any judgments at all. This result is neither an independent nor efficient system of justice. With roots stretching back to the imperial civil service system, Chinese judges continue to act as bureaucrats in a governmental system charged with processing disputes rather than as independent adjudicators determining right from wrong.

Undeniably, Chinese courts and the law are tied to tradition, with the Chinese legal system often drawing on both its socialist and Confucian past. Cultural receptivity to legal reforms is shaped by institutional memory, and reform efforts are offspring of historical traditions. For Landry, the general population's trust in legal institutions can be traced not to the recent reforms, but to the longevity of legal institutions in Chinese history. For Minzner, judicial reforms are also limited by their historical roots. Thus, if the historical legal culture that informs the norms and expectations of legal actors is at odds with the new legal culture imposed by rule of law reforms, displacing these habits and interests may be more realistic in new rather than in existing legal institutions. Unsurprisingly, reform finds more fertile soil if it can germinate to be consistent with historical legacies.

But what happens when a legal culture informed by historical legacy encounters actual present-day experiences? This is a topic of interest for Michelson and Read and for Gallagher and Wang. Several of the chapters in this book suggest problems for legal reform when expectations outpace reality and rhetoric is met with actual experience.

LEGAL CULTURE AS SHAPED BY ACTUAL EXPERIENCES

Whereas Landry and Minzner focus on the historical determinism underlying legal reforms in China, other authors in this volume emphasize the importance of legal culture as shaped by actual experiences. For these authors, judicial reform is only effective if it is being used and the reality today is that Chinese citizens are making use of the courts and using the language of "rights."

Indeed, although Chinese courts are used primarily to assert private socioeconomic rights against other private individuals, as in debt, contract, and family law cases, an increasing number of lawsuits are seeking greater structural change. China's lawyers are filing lawsuits over discrimination and poor labor conditions, and sometimes they do win (see Gallagher and Wang, Chapter 7; Kellogg, Chapter 11). After the 2008 massive earthquake that rocked Sichuan province and resulted in a loss of tens of thousands of lives and immense property damage, initially there was social unrest, followed, as in rights-based societies, by calls for litigation. With many citizens blaming local party officials for faulty construction, the survivors sought to sue the government.[10] At camps for survivors, volunteers distributed "law promotion" handbooks published by the Chengdu Justice Bureau to explain how to use the law to sue the government for building-code violations. It appeared that local governments preferred to face citizens in court rather than on the streets.

However, the details of Chinese citizens' experiences with the legal system are telling. First, the urban/rural divide that is so prominent in economic disparities seems to be replicated in Chinese legal institutions and culture (see Gallagher and Wang, Chapter 7; Michelson and Read, Chapter 6; and Landry, Chapter 5). But the verdict is still out regarding whether these disparities mean that rural disputants are more likely to trust official justice. In Chapter 6, Michelson and Read conclude that rural disputants are more likely to "lump" their disputes or utilize traditional administrative and/or neighborhood mediation and that they rate bilateral negotiations and informal relations as more trustworthy than official justice officials. By contrast, in those districts where the historical legacy of official justice is longer and more positive, Landry finds that rural disputants tend to trust official justice more than informal justice.

These differing results point to the importance of disaggregating data and to the need for further research. For one, the differing results may be explained by the different research sites. More significantly, however, the different conclusions may reflect the disparities between actual experiences and rising abstract expectations of the legal system and the collision of rural litigants' informed assessments with their uninformed expectations. Indeed, higher expectations, whether formed by legal propaganda or historical memory, may stall legal reforms. As Gallagher and Wang discovered, unrealistic expectations have far outpaced realistic reform efforts, leading to greater disenchantment. The closer one brings a legal dispute to the Chinese legal system, the less positively he or she will assess the experience.

Such a downbeat assessment of official justice by those who use the system is particularly understandable in those rural areas with limited funding for the courts. Rural residents who actually try to use the courts face high court fees and other related expenses that result in financial barriers to official justice. More economically developed areas, meanwhile, enjoy

[10] Geoffrey A. Fowler, Sky Canaves, and Juliet Ye, "Chinese Seek a Day in Court: With New Faith in Rule of Law, More Citizens File Suits," *Wall Street Journal*, July 1, 2008, p. A12.

greater geographical proximity to the courts and more resources, resulting in more favorable experiences and assessments by litigants. Rural areas with limited funds also may lack a positive historical legacy of legal institutions.

Indeed, even in areas with a positive historic legacy, Landry may have measured villagers' general perceptions of official justice, untested by actual experience. Landry's rural informants have high expectations in this instance, formed more by historical legacy and less by legal propaganda but nonetheless still untarnished by actual experience with the current legal system. It would have been informative to test the strength of historical legacy in the face of actual experience and vice versa. A return visit to either of these test sites would provide valuable information about the enduring factors of history and cultural change. Certainly, trust in the legal system in China is shaped as much by actual experience as by historical legacy and legal propaganda.

Furthermore, actual experience with and perceptions of the legal system also seem to depend on the litigants' insider/outsider status. In their study of labor litigants, Gallagher and Wang (see Chapter 7) conclude that older, urban disputants employed in the state sector are more likely to feel powerless and that younger, rural disputants employed in the non-state sector are more likely to embrace their legal experience. Older state workers are more inclined to stay within the system and petition the state for recourse, whereas younger, non-urban workers tend to resort to the legal system. Disenchantment is most profound among those who are relatively well-off and protected by the socialist system of employment, whereas those who remain on the outside by virtue of age or birthplace are more sanguine about the law. In other words, outsiders trust the legal system because it represents an opportunity to challenge the status quo.

If so, trust in the legal system will depend on legal propaganda, a positive historical legacy, and a litigant's own status within the legal system. Those who receive more propaganda, live in areas with a positive historical legacy of legal institutions, or live outside the status quo are more likely to resort to the legal system. However, the danger is that such greater awareness of rights and trust is be translated into higher expectations and greater disenchantment with the legal system when experiences do not comport with expectations. Rights consciousness raised through legal propaganda can create unrealistic expectations that are exacerbated by the unequal distribution of legal services. From a policy standpoint, rather than alleviating inequalities, the Chinese legal system may be replicating existing disparities and widening the urban/rural gap caused by market reforms. Although economic development can serve to raise expectations of official justice, economic development has and will continue to be uneven across China's vast geography, coloring in the different experiences of everyday litigants.

Until court performance improves or greater access to legal assistance is provided, rights education may be counterproductive, as the high expectations fueled by legal propaganda can backfire from unrealistic expectations, higher levels of disillusionment, and more negative perceptions of the legal system's effectiveness and fairness. Although a modest dose of distrust is needed for the health and well-being of rule of law systems by keeping them under constant scrutiny, high levels of disillusionment fueled by high expectations ultimately may undermine the legitimacy of the legal system and, by extension, the Chinese state.

LEGAL TECHNOCRATS OR LEGAL PROFESSIONALS?

If the legality and formality of the past thirty years of legal reforms have indeed led to greater "disenchantment," one final reason may be that law has not become an organic part of social life. According to Liu (see Chapter 8), formalistic law has become more technocratic, authoritative, and sometimes even incoherent. As such, formality has become a barrier to rights attainment rather than an equalizer enabling citizens to access justice. Legal technicalities can even legitimize state repression as long as the state acts "in accordance with the law." Formal processes in China have led to greater responsibilities for litigants, but absent greater legal assistance, those with more resources will be able to use legal niceties against those with fewer resources.

Indeed, even in light of recent shifting policy changes, it is important to note that the baseline for legal formality apparently has shifted. Liu's analysis reveals an overall shift from 1979 to 2003 toward a greater propensity by legal professionals to give technical legal answers in response to questions regarding civil disputes. For example, legal professionals in popular legal magazines are not reverting back to political responses. Rather, they are exuding an increased reverence for legal technicalities.

Although thirty years of legal reforms have meant greater legality and technical niceties, greater formal process unmatched by increased voice and access will not foster the ordinary citizen's sense of empowerment. Indeed, a rural litigant's negative view of the legal system can be explained in part by an inability to separate outcome from process, such that losing litigants have negative views of the legal system (see Michelson and Read,

Chapter 6). This is particularly true of older litigants who tend to judge their experience by distributive outcomes, whereas younger litigants seek improved procedures (see Gallagher and Wang, Chapter 7). But the "disenchanting" experiences of Chinese litigants may ultimately be explained by the ongoing lack of true procedural justice even after the thirty years of legal reform in the direction of greater formality.

Procedural justice is only valued when a disputant feels that he or she has been heard in the legal process. Rather than conflating substantive outcomes with procedural justice, Chinese litigants may not be receiving procedural justice if their experiences with the courts do not truly provide them with an opportunity to be heard. Chinese litigants' disappointment with the legal system cannot be attributed solely to not obtaining winning outcomes. Rather, litigants are disappointed with the legal system because they do not have a sense of participation in the process and do not feel that their stories have been heard.

From my own research, I have found that although litigants are more "rights" conscious and the litigation experience may be educational, few litigants feel a sense of participation in the process.[11] In my survey of sixty-four litigants in a Beijing legal-aid office in 2002, for example, the majority demonstrated a preference for rights and chose "enforced rights" as a preferred outcome, indicating a greater "rights" consciousness. By contrast, the option of "benefits to both sides" came in a distinct second, and only a very few respondents selected "restoring relationships" as their preferred outcome. But even though litigants are more rights conscious, more litigants perceive that they have little influence over the decision-making process. After the legal process, these same litigants reported a sense of greater self-respect but little sense of empowerment from the experience. Legal propaganda may have led to greater "rights" awareness and expectations in the legal process, but the turn to a more formal legal process has not necessarily added to a greater sense of participation for Chinese citizens.

A more formal process works if it can render the court process more transparent and predictable, even the playing field between judges and litigants, and increase participation by lawyers and litigants. At its most basic, a legal system relies on a process that will support "hearing the

[11] Margaret Y. K. Woo, "Law, Development and the Rights of Chinese Women: A Snapshot from the Field," *Columbia Journal of Asian Law* 19, no. 1 (spring–fall 2005): 345–360.

other side/*audi alteram partem*," whatever the subject matter. A process that allows both sides to be heard means a greater sense of democratic participation by litigants who have a hand in shaping state norms from the top, as they can argue how such norms may be applied to local conditions from below. Absent that kind of participation within the legal system, ordinary citizens are apt to go outside the system to seek their redress.

Chinese litigants, therefore, will and have gone outside the courts to apply popular pressure on the court with such strategies, continuing to challenge court reforms and professionalization of the judiciary. Where critics of Chinese legal reforms are more concerned with the influence of the CCP in politically sensitive cases, Ben Liebman returns our focus to the day-to-day popular and institutional pressures faced by Chinese courts. According to Liebman, professionalizing the judiciary alone is insufficient to establish judicial independence without an understanding of how the *xinfang* (letters and petitions) system and the less institutionalized methods of popular protest check the judicialization process in China.

Undoubtedly, Chinese courts today view popular opinion and individual protests as challenges to their authority, and , as Liebman points out, these courts may also be too responsive to popular pressures (see Chapter 9). When cases rise to the level of popular attention, either through the media or mass protests, Chinese judges will move beyond the legal technicalities and adjust their decisions to meet popular demand. Although this may serve as a necessary route to buffer the bluntness of legal technicalities, the problem is that when popular pressures change judicial outcomes, this change occurs through the media or mass protests rather than through the orderly presentation of information or through the deliberation of fair and open contestation that can be provided by court procedures. This makes for neither a predictable nor consistent legal system. Liebman thus concludes that "the determination of petitioners to pursue their grievances may reflect greater awareness of rights among litigants. But it also suggests that a system that is increasingly focused on rights will not necessarily lead to a system in which judges and courts are the central players, or make the final determinations."

In sum, not only are Chinese courts subject to political pressures, but surprisingly, they also are susceptible to popular pressures. Law reform efforts may add greater rights awareness, but such rights awareness has had the contrary effect of placing greater popular pressures on the courts, with the popular pressures checking the judicialization process.

Professionalization of the judiciary is important, but legal reformers also will do well to refocus their energies on popular rights education and to provide legal assistance to those seeking to assert rights and steer disputes properly within the legal system.

Indeed, true access to justice and greater participation by litigants require the assistance of independent and powerful mediating legal institutions – whether the judiciary or the bar – to navigate the legal system and to mediate between citizens and the state. Disenchantment with and alienation from the technicalities of the legal system can only be mitigated by constant contact with legal-aid staff, a supportive social network, and a less bureaucratic judiciary. There must be a sufficient number of these institutions so they are readily accessible to ordinary citizens. As important as actual numbers, legal experts should be part of a "profession" that can give voice to clients and to the broader public interest.

Yet such conditions are still evolving in China today. First, poor distribution continues to exist, with a lack of legal professionals in some areas of China (see Peerenboom, Chapter 4). The move toward a private marketplace for legal services, although adding more lawyers in sheer numbers, nevertheless has created an inequality gap that has triggered social discontent and a resurgence of state involvement in the legal profession. What we are seeing is a bifurcated system, not only between political and less political cases (in politically sensitive cases, Chinese courts are known either to turn away the case or to solicit the case and carefully construct the parties, issues, and remedies to ensure a global settlement of the dispute),[12] but also between those with legal assistance and those without.

Away from big cities such as Shanghai and Beijing, lawyers are still few and far between. Whereas there is one lawyer for every 270 people in the United States, there is one lawyer for every 10,650 people in China. China has made progress toward its target goal of 150,000 lawyers nationwide. China now has reportedly 122,000 full-time lawyers, up from 48,000 in 1997. But lawyers are poorly distributed, with more lawyers in the cities than in the countryside, and more lawyers in the lucrative areas of commerce than in the less lucrative areas of family law, debt, and employment. With the latter areas being of greatest concern to ordinary citizens, there exists a tremendous gap in the availability of services between those

[12] Margaret Y. K. Woo, "China's Developmental State and the Challenge of Formal Process." In *Common Law, Civil Law and the Future of Categories*, ed. Janet Walker and Oscar Chase (Lexis/Nexis, 2010).

with commercial disputes and those with more mundane disputes, and between the urban rich and the rural poor.

The Chinese government recognizes the needs of the rural poor for legal assistance, and during the last ten years it has devoted substantial funds to establishing a nationwide legal-aid system complementing the system of rural township legal services/ "justice offices" (*sifasuo*), the lowest branch in the Ministry of Justice bureaucracy. But these efforts vastly underserve the rural poor. As pointed out by Fu Yulin (see Chapter 10), legal services and local justice offices rise and fall, depending more on central policy dictates than on local populist needs and demands. Thus, despite the fact that in the first six months of 2007, China's three-thousand-plus legal-aid offices handled 172,600 cases, a jump of nearly 40 percent from the previous year, only one-quarter of the existing rural cases had legal representation. Many legal-services providers, despite the recent influx of funds, are still hampered by resource limitations. In addition to minimal funds, they lack staff, means of publicity, legal training, and recognition by state agencies.

More problematically, the call for better training of judges and lawyers has meant a body of legal professionals more educated in the technicalities of the law but less trained in the nuances of representation and serving their clients. The focus on professional independence has urged independence from the state, but this has met with limited success, as undue influences – be it from popular pressures (see Liebman, Chapter 9) or internal salary incentives and disincentives (see Minzner, Chapter 2) – still pervade the judiciary.

Apart from sheer numbers, each member of the judiciary and the bar needs to have an identity as a "democratic professional." A "democratic professional" utilizes legal skills and expertise to include rather than exclude the participation of clients and to uphold the social conception of justice.[13] Technocratic authority grounded in the expertise of legal methods and language can block local knowledge of the disputants. "Technocrats" can take the most critical aspects of decisions out of the hands of those they serve and thus immobilize citizens. Access to justice requires a vast number of legal professionals, but these professionals must be able to play the role of buffers between citizens and elites by

[13] Talcott Parsons, "Professions." In *International Encyclopedia of the Social Sciences*, ed. David L. Sills (New York: MacMillan and The Free Press, 1968), vol. 12, p. 536. In addition to defending the rights and advancing the interests of particular clients, the legal profession embodies and upholds the social conception of justice.

accommodating their clients' needs and problems within a larger system of domination and control.[14]

Such a vision of legal professionals has yet to take root in China. Bar associations remain weak, with key positions often filled by state justice officials. Legal education is more theoretical than practical, with a greater emphasis on memorization of the law than on problem solving and shaping legal solutions. Furthermore, the role of the lawyer is often poorly understood. Chinese lawyers encounter frequent problems in representing their clients and at times are even subject to physical abuse from the public or arbitrary arrest by the state. At the same time, Chinese judges increasingly are acting to process disputes rather than solve them (see Minzner, Chapter 2). My own research showed that litigants expressed vast dissatisfaction when judges acted "too simply," "too quickly," or were too "cold and bureaucratic."[15] These litigants felt that the judges were acting as mere administrators rather than as administrators of justice.

Still, there are some promising signs. The constraints caused by the limited resources have meant that some public-interest or "cause" lawyers are beginning to network, interact, and cooperate with one another. Through their interactions, "cause" lawyers, as "gatekeepers" to the legal system, are developing some public space in which an identity of public service is evolving.[16] Piggybacking on the government's goal of enforcing social controls, some individual lawyers have sought to enforce laws on behalf of the public, and there are pockets of progressive lawyers who have developed a public consciousness that is commensurate with their professional identity.

Although the All-China Lawyers Association remains conservative – for example, by issuing a 2006 "guiding opinion" instructing law firms to assign only "politically qualified" lawyers to cases involving ten or more litigants – there are individual lawyers who take great risks to

[14] Dewey conceived of democratic professionals as task sharers who seek to produce social goods for the public and to solve problems by organizing the public. John Dewey, "Practical Democracy [1925]." In *John Dewey, The Later Works: 1925–1953*, ed. Jo Ann Boydston (Carbondale: Southern Illinois University Press, 1981–1990), vol. 2, p. 219; see also Susan M. Olson and Albert W. Dzur, "Revisiting Informal Justice: Restorative Justice and Democratic Professionalism," *Law & Society Review* 38, no. 1 (March 2004): 150.

[15] Woo, "Law, Development and the Rights of Chinese Women: A Snapshot from the Field," 345–360.

[16] Margaret Y. K. Woo, Christopher Day, and Joel Hugenberger, "Migrant's Access to Civil Justice in Beijing," *Loyola University of Chicago International Law Review* 4, no. 2 (2006–2007): 167–209.

litigate discrimination cases and environmental protection or property rights cases even as they often face retribution by the state. This was evident in the numerous discrimination cases brought by carriers of hepatitis B, as lawyers sought to enforce constitutional norms through ordinary civil litigation (see Kellogg, Chapter 11). More recently, several lawyers have even filed suits to test the new government information law, which took effect on May 1, 2008, trying to hold the government to a standard of to greater transparency. According to one lawyer, Liu Xiaoyuan, "You do not have to kill yourself to be a rights lawyer.... You just have to be careful about the methods you use and the way you approach the truth."

With more predictable and formal procedures, some Chinese "cause" lawyers may be able to utilize court procedures strategically by appealing to judges through seemingly less political procedural arguments rather than by directly attacking substantive policies. Yet, undeniably, these legal professionals take enormous risks in bringing litigation challenging the state. "Cause" lawyers face threats from the state when they become too public in their advocacy. Because of its fear of instability and social unrest, the Chinese government will clamp down (as it already has) on the more visible legal activists, detaining lawyers representing migrant workers, death row inmates, or mass tort victims.[17] For example, lawyers who signed a petition in support of Tibetan protestors now find their licenses under threat of nonrenewal and may even face disbarment.[18]

Although there are some promising signs, then, the legal profession in China has yet to become the "trustee" of the public interest. It is just as important in the development of a legal culture that legal expertise include rather than exclude local knowledge of the disputants. Absent local knowledge of the communities affected by social problems, the legal expert cannot adequately solve such problems. Legal professionals can serve as intermediary catalysts between a fragmented and underinformed public and a distant and increasingly complex political system.

[17] Xu Zhiyong, aged thirty-six, a soft-spoken and politically shrewd legal scholar who made a name for himself by representing migrant workers, death row inmates, and the parents of babies poisoned by tainted milk, was accused of tax evasion. Released after a one-month detention, the charge was seen almost universally as a cover for his true offense: angering the Communist Party leadership through his advocacy of the rule of law. Mr. Xu also had been the director of the now-closed Open Constitution Initiative. Others include Chen Guangcheng, a blind activist who exposed abuses in China's birth control program, and Gao Zhisheng, who worked on behalf of underground Christian churches and practitioners of Falun Gong. He mysteriously "disappeared" for fourteen months in 2009–10.

[18] Jim Yardley, "China Disbars Lawyers Who Offered to Defend Tibetans," *International Herald Tribune*, June 3, 2008, http://www.nytimes.com/2008/06/03/world/asia/03iht-04tibet.13432270.html (accessed December 16, 2010).

Democratic legal professionals work with lay participants in the construction of norms that constrain and direct professional action. Neither the Chinese judiciary nor the legal profession has yet to fully embrace such a concept of law and legality.

Ultimately, mediating actors in China may take the form of semiprofessionals, such as "barefoot lawyers" who straddle the field between lawyering and activism in lending advice to the rural poor. In the rural areas, far away from central directives, there is of necessity a synchronization of legal norms with local dictates. In norm setting, we see local legal affairs offices massaging national legislation to local conditions through local administrative rule making and administrative reconsideration (see Grob, Chapter 3). These local offices are often staffed by semiprofessional legal workers rather than full-time lawyers. And traditional values still dominate, as grassroots residents prefer those with whom they have a relationship, whether legal professionals – a lawyer, judge, public security officer, or procurator – or, more frequently, semi-professional legal workers (see Fu Yulin, Chapter 10). Thus, in a number of fora, we are seeing semiprofessional legal actors carving out openings through which ordinary citizens, with greater support, can access the law.

In sum, if Chinese litigants by and large are dissatisfied with their experiences in the courts, it may be the case that judges and lawyers as technocrats are not giving voice to the participants. The focus on formality has meant the rise of technocratic control. Absent the consistent development of a profession more oriented toward the public good than toward commercial gain, more oriented toward problem solving than toward technocratic application of the law, and more directed toward independent adjudication than toward bureaucratic processing of claims, the role of the Chinese legal system will continue to be the processing and, at times, the resolver of individual disputes rather than the broader role of encouraging the formation of a more engaged and democratic citizenry.

THIRTY YEARS OF CHINESE LEGAL REFORMS (1979–2009)

In enforcing rights in ordinary litigation, a legal system not only produces decisions, but it also sends messages about entitlement and vindication.[19] In applying top-down norms to individual disputes, a legal

[19] Lawrence M. Friedman, "Courts Over Time: A Survey of Theories and Research." In *Empirical Theories About Courts*, ed. Keith O. Boyum and Lynn Mather (New York:

system conveys messages from the state as reconciled with local social values.[20] Even if an ordinary dispute is not a direct and open challenge to the state, the contest of how a legal norm is to be applied in a particular dispute provides an opportunity to mediate and redefine state messages with local values. In the ideal, then, civil disputes as funneled through a legal system can be the locus for local resistance, for a reshaping of the legal culture, and for participation in the political system by ordinary citizens.

Quite apart from a state's goals for the legal system to be a coercive force, legal mechanisms for dispute resolution have the potential of changing people's interactions with the state.[21] The experience of vetting conflicts between different interests and through legal procedures can change the interactions between citizens and officials to those of equal exchange between citizens and government officials. If the legal disputing process allows the citizen a say in the enforcement of public norms, as, for example, litigants in public interest litigation, a legal system can alter citizens' self-perception – from governed subordinates to responsible citizens in a more participatory society.

Thus, the process of asserting legal claims in a formal legal context, even in ordinary litigation and, arguably, nonpolitical cases, is important. In adjudicating, courts can teach individuals the language of rights and the skills of participation. By institutionalizing conflicts through dispute resolution methods, a legal system teaches ordinary citizens the language of rights and equal justice, the "grammar of justice," so to speak.[22] Citizens may learn the language of rights as "part of a repertoire of skills used, either individually or collectively, as a weapon against recalcitrant

Longman, 1983). As Galanter has noted, "[C]ourts produce not only decisions, but messages. These messages are resources which parties . . . use in envisioning, devising, negotiating and vindicating claims (and in avoiding, defending and defeating them). . . . " Marc Galanter, "Justice in Many Rooms." In *Access to Justice and the Welfare State*, ed. Mauro Cappelletti (Alphen aan den Rijn: Sijthoff, 1981), p. 158.

[20] Laura Nader, "The Crown, the Colonists, and the Course in Zapotec Village Law." In *History and Power in the Study of Law: New Directions in Legal Anthropology*, ed. June Starr and Jane F. Collier (Ithaca: Cornell University Press, 1989), pp. 320–344.

[21] Juan Linz posits that five interacting arenas need to reinforce one another in order for democratic consolidation to occur: a free and lively civil society, an autonomous and valued political society, institutions that carry out the value of the rule of law, effective state bureaucracy, and institutionalized economic society. Juan J. Linz and Alfred Stepan, *Problems of Democratic Transition and Consolidation: Southern Europe, South America, and Post-Communist Europe* (Baltimore: Johns Hopkins University Press, 1996), pp. 3–15.

[22] The term "grammar of justice" comes from Elizabeth H. Wolgast, *The Grammar of Justice* (Ithaca: Cornell University Press, 1987).

husbands, in-laws, or officials."[23] Courts can be a site for micro-assertions of rights, and, in determining rights, court adjudications are distinctly different from community compromises.

In this way, use of the legal system may shape a culture that is more conducive to the assertion of rights, with the micro-assertion of rights one of the first steps in democratic development. The process of rights of assertion through the legal system has the potential to go beyond adjudicating norms and resolving disputes, allowing citizens to think of themselves as equal to others and able to claim their rights vis-à-vis others.[24] Although some may criticize law and litigation as self-centered individualism, litigation and the use of the formal legal process can represent an expression of one's belief in justice, a growing sense of rights consciousness, and an emerging desire to participate in the public process.

But if the legal disputing experience is negative, giving no voice to participants, then the learned grammar of rights is met with an experience of disempowerment even beyond the outcome of the dispute. Law and courts then become an oppressive space, posing barriers rather than providing routes to relief and depriving citizens of the dignity and participation that is so necessary for the realization of equal citizenship.

In the last thirty years, Chinese legal reformers, arguing for more adjudication and greater judicial independence, have shared the state's goal of moving toward legalism. Chinese state authority wants law and the courts to promote the state goals of economic development, state legitimacy, and social stability. This confluence of factors has served as fertile ground for the growth of legal formality. Substantive laws were enacted, legal procedures were formalized, and the use of the courts was encouraged.

The increased utilization of the courts can be explained as the result of various factors: some political, such as the state's desire to ensure stability by channeling disgruntled citizens through the legal system; some economic, in that increased economic activity may lead to additional disputes requiring resolution; and some social, such as the loosening of the household registration system that created more mobility and opportunities for disputes outside the traditional social milieu. Certainly the presence of courts and legal institutions has helped to establish legitimacy for the state by routing disputes to the central government for determination

[23] Neil J. Diamant, *Revolutionizing the Family: Politics, Love, and Divorce in Urban and Rural China, 1949–1968* (Berkeley: University of California Press, 2000), p. 12.
[24] Ibid., 31.

of right and wrong. But the question is whether Chinese courts and legal reforms have done more than legitimize state authority and provide some measure of social control.

The formal legal system in China is evolving and shifting along a continuum. The path of Chinese legal reform, however, is not simply an inevitable and unidirectional trajectory from enforcing central policy and asserting social control to performing the task of conflict resolution and, ultimately, building a sense of rights consciousness and participation. There are and will continue to be shifts and turns. Correctly or not, rather than serving simply as adjudicators of opposing interests, courts in China are increasingly called upon to serve as a much-needed social lubricant to adjust social values. This role is vital to the stability of the government, particularly in light of an arguably retreating moral authority of the party-state, and it also is critical to the development of a rights-conscious populace. In deciding right from wrong, courts can provide the social stability that is necessary for democratic development as individuals are protected from arbitrary infringement of their rights. But recent escalating unrest suggests that Chinese courts and Chinese legal reforms have failed to provide the social stability desired by the state and the populace. The thirty years of legal reform has reached a juncture at which new and different reform strategies are needed.

For the Chinese state, law and courts can legitimize state authority, protect the market economy, and centralize its power. Formal procedural regularity bolsters the legitimacy of the courts and of the state. For Chinese citizens, formal legal process can resolve disputes, instill a culture of participation, and develop a sense of rights consciousness. Whether such process will serve ordinary citizens in these ways will depend on whether citizens view the legal authority as having a legitimate right to dictate their behavior and whether the citizens, when using the courts, experience some semblance of participation.[25]

The extent to which and the direction in which Chinese legal reforms will continue are highly contested. Despite the significant limitations on the range of viewpoints that can be publicly expressed, there has been robust debate on the extent to which China should emulate the

[25] Legitimacy itself has a reciprocal relationship with beliefs about the fairness of the procedures and social process experienced in encounters with authority. Tom R. Tyler, *Why People Obey the Law* (New Haven: Yale University Press, 1990), p. 25. *See also* Tom R. Tyler, "What is Procedural Justice? Criteria Used by Citizens to Assess the Fairness of Legal Procedures," *Law & Society Review* 22, no. 1 (1988): 103–135; Tom R. Tyler, "The Role of Perceived Injustice in Defendants' Evaluations of Their Courtroom Experience," *Law & Society Review* 18, no. 1 (1984): 51–74.

political and legal systems of Western liberal democracies. Liberal reformers view Western liberal democracies as the blueprint for Chinese development and see market integration as leading inevitably to political reform. Those who believe in the link between economic development and greater political liberalization would argue that China's increasing wealth has and inevitably will lead to greater use of courts in a democratic manner.

By contrast, the "New Left" increasingly argues that China's attempt to emulate the West has significantly increased inequality and further strengthened the existing authoritarian regime. Within this debate, we have seen support for some increased legal aid (or government-sponsored legal services for the economically disadvantaged) and some growing public interest litigation (*gongyi susong*), a form of litigation and related activities that seeks to represent the broad public interest and have a norm-setting impact. Wealth and markets alone are insufficient to create a legal system open to rights assertion and participation.

What this debate has not acknowledged is what scholars in this volume have unearthed – that is, the danger of high levels of unmet expectations, the constant tug and pull between historical determinism and actual experience, the potential fragmentation of diffuse sources of law, and, finally, the growing technical alienation posed by legal professionalism. Given the inconclusive experiences of ordinary citizens in the courts, the transition to greater participation and rights consciousness may not necessarily be equated with the latest set of legal reforms in China. Disparities in economic power promoted by market reforms are replicated, rather than alleviated, by the legal system. Legal technicalities have replaced legal justice. Until reformers pay close attention to these issues, the role of law and courts in China cannot be accurately gauged or fulfilled. It will continue to be a messy and complicated picture. Perhaps, then, the most important impact of the Chinese legal reforms in the last thirty years is the rising expectation among Chinese people that law and the legal system can and should be used to address their grievances. What remains to be seen is whether the system will meet these expectations and whether reforms can be carefully calibrated to avoid the pitfall delineated in this volume.

Index

Activists, 343, 378
Adjudication, 4, 8, 17, 28–30, 34–38, 45, 49, 51–52, 384, 400
  constitutional, 354, 362
Administrative disputes, 95, 158
Administrative litigation, 39, 95, 99, 104, 106, 111, 320
Administrative Litigation Law, 70, 92, 99, 102, 104, 110, 371
Administrative reconsideration, 95, 97–98, 100, 102–5, 107, 109, 116, 368, 398
Administrative Reconsideration Law (ARL), 96, 98, 102, 104
Administrative Reconsideration Regulation (ARR), 102
All-China Lawyers Association, 396
Amherst School, 14, 238–39
Anhui Province, 67, 94, 111–12, 157, 284, 302–3
Arbitration, 3–4, 116, 120, 129–30, 206–7, 211, 226–28, 230–31, 306, 386
Authoritarian regimes, 149, 210, 270–73, 307, 313, 381

Basic people's court (BPC), 63, 68
Beijing, 12, 32, 44–45, 49, 55, 68, 120, 127–28, 135, 170–73, 175, 181, 187, 192–93, 284
  Bureau of Justice, 127, 134
  First Intermediate People's Court, 68
  Higher People's Court, 293
  survey, 12, 172, 182, 187–88
Beijing University, 351, 361, 377

Cai, Dingjian, 353
Caijing, 369
China Law Society, 240, 349
Chinese Communist Party. *See* CCP
Chinese Communist Party (CCP), xxii, 8, 26–28, 30, 44–46, 51, 54–57, 64, 140, 142, 164–65, 167–68, 204, 317, 382
Citizens, rural, 221–22, 315, 328–29
Citizenship, 4, 19, 223–24
Civil cases, 18, 26–27, 29, 35, 40–41, 44, 281, 303–4, 332, 381–82
Civil justice, 25–30, 32, 38, 40–41, 44, 46, 48, 53–57
Civil litigation, 7, 19, 29, 41, 49, 317, 347
Civil procedure, rules of, 27–28
Civil Procedure Law, 36, 38–39, 41, 247–48, 304
Constitution, 17–18, 60, 77–78, 102, 311, 340–61, 363–65, 367–79, 383
  arguments based on, 363, 369, 371–72, 378
  development, 340–41, 362–63
  enforcement, 346–47, 350
  interpretation, 18, 342, 344–45, 352, 359
  law, 244, 247–48, 261, 340, 345, 350–51, 353, 355, 361
  litigation, 17–18, 343, 349, 357, 360–61, 363, 369, 376–77
  norms, 18, 341–42, 346–47, 352, 354, 358, 372, 378, 397
  review, 343–46, 348–49, 353–54, 359–60, 369
  rights, 17, 340, 342–45, 348, 352–53, 356, 358, 361, 364, 371, 378

Courts, 11–13, 16, 18–21, 30–55, 104–7, 173–78, 180–87, 269–313, 327–30, 332–35, 341–43, 345–48, 350–58, 371–76, 398–402
  adjudication committees, 60, 62, 65, 72, 285, 294
  appellate, 34, 68, 75
  basic-level, 18, 53, 59, 75, 117, 121, 276, 285, 291, 351, 355, 358
  higher-level, 9, 46, 50, 58–59, 74–80, 117, 284, 298–99, 306
  party committees in, 65
  provincial-level, 277, 302–3, 318
  responsibility systems, 9, 58–60, 63–64, 66–68, 71–74, 77, 80, 85–89, 284
Criminal cases, 70–71, 81, 120, 123, 125, 141, 147, 189, 243–44, 280, 293, 322
Criminal law, 124, 133, 234, 247–48, 336, 356
Criminal Procedure Law, 15, 125, 235, 245, 247–48
Cui Zhiqing, 142–43
Cultural Revolution, 11, 30, 147, 154, 156–57, 161, 225–26, 234–36, 240, 272, 282

Democratization, 89, 204
Discrimination, 18, 364–68, 375, 388
  hepatitis, 18, 364–71, 373–77, 397
Disenchantment, 20, 192, 217, 220–21, 233, 390–91, 394
Dispute resolution, i, iv, 1, 3–4, 11, 13, 15, 19, 37, 45, 94, 129, 204–5, 211, 329
  civil, iii–iv, 3, 58, 320, 338
  legal triad, 3–6
Disputes
  civil, 1, 3, 7, 26–27, 42, 46, 49, 54, 120, 255, 320, 332, 338, 358, 399
  commercial, 3, 27, 48, 116, 395
  employment, 204, 220, 222–23
  family, 326, 331
  inheritance, 14–15, 243, 249–52, 254, 262, 265–66
  labor, 3, 15, 116, 205–7, 221–22, 258–59, 261–62
  pension, 116, 213, 226–27
  pyramid of, 205, 207
Distributive justice, 13, 171, 174, 180–81, 197

Economic growth, 10, 114, 117–19, 132–33
Enforcement, 36, 96, 101, 103, 121, 255, 285, 342, 345, 399
External efficacy, 13, 209, 211, 217, 220–21, 233

Fazhi bangongshi (FZB), 7, 9–10, 93–104, 108–12, 385
  local, 93–95, 98, 100, 111–13, 386
Fees, 124, 321, 324–25, 329, 336, 338
Firms, 120, 123, 126–29, 131–34, 207, 211, 222, 224
  Chinese, 129–31
  foreign, 130–31, 133
  non-state, 14, 142, 205, 223–25, 390
  state-owned. *See* state-owned enterprises
Foreign investors, 130

Gazetteers, 51–53, 139–40, 145–48, 157, 357
Gongmeng, 376–77
Guangzhou, 32, 128, 141–42
Guomindang. *See* KMT

Henan Province, 12, 172, 300, 318
Higher people's courts (HPCs), 28, 32, 68, 77
Historical legacies, 9, 11–12, 20, 90, 141, 383–84, 388–90
HPCs. *See* higher people's courts
Hu, Jinguang, 350–51
Huang, Songyou, 25, 36, 42, 363
Hunan Province, 12, 172

Imperial China, 59, 80–81, 234
  civil service system, 387–88
  criminal codes, 83–84
Incorrectly decided cases. *See* judicial error
Industrial injury, 261–62
Intermediate people's court (IPCs), 63, 68, 77, 121, 279, 283–84, 291, 340
Internal efficacy, 14, 209, 215, 220–21, 232
IPCs. *See* intermediate people's court

Jiang Ping, 360n48
Judicial authority, 48, 74, 80, 85, 87, 90, 291, 346, 348
Judicial decisions, 66, 71, 105–6, 121, 237, 346–47, 383

Judicial disciplinary sanctions, 58–59, 61–63, 65, 67–69, 71, 73, 75, 77, 79, 81, 83, 85, 87–89
Judicial error, 64–68, 71, 77, 80, 84–87
Judicial exam, 31, 118, 122–23, 325, 332
Judicial independence, 8–9, 94, 113, 141, 345, 360, 381, 385, 393
Judicial interpretations, 25, 49–50, 52, 56, 75–76, 235, 245, 253, 257, 261
Judicialization, 3, 17–18, 116, 343, 346–48, 350–52, 354, 359–60, 378–79, 393
Judicial reform, 8, 30, 33, 39–40, 43, 46–50, 89, 388
Judicial review, 248, 270, 343, 346, 348, 350–51, 354, 361
Judiciary, 5–9, 19, 25–27, 29–31, 33, 37–38, 45, 47–50, 53, 56, 74–76, 120–22, 234–35, 387, 393–95
Junhe, 127–28

King & Wood, 127–28

Labor
  contracts, 231, 261, 355
  law, 129, 207, 213, 227–29, 247, 261–62, 355, 364
  strikes, 213, 215, 229, 348
Landry, Pierre, 175, 178, 308
Law firms, 118, 123, 126, 129, 133–34, 214, 238, 315–17, 320, 322–24, 326, 331, 337, 383
  elite, 10, 125, 127–29, 131–33
  foreign, 117, 128, 130
Law scholars, constitutional, 343, 349
Law schools, 30, 117, 125
Lawyers, 10, 114–20, 122–30, 132–35, 181–82, 235–41, 243–45, 247–48, 250–52, 254–58, 262–64, 322–35, 337–39, 378–79, 394–98
  activist, 18, 116, 343, 368
  barefoot, 123–24, 133, 263, 398
  cause, 396–97
  criminal, 125
  per capita, 120, 123
  private, 7, 12, 165, 331, 336
  pro-bono, 336
  role of, 134, 261–62
  weiquan, 211, 377, 397
Legal affairs office. *See* fazhi bangongshi (FZBs)
Legal aid, 111–12, 205, 228, 315
Legal assistance, 221, 233, 321–24, 326, 332, 336–37, 339, 391, 394–95
Legal consciousness, vi, 5–6, 10–11, 13, 17, 20–21, 169, 204, 210–11, 220, 232, 235, 238, 253, 312
Legal culture, 6, 11, 20–21, 113, 142, 197, 234, 264, 312, 383–84, 387–88, 397, 399
Legal development, v, 1–2, 6–7, 31, 90–91, 94–96, 98, 100, 109–10, 112–13, 368, 386
Legal errors, 9, 58–60, 62–63, 67–68, 71–72, 83, 87–88
Legal knowledge, 36, 47, 100, 212–14, 220–21, 280, 318, 328
Legal mobilization, vii, 2, 13, 175, 191–92, 205–7, 210–11, 213, 217, 220, 222, 225, 229–33
Legal profession, v, 5, 10, 31, 114–15, 117–19, 122, 125, 127–28, 131–34, 210–11, 234–35, 264, 394–95, 397–98
Legal propaganda, 389–92
Legal reasoning, 47–48, 53, 236, 251, 254, 260, 262, 356
Legal reformers, 20–21, 87, 383, 394, 400
Legal services, 17, 134, 264, 314–29, 331–32, 335–39, 377, 386, 390, 394–95
  markets for, 131, 324, 326, 328–31, 337
  workers of, 7, 10, 126, 317–18, 320, 322–39
Legal workers, 123–24, 133–34, 328, 336, 398
Legislation Law, 92, 98, 345
Legislature, 5, 27, 344, 346, 374
Litigation, 17–20, 47–48, 105, 107–10, 120, 129, 197, 206–7, 217, 219–20, 277–78, 284–85, 301–2, 364–66, 372–74
  fees, 105, 214, 330
  masters, 234
  related to petitioning, 277–78, 280, 283, 285, 291, 295, 297, 301, 304
Liu, Sida, 391
Luban, David, 37

Marriage Law, 147, 247–50, 252, 255, 264–65

Media, 4, 16, 18, 160–61, 163, 184, 212, 214, 230, 271–72, 287–88, 300, 307, 309, 393
  Southern Weekend, 360, 369
Mediation, xviii, 3–4, 8, 17, 28–30, 33–43, 47–54, 116, 206–7, 303–4, 314–16, 320–21, 324–26, 333–34, 384–86
  administrative, 315
  commission, 322–23, 325, 333–34, 337
  committees, 17, 161, 320, 334
  firm-based, 206
  judicial, 25–26, 28, 33, 36–37, 41–42, 44, 49–54, 56, 206, 337
  people's, 49, 161, 315–16, 320–21, 325, 333–34, 337
  rate, 38, 42, 53, 64
  social conflict centers, 324
  teams, 333–34
Michelson, Ethan, 207, 240, 388–89
Ming Code, 84–85
Ministry of Health, 366, 374–75
Ministry of Justice, xxi, 32, 49, 111, 123, 134, 315, 317–21, 323, 325, 333, 335
MoJ. *See* Ministry of Justice

Nationalist Party (KMT) (Guomindang), 140–41, 143, 154, 164–65, 167
National People's Congress (NPC), 18, 27, 51–53, 59, 102, 118, 175, 235, 243, 250, 284, 341, 343–49, 359, 370
National People's Congress Standing Committee (NPCSC), 18, 343–45, 352–54, 359, 366, 375–76, 379
Negligence, 61–62, 68–69, 178
NPC. *See* National People's Congress
NPCSC. *See* National People's Congress Standing Committee

Open Constitutional Initiative. *See* Gongmeng
Organic Law of the PRC Courts, 60, 77–78, 92

People's Congresses, 27, 49, 93, 112, 284, 287, 345, 347, 351
  local, xv, 65, 92–93, 96–100, 102–3, 275, 298, 345, 372
Petitioners, 16, 44, 88, 209, 230, 270, 273–77, 279, 282–94, 297–313, 393
Petitioning, 4, 8, 15–16, 20, 44–45, 51–52, 88, 95, 225, 228–31, 269–70, 272–309, 311–13, 366–67, 393
  constitutional, 345n11
  court-related, 45, 276–77, 285, 308–9
  influence of, 307–8, 310, 312
Police, 12–13, 27, 31, 133, 135, 170, 173–77, 180–82, 184–89, 192–94, 201–2, 214, 278, 312, 377
Political efficacy, 208–9, 212
Political identity, 13, 205, 221–25, 233
Political liberalism, 115, 132–34
Political participation, 208, 210–11, 232
Political reforms, 20, 115, 134, 211, 359, 402
Political system, 8, 44, 48, 119, 150, 210, 234, 269–71, 306–7, 311, 399
Populism, 270–71, 309, 311, 313
Procedural justice, i, 13, 39–40, 42, 171, 174, 178, 180–81, 197, 225, 310, 392, 401
Professionalism, 47–48, 103, 118, 121, 124, 128, 133, 206
Prosecutors, 99, 118, 123, 125, 133, 241
Protestors, 281, 291
Protests, 74, 86, 269–70, 272, 274, 279–83, 285–86, 289–90, 294, 297–98, 306, 309
PSB. *See* public security bureau
Public opinion, 140, 144, 149–50, 161, 183, 269–73, 308–9, 311, 313, 362
Public security bureau (PSB), 99, 108
Public security offices, 328–29, 331, 337–38
Public security organs, 12, 151, 154–55

Qing Code, 84–85
Qingshi (requests for advisory opinions), 59, 74–80, 88–89, 347
Qi Yuling case, 352, 354, 358–63

Reconsideration. *See* administrative reconsideration
Reformers
  judicial. *See* judicial, reform
  scholars, 378–79
Reforms, 19, 21, 25–26, 28–29, 32, 38, 44–45, 48, 52, 54–56, 77, 109, 139–41, 158, 303–4
  constitutional, 360, 379
  economic, 91, 117, 144, 158, 380, 382
  enterprise, 224, 282
  institutional, 149, 349, 351, 386–87
  top-down, 19, 21, 383, 385

Rehearing procedures, 288, 290–91, 304
Republic of China (ROC) (Taiwan), xv, 2, 25, 28, 39, 49, 51–53, 60, 92, 114–15, 139, 143, 148–49, 345–46, 364
Reversals, appellate, 58, 63, 68, 83, 86
Rights, 7, 15, 37, 78, 170, 211, 221, 239, 322, 342, 360, 364, 369–70, 392–95, 400–401
  consciousness, 390, 392, 400–402
  greater awareness of, 312–13, 390, 393
  individual, 78, 269, 344, 353, 358, 363, 378
Rights claims, constitutional. *See* Constitution, rights

Shaanxi Province, 12, 172, 318
Shanghai, 32, 81, 94, 120–21, 127–28, 135, 142, 172, 180, 184, 208, 220, 222, 227–29, 240–41
Shenzhen, 32–33, 35, 42, 127–28, 288
Shuanggui, 363
Sifa ting (SFT), 10, 95–96, 111–12, 318
Social stability, 17, 51, 55, 86, 116, 270, 277–78, 281, 294, 310, 337, 400–401
SPC. *See* Supreme People's Court
State Council, 92–94, 98, 103, 109, 118, 148, 235, 285, 317, 321, 371, 374
State Letters and Visits Bureau, 274
State-owned enterprises, xv, 131–32, 214, 224, 230, 232
Statistics, official, 172, 276–77, 381
Supervision, 34, 51, 81, 97, 99, 110, 287, 307, 320–21, 345, 359
Supreme People's Court, 7–8, 25–29, 32, 38–41, 49–52, 54–56, 58–59, 61–63, 76–77, 105, 252–53, 276, 294–97, 349–52, 355–62
  directives, 61–63, 67–68, 71–73, 85–87, 89
  judges, 36, 362
  opinions, 38, 254, 257–58
  work reports, 43, 49, 51, 53, 275–76, 279, 288, 301, 381–82
Survey data, 11, 145, 168, 170–71, 176, 186, 193–95, 215

Taiwan. *See* ROC
Television. *See* media
Tianjin, 128, 142, 318, 355–56
Tribunals, 64–66, 69, 72–73
Trust, 11–12, 17, 140, 144–45, 149–52, 158–60, 163–64, 166–68, 170, 175, 185, 238, 312, 327–28, 389–90
  institutional, 149, 151, 164, 168
  level of, 12, 149–50, 158–59, 163, 167
Tyler, Tom R., 171, 173–74

United States, 125–26, 210, 221, 310, 352, 365, 394
Urbanization, 142, 165, 167–68

Wang, Lei, 348, 351–52, 354
Weber, Max, 237–38, 258
Western legal systems, 348
Workers, 48, 206, 213–14, 216, 222–24, 227, 229–30, 233, 259, 261–62, 338–39
  migrant, 213, 222, 229, 328, 397
  older, 223, 226, 229
  retired, 226–27
Wuxi, 213–14, 218, 222, 229

Xi'an, 128, 281
Xiao Yang, 25–26, 39, 41, 51, 55
Xinfang. *See* petitioning
Xuan Ke, 340–41

Yang Xiancai, 363
Yu Jianrong, 44, 274
Yunnan, 63–64, 135

Zhang Qianfan, 345, 349, 354, 361
Zhang Qingguo, 76–78
Zhang Xianzhu, 364, 367–76
Zhonglun, 127–28
Zhou Wei, 352–53, 357, 368–71, 373–74

CPSIA information can be obtained at www.ICGtesting.com
Printed in the USA
BVOW032019130212

282706BV00004B/2/P

9 781107 006249